The Musical Classroom

The Musical Classroom: Models, Skills, and Backgrounds for Elementary Teaching

Patricia Hackett ● Carolynn A. Lindeman ● James M. Harris

San Francisco State University

Prentice-Hall, Inc. Englewood Cliffs, New Jersey 07632

Library of Congress Cataloging in Publication Data

HACKETT, PATRICIA [date]
   The musical classroom.

   Bibliography: p.
   1. School music—Instruction and study. I. Lindeman,
Carolynn A. (date) joint author. II. Harris, James M. (date) joint
author. III. Title.
MT1.H12   372.8'7'044   77-27646
ISBN 0-13-608356-0

10   9   8   7   6   5   4   3   2   1

Prentice-Hall International, Inc., *London*
Prentice-Hall of Australia Pty. Limited, *Sydney*
Prentice-Hall of Canada, Ltd., *Toronto*
Prentice-Hall of India Private Limited, *New Delhi*
Prentice Hall of Japan, Inc., *Tokyo*
Prentice-Hall of Southeast Asia Pte. Ltd., *Singapore*
Whitehall Books Limited, *Wellington, New Zealand*

Contents

SECTION TWO *Playing Instruments* 209

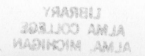

SECTION THREE   *Backgrounds for Teaching Music   297*

Appendix   337

To Instructors

The Musical Classroom: Models, Skills, and Backgrounds for Elementary Teaching is designed for use in a one-semester music course for the elementary education major and can also serve as a resource book for in-service teachers. It enables students to develop skills in music teaching, while at the same time providing introductory experiences in playing and reading music.

The text is divided into three sections:
One: Model Experiences for Teaching Music
Two: Skills in Playing and Reading Music
Three: Backgrounds for Teaching Music

Section One consists of 63 model experiences for teaching music. Each of these focuses on a single learning about music, within a framework of musical elements: melody, rhythm, harmony, form, and expressive qualities. Each model experience provides for measurement of pupil success through stated behavioral objectives. Each uses a specific musical selection to provide a musical context for every learning experience. The 118 musical selections, chosen from the basal music series represent a wide variety of musical styles. The 63 model experiences are organized to proceed from simple to more complex understandings about music. They may be taught either by instructors or students, in the college classroom or the elementary school. They may be used at many educational levels by altering the vocabulary and perhaps the musical selection. Though statements to pupils are suggested (in small capital letters in the text), these experiences are truly *models* and should be modified to reflect varying goals, skills, and personalities.

Section Two provides introductory experiences in reading and playing music, using the Autoharp, guitar, piano, and soprano recorder. They are written for independent or small-group use by college students and require only minimal assistance from an instructor. These programs of study are complementary to Section One and use some of the same songs. A total of 78 songs are notated. This instrumental instruction is deliberately separated from Section One, so that model experiences in the latter may be used by the student without performance skills.

Section Three is a concise introduction to the teaching of music in the elementary classroom. It describes the musical elements and behavioral objectives that are exemplified in the model experiences of Section One, and discusses the role of singing and other music-making activities. A feature of this section is a description of each basal music series; several of these descriptions are provided by the series authors themselves. This section concludes with a brief account of the eclectic curriculum in music education.

Annotated bibliographies appear throughout to inspire and spur the student to explore areas of individual concern. A Glossary and an Appendix of music theory are also included, as are specialized indices and pronunciation guides.

Preliminary manuscripts of this text have been used by six instructors with nearly 1300 students from widely varying music backgrounds. Over a period of two years, hundreds of sound and video tapes recorded the success of energetic students who used these materials in college and elementary classrooms.

To Students

Creating *The Musical Classroom* required tremendous commitment from three authors who frankly admit a preference for spending precious free hours with friends, food, and fresh earth. The result is a book that presents deep feelings and beliefs about music and about learners of all ages.

College students who lack performance skills often postpone enrolling in a music methods course. They are certain that without playing skills they will be unsuccessful in their teaching. Yet one does not need to be an accomplished performer to teach music. The teacher *does* need a fundamental understanding of how music "works," and must learn how to convey this understanding to others.

The Musical Classroom begins with model lessons in music which may be understood (and taught) by college students who have absolutely *no* musical background. It *is possible* for a teacher to develop understandings about music while teaching others. And this active involvement in teaching nearly always leads to a desire to develop performance skills. The authors of *The Musical Classroom* believe it is possible to do all of these simultaneously: to develop understandings about music, to share this understanding while teaching others, and to learn to play a musical instrument.

This text succeeds only when those who use it say, "We did it ourselves." As every journey begins with a single step, the use of this text in a one-semester course represents that first step. Its music and models should be used to develop a philosophy and style so meaningful and so personal that the model will hardly be remembered. Only *you,* the learner, can plan the lifetime journey that will expand *your* musical literacy, refine *your* performance skills, and perfect *your* teaching skills. Those who love music and children with equal passion will never cease to develop their own ingenious means for bringing children into intimate touch with all the excitement of the world of *music*.

Patricia Hackett
Carolynn A. Lindeman
James M. Harris

Acknowledgments

We are deeply indebted to our students in the Music for Children classes at San Francisco State University. Working with students from richly varied cultural backgrounds has been an exciting experience. It is truly *we* who have been educated.

We also wish to express appreciation to our colleagues in the Music Department and to the administration of the School of Creative Arts, San Francisco State University, for their continuous encouragement and support of our efforts.

Credit and appreciation are due publishers and copyright owners for use of the following:

● ALL AROUND THE KITCHEN from *Silver Burdett Music (Book 1)*. © 1974 General Learning Corporation.

● A RAM SAM SAM from *Sing It Again*. © CRS 1958 by permission of World Around Songs, Burnsville, N.C.

● CLAP YOUR HANDS from *American Folk Songs for Children* by Ruth Crawford Seeger. Copyright 1948 by Ruth Crawford Seeger. Reprinted by permission of Doubleday & Company, Inc.

● FIVE ANGELS from *Making Music Your Own (Book 1)*. © 1971 General Learning Corporation. Reprinted by permission of Silver Burdett Company.

● GRIZZLY BEAR. © Copyright 1965 by Stormking Music, Inc. All rights reserved. Used by permission.

● HARI KRISHNA from *New Dimensions in Music (Book 5)*. © 1970, American Book Company.

● HOLD ON from *Silver Burdett Music (Book 4)*. © 1974 General Learning Corporation.

- JAMAICA FAREWELL. © Copyright 1955 by Shari Music Publishing Corp. All rights reserved. Used by permission.

- JANE, JANE reprinted from *Sing Out! The Folk Song Magazine,* 270 Lafayette St., New York, N.Y. 1002. Used by permission.

- JOE TURNER BLUES from *Making Music Your Own (Book 6).* © 1971 General Learning Corporation.

- JOHN THE RABBIT from *Making Music Your Own (Kindergarten).* © 1971 General Learning Corporation.

- LADY, COME from *Silver Burdett Music (Book 2).* © 1974 General Learning Corporation. Reprinted by permission of Silver Burdett Company.

- LA VÍBORA from *Making Music Your Own (Book 1).* © 1971 General Learning Corporation. Reprinted by permission of Silver Burdett Company.

- LITTLE DAVID, PLAY ON YOUR HARP from *Silver Burdett Music (Book 3).* © 1974 General Learning Corporation.

- MINKA from *Making Music Your Own (Book 6).* © 1971 General Learning Corporation. Reprinted by permission of Silver Burdett Company.

- POOR TOM (GHOST OF TOM) from *101 Rounds.* World Around Songs, Burnsville, N.C.

- ROLL AN' ROCK from *Silver Burdett Music (Book 3).* © 1974 General Learning Corporation.

- SERAFINA from *Shanties from the Seven Seas.* By permission of Routledge & Kegan Paul, Ltd.

- SING HALLELU from *Silver Burdett Music (Book 1).* © 1971 General Learning Corporation. Reprinted by permission of Silver Burdett Company.

- SKIN AND BONES by Jean Ritchie. Copyright © 1953 and 1964 by Geordie Music Publishing, Inc., New York, N.Y. All rights reserved. Used by permission.

- SWEET POTATOES from *Exploring Music (Book 5).* © 1966, Holt, Rinehart and Winston, Publishers.

- THE FROG AND THE MOUSE from *Exploring Music (Book 3).* © 1966 Holt, Rinehart and Winston, Publishers.

- THE WIND BLEW EAST, Collected, adapted, and arranged by John A. Lomax and Alan Lomax TRO. © 1941 and renewed 1969 by Ludlow Music, Inc. Reprinted by permission.

- THESE BARNACLED ROCKS. . . from *The Way of Haiku,* original verses in English by J. W. Hackett. © 1968 by Japan Publications, Inc., Tokyo and New York.

- TUTÚ MARAMBA from *Silver Burdett Music (Book 5).* © 1974 General Learning Corporation. Repinted by permission of Silver Burdett Company.

- WE ARE GOING DOWN THE NUMBERS from *Making Music Your Own (Book 1).* © 1971 General Learning Corporation.

SECTION ONE

Model Experiences for Teaching Music

A Word About the Format

> Each model experience is organized in the same manner. An explanation of this organization and of the labels utilized is provided below. Experiences intended for group work-through are slightly different and are described at the end of this explanation.

Music Learning

This is the single understanding that will result from using the music and the process of the model experience. Other music learnings will follow, in association with the same music. These are suggested under "Another Time." (See below.)

Musical Context

This is the musical selection upon which the model experience is based. These are to be found in the basal music series for elementary grades. The abbreviations used throughout are:

AIM: *Adventures in Music*
BOL: *Bowmar Orchestral Library*
CMCM: *Comprehensive Musicianship Through Classroom Music*
DMT: *Discovering Music Together*
EM: *Exploring Music*
MMYO: *Making Music Your Own*
NDM: *New Dimensions in Music*
SBM: *Silver Burdett Music*
SOM: *Spectrum of Music*

(These texts are described in detail in Section Three.)

Reading Objective

When appropriate and meaningful, an objective is included which may be used to develop skills in interpreting the special notation or vocabulary of music.

Behavioral Objective

This is a statement that specifies what students will be able to *do* as a result of the musical experience. Teachers should note *how* students will demonstrate their music learning: through singing, playing instruments, or body movements, and so forth.

Grade

Lower and *upper* suggest the possible level of use with children. It must be understood that this is only a guideline and that the use of the model experience will vary greatly according to the background, age, and maturation of the children. It is quite possible that differences within a grade will be greater than between grades.
  Lower—lower grades; grades 1 to 3
  Upper—upper grades; grades 4 to 6

Materials

Recordings, books, and other equipment are specified.
  Page and recording numbers are listed whenever possible. This information applies to the *latest* (as of 1977) teacher's edition. Pagination may be different in earlier editions; refer to indices.
  Worksheets which are shown for children's use must be prepared in advance.

Classroom work begins here →

WHEN A SENTENCE IS WRITTEN IN SMALL CAPITAL LETTERS, IT SUGGESTS A PHRASE THAT MAY BE SPOKEN BY THE TEACHER, EXACTLY AS IT APPEARS. Often these sentences are carefully formulated questions (or summary statements).

Focusing Statement

To capture the attention of your students, a focusing statement is suggested for your consideration. To reflect better *your* personality and style, create your own! Although the focusing statements in *The Musical Classroom* are brief and concise, some teachers can elaborate and expand without losing the interest of their class. Remember that a *music learning* is the purpose of the model experience, and, therefore, it should not be obscured.
  Symbols occur throughout, principally as a space-saving device, though they are also a guide to the "operations" involved in the model experiences.

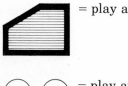 = play an Autoharp

 = sing

 = use a reel-to-reel tape recorder

 = play an instrument

 = speak or chant

 = use a cassette recorder

 = play a recording

 = silently "mouth" words

6:99 = level 6, page 99
EC = early childhood book

Summary

Classroom work ends here →

At the end of an experience, it is important to summarize the music learning. Rather than announcing this summary to the students, elicit it *from* them.

ANOTHER TIME

To be enjoyed, music usually must be heard until it becomes an old friend. Exciting music contains much that can be discovered on subsequent days. Suggestions for further music learning are included here.

ELABORATION

Students need many opportunities to discover the same musical understanding using other modes of learning. Techniques for this elaboration and exploration are suggested here.

OTHER MUSIC

Every model experience in *The Musical Classroom* includes a list of "Other Music." These alternate selections exemplify the *same* music learning, and most may be used with parallel techniques. Thus teachers may use musical materials which are more familiar, more accessible, or more appropriate for particular students.

BIBLIOGRAPHY

References to relevant information are presented here, inviting individual research in areas of special concern.

WORK-THROUGH EXPERIENCE

These experiences are designed for use by students in college classes. They may be used in small, independent groups because they contain specific, step-by-step instructions. The musical learnings in these experiences are more complex than in the other model experiences. If they are used in an elementary classroom, the children must have adequate background.

Now, turn to p. 21 and take a look at this format in the model experience *Stomp Dance*.

To Students

BEFORE PRESENTING A MODEL EXPERIENCE

1. Study the entire model experience carefully. Be sure the music learning and the procedures described are clear to you. See your instructor about any uncertainty.

2. Find out as much as possible about the background of your learners. If possible, visit the group prior to your teaching. Learn what books, materials, and audiovisual equipment are available in your particular school.

3. Listen to any recording several times. Be sure to practice finding the specific band on a recording, so that you can find it quickly *during* the presentation.

4. Practice using any materials (recordings, demonstration of instruments, setting up pegboard, etc.).

5. Study the behavioral objective stated for the experience. Be prepared to observe the learners' demonstrations of their understandings.

6. Prepare yourself fully as to the sequence of the lesson so that you can be secure in knowing "what comes next."

7. If possible, secure a cassette tape recorder and a tape cassette to use for recording your presentation.

WHILE PRESENTING A MODEL EXPERIENCE

8. The "opener" is all important for "turning the learners on." Use the suggested "focusing statement," or use a similar idea that reflects your own personality. Make it as brief and concise as possible, keeping in mind that you must capture their interest in the music to follow.

9. Involve students *actively* as soon as you can, and as frequently as you can. These involvements suggested in the model experience (clapping, singing, moving, playing instruments, etc.) will lead in this direction.

10. Try to keep interest high and to maintain excitement by moving at an appropriate pace. Observe the students, and let their degree of success dictate the tempo of the work. You must move quickly enough to keep students intrigued and involved, but slowly enough to let ideas sink in, so students feel comfortable with the material.

11. Close eye contact must be maintained with the class. Be enthusiastic and expressive; humor never hurts!

12. Ask clear, direct questions. With children, it is important to direct and phrase questions in such a manner that you do *not* elicit a response from all twenty-five at the same time! STATEMENTS IN SMALL CAPITAL LETTERS within the model experiences should provide ideas. And with young children, you may first want to ask *"show* me . . ." before you ask *"tell* me . . ."

13. When using the phonograph, adopt the technique of turning the volume knob to low before placing the needle on the record. Then, with the needle in place, increase the volume. When the selection ends, fade the volume before lifting the needle.

AFTER PRESENTING A MODEL EXPERIENCE

14. If you were able to record your presentation, replay the tape. Assess your effectiveness. Did you give clear directions? Did you involve the students actively in meaningful work? Did you manage the materials and the class well?

15. Assess your learners. Were you able to observe or record evidence of their learning?

16. Using the *self-evaluation* column at the beginning of the section containing this specific model experience, evaluate and then check your degree of assurance in communicating the specific music learning of that experience.

17. Review the observations made by your instructor or by others present during your presentation.

Rhythm: all of the durations that occur in music.

ENGINE, ENGINE
    Chants can suggest the presence of steady beats.

THE WIND BLEW EAST
    Music can suggest the presence of steady beats.

Harmony: the simultaneous sounding of two or more pitches; the vertical structure in music.

SKIP TO MY LOU
    Chords can accompany melodies.

Expressive qualities: those qualities (dynamics, tempo, timbre) which, combined with other musical elements, give a composition its unique musical identity.

THE ELEPHANT
    Music can move in a fast tempo or in a slow tempo.

SERAFINA; FOG
    Tempo, combined with other musical elements, gives a composition its unique musical identity.

Form: the shape, order, or design of a musical composition.

STOMP DANCE, etc.
    In "call-and-response" form, responses can be identical to the call, or contrasting.

After completing each model experience, decide how successfully you are able to identify, explain, or demonstrate the music learning that was the focus of the experience. Check the appropriate box.

Secure   Fairly secure   Insecure

8

Pre-music Learning	Chants can suggest the presence of steady beats.
Musical Context	ENGINE, ENGINE (traditional children's chant)
Behavioral Objective	To identify aurally a chant that moves in steady beats; and to demonstrate that recognition in body rhythms
Grade	Lower
Materials	Your voice and body

Focusing Statement

TRY SOME STEADY BEATS WITH ME.

Patsch (or *patschen*) means to slap tops of thighs.

Patsch, repeating until steady beat is well established.
　　Body rhythms (lap, lap, lap, etc.)

KEEP THOSE STEADY BEATS GOING WHILE I ADD SOME WORDS. Chant rhythmically:

　　ENG-ine, ENG-ine, NUM-ber NINE
　　|　　　　|　　　　|　　　　|
　　GO-ing DOWN Chi-CA-go LINE
　　|　　　　|　　　　|　　　　|
　　IF the TRAIN comes OFF the TRACK
　　|　　　　|　　　　|　　　　|
　　DO you WANT your MON-ey BACK?
　　|　　　　|　　　　|　　　　|

Review words with questions about the chant.
(WHO REMEMBERS THE NUMBER OF THE ENGINE? WHERE WAS IT GOING?)
START THE STEADY BEATS AGAIN AND REPEAT THESE WORDS <u>AFTER</u> ME:
　　Body rhythms　　(At first, chant one line at a time for
　　Chanting　　　　echoing; progress to two lines at a time.)
WE'RE READY TO DO THE WHOLE CHANT TOGETHER. I'LL KEEP THE STEADY BEATS GOING; YOU JUST CHANT THE WORDS.
　　Body rhythms　　(repeat several
　　Chanting　　　　times)
　　Students enjoy many repetitions of such chants. If they are able, have them repeat the chant as they *patsch*. WHEN DO <u>YOU</u> LIKE TO SAY CHANTS? Elicit jumping rope, bouncing a ball, etc.

Summary

IT'S EASY TO KEEP BALL-BOUNCING AND ROPE-JUMPING STEADY WHEN WE USE A CHANT WITH A STEADY BEAT.

ANOTHER TIME

1. Body rhythms could be expanded to emphasize the grouping of four steady beats. For example:

　　ENG-ine, ENG-ine, NUM-ber NINE
　　lap　　　*clap*　　*clap*　　*clap*
　　　　　　　　　　or
　　lap　　　*clap*　　*snap*　　*lift* (hands up)

2. Students can move to the steady beats as they chant. Arm movements might represent train wheel movement. The "train" might change directions with each line of words (phrase).

OTHER CHANTS

HAMBONE. SOM 2 (song, sometimes used as a chant)

HEAD SHOULDERS, BABY (Black American). SBM (EC) (Listen to this chant in *Music from the South*, V, "Song, Play, and Dance," Library of Congress FA 2654.)

HICKORY, DICKORY DOCK. CMCM 1A; MMYO (Kg) (song, sometimes used as a chant)

I LOVE COFFEE

MISS MARY MACK. SOM 2 (song, sometimes used as a chant)

MOTHER, MOTHER, I AM ILL

OLD MOTHER WITCH. SBM 2

OLIVER TWIST. SBM 1

ONE POTATO, TWO POTATO

SPANISH DANCERS

TEDDY BEAR

WHO TOOK THE COOKIE FROM THE COOKIE JAR? NDM (EC)

BIBLIOGRAPHY

Abrahams, Roger D. *Jump-rope Rhymes.* Austin, Tex.: University of Texas Press, 1969. Informative history for the general reader.

Jones, Bessie, and Bess Loman Hawes. *Step It Down.* New York: Harper & Row, Publishers, 1972. An outstanding source of games, plays, songs, and stories from the Afro-American heritage. Includes notation of many songs, as well as much information for the general reader.

Kenney, Maureen. *Circle Round the Zero.* St. Louis, Mo.: Magnamusic–Baton, Inc. The singing games of Black children; highly recommended.

Knapp, Mary, and Herbert Knapp. *One Potato, Two Potato . . . The Secret Education of American Children.* New York: W. W. Norton & Co., Inc., 1976. Children's folklore, containing descriptions of hundreds of games, songs, scary stories, etc.

Wuytack, Jos, and Tossi Aaron. *Joy.* Paris: Alphonse Leduc and Co., 1972. A collection of American play-party songs for singing, movement, recorder, and Orff instruments.

Listen to these recordings:

AMERICAN FOLK SONGS FOR CHILDREN, rec. in the field and edited by Alan Lomax, Southern Folk Heritage Series, Atlantic 1350. Bessie Jones may be heard on this recording.

1, 2, 3 AND A ZING, ZING, ZING. Folkways FC 7003 (street songs).

SOUTHERN MOUNTAIN CHILDREN'S SONGS AND GAMES. Folkways FC 7054.

LINE GAMES AND PLAY-PARTY SONGS FROM ALABAMA. Folkways FC 7004.

SKIP ROPE GAMES. Folkways FC 7029 (recording by Pete Seeger includes TEDDY BEAR, FUDGE, and others; also, a short history of rope skipping).

MUSIC FOR CHILDREN* (Carl Orff and Gunild Keetman). Angel Records 3582B. This recording presents children performing many examples of rhythmic speech and song.

*The film *Music for Children* (Carl Orff and Gunild Keetman) presents children performing in rhythmic speech ensembles. New York: Contemporary Films, 1958.

Music Learning	Music can suggest the presence of steady beats.
Musical Context	THE WIND BLEW EAST (folk song from the Bahamas). CMCM 1B; DMT 1; MMYO 1; SBM 1
Behavioral Objective	To identify aurally the section of the song with a steady beat; and to demonstrate this recognition by steady clapping during section B
Grade	Lower
Materials	Recording: DMT 1; MMYO 1, rec 1; SBM 1, rec 2

Teacher should learn the song ahead of time. (If you are uncomfortable singing, lyrics may be chanted rhythmically. Modulate your voice for interest.)

Focusing Statement

LISTEN TO THIS SONG, AND CLAP WHEN YOU FEEL THE BEAT.

(Clap during B section.)

IT WAS EASY TO CLAP ON THE SECOND PART OF THE SONG, BECAUSE IT HAS A STEADY BEAT.

Repeat the listening and clapping. Some classes may be ready to join in singing the words of the B section.

LET'S TRY SOME DIFFERENT MOVEMENT ON THE <u>FIRST</u> PART OF THE SONG.

Suggest moving one arm away from the body on the first phrase, "the wind blew east" (use arc shape, down to up).

Move the other arm similarly on the second phrase, "the wind blew west."

Both arms may go up together, drawing a circle in the air on "the wind blew the sunshine right down to town."

Try the movements while speaking the words, and then try the movements with the recording. Involve students in clapping steadily during the B section of the song this time, too.

(Move.)

Students should be ready to sing all the words along with the movements.

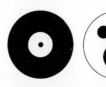

(Move.)

Summary

WHAT A GOOD JOB YOU DID SHOWING THE STEADY BEATS IN THE SECOND SECTION OF OUR SONG!

ANOTHER TIME

Follow the suggestions in MMYO 1, Teacher's Edition, for working with understandings of higher and lower pitches in *The Wind Blew East.*

ELABORATION

1. Young children should have many opportunities to respond to the steady beat of music. They can move to the music with locomotor movements (marching, walking) or non-locomotor movements (moving arms, swaying, twisting, stepping in place.) They can use body rhythms (clapping, patching, snapping) to *show* their aural perceptions. They might even play percussion instruments and draw lines on paper or chalkboard to *show* steady beats. Many musical materials are presented below. Select appropriate songs and listening selections to use with your students.

2. Use the Crayon Activities (nos. 9 and 12) in SBM (EC) and the "What Do You Hear?" charts in SBM 1:129 and SBM 2:33 to evaluate perception of "beat" and "no beat."

3. Follow this experience with model experience *Serafina,* p. 19, for young students and *War Dance Song,* p. 151, for older groups.

4. Older students may wish to use the graph in SBM 6:44 to create a sound piece strongly related to the beat.

Consider taping this experience for students to use individually.

5. Create your own *evaluatory* listening experience based on "beat" and "no beat." Choose three or four musical selections from the lists of materials below. Devise a worksheet on which students may indicate their "beat" or "no-beat" answers for each selection they hear. Young children might use a worksheet that uses symbols such as:

(beat)

(no beat)

Older students can simply circle the words "beat" or "no beat" on a worksheet. After students have listened and made choices, replay excerpts of the selections in order for students to associate the music with the correct answers. Students might clap lightly as "beat" selections are replayed and move one hand freely through the air as the "no-beat" selections are replayed.

OTHER MUSIC

● *Songs with a steady-beat section*

DUMPLIN'S. MMYO 3

GO TELL IT ON THE MOUNTAIN. MMYO 5

GREY MONDIE. SBM 2

NOAH. SBM 4

ROLL AN' ROCK. p. 120

● *Songs with a steady beat throughout*

ALL AROUND THE KITCHEN, p. 68

CLAP YOUR HANDS, p. 105, CMCM 1A and 2B; DMT (EC); MMYO 1 and 2; NDM Beg., 1, and 2; SBM 1

ELEPHANT SONG. CMCM 1B; EM 1; MMYO 2

HAND GAME SONG. SBM (EC)

MARCHING TO PRETORIA. CMCM 1B; EM 4; MMYO 2 and 3; NDM 3

WAKE ME. SBM 2

YANKEE DOODLE. CMCM 2A; EM 2; MMYO 3; NDM 3; SBM (EC)

● *Other music with a steady beat*

BOSS WALK. SBM 2

DANCE by Cage. EM 2

FANFARE IN C MAJOR by Purcell. SOM 3

MARCH from *Thesée* by Lully. SOM 3

MARCH from *Suite No. 2 for Small Orchestra* by Stravinsky. EM 2; NDM 2; SBM 2; SOM 3

See MARCHES recording, BOL 54.

MENUETTO from *Royal Fireworks Suite* by Handel. SBM 2

TRUMPET TUNE by Purcell. MMYO 3

VIENNESE MUSICAL CLOCK from *Háry János Suite* by Kodály. AIM 2, vol. 1; BOL 81; EM 4; NDM 4

THE WASHINGTON POST by Sousa. EM 3; SOM 3

● *Music with no steady beat*

THE BANSHEE by Cowell. EM 3; MMYO 3; NDM 2

ELECTRONIC STUDY NO. 1 (excerpt) by Davidovsky. SBM 2

O COME, O COME, EMMANUEL. SOM 6

POÈME ÉLECTRONIQUE by Varèse. NDM 5; SBM 4

SOUND PATTERNS (excerpt) by Oliveras. SBM 2; SOM 6

VOILES by Debussy. EM 6; MMYO 5

● *Other sound experiences with both beat and no steady beat*

CLOUDS. SBM 2:30 (poem recited with beat and with no beat)

SOUND EFFECTS. SBM 2:28 (natural sounds with beat and with no beat)

BIBLIOGRAPHY

Beer, Alice S., and Mary E. Hoffman. *Teaching Music What, How, Why.* Morristown, N.J.: Silver Burdett Co., 1973, pp. 27–28. A "beat" and "no-beat" teaching strategy designed for seven- to nine-year-olds is presented.

Robinson, Doris. "Is There a Correlation between Rhythmic Response and Emotional Disturbance?" *Journal of Music Therapy,* 2 (Summer, 1970), p. 54. The author speculates that an emotionally disturbed child may have "his own beat": one that suggests his emotions are disconnected from his rhythmic response. Thus, "his beat" may not coincide with that in the music.

THE WIND BLEW EAST

Folk Song from the Bahamas

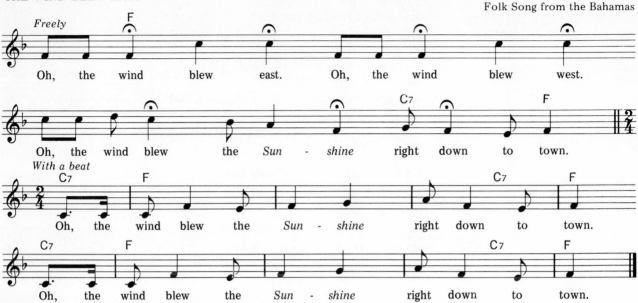

Collected, adapted and arranged by John A. Lomax and Alan Lomax. TRO – © Copyright 1942 and renewed 1969 Ludlow Music, Inc., New York, N.Y. Used by permission.

Music Learning	Chords can accompany melodies.
Musical Context	SKIP TO MY LOU (American singing game). CMCM 1A; DMT (EC), 2, 3; MMYO 1 and 4; NDM (EC); SBM 1; SOM 4
Behavioral Objective	To identify aurally the simultaneous sounding of two or more pitches on the Autoharp; and to demonstrate that recognition by strumming chords on the Autoharp.
Grade	Lower and upper
Materials	Autoharp(s) Chord chart (See below.) Students should be able to sing *Skip to My Lou*.

Focusing Statement

Summary

Song notation, p. 76.

LET'S SING <u>SKIP TO MY LOU</u> WITH AUTOHARP ACCOMPANIMENT. Point to chord chart. Note that the F and C₇ chords will be used. Explain that each letter of the chart indicates a steady beat strum.

F	F	F	F
C₇	C₇	C₇	C₇
F	F	F	F
C₇	C₇	F	F

Select two students, one for the strumming and one to press the chord buttons. Have the Autoharp players play through the chart once while you point to each strum on the chart.

AUTOHARP PLAYERS, PLAY THROUGH THE CHART TWICE THIS TIME. THE
FIRST TIME, YOU'LL PLAY ALONE. THE SECOND TIME, WE'LL SING WITH YOU.

(Don't allow Autoharp players to
pause between the two playings;
class sings song once, on second
playing)

PLAYING THE AUTOHARP WITH OUR SINGING ADDS <u>HARMONY</u>. Discuss
the idea of *harmony* with students: the multiple pitches (strings)
sounding as each chord is strummed; the compatibility of these
combined pitches.

NOTE: In the broadest sense, *harmony* is the simultaneous sounding of two or more pitches. This may be "proved" on the Autoharp
by having one student press the *G-major* bar while a second student
plucks each individual string. Three different pitches (G, B, D), in
several octaves, will be heard.

Consider changing Autoharp players at this point. THIS TIME,
LET'S HAVE THE PLAYERS STRUM JUST THE FIRST LINE OF THE CHORD
CHART FOR AN INTRODUCTION. Remind students to begin singing after
the introduction.

(Sing song once,
after introduction.)

THE AUTOHARP CHORDS SOUND MANY DIFFERENT STRINGS AT THE SAME
TIME. WHEN WE SING, OUR VOICES MAKE JUST ONE SOUND AT A TIME.

ELABORATION

1. Follow this experience with model experiences *Bow, Belinda* and
Skip to My Lou, p. 173.

2. To practice playing harmony and singing melody, see the list of
two chord songs, p. 214 and p. 217. Chord these songs "by ear," if
you are able. Otherwise, refer to the basal music series indicated.

3. Use these *"What Do You Hear?"* charts to evaluate perception of
harmony and no harmony: SBM 1:128, rec 7, and SBM 2:196, rec. 8.

● *Other songs with F and C₇ chords*

A RAM SAM SAM, p. 233

ALOUETTE. CMCM 2A

BOW, BELINDA, p. 176

CLAP YOUR HANDS, p. 105

DOWN IN THE VALLEY. DMT 4; SOM 4 and 5

HE'S GOT THE WHOLE WORLD IN HIS HAND. MMYO 6

HUSH, LITTLE BABY. DMT 4

SANDY LAND. MMYO 2, 3, and 4

SWEET POTATOES, p. 287

THE MORE WE GET TOGETHER. CMCM 2A

THE WIND BLEW EAST, p. 14

BIBLIOGRAPHY

Holt, Dennis, and Betty R. Flinchum. "Feel the Sound," *Music Educators Journal,* 63, 4 (December, 1976), p. 51. A sample lesson, using the song *Skip to My Lou* to illustrate an integrated approach to music and movement. Students are directed to perform eye-hand coordination skills of ball bouncing to the verse section, and throwing and catching skills on the refrain.

Wheeler, Lawrence, and Lois Raebeck. *Orff and Kodály Adapted for the Elementary School.* Dubuque, Iowa: Wm. C. Brown Co., 1972, pp. 31–33. Ideas are presented for creating rhythmic and melodic ostinati to accompany *Skip to My Lou.*

Music Learning	Music can move in a fast tempo or in a slow tempo.
Musical Context	THE ELEPHANT by Hap Palmer. SBM 1
Behavioral Objective	To identify, both aurally and visually, objects, people and music that move fast and slow; and to demonstrate this recognition in body movements.
Grade	Lower
Materials	Recording: SBM 1, rec 3 Photographs of objects and people moving fast *and* slow (person walking, person running; airplane on runway, airplane in air, etc.) Photographs of elephants moving fast and slow, if possible.

Focusing Statement

PEOPLE AND THINGS CAN MOVE EITHER FAST OR SLOW. MUSIC CAN, TOO.

Display photographs, and discuss with students those that suggest fast movements, and those that suggest slow movements. Young children may wish to try some of the movements suggested by the photographs. Finally, show pictures of elephants. Ask students to describe or show you the kinds of movements an elephant might make. ARE THEIR MOVEMENTS ALWAYS SLOW? CAN AN ELEPHANT MOVE FAST? HERE'S A SONG ABOUT THE ELEPHANT. LISTEN TO THE BEGINNING OF THE SONG AND DECIDE IF THE MUSIC MOVES FAST OR SLOW.

 (Play only first section A, the slow part)

(Students will, undoubtedly, notice the slow tempo.) LET'S TRY SOME MOVEMENTS WITH THE SONG.

Choose a small group of students. Space them informally around the room. Direct them to listen carefully and to move just as the music suggests. BE READY TO CHANGE YOUR MOVEMENTS IF THE MUSIC CHANGES.

In some classes, all students may be able to try these movements at the same time.

 (Move to entire song.)

Summary

YOU WERE REALLY LISTENING! YOUR MOVEMENTS CHANGED WHEN THE TEMPO CHANGED FROM SLOW, TO FAST, AND BACK TO SLOW.

Discuss the first words of the fast section ("rumble, rumble . . .") and why the elephants were moving *fast*. Reiterate that the beginning and ending sections were *slow*.

Choose another group to move, or choose two groups, one for the slow sections and one for the fast. Some classes may be ready to sing some of the words.

 Move

Summary

Encourage students to verbalize their understandings of fast and slow movement in music.

ANOTHER TIME

Focus on the form (A B A) of this song. The students have already demonstrated, through movements, the different sections: A, slow; B, fast; A, slow. Now they should be ready to identify these sections through shapes, letters, or perhaps with photographs, the form of *The Elephant*. Use ▲ ● ▲ , or two photographs depicting slow movement and one photo depicting fast movement.

ELABORATION

1. Select music in a slow and in a fast tempo. Create a movement game for each tempo. Ideas for the fast tempo might include a relay game in which the students skip around a predetermined circle, holding a stick, and passing it to another student at the completion of one circuit. The slow tempo might be expressed through flowing movements, perhaps using a scarf. The idea of "slow motion" might also be explored.

2. See "Crayon Activities" 5, 6, 12, and 20, and "What Do You Hear?" charts, SBM (EC.), SBM 1:9, rec 1; SBM 1:68, rec 4; SBM 2:12, rec 1

OTHER MUSIC

● **Music with both fast and slow tempos**

ADAGIO AND ALLEGRO from *Divertimento in B♭* (K. 186) by Mozart. EM 1
A-TISKET, A-TASKET (Versions 1 and 2). SBM 1
FINALE from *Divertissement* by Ibert. DMT 1
MINUTE WALTZ IN D♭ MAJOR by Chopin. EM 3
PLAY FOR MA DOGOMA. SBM 2
PRESTO AND PASTORALE from *Scuola di Ballo* by Boccherini. MMYO 1
SCHERZO from *Septet, Op. 20* by Beethoven. EM 1
SLOW AND STEADY. SBM (EC)
SPEED OF THE BEAT by Bogusky. SBM 2

● *Music in a slow tempo*

ADAGIO FOR STRINGS by Barber (excerpt). NDM 5; SBM 1
AIR from *Suite No. 3 in D* by Bach. EM 3

NOCTURNE FOR STRING ORCHESTRA by Borodin. NDM 5

PRELUDE TO ACT I from *Carmen Suite* by Bizet. DMT 1

THE SWAN from *Carnival of the Animals* by Saint-Saëns. BOL 51; EM 2

● *Music in a fast tempo*

BALLET OF THE UNHATCHED CHICKS from *Pictures at an Exhibition* by Moussorgsky. AIM 1; EM 4

BOURÉE from *Water Music Suite* by Handel. EM 5

CANON FOR STRING QUARTET by Schoenberg. EM 5

DEVIL'S DANCE from *A Soldier's Tale* by Stravinsky. BOL 68; MMYO Kg

HALLOWEEN by Ives. EM 1

ILE DE FRANCE from *Suite Française* by Milhaud. DMT 1

ITALIAN CONCERTO, Movement 3 (excerpt), by Bach. SBM 1

OTHER RECORDINGS

The Elephant (Hap Palmer) is recorded on *Learning Basic Skills Through Music,* I (Hap Palmer: Activity Records, Freeport, N.Y.).

While *music learning* is not the focus of the Hap Palmer recordings, teachers can adapt and utilize such activity recordings for music learning experiences.

Recordings of the Children's Record Guild and Young People's Records (Educational Activities Division of The Greystone Corp., 100 Sixth Ave., New York, N.Y. 10013) may also be utilized to focus on music learnings.

BIBLIOGRAPHY

Doll, Edna, and Mary Jarman Nelson. *Rhythms Today!* Morristown, N.J.: Silver Burdett Co., 1965. Many outstanding ideas for relating movement to musical understanding.

Taylor, Elizabeth Medert. "Teaching Music Concepts Through Body Movement," *Music Educators Journal,* 59, 8 (April, 1973), p. 50. Many ideas for using beanbags, hoops, feathers, scarves, etc., for illustrating concepts.

Zimmerman, Marilyn P. *Musical Characteristics of Children.* Washington, D.C.: Music Educators National Conference, 1971. Report of research that suggests music with a fast tempo should be used in first experiences with rhythmic movement, because children seem better able to keep time with fast tempi than with slow. Technical.

Precede this lesson with a brief discussion of the many jobs done on board an old sailing vessel (swabbing the deck, polishing wood and brass, hoisting the mains'l, weighing anchor, winding the capstan, steering, mending nets, lookout duty in the crow's nest, etc.). Mention the important role of the *shanteyman,* who led the sailors in songs to coordinate work efforts and to entertain.

Music Learning

Tempo, combined with other musical elements, gives a composition its unique musical identity.

Musical Context

SERAFINA (sea shantey). MMYO 1
FOG by Alan Hovhaness (American, b. 1911). MMYO 6

Behavioral Objective

To identify aurally the tempos of two songs, and to demonstrate this recognition through body movements.

Grade

Lower

Materials

Recordings: MMYO 1, rec 4; MMYO 6, rec 2
Large triangle, cowbell, or similar-sounding object

Place students informally around the room, so that each has plenty of space for movement.

Focusing Statement

SILENTLY CHOOSE A SHIPBOARD JOB FOR THE MUSIC WE'RE ABOUT TO HEAR. THE BOSUN'S WHISTLE, AT THE BEGINNING OF THE RECORD, IS THE SIGNAL TO BEGIN YOUR JOBS. TRY TO DO YOUR JOB TO THE BEAT OF THE MUSIC.

 Recording (SERAFINA)

Body movements

Comment on the *tempo* of the steady-beat movements. Repeat, this time with just a few students demonstrating their jobs for the entire class.

 Recording

Body movements

Song notation, p. 284.

EACH TIME YOU HEAR THIS SIGNAL (strike triangle or cowbell), EACH PERSON IS TO CHANGE TO ANOTHER JOB. START A JOB WHEN YOU HEAR THE BOSUN'S WHISTLE.

Recording

Body movements

 Instrument (teacher)
(Signal strongly at
end of each verse.)

Comment upon and discuss the variety of movements used and students' sensitivity to the rhythm and tempo of the shantey. (JOHN SWABBED THE DECK RIGHT ALONG WITH THE BEAT OF THE MUSIC.)

Now, ask each student to *silently* choose a favorite job from those explored earlier.

HOW WOULD IT LOOK AND FEEL IF THAT SAME MOVEMENT WERE DONE IN SLOW MOTION OR IN A THICK, DARK FOG?

Discuss, stressing exaggeration (*very* slow and *very* large movements), with little rhythmic regularity.

TRY TO DO YOUR MOVEMENTS WITHOUT A SOUND.

Body Rhythms

Functional, realistic movements become abstract movements through exaggeration.

Select a few students whose new movements seem most drastically altered (or abstracted) and have them demonstrate. Ask others to guess what the *original* movement must have been.

Encourage half the group to do their abstract movements while the others observe and discuss. Exchange roles.

Ask everyone to get ready to move again, stressing the slowness and largeness of movement. Ask them to WATCH FOR MY SILENT SIGNAL TO BEGIN AND MOVE AS QUIETLY AS YOU POSSIBLY CAN.

Musical styles are a secondary focus of this experience: *folk song style* and *impressionism*.

 Recording (FOG)   (Begin the record *after* all are moving. Then start inaudibly, increasing the volume just enough for all to hear.)

Body Rhythms   (As recording ends, whisper FREEZE! Hold for several seconds.)

Summary

DID THAT SONG FIT YOUR MOVEMENTS BETTER THAN THE FIRST ONE WOULD HAVE? WAS IT SLOWER OR FASTER? WAS IT LOUDER OR SOFTER? DID IT HAVE THE SAME STRONG RHYTHM AS SERAFINA? WHAT OTHER DIFFERENCES DID YOU NOTICE IN THE TWO SONGS? (INSTRUMENTS, DURATIONS, ETC.) I THINK THAT MUSIC HELPED YOUR BODIES MOVE THEIR SPECIAL WAYS.

ELABORATION

Have students examine the two sea pictures (MMYO 5, pp. 140–141) for visual contrasts similar to the movement and sound contrasts of this model experience. Or use these examples to help you select other appropriate pictures for this use.

OTHER MUSIC

Shanties

A-ROVIN'. MMYO 6
AUSTRALIA. NDM 6
AWAY FOR RIO. MMYO 4
HAUL AWAY, JOE. EM 2

Music for slow movement

BERCEUSE from *The Firebird Suite* by Stravinsky. AIM 1
CLOUDS by Debussy. BOL 70
FOG HORN by W. S. Haynie. EM 1
VOILES by Debussy. EM 6; MMYO 5

Music Learning	In "call-and-response" form, responses can be identical to the call, or contrasting.

Musical Context

STOMP DANCE (Cherokee Indian). SBM 3

HO JAMALO (India). SBM 5

MAI WAKARINGANO (Africa). SBM 5

Behavioral Objective

To identify aurally and visually the *responses* that are identical or contrasting to the *call;* and to demonstrate this awareness by using body rhythms and by visually identifying design A or B.

Grade

Upper

Materials

Recordings: SBM 3, rec 4; SBM 5, recs 1 and 6

Paper and pencil for each student

Chart of designs A and B on chalkboard or small chart

Focusing Statement

IF I ASK YOU TO RESPOND TO MY CLAPPING (X X XX X), I WONDER WHAT YOU WILL DO? TRY IT, AFTER I CLAP AGAIN.

Teacher claps: x x xx x   (The most probable response is an exact repetition.)

Encourage students to clap a clear echo. Then begin a series of *calls* which they are to repeat. Establish an underlying framework of four beats. LISTEN AND CLAP AN EXACT RESPONSE TO MY CALL.

Teacher claps	*Students clap*
1. X XX X X	1. X XX X X
2. XX XX X X	2. XX XX X X
3. XX X XX X	3. XX X XX X
4. X X XX X	4. X X XX X

Compliment students on the accuracy of their clapped responses and on their good listening, if appropriate.

LOOK AT THE TWO SETS OF DESIGNS ON THE BOARD. WHICH ONE LOOKS LIKE THE CLAPPING WE JUST DID? (A) Discuss why.

NOW, WE'RE GOING TO HEAR MUSIC BY AMERICAN INDIANS. THE SINGERS ECHO THE LEADER EXACTLY. WATCH DESIGN A AS YOU LISTEN.

Recording: STOMP DANCE *(Play only the first third.)*

Focus attention on design B. Ask HOW IS IT DIFFERENT FROM A? Discuss. TO MAKE OUR SOUNDS LIKE THIS DESIGN, WE NEED A RESPONSE PATTERN WE CAN REPEAT. Elicit clapped patterns from individual students. Before each student begins, you might say ONE, TWO, READY, BEGIN.

Student claps   (Encourage staying within a four-beat framework.)

Select a pattern that seems to "work," and encourage the entire class to clap it several consecutive times. Then explain that they should insert a space between each pattern. MAKE THE SPACE JUST AS LONG AS THE PATTERN. Teacher should demonstrate, if possible:

Teacher claps: pattern; $\left(\begin{array}{c}1\text{-}2\text{-}3\text{-}4\\ \text{space}\end{array}\right)$; pattern; $\left(\begin{array}{c}1\text{-}2\text{-}3\text{-}4\\ \text{space}\end{array}\right)$

LET'S ALL TRY IT.

All clap   (Alternate pattern with space; think beats 1–2–3–4 or count them, if it aids the rhythmic regularity.)

NOW, I'M GOING TO PUT IN A <u>DIFFERENT</u> PATTERN DURING THAT SPACE. DON'T LET ME THROW YOU OFF! Get the process going with ONE, TWO, READY, GO:

Inexperienced classes will need practice using this technique.

All clap   (Establish as before. Then teacher inserts varying patterns. Continue until objective is achieved.)

WATCH DESIGN B AS WE HEAR MUSIC FROM INDIA. LISTEN AS THE MEN SING THE SAME RESPONSE AFTER EACH CALL THEY HEAR.

Many students will be able to sing the *Ho Jamalo* response, which means "let us be together again."
The response, "Mai Wakaringano," means "Mother of Karingano."

Recording   (HO JAMALO: play about 50 seconds.)

Distribute small sheets of paper, one to each student. Have them place their names at the top. WE ARE GOING TO HEAR AFRICAN MUSIC. IF YOU HEAR RESPONSES THAT ECHO THE CALL, MARK A ON YOUR PAPER. IF YOU HEAR RESPONSES THAT CONTRAST TO THE CALL AND KEEP THEIR OWN PATTERN, MARK B ON YOUR PAPER. LISTEN CAREFULLY.

Recording   (MAI WAKARINGANO: design B)

Replay the composition, so that all students are sure of the correct response.

Summary   WHO WILL DESCRIBE ONE OF THE CALL-AND-RESPONSE STYLES WE HEARD TODAY? WHO WILL DESCRIBE THE OTHER RESPONSE? Ask students to

Cultural musical styles are a secondary focus of this experience.

recall what peoples were represented by this music. Discuss how each has a different, characteristic musical sound.

ANOTHER TIME

Listen for a periodic expansion of the call and an identical response in *Ho Jamalo.* Discover the caller repeats his melody on occasion:

△ ●
△ ●
✕ ●

□ ●
□ ●
○ ●

ELABORATION

1. Use songs from the lists which follow and design a similar model experience for lower grades.

2. As an evaluatory experience, tape three selections from those listed below. Make the tape and a worksheet available at a learning station for students to work with on their own.

OTHER RECORDED MUSIC USING "CALL-AND-RESPONSE" FORM

CHITIRUANO TRIBAL DANCE SONG, *Samandoza-Iwe* (Africa). SBM 2 (This selection is also included in model experience *War Dance Song,* p. 151, with a focus on beat and pattern.)

KALANGA DANCE (Africa). SBM 5

NFENI NEUGOMA (Africa). NDM 5

SONG FOR THE HAI (Near East). SBM 6

SONGS OF THE MUSKOGEE CREEK, I, and II. Indian House Recording (P.O. Box 472, Taos, N.M. 87571), 1970. A fine recording of contemporary Indian singers performing several stomp dance songs.

OTHER "CALL-AND-RESPONSE" SONGS

● *Songs with design A*

CHE CHE KOOLAY. SBM 2 and 3

THE GOAT. MMYO 4

JOHN HENRY. NDM 5

JOHNNY ON THE WOODPILE. DMT 1

LONG GONE. SOM 5

LONG JOHN. MMYO 6

OLD TEXAS. SBM 4; SOM 3

TONGO. DMT 2 and 3; SBM 4, SOM 2

WHO HAS THE PENNY? NDM 1

● *Songs with design B*

ALL AROUND THE KITCHEN, p. 68

THE FROG AND THE MOUSE. See p. 212.

GOGO. MMYO 2

HILL AND GULLY. MMYO 5; SBM 3

JANE, JANE, p. 227

LIMBO LIKE ME. NDM 6

OZIBANE! OZIBANE! OZIBANE! SBM 3

WON'T YOU LET THE BIRDIE OUT? SBM (EC)

BIBLIOGRAPHY

Christ, Christine, Jon Dunn, and Robert Revicki. "Song as a Measure of Man," *Music Educators Journal,* 62, 9 (May, 1976), p. 26. A stimulating article which discusses the relationship of vocal folk song style to social structure.

Herzog, George. "African Influences in North American Indian Music," in *Papers of the International Congress of Musicology,* American Musicological Society, 1944. The "call-and-response" music of the American Indians *may* have been influenced by Negro slaves who took refuge with Indian groups.

Lomax, Alan. *Cantometrics: A Method in Musical Anthropology.* Berkeley, Calif.: University of California Extension Media Center, 1976. Book and seven training tapes. The geography of song style, pp. 22–47, will be especially valuable to teachers of social studies. The training tapes provide an unparalleled opportunity to gain an insight into the relationships between folk song style and social organization.

McAllester, David P. "Musics of the Americas," *Music Educators Journal,* 59, 2 (October, 1972), p. 54. A brief discussion of Indian music of North and South America and of influences from Europe, Asia, and Africa. For the general reader.

Merriam, Alan P. "African Music," in *Continuity and Change in African Cultures,* eds. William R. Bascom and Melville Jean Herskovits. Chicago, Ill.: University of Chicago Press, 1959, p. 49.

Parthun, Paul. "Tribal Music of North America," *Music Educators Journal,* 62, 5 (January, 1976), p. 32.

Reimer, Bennett. "Patterns for the Future," *Music Educators Journal,* 63, 4 (December, 1976), p. 22. A thoughtful analysis of emerging patterns in music education, including the trend to study musical qualities in a wide variety of styles from many cultures.

B

Melody: a linear succession of pitches; the horizontal structure in music.

BARCAROLLE; POLKA
The pitches of melodies can be mostly connected or mostly disconnected.

JOHN THE RABBIT
Pitches in a tonal pattern can repeat.

THE FROG AND THE MOUSE
Melodies can include skips of an octave.

SCOTLAND'S BURNING
A melody can include repeated tonal patterns.

GRIZZLY BEAR
Pitches in a tonal pattern can repeat or can move by skipping up.

Expressive qualities: those qualities (dynamics, tempo, timbre) which, combined with other musical elements, give a composition its unique musical identity.

PARADE
Musical sounds can be soft or loud or can gradually become softer or louder.

After completing each model experience, decide how successfully you are able to identify, explain, or demonstrate the music learning that was the focus of the experience. Check the appropriate box.

Secure
Fairly secure
Insecure

Music Learning	The pitches of melodies can be mostly connected or mostly disconnected.

Musical Context

BARCAROLLE from *Tales of Hoffman* by Jacques Offenbach ("AWE-fn-bok") (German, 1819–1880). AIM 3 (I); DMT 5; NDM 1

POLKA from the ballet *The Golden Age* by Dmitri Shostakovich ("shaw-stuh-KOE-vich") (Russian; b. 1906). DMT 3; EM 2; MMYO 2

Behavioral Objective

To identify melodies with pitches mostly connected and mostly disconnected; and to demonstrate that recognition by drawing abstract figures on paper while listening to music.

Grade

Lower

Materials

Recordings:

BARCAROLLE — AIM; DMT 5; NDM 1; SBM 6, rec 2

POLKA — DMT 3; EM 2, rec 7; MMYO 2, rec 2

Two sheets of construction paper for each student: one light, bright color; one darker color. Give each student two different colors.

Two crayons of contrasting color for each student

Withhold titles of compositions to be played until later in this experience.

Focusing Statement

WHEN I CALL OUT A WORD, USE ONE HAND TO DO WHAT THE WORD SUGGESTS. FOR EXAMPLE, IF I SAY "POPCORN POPPING," WHAT KIND OF LINE WILL YOU DRAW IN THE AIR? SHOW ME.

Continue with several examples to be drawn in the air: airplane taking off; hamburgers frying; pouring syrup over pancakes; pebbles dropped into water, etc.

THOSE WORDS SUGGESTED DIFFERENT KINDS OF LINES. MUSIC CAN DO THAT, TOO.

WE'RE GOING TO LISTEN TO TWO PIECES OF MUSIC AND DRAW SOMETHING THAT WILL MATCH EACH PIECE. WE'LL USE A DIFFERENT COLOR PAPER FOR EACH PIECE.

Distribute colored paper, two different colors to each student. Students may help you with this.

FIRST, LET'S LISTEN TO PART OF EACH PIECE. AFTER YOU HAVE HEARD BOTH, CHOOSE THE COLOR YOU WANT TO USE FOR EACH.

 Play excerpts; emphasize listening to *both* pieces before making a final choice of colors.

NOW, LET'S USE CRAYONS AS WE LISTEN TO THE MUSIC. DRAW THE SAME KINDS OF THINGS YOU DREW IN THE AIR.

Distribute crayons, two colors to each student. Caution students to avoid drawing pictures of things (objects) we can recognize.

BARCAROLLE (Consider starting at the end of the long introduction.)

 POLKA

Substitute titles for numerals, if you wish.

BARCAROLLE: a boat-song of Venetian gondoliers; always in $\frac{6}{8}$ or $\frac{12}{8}$ meter, in moderate tempo.

Summary

Have students write the number "1" on the back of the first drawing and "2" on the back of the second.

Write *Barcarolle* on one side of the chalkboard. Select No. 1 drawings from about half the class and place them on the chalk tray. (A student might collect all the crayons while you are doing this.)

Ask, DO THESE DRAWINGS LOOK AT ALL SIMILAR? Discuss. Consider displaying the drawings one at a time as you replay *Barcarolle.*

Write *Polka* on the other side of the chalkboard. Place No. 2 drawings from the other half of the class under this title. Discuss similarities and replay *Polka,* if appropriate.

YOUR DRAWINGS CERTAINLY SUGGEST A CONNECTED MELODY <u>LINE</u> (point to *Barcarolle* drawings) AND A DISCONNECTED MELODY <u>LINE</u> (point to *Polka* drawings.)

ANOTHER TIME

This model experience might be done with body movements serving as the students' medium of expression. The exploration of *line* should involve total body movement. Use *locomotor* or *axial* (nonlocomotor) movements, depending on available space.

ELABORATION

Tape two different selections (see "Other Music") for individual students to use at a learning station or listening post. Make paper and crayons available for drawing.

OTHER MUSIC

● *Pieces with mostly connected melodies*

AIR from *Suite No. 3 in D* by J.S. Bach. EM 3

NOCTURNE (for string orchestra) by Borodin. NDM 5

PASTORALE from *Presto and Pastorale* by Boccherini. MMYO 1

THE SWAN from *Carnival of the Animals* by Saint-Saëns. BOL 51; EM 2

● *Pieces with mostly disconnected melodies*

DEVIL'S DANCE from *A Soldier's Tale* by Stravinsky. BOL 68; MMYO-Kg.

FANFARE FOR THE COMMON MAN by Copland. NDM 5

GAVOTTE from *Classical Symphony* by Prokofiev. NDM 4; SBM 2, 4, 6

BIBLIOGRAPHY

Nye, Robert Evans, and Vernice Trousdale Nye. *Music in the Elementary School.* Englewood Cliffs, N.J.: Prentice-Hall, Inc., 1970, pp. 202–203. Song approach to connected and disconnected sounds is presented; includes list of standard recordings, illustrating articulation of melodic line.

BARCAROLLE: THEME

from *The Tales of Hoffman* by Offenbach

Music Learning

> Pitches in a tonal pattern can repeat.

Musical Context

JOHN THE RABBIT (American folk-game song). MMYO-Kg; SBM 2

Reading Objective

Behavioral Objective

To identify aurally the repeated pitches heard in the "response"; and to demonstrate that recognition by singing and playing the response.

Grade

Lower

Materials

Recording: MMYO Kg; SBM 2

Resonator bell (low E) and mallet

Teacher should learn the song ahead of time. (If insecure about singing the song, chant the lyrics rhythmically, with expressive inflection.)

Focusing Statement

I'M THINKING OF TWO WORDS AND WANT YOU TO TRY SAYING THOSE WORDS SEVERAL DIFFERENT WAYS.

WHEN I GIVE YOU A SIGNAL, LIKE THIS (raise one hand), SHOW HOW QUIETLY YOU CAN SAY THE WORDS "OH YES." REMEMBER, WAIT FOR MY SIGNAL.

Song notation, p. 266

Repeat this procedure, having them say "Oh, yes" *quickly, slowly, scarily,* etc. (They will carry this to outrageous extremes with little encouragement!)

HOW MANY TIMES WOULD YOU NEED TO <u>CLAP</u> TO MAKE YOUR <u>HANDS</u> SAY "OH, YES?" (twice) Have them do this on signal.

HOW MANY TIMES WOULD YOU <u>PATSCH</u>? (two) STAMP YOUR FEET? (two)

NOW LET'S <u>SING</u> THE TWO WORDS. BEFORE WE DO, TELL ME HOW MANY BELLS YOU SEE. (Display the low-E bell only.) YES, ONLY ONE. WHEN WE SING "OH YES," WE'LL SING BOTH WORDS ON THE <u>SAME</u> PITCH. LISTEN TO IT.

Play ♪ ♩

("Oh, Yes") on E bell

(teacher)

NOW, SING "OH, YES" AS I PLAY IT.

Repeat several times, if appropriate.

I KNOW A SONG THAT HAS "OH, YES" IN IT. EACH TIME YOU SEE ME GET READY TO PLAY "OH, YES" ON THE BELL, YOU GET READY TO SING ALONG.

Sing (or chant) the song with deliberate rhythm. Exaggerate your preparation to play the bell for each "Oh, yes" and sing these responses with the students.

Old John the rabbit (play and sing "OH, YES")
Old John the rabbit (play and sing "OH, YES")
Got a mighty bad habit (play and sing . . .) etc.

Next, play the recording of the song. Remind students that their job is to sing the *responses* ("Oh, yes.")

Maintain good eye contact to encourage singing.

A good technique to use with *call-and-response* songs, such as JOHN THE RABBIT, is to keep one hand on the volume control of the record player. You can, by quickly lowering and raising the volume, "remove" each "Oh, yes," so the students' responses become more prominent. They also feel more responsible for filling the silence.

Summary

WHO REMEMBERS HOW MANY DIFFERENT PITCHES WE USED TO SING THE "OH, YES" RESPONSES IN <u>JOHN THE RABBIT</u>? (One; display E bell again.) ONE IS RIGHT. WE SANG TWO WORDS, BUT ON THE SAME PITCH.

ANOTHER TIME

1. Provide a cassette of *John the Rabbit* for individual students to use at a tape recorder with earphones. They can play the responses on bells as the tape plays. Some might read the responses from the song notation. (See "Reading Objective," p. 28, or song notation, p. 266.)

2. Have students sound the responses by playing the E bell. As the song is sung, move from student to student, inviting each to play a response as the class *sings* the response. Teacher should hold the bell and move the mallet *quickly* from student to student so that each is ready to play the response on time. Encourage individuals to sing as they play the bell.

3. A percussion instrument might be used to "fill in" the responses. Or, the responses can be shown with a body movement. (SAY "OH, YES" WITH ONE FINGER, ONE SHOULDER, ONE ARM, YOUR HEAD, etc.) These techniques will stress the rhythm of the response. The short-long (♪ ♩) durations produce *syncopation* in the responses.

4. Encourage students to learn the easier lines of the lyrics immediately. ("He ate tomatoes, and sweet potatoes," for instance.)

See Glossary.

OTHER SONGS WITH CONSPICUOUS REPEATED PITCHES

CATCH A FALLING STAR. SOM 6

DOWNRIGHT UPRIGHT. SOM 4

KOOKABURRA, p. 285

OLD BRASS WAGON. CMCM 1B; EM 2; SOM 2

SING HALLELU, p. 261

TIRITOMBA. SOM 5

WAKE UP NOW. SOM 4

See model experience *Minka,* p. 167

RECORDINGS

Listen to OLD UNCLE RABBIT in *Afro-American Blues and Game Songs,* Library of Congress AFS L4, ed. Alan Lomax. It is a charming variant of *John the Rabbit.*

BIBLIOGRAPHY

Ludwig, Alice Jean, and Florence Tyson. "A Song for Michael," *Journal of Music Therapy,* 6, 3 (Fall, 1969), pp. 82–86. How the song *John the Rabbit* was used to establish positive verbal communication with a twelve-year-old aphasic boy.

These therapy sessions are documented in a 16mm sound film *Song for Michael* (1966). It is available, for educational or clinical use only, from Music Therapy Center, 18 West 74th Street, New York 10023.

Music Learning	Melodies can include skips of an octave.
Musical Context	THE FROG AND THE MOUSE (English folk song). EM 3
Reading Objective	 (optional)

Behavioral Objective

To identify aurally the interval of an octave; and to demonstrate that recognition by singing the interval and by playing it on resonator bells.

Grade

Lower or upper

Materials

Recording; EM 3, rec 3
Resonator bells D E F G A B♭ C D and one mallet. (Melody bells may be used.)

Focusing Statement

Song notation, p. 289.

AS THIS RECORDING PLAYS, LISTEN FOR THE WORDS "WHIPSEE DIDDLE DEE DANDY O!" BE READY TO TELL HOW THE VOICES MOVE WHEN THEY SING THE "WHIPSEE" PART.

   (Play one verse, then fade out.)

See Appendix for Curwen hand signs.

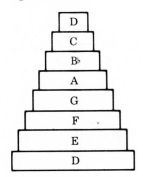

(whip - see)

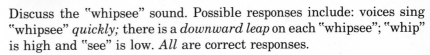
ta   *ti*

If appropriate, elaborate on the relation of the word *octave* to such words as octopus, octagon, etc.

Use octave notation, if appropriate.

Discuss the "whipsee" sound. Possible responses include: voices sing "whipsee" *quickly;* there is a *downward leap* on each "whipsee"; "whip" is high and "see" is low. *All* are correct responses.

Play the recording again, encouraging students to sing each "whipsee." Curwen hand signs *(la)* may be used during the singing of the high and low pitches (D.) Or, students may move their hands from high to low, or clap high on the high D and *patsch* on the low D.

   Body movement   (Play all or part of recording. Try to help students to be ready for the third "whipsee" of each verse.)

LET'S PLAY THE "WHIPSEE" PART ON BELLS. Display the eight resonator bells (see margin.) Ask students to count the bells from D to D (1–8.)
   WE NEED ONLY THE TWO D BELLS FOR PLAYING "WHIPSEE." (Display these two bells.) WHEN TWO BELLS WITH THE SAME LETTER NAME ARE EIGHT BELLS APART, WE SAY THEY ARE AN <u>OCTAVE</u> APART.
   Elicit from students that the smaller D bell will make the higher sound and the larger D bell, the lower sound; discuss why.
   Invite several students to play the D–D octave. BE SURE TO PLAY THE OCTAVE QUICKLY, JUST AS THE SINGERS SING IT ON THE RECORD.
   Teacher and class should try singing the words "whipsee diddle dee dandy o" as each player plays the octave.

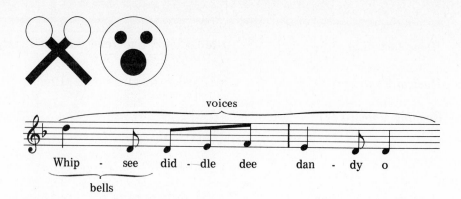

voices

Whip - see did - dle dee dan - dy o

bells

Very young students may enjoy dramatizing this ballad.

Assign several students to take turns playing the octaves with the recording. (Three students can have turns during each verse.) Encourage the other students to sing each "whipsee diddle dee dandy o," and as much of the rest of the song as they are ready to sing.

(Play entire recording.)

Summary

WHO CAN REMEMBER HOW MANY TONES MAKE UP AN OCTAVE? (8) DO TWO PITCHES AN OCTAVE APART HAVE THE SAME OR DIFFERENT LETTER NAMES? (same) THE OCTAVES GIVE <u>THE FROG AND THE MOUSE</u> A REAL ZIP!

The Frog and the Mouse in MMYO 5 is in the key of C minor. Simply substitute two C bells, an octave apart, to do this model experience with the MMYO recording.

ANOTHER TIME

Encourage students to learn to play the entire melodic fragment, "whipsee diddle dee dandy o." Further, the entire song can be played, using the pitches of the D-minor scale, as displayed in the "bell pyramid" in this model experience.

OTHER MUSIC WITH OCTAVE SKIPS

AMAHL AND THE NIGHT VISITORS by Menotti ("Look, mother . . ." octave E–E). SOM 5

BONSOIR, MES AMI. MMYO 5

BYE'M BYE. EM 2; SBM 2

FOR HEALTH AND STRENGTH. MMYO 3 and 4; SOM 1 and 3

GAVOTTE from *Classical Symphony* by Prokofiev. NDM 4; SBM 2, 4, and 6

HOP UP, MY LADIES. DMT 3; SBM (EC); SOM 2

THE KEEPER. MMYO 4

NIGHT HERDING SONG. MMYO 3

OLD ABRAM BROWN. MMYO 4

THE OLD WOMAN AND THE PEDDLER. MMYO 2; SOM 2

QUAIL'S CALL. MMYO 3

SARASPONDA. CMCM 2B; DMT 3; EM 3

SCOTLAND'S BURNING. p. 283

THE TAILOR AND THE MOUSE. DMT 3

THIS IS MY COUNTRY. SOM 5

WAIT FOR THE WAGON. MMYO 3; SOM 3

WHATEVER CAN THAT BE? MMYO 1 (C–D pattern repeats at the octave)

BIBLIOGRAPHY

Duell, Orpha K., and Richard C. Anderson. "Pitch Discrimination Among Primary School Children," *Journal of Educational Psychology*, 58, 6 (1967), p. 315. This research indicates that wider intervals seem to be easier for young children to perceive.

Music Learning	A melody can include repeated tonal patterns.
Musical Context	SCOTLAND'S BURNING. MMYO 3; NDM 4
Behavioral Objective	To identify aurally a rhythmic and melodic pattern; and to repeat that pattern exactly with clapping and singing.
Grade	Lower
Materials	None

Focusing Statement

LET'S TRY AN ECHO GAME.

Explain to students that you will first clap a pattern, then they will echo it exactly. Demonstrate by clapping this pattern:

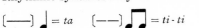

Clap the same pattern again, identifying it as the echo:

Rhythmic syllables may also be used:

Now, try a few more patterns with the students. Remind them to listen carefully and to wait until they have heard the *whole* pattern before starting the echo.

Examples:

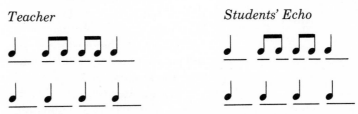

| *Teacher* | *Students' Echo* |

Now, try for continuity by moving from one pattern and echo to the next, without any breaks. Keep the game going as long as interest is high.

Body rhythms

Summary

YOU LISTENED WELL. IT TAKES GOOD LISTENING TO REPEAT THOSE PATTERNS EXACTLY.

NOW, LET'S PLAY THE ECHO GAME WITH OUR VOICES.

Song notation, p. 283.

Explain to students that they should repeat everything they hear you say. Chant rhythmically each measure of the lyrics of *Scotland's Burning,* and then gesture for students to repeat the measure just chanted.

Teacher	*Students' echo*
● SCOTLAND'S BURNING,	● (SCOTLAND'S BURNING,)
● LOOK OUT!	● (LOOK OUT!)
● FIRE! FIRE!	● (FIRE! FIRE!)
● POUR ON WATER!	● (POUR ON WATER!)

Words might be written on board.

Repeat until class is comfortable with the lyrics.

Sound D for the starting pitch.

THESE WORDS GO WITH A SONG. Sing the song. Ask students to listen and raise their hands each time they hear the *repeated part* (echo).

Some classes may be ready to use Curwen hand signs. See "Another Time," below.

LET'S ALL SING THE SONG! After singing a measure, gesture for students to sing the echo, and continue throughout song.

WE'RE READY TO SING ALL THE WORDS NOW. WE ALL HAVE TO DO EVERYTHING. HOW MANY TIMES WILL WE SING "SCOTLAND'S BURNING"? (2) HOW MANY TIMES WILL WE SING "LOOK OUT"? (2) "FIRE! FIRE!"? (2) "POUR ON WATER!"? (2)

Summary

IT CERTAINLY MAKES A SONG EASY TO SING WHEN WE REPEAT THE SAME WORDS, THE SAME MELODY, AND THE SAME RHYTHMS.

ANOTHER TIME

1. Challenge more able classes to learn the Curwen hand signs for do, re, mi, and so, and use them with *Scotland's Burning*.

Teach the hand signs, using the echo technique: teacher sings and pantomimes each of the four tonal patterns of *Scotland's Burning;* then the students sing and pantomime.

For greater physical involvement, strike the hands together in front of the body on each syllable:

See Appendix.

> do = clenched fists strike, thumbs together
>
> re = slanted fingers strike, index fingers touching
>
> mi = horizontal fingers strike, index fingers touching
>
> so = palms touch, thumbs on top and pointing the same direction as the fingers

2. Four students could play the four tonal patterns on the melody bells. When they are ready, encourage them to play the song for the class.

3. Add a drone accompaniment to the singing: sound the G and D bells together and play in a slow, steady rhythm.

4. Add an Autoharp drone. Press the G minor and G₇ buttons simultaneously. Two students can play, by assigning one student to press the buttons and the other to strum a steady rhythm.

ELABORATION

1. Individuals can serve as leaders and create new echo patterns for the class (or a small group).

2. For more challenge in the rhythmic echo game, lengthen the pattern or create more difficult patterns. Combine other body rhythms (*patsch,* stamp) with the hand clapping. To add tone-color interest, substitute percussion instruments for body rhythms.

3. Use "Rhythm Echoes": SBM 1, rec 6; SBM 2, rec 6; and SBM 4, rec 3. Rhythm patterns are played on percussion instruments. Students may clap, tap, or play the patterns on a percussion instrument for the echoes. Give experienced students the more difficult patterns to echo.

4. Encourage students to sing or play echoes. Begin with the so-mi (G–E) interval. Improvise various melodic patterns on this interval and have the class echo them. Hand signs are appropriate.

OTHER MUSIC

● *Songs with repeated tonal patterns*

ARE YOU SLEEPING? pp. 163, 259

CHE CHE KOOLAY. SBM 2

THE GOAT. MMYO 4

I'M ON MY WAY. SOM 5

JOHN HENRY. NDM 5

JOHNNY ON THE WOODPILE. DMT 1

LONG JOHN. CMCM 3C; MMYO 6 (LONG GONE, SOM 5)

OLD TEXAS. SBM 4; SOM 3 (TEXAS COWBOY'S SONG, DMT 4)

TONGO. DMT 2 & 3; SBM 4; SOM 2

See also SCOTLAND'S BURNING (F major). EM 2

● *Music with identical melodic phrases*

STOMP DANCE (Cherokee Indian). SBM 3

SHEPHERD'S DANCE from *Amahl and the Night Visitors* by Menotti. BOL 58; SOM 5

BIBLIOGRAPHY

Aronoff, Frances Webber. "Games Teachers Play: Strategies to Make Music Move Children," *Music Educators Journal* 58, 6 (February, 1971), p. 28. The echo song *Tongo* is used in a music-and-movement game strategy.

Music Learning	Pitches in a tonal pattern can repeat or can move by skipping up.
Musical Context	GRIZZLY BEAR (Negro work song). MMYO 6
Reading Objective	

(See blank notation below.)

Behavioral Objective	To identify aurally and visually the pitches that repeat and move up; and to demonstrate that recognition by singing and playing the two melodic patterns.
Grade	Lower or upper.
Materials	Recording: MMYO 6, rec 8
	Resonator bells or melody bells; mallet (Use bells with recording *only if they are in tune with each other.*)

Focusing Statement

CAN YOU HEAR A PART IN THIS SONG THAT IS REPEATED?

 (Play enough of recording for students to identify responses.)

Students will readily recognize the "griz-ze-ly bear" part was repeated. *Write those words on the board.*

    LISTEN TO A BIT OF THE SONG AGAIN AND DECIDE IF THE "GRIZ-ZE-LY BEAR" PART IS ALWAYS SUNG THE SAME WAY.

 (Play excerpt.)

Most students will notice that "griz-ze-ly bear" sometimes goes up and sometimes stays the same. Place lines showing melodic direction above the words on the board, adding a second set of words:

    (1) griz- ze- ly bear   (2) griz- ze- ly bear

LET'S SING THE "GRIZ-ZE-LY BEAR" PARTS THIS TIME.

    Indicate that half the class will sing the *first* response (skips up) and the rest of the class will sing the *second* response (pitch repeats). Remind students that the two patterns alternate throughout the song.

 (Play *entire* recording.)

WE'RE READY TO ADD SOME BELL PLAYERS.

Use staff notation with more experienced classes. See "Reading objective."

Ask how many bells will be needed to play the first response, the one that *skips up*. Sing it for them if they are not sure. Two bells will be needed. Indicate that the D bell will begin the pattern and the other bell will be F♯. Select a student who can play the response that skips up.

If students are ready, help them discover that D-F♯ is an interval of a *third*.

$$\overline{}\ \ \begin{array}{ccc} \text{—} & \text{—} & \text{—} \\ (1)\ \text{D} & \text{D} & \text{D} \end{array}\ \ \overline{\text{F♯}}$$

Ask how many bells will be needed to play the *second* response, the one with repeated pitches throughout. Students should respond that only one bell will be needed. Select the D bell and select a student to play the repeated pitch response.

The class might use Curwen hand signs to show melodic direction.

$$\begin{array}{cccc} \text{—} & \text{—} & \text{—} & \text{—} \\ (2)\ \text{D} & \text{D} & \text{D} & \text{D} \end{array}$$

Try each bell player's part as the class sings each response.

WE'RE READY TO SING <u>AND</u> PLAY THE "GRIZ-ZE-LY BEAR" PART WHEN IT COMES IN THE SONG.

All students should sing both responses. In fact, some students may be ready to sing *all* the words.

Summary

HOW DID THE PITCHES IN RESPONSE NO. 1 MOVE? (up) BY SKIPPING OR STEPPING? (skipping) HOW DID THE PITCHES IN RESPONSE NO. 2 MOVE? (repeated pitches or stayed on same level)

ANOTHER TIME

Add the offbeat snapping suggested in MMYO 6 for *Grizzly Bear.* This will emphasize the syncopation.

ELABORATION

Model experience *Pianists,* p. 84, would be a logical follow-up.

OTHER SONGS WITH REPEATED MELODIC PATTERNS

ALL AROUND THE KITCHEN, p. 68

GOGO. MMYO 2 (repeated and upward movement in responses)

HILL AND GULLY. MMYO 5 (pattern of repeated pitches)

JANE, JANE, p. 227 (stepwise pattern, D-E)

JOHN THE RABBIT, p. 266 (pattern of repeated pitches)

JOHNNY ON THE WOODPILE. DMT 1

BIBLIOGRAPHY

Bergethon, Bjornar, and Eunice Boardman, *Musical Growth in the Elementary School* (2nd ed.) New York: Holt, Rinehart and Winston, 1970. Contains a discussion of the vocal range of the young child, which is generally quite limited:

Debban, Betty. "The Direct Link in Reading Readiness, *Music Educators Journal*, 63, 5 (January, 1977), p. 42. An article focusing on the link between readiness to read music and successful reading of traditional notation.

GRIZZLY BEAR

Negro Work Song

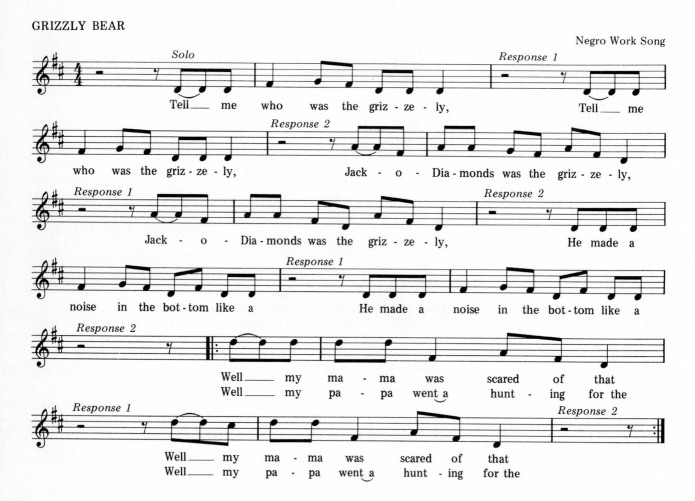

Music Learning	Musical sounds can be soft or loud or can gradually become softer or louder.

Musical Context

PARADE from *Divertissement* by Jacques Ibert ("ee-bear") (French, 1890–1962). AIM 1; SBM 3

Behavioral Objective

To identify aurally the rhythmic phrases and parts of musical composition that are soft and loud, and to demonstrate that recognition by responding in appropriate body rhythms.

Grade

Lower

Materials

Recording: SBM 3, rec 3; AIM 1

(Withhold title of the composition until end of lesson.)

Before proceeding with this experience, students should have explored echo clapping. See p. 21 and p. 33.

Focusing Statement

See Glossary

Forte (FOHR-tay) (Italian term for *loud*)

Piano (pee-AHN-oh) (Italian term for *soft*)

Pianoforte is the precise name for the instrument we call *piano*.

LET'S PLAY AN ECHO GAME. BE READY FOR SOME NEW IDEAS.

Create rhythmic phrases for students to repeat. Clap some phrases *loud* and some *soft*. Make sure students respond with appropriate *dynamics*. If students are able, try dynamic changes *within* a phrase.

Body rhythms

YOU MADE A BIG DIFFERENCE BETWEEN YOUR LOUD AND SOFT CLAPPING!

WE'RE GOING TO LISTEN TO A PIECE OF MUSIC THAT BEGINS SOFTLY, BUT HAS LOUD PARTS, TOO. WE'LL CLAP THE STEADY BEATS AS WE LISTEN.

WHO CAN SHOW ME SOFT STEADY BEAT CLAPPING? AND LOUD STEADY BEAT CLAPPING? Have students demonstrate this.

Ask students to be ready to begin clapping the steady beats softly, but to listen carefully for *any* and *all* changes in dynamics.

(Encourage students to adjust to tempo changes, too.)

Body rhythms

Students will discover that the music begins softly, gradually increases in volume to loud, and then decreases to a soft ending.

$$p \underline{\hspace{1.2cm}} f \hspace{0.6cm} \underline{\hspace{1.2cm}} p$$

HOW COULD YOU SHOW SOFT STEPS WITH YOUR FEET? (tiptoe, etc.) HOW ABOUT LOUD STEPS? (stamping, etc.) WHAT KINDS OF STEPS COULD YOU TAKE WHEN THE MUSIC IS IN BETWEEN SOFT AND LOUD AND LOUD AND SOFT? (walking, marching, etc.)

LET'S TRY SOME OF THOSE MOVEMENTS WITH THE MUSIC NOW.

In some classes, all students may be ready to try movements.

Choose a small group (up to half the class) to move to the music. The rest of the students can again clap the steady beats.

Body rhythms

Repeat, giving remaining students an opportunity to move to the music. Consider giving a few percussion instruments to students who are not moving.

Body rhythms

Summary

YOU CHANGED FROM SOFT TO LOUD, AND BACK TO SOFT AGAIN WITH HAND CLAPPING AND WITH YOUR FEET. CAN YOU DECIDE WHY THE COMPOSER CALLED THIS PIECE <u>PARADE</u>? Ask students to decide where the parade might have been when the music was soft, and also when the music was loud.

ANOTHER TIME

Use the many ideas for *Parade,* suggested in the Teacher's Guide, AIM 1.

ELABORATION

1. Write several dynamic symbols on cards:

Arrange in any order. Then, using percussion instruments, create a "sound piece" with dynamic contrasts. A conductor may be needed to indicate changes!

2. See "Crayon Activities" 7, 8, 10 and 11 in SBM (EC), pp. 40 and 48.

3. See "Sound Effects, Soft and Loud," SBM 1:34, rec. 2.

4. Create a "sound piece" using dynamic changes. Follow the ideas suggested in *Sound Piece 1* by D. Walker, SBM 3:50.

5. To evaluate perception of loud and soft dynamics, use the following "What Do You Hear?" charts in SBM: SBM 1:36; rec 2; SBM 2:43, rec 2; SBM 3:52, rec 3; SBM 4:59, rec. 4.

OTHER MUSIC

DREAM MARCH by Copland. AIM 2, vol. 2; EM 1

PARADE by Gould. EM 1

WHEAT DANCE from *Estancia* by Ginastera. AIM 4, vol. 1; CMCM 3A

BIBLIOGRAPHY

Zimmerman, Marilyn P. *Musical Characteristics of Children*. Washington, D.C.: Music Educators Conference, 1971, p. 11. A report of research that suggests that strong dynamic contrasts do *not* need to be unduly emphasized, because perception of loudness develops early and with little formal training. It is reported, however, that specific vocabulary must be utilized, because *high* and *low* are often applied to dynamics. The following resources discuss research on dynamics: Andrews, Frances M., and Ned C. Deihl. "Development of a Technique for Identifying Elementary School Children's Musical Concepts," *Journal of Research in Music Education*, 18, 3 (February, 1970), p. 214.

Laverty, Gladys E. "The Development of Children's Concepts of Pitch, Duration, and Loudness as a Function of Grade Levels," as reviewed by David Swanzy in *Council of Research in Music Education*, 23 (Winter, 1971), p. 33.

Rhythm: all of the durations that occur in music.

KANGAROO
> A melodic rhythm usually includes long and short sounds.

MARCH, LITTLE SOLDIER
> The prevailing rhythm of a musical composition can include consecutive long sounds, consecutive short sounds, or combinations.

BINGO
> Rhythm patterns can include sounds of long and short duration.

Expressive qualities: those qualities (dynamics, tempo, timbre) which, combined with other musical elements give a composition its unique musical identity.

TOCCATA FOR PERCUSSION, etc.
> Instrumental families (woodwind, string, brass, percussion) can be identified by their timbres.

*OVEN GRILL CONCERTO; POÈME ÉLECTRONIQUE
> Timbre, duration, and volume can be altered electronically.

After completing each model experience, decide how successfully you are able to identify, explain, or demonstrate the music learning that was the focus of the experience. Check the appropriate box.

Secure Fairly secure Insecure

*Group work-through experience.

42

Music Learning	A melodic rhythm usually includes long and short sounds.
Musical Context	KANGAROO from *Carnival of the Animals* by Camille Saint-Saëns ("sa[n] saw[n]s") (French, 1835–1921). BOL 51; EM 2; SOM Kg
Behavioral Objective	To identify aurally the long and short durations in a melodic rhythm; and to demonstrate this recognition by manipulating puppets appropriately.
Grade	Upper

Materials	Recording: BOL 51; EM 2, rec 8; SOM Kg, rec 7
	A small branch of a tree, about 2 ft. tall
	Two puppets:
	    1. resembling a cat (use a sock)
	    2. small, artificial bird on a stiff wire (wire about 15 in. long)

Focusing Statement

PRETEND YOU ARE CATS, LOOKING AROUND FOR A BIRD. SHOW ME WHAT TYPE OF MOVEMENT YOU MIGHT MAKE. Select a few students to act out their ideas.

    Body movement (cats)

IF YOU WERE A BIRD, WHAT KIND OF MOVEMENT MIGHT YOU MAKE? Encourage "actors" to think about crouching, stalking, leaping, and other catlike movements. Select a different group of students to act out their ideas for bird movements.

    Body movement (birds)

NOW, LET'S HEAR SOME MUSIC THAT SEEMS TO SUGGEST THESE MOVEMENTS. LISTEN TO HEAR IF A BIRD AND A CAT WOULD MOVE AT THE SAME TIME.

 (Listen to KANGAROO.)

Students will also be responding to high pitches (bird) and low (cat).

A bird and a cat would *not* move at the same time. Discuss the jerky, uneven sounds and their appropriateness to the bird movements. Decide WHEN THE SHORT (or fast) SOUNDS ARE HEARD, WHICH CREATURE IS MOVING? (the bird) DURING THE LONGER (and slower) SOUNDS, WHICH? (the cat) Listen again, if appropriate.

    Show the students the two puppets, the bird and the cat. WE NEED PUPPETEERS TO USE THE CAT AND BIRD PUPPETS. Select two students.

    Remind puppeteers to MOVE ONLY WHEN YOU HEAR "YOUR" MUSIC. The teacher may sit between the puppeteers, holding the branch, as a part of the scene. (And perhaps acting as a prompter!)

 Puppetry

DOES THE BIRD MOVE FIRST? (yes) FOLLOWED BY THE CAT? (yes) Discuss how the two musical ideas alternate. Listen to discover that the "bird music" ends the composition on a high-pitched chord.

Select two more students as puppeteers, and urge them to think of a story for the music.

 Puppetry

Discuss students' ideas for a story, using birds and cats. (Classes have created a chase in which the bird hops from branch to branch, but the cat never climbs high enough to catch it. The bird flies away on the final chord, perching on some high place.)

NOW, LET'S FIT YOUR STORY TO THE MUSIC.

 (Allow several pairs of pupils to act as puppeteers. A third person may hold the branch.)

Summary

THE LONG AND SHORT SOUNDS (AND THE HIGH AND LOW SOUNDS) MADE THAT VERY GOOD MUSIC FOR OUR PLAY. BUT THE COMPOSER OF THE MUSIC TITLED IT "KANGAROO"! CAN YOU IMAGINE WHY? (Discuss the long and short durations, up-and-down melodies.)

ELABORATION

1. For very young children, try movements that will enable them to "show" that they hear the short and long sounds. An excellent choice is the A section of "Ballet of the Unhatched Chicks" from *Pictures at an Exhibition* by Moussorgsky, AIM 1; BOL 82; DMT (EC); EM 4; SBM 6. Encourage children to move with short steps to the short sounds, but to "freeze" when they hear the single long sound at the end of the A section. (The form of the composition is A A B A.)

2. To evaluate perception of long and short sounds, use "What Do You Hear?" chart 5, SBM (EC): 134, rec 6, and "What Do You Hear?" chart in SBM 1:74, rec 5.

OTHER MUSIC WITH SHORT AND LONG SOUNDS

THE BANSHEE by Cowell. EM 3; MMYO 3

BRANDENBURG CONCERTO NO. 3, second movement, by Bach (electronic synthesizer). SBM 1

COMPOSITION FOR SYNTHESIZER by Babbit. EM 6

HALLOWEEN by Ives. EM 1

LONG-EARED PERSONS and HENS AND ROOSTERS from *Carnival of the Animals* by Saint-Saëns. BOL 51; EM 2; SOM 1

TUILERIES from *Pictures at an Exhibition* by Moussorgsky. BOL 82; EM 4

Use these compositions from SBM 6 (see *Style: New Music,* p. 118, rec 5): DRIPSODY, ATMOSPHERES, BOWERY BUMS, DAWN FIGURES.

BIBLIOGRAPHY

Cornell, Helen L., "Drums and Dumpsters, Puppets and Pods," *Music Educators Journal,* 60, 8 (April, 1974), p. 60. Many excellent ideas for individualized projects.

Music Learning

> The prevailing rhythm of a musical composition can include consecutive long sounds, consecutive short sounds, or combinations.

Musical Context

MARCH, LITTLE SOLDIER from *Memories of Childhood* by Octavio Pinto ("PEEN-toh") (Brazilian, 1890–1950). BOL 68; DMT (EC); MMYO 2

Behavioral Objective

To identify aurally long and short sounds when played on a percussion instrument and when heard in a musical selection; and to demonstrate this recognition in body movements.

Grade

Lower

Materials

Recording: BOL 68; DMT (EC); MMYO 2, rec 1
Claves or drum

On claves or drum, play steady beats in a "walking tempo" appropriate to students' age level.

   etc.

Focusing Statement

HOW WOULD YOU MOVE TO THIS SOUND?
   Students will probably suggest walking, marching, etc. Stress the evenness of the beats.
   WHAT DOES THIS SOUND SUGGEST?

 Play a "running tempo," twice as fast as the even, steady beats above:

Responses will possibly indicate running, racing, etc. Emphasis should be on shorter steps and on movement that would be *faster than walking.*
   HERE'S A HARD ONE! WHAT MOVEMENT DOES THIS SUGGEST?

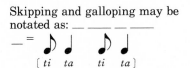 Play a combination of short and long sounds (____ ___ ___), as in a skipping rhythm.

Skipping or galloping may be suggested by students. Stress the *uneven* movement, and the combined short and long steps.
   LET'S TRY A LISTENING-AND-MOVING GAME.
   Choose a group of students. Arrange groups about the room so that all have sufficient space for moving.

LISTEN TO THE CLAVES (or drum), AND MOVE TO THE SOUNDS THEY SUGGEST. (Be ready to change your percussion patterns without pausing: walk, run, skip, run, walk, etc.)

   Body movement   (Have students *walk* back to their seats, as you play your final "walking pattern.")

Summary

YOU WERE VERY GOOD LISTENERS. YOU MOVED TO THE SHORT SOUNDS AND THE LONGER SOUNDS SO WELL!

NOW, LET'S DECIDE WHICH MOVEMENT WILL WORK BEST WITH THIS MUSIC. JUST LISTEN AND THINK THIS TIME.

   (Play excerpt.)

Invite students to try their movement ideas to the music. All can probably participate in this experience, space allowing.

   (Play entire recording.)

Move

Summary

YOUR MARCHING AND WALKING (and other) STEPS WERE EVEN AND JUST PERFECT FOR THE SOUNDS OF THIS MUSIC.

ANOTHER TIME

1. Place this design on the chalkboard:

1 ___ ___ ___ ___
2 __ __ __ __ __ __ __
3 __ ___ __ ___ __ ___ __ ___

Some sources suggest that ♩. ♪ expresses the skipping rhythm.

(Use traditional notation, if your class is ready:

___ = ♩ ; __ __ = ♫ ♫ ; ___ ___ = ♪ ♩.)

Ask students to decide which lines (or notes) show the pattern of running (No. 2), of walking (No. 1), and of skipping or galloping (No. 3). Help students decide that running takes short steps, that walking takes longer steps, and that skipping takes short *and* long steps.

ELABORATION

1. Choose a selection from "Other Music," below, for more experience moving to music.

2. To review fundamental movements, use BOL 51, *Animals and the Circus.*

3. See model experience *Bingo,* p. 48.

OTHER MUSIC

● *Music suggesting walking or marching*

EL CAPITAN by Sousa. DMT 4

MARCH from *The Nutcracker Suite* by Tchaikovsky. BOL 58; EM 2; DMT 3; NDM 1

MARCH OF THE TOYS by Herbert. NDM (EC)

PRINCE OF DENMARK MARCH by Clarke. EM 2; SOM Kg

SEMPER FIDELIS by Sousa. AIM 3, vol. 2; EM 2; NDM (EC); SOM 4

VIENNESE MUSICAL CLOCK from *Háry János Suite* by Kodály. BOL 81; AIM 2; EM 4; NDM 4

● *Music suggesting running*

AIR GAI from *Iphigenia in Aulis* by Gluck. AIM 1

AVIARY from *Carnival of the Animals* by Saint-Saëns. BOL 51; DMT 3; EM 2

THE BALL from *Children's Games* by Bizet. AIM 1

CHILDREN'S BALLET by Turk. EM 1

● *Music suggesting skipping or galloping*

ENGLISH JIG by Telemann. EM 1

GIGUE from *Suite for Strings* by Corelli. NDM 4; SOM Kg

GIGUE from *Suite No. 3* by Bach. AIM 1

WILD HORSEMAN from *Album for the Young* by Schumann. BOL 64; MMYO 1

● *Music suggesting combined movements*

MARCH AND COMEDIANS' GALLOP from *The Comedians* by Kabalevsky. AIM 3, vol. 1; EM 1

RIG-A-JIG-JIG (song). CMCM 2B; EM 2; MMYO Kg; NDM 1 (verse — walking; refrain — skipping)

BIBLIOGRAPHY

Doll, Edna, and Mary Jarman Nelson. *Rhythms Today!* Morristown, N.J.: Silver Burdett Co., 1965, pp. 16–18. Description of fundamental movements. Accompanying recordings include five selections for basic locomotor movements: walk, run, gallop, skip, step-hop.

Rosenkranz, Peggy A. "Perceptual-Motor Development," *Music Educators Journal,* 61, 4 (December, 1974), p. 57. Ideas for using music and movement in special education; discussion of locomotor movement.

See the film *Building Children's Personalities with Creative Dancing,* University of California, Extension Division, film no. 5844. Gertrude Knight spends a summer working with children, ages 6–10. Individual development and expressiveness are lovingly documented in this color film.

Music Learning	Rhythm patterns can include sounds of long and short duration.
Musical Context	BINGO (American folk song). DMT 1 and 3; EM 1; SBM (EC)
Reading Objective	♩ ♩ ♫ ♩ or __ __ __ __ __
Behavioral Objective	To identify aurally and visually the long and short sounds in the rhythm pattern of the word "Bingo"; and to demonstrate that recognition in clapping and singing.
Grade	Lower
Materials	Ability to sing the song; or Song recording: DMT 1 or 3; EM 1:21, rec 2; SBM (EC): 169, rec 7

Some classes may use blank notation:
__ __ __ __ __
ta   ta   ti -ti   ta

Either clap or write on the chalkboard the rhythm pattern shown above. Invite the class to clap or speak the pattern.

Focusing Statement

THIS PATTERN OF LONG AND SHORT SOUNDS IS <u>VERY</u> IMPORTANT IN A SONG I WANT TO SHARE WITH YOU. WHEN YOU HEAR THE PATTERN, CLAP OR SING WITH ME.

 Clap   (Pattern occurs three times, each time "B-i-n-g-o" is *spelled* in the song.)

WONDERFUL! WHAT GOOD LISTENERS YOU ARE! WHO CAN TELL US WHAT WAS BEING SUNG WHEN WE CLAPPED THE RHYTHM PATTERN? ("B-i-n-g-o")

     LET'S ALL CLAP AND SING THAT RHYTHM PATTERN AT THE SAME TIME. Tune up for singing on B.

 Clap   (Last half of song: "B-i-n-g-o")

LET'S SING THE ENTIRE SONG. <u>EVERYONE</u> SING AND CLAP THAT RHYTHM PATTERN, WHEN IT'S TIME. Tune up for singing on D–G.

 Clap pattern at proper time

Now, try the traditional "game" with this rhythm pattern: omit one letter each of the five times the song is repeated, inserting a clap where a letter should occur:

Letters that sound "faster" are actually *shorter* in duration.

- i ng o, - i ng o, - i ng o,
- - ng o, etc.
- - -g o, etc.
- - -- o, etc.
- - -- -, etc. (This last time, only the clapped pattern will be heard; no singing!)

 Clap

Summary

It will be almost impossible for young children to verbalize this understanding, but some will be able to *show* you.

WHO CAN SHOW ME (or tell me) WHICH LETTERS SOUNDED SHORTER THAN THE OTHERS? ("n" and "g") TOGETHER WITH THE OTHER LONGER LETTERS, THAT CREATED A RHYTHM PATTERN OF SHORT AND LONG SOUNDS.

ELABORATION

Children who have difficulty with the concept of shorter and longer sounds will need experiences similar to these:

1. Clap patterns in song, chants, and poems whenever the opportunity presents itself. Use other body sounds in place of clapping (*patsch*, snap, stamp, etc.)

2. Place strips of masking tape on the floor, showing the long and short durations in a pattern (as, ___ ___ _ _ ___ in *Bingo*). Ask students to "walk the pattern," being sure to take *faster (and shorter) steps on the shorter lengths of tape.*

3. Obtain short (5-in.) lengths of doweling or popsicle sticks, and give each student a bundle of eight or ten. Have students place the sticks *vertically* in front of themselves, creating various rhythm patterns, so that ___ ___ _ _ ___ is now expressed as:

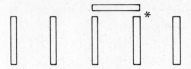

4. Clap or make body rhythms to express the patterns created. Use rhythm syllables (ta, ti).

5. Use sticks to "notate" the patterns in the names of people, places, and things.

$$\left[\quad \text{Ke - o - kuk} \quad \right]$$

Music Learning	Instrumental families (woodwind, string, brass, percussion) can be identified by their timbres.
Musical Context	TOCCATA FOR PERCUSSION by Carlos Chávez ("CHAH-vez") (Mexican, 1899–1978). EM 3, NDM 5
	SARABANDE by Johann Christoph Pezel ("PET-zl") (German, 1639–1694). NDM 5
	CANON FOR STRING QUARTET by Arnold Schoenberg ("SHURN-bergh") (Austrian–American, 1874–1951). EM 5
	WALTZ from *Suite No. 2 for Small Orchestra* by Igor Stravinsky ("strah-VIHN-skee") (Russian–American, 1882–1971). EM 2; NDM 2; SBM 2; SOM 3
Behavioral Objective	To identify aurally the instrumental families; and to demonstrate that recognition by circling the appropriate word on a worksheet.
Grade	Lower and upper

Materials	Recordings: TOCCATA FOR PERCUSSION—EM 3, rec 8; NDM 5, rec 11
	        SARABANDE—NDM 5, rec 11
	        CANON—EM 5, rec 9
	        WALTZ—EM 2, rec 7; NDM 2, rec 8; SBM 2, rec 7; SOM 3, rec 8

	Worksheet for each student (see below)
Focusing Statement	Display photographs of the brass instruments. Point to those you think will be most familiar to your students, and ask WHAT IS THE NAME OF THIS INSTRUMENT? Continue with strings, percussion, and woodwinds. Because this model experience focuses on the "family" sound, it may only be necessary to identify representative instruments, or those of greatest interest to students.

---

*Note that *the short sounds must be joined at the top* by another stick. You can see how readily this patterning leads to musical notation (vertical note stems, and beamed groups of eighth notes).

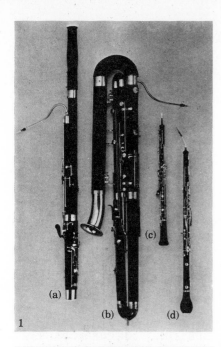

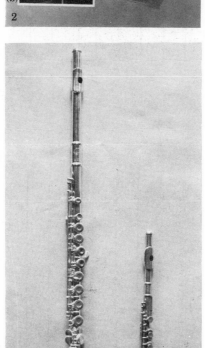

1. WOODWINDS: (a) bassoon, (b) contra bassoon, (c) oboe, (d) English horn. 2. PER-CUSSION: (a) tympani, (b) snare drum, (c) bass drum. 3. PERCUSSION: (a) gong, (b) bells, (c) chimes, (d) xylophone. 4. WOODWINDS: (a) bass clarinet, (b) clarinet, (c) saxophone. 5. WOODWINDS: (a) flute, (b) piccolo. 6. BRASS: (a) trumpet, (b) French horn, (c) tuba, (d) trombone. 7. STRINGS: (a) violin, (b) viola, (c) cello, (d) bass.

51

Distribute this worksheet to each student:

1	2	3	4
Woodwind *String* *Brass* *Percussion*	*Woodwind* *String* *Brass* *Percussion*	*Woodwind* *String* *Brass* *Percussion*	*Woodwind* *String* *Brass* *Percussion*

Read the words aloud, and help students understand that FOUR SELECTIONS WILL BE HEARD. FIRST, LISTEN TO NUMBER ONE, AND MARK WHAT YOU HEAR: WOODWIND, STRING, BRASS, OR PERCUSSION.

 Play TOCCATA. (See left margin for answers.)

Consider verifying correct answer after each selection, rather than waiting until the conclusion of the experience.

If necessary, remind students that THERE IS ONLY <u>ONE</u> CORRECT ANSWER FOR EACH COMPOSITION. Continue playing each recording in turn.

 Play SARABANDE.

 Play CANON.

 Play WALTZ.

Summary

Identify correct responses. Be sure to replay each selection, so that students can associate the correct response with the corresponding musical sound. Help students conclude that each orchestral family has its own characteristic *timbre*.

ANOTHER TIME

1. Tape-record this model experience for individuals to use at a learning station. Provide a worksheet, or photographs of each instrumental family.

2. Create an experience in which students identify the sound of a single instrument. Use selections from the lists which follow, or locate recordings from your own library.

3. View *The Symphony Orchestra,* Encyclopaedia Britannica Films, 425 N. Michigan Ave., Chicago, Ill., 60611. Film for upper grades.

Answers
1. percussion
2. brass
3. strings
4. woodwinds

ELABORATION

Every recording used in the classroom offers opportunities to develop sensitivity to instrumental tone color. When attempting to "listen into" music, for a specific melody or rhythm, listeners are greatly aided by the timbre of the instrument(s) playing that melody or rhythm. Thus it becomes extremely important to be able to identify these instruments by sound, by sight, and by name.

Utilize the excellent *Meet the Instruments* posters from Bowmar, P.O. Box 3623, Glendale, Calif., 91201. Full-color posters (25) on art board, 14 in. x 22 in.

1. Create an experience in which students identify the sound of folk or popular instruments.

2. Listen to *The Young Person's Guide to the Orchestra* by Britten, BOL 83; NDM 3.

3. Very young children may enjoy hearing these well-known recordings:

> CHILD'S INTRODUCTION TO THE ORCHESTRA (Golden Records)
>
> THE KING'S TRUMPET (Children's Record Guild)
>
> LICORICE STICK: STORY OF THE CLARINET (Young People's Records)
>
> SAID THE PIANO TO THE HARPSICHORD (Young People's Records)
>
> TUBBY THE TUBA (Decca Records)
>
> THE WONDERFUL VIOLIN (Young People's Records)

4. Young children may dramatize *Peter and the Wolf* by Prokofiev. (EM 1 and several commercial recordings).

5. Use the *Meet the Instruments* recordings with two filmstrips produced by Bowmar Records.

6. See these sections in NDM 4: *Music Has Color;* NDM 5: *Musical Colors;* and NDM 6: *Color.*

7. To develop skills in recognizing tone color, use these Call Charts from SBM:

> SBM 2:125, rec 6, THE SOUNDS OF INSTRUMENTS
>
> SBM 2:125, rec 6, TONE-COLOR IMPROVISATION, in which students may join.
>
> SBM 5:91, rec 4, CANON from *Five Miniatures for Brass* by Starer
>
> SBM 5:94, rec 4, ANDANTE CANTABILE from *String Quintet in E♭* by Beethoven
>
> SBM 6:9, rec 1, THREE DANCES FOR SOLO SNARE DRUM, by Benson
>
> SBM 6:15, rec 2, ALLEGRO DECISO from *Water Music Suite* by Handel

8. Evaluate students' perception of instrumental timbre through the following "What Do You Hear?" charts: SBM 1:85, rec 5, *Tone Colors* (of classroom instruments); SBM 1:90, rec 6; SBM 2:129, rec 6; SBM 3:93, rec 6; SBM 3:96, rec 6; SBM 4:114, rec 7 (includes Baroque recorder); SBM 5:95, rec 4; SBM 6:46, rec 2 (includes Baroque recorder and electronic sound sources).

OTHER MUSIC

● *Music demonstrating sounds of instrumental "families"*

● AIR from *Suite No. 3 in D* by Bach. EM 3; SOM 2 (strings)

STRING QUARTET NO. 10, first movement, by Mozart. EM 4

GIGUE from *Suite for Strings* by Corelli. NDM 4; SOM Kg (strings)

NOCTURNE from *Quartet in D Major* by Borodin. NDM 5 (strings)

PORKCHOP, third movement, from *String Quartet No. 3* by Balazs. SOM 4

● FANFARE FOR THE COMMON MAN by Copland. NDM 5; SOM 4 (brass)

PRAISE THE LORD (Moravian hymn) by Bechler. MMYO 5 (brass)

CANZON À 12 IN ECHO by Gabrieli. EM 5

● ANDANTE from *Trois Pièces Breves* by Ibert. NDM 5 (woodwinds)

ARIA by Scarlatti. SOM 3 (woodwinds)

GAI from *Kleine Kammermusik* by Hindemith. NDM 5 (or Fifth movement, EM 6) (woodwinds)

THE HEN, THE DONKEY, AND THE CUCKOO by Huguenin. SOM 3 (woodwinds)

RONDO from *Serenade in B♭ Major* by Mozart. NDM 5 (woodwinds)

● IONISATION by Varèse. EM 4; NDM 5 (percussion)

NUMBER NINE ZYKLUS FOR ONE PERCUSSIONIST by Stockhausen. EM 5

PERCUSSION MELÉE by Ganz. EM 2

PERCUSSION RONDO by Mitchell. SOM 3

SYMPHONY NO. 11, second movement (first section), by Cowell. EM 4 (percussion)

● *Music demonstrating solo instrumental timbre*

JIMBO'S LULLABY from *Children's Corner* by Debussy. BOL 63; SOM Kg (string bass; strings)

THE SWAN from *Carnival of the Animals* by Saint-Saëns. AIM 3, vol. 2; BOL 51; EM 2 (cello)

SYMPHONY NO. 1, Horn Theme, by Brahms. SOM 2 (French horn)

PRINCE OF DENMARK MARCH by Clarke. EM 2; SOM Kg (trumpet)

SIGNS OF THE ZODIAC from *The Adventures of Mercury* by Satie. EM 1 (trumpet and tuba)

THE ALLIGATOR AND THE 'COON from *Acadian Songs and Dances* by Thomson. EM 5 (bassoon)

AVIARY from *Carnival of the Animals* by Saint-Saëns. BOL 51; DMT 3; EM 2 (flutes)

SONG by Miller. SOM 4 (flute)

SCHNELLE VIERTEL from *Kleine Kammermusik* by Hindemith. MMYO 3 (several woodwind solos)

FOSSILS from *Carnival of the Animals* by Saint-Saëns. BOL 51; EM 2 (xylophone)

BIBLIOGRAPHY FOR YOUNG PEOPLE

Collier, James. *Which Musical Instrument Shall I Play?* New York: W. W. Norton & Co., 1969. Grades 4–6; a children's aid in selecting an instrument to study. (Also includes electrically amplified instruments.) Good photos.

Craig, Jean. *Woodwinds.* Minneapolis: Lerner Publications, 1962. An introduction for upper grades.

Davis, Lionel, and Edith Davis. *Keyboard Instruments.* Minneapolis: Lerner Publications, 1962. Upper grades; history and mechanical functioning of the instruments.

Kettlekamp, Larry. *Horns.* New York: William Morrow, 1964. Upper grades.

Posell, Elsa. *This Is an Orchestra.* Boston: Houghton Mifflin, 1950. Upper grades; photographs and descriptions of instruments; advice on choosing and purchasing an instrument.

Surplus, Robert W. *Beat of the Drum.* Minneapolis: Lerner Publications, 1962. Upper grades; introduction to percussion.

WORK-THROUGH EXPERIENCE

Music Learning

> Timbre, duration, and volume can be altered electronically.

SOUND EXPERIMENT WITH TAPE RECORDER: TIMBRE, VOLUME, AND DURATION

Musical Context

OVEN GRILL CONCERTO by Biasini and Pogonowski. SOM 5

POÈME ÉLECTRONIQUE by Edgard Varèse ("vah-REZZ") (French-American, 1885–1965). NDM 5

Grade

Upper

Materials

Recordings (see below)

Reel-to-reel tape recorder

Microphone

Recording tape (clean)

Large cymbal or gong (or very large triangle)

Large padded mallet

Pair of claves (or hardwood sticks)

Autoharp (or other stringed instrument)

Part I

Musical Context

OVEN GRILL CONCERTO by Biasini and Pogonowski. SOM 5, rec 7

Behavioral Objective

To identify aurally and compare timbre, duration, and volume of sound, first when there is some distance between the sound source and the receiver (between the musical instrument and the ear or microphone), and second, when sound source and receiver are in direct contact; and to demonstrate this recognition by describing the sound qualities perceived when the tape recorder microphone and the ear are placed against the back of the sound source (Autoharp) and when a recorded composition is heard.

1. Select individuals to manipulate each piece of equipment: tape recorder, microphone, reel of tape, and Autoharp.

2. Discuss why the microphone might be called "the ear of the tape recorder."

3. Have one person strum across all the strings of the Autoharp *without pressing any chord buttons.* Everyone should listen to this sound for timbre, volume, and duration. Describe these qualities as heard.

4. Now, listen to the same sound as follows:

    a. the person who strums holds the Autoharp in a vertical position so that someone else can press one ear against the underside of the instrument;

    b. listener should close "free" ear with a finger;

    c. strummer then gives one long strum across the strings, as before, and

    d. listener continues to listen until the sound has completely died away.

timbre = TAM-br

5. Allow several persons in the group to listen, as in step 4 above. Discuss individuals' perceptions of the sound as it is altered by their ear placement. (Discuss in terms of volume, duration, and timbre.)

6. Follow the procedure in step 4 above, but use the microphone and tape recorder as the "ear" and the "listener."

    Try two ways:

    —first, record with the microphone several feet away from the Autoharp (comparable to No. 3 above).

    —next, as in step 4 above, record with the microphone against the underside of the Autoharp; some experimenting with the volume level may be necessary to avoid excessive distortion.

7. Discuss and compare the recorded sounds. Note the similarities between listening with one's *ear* in contact with the instrument and recording with the *microphone* in contact with the instrument.

8. To hear an example of how contemporary composers employ this contact mike technique, play recording of *Oven Grill Concerto.* Notice the exaggerated durations of sound and the drastically altered timbre.

Part II

Music Learning

POÈME ÉLECTRONIQUE by Varèse. NDM 5, rec 11

Behavioral Objective

To identify aurally the effects of microphone placement and volume-control manipulation upon the volume, duration, and timbre of sound; and to demonstrate this recognition by using the tape recorder's microphone and volume control to increase the volume of a cymbal sound artificially.

1. Select a new team to manage tape recorder, microphone, tape, cymbal with mallet, and claves.

2. Without any reference to music, discuss your understanding of the word *decay*.

See Glossary.

Now try to decide what happens when we say that *musical sounds decay*.

3. Strike the claves together just *once*.

Was the decay fast or slow?

4. Using the padded mallet, give the cymbal a fairly strong strike. Notice how long it takes for the sound to disappear completely.

5. Try this again, as follows:

a. scatter the group around the room.

b. ask each person to raise a hand when the sound can no longer be heard.

6. Decide why those standing near the cymbal hear the sound for a longer time than those standing farther away from the cymbal.

7. Think of some ways to use the tape recorder to suggest that the cymbal sound will seem to *crescendo*, rather than to *decrescendo*.

Try your ideas, and replay each one for evaluation. Don't hesitate to try one idea several times to achieve the most dramatic result.

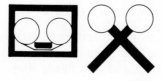

8. Combine the uses of volume control *and* microphone placement (or movement) to achieve a more striking example of decay *reversal*.

9. Discuss changes in the instrumental timbres in terms of volume and duration. Write your observations below:

Summary

10. Play recording of *Poème Électronique*. Discuss possible sound sources the composer manipulated on tape to create the many expressive effects.

ELABORATION *(PART I)*

1. Encourage individuals or small groups to use the *contact mike* technique to record sounds *other than* musical instrument sounds: machines, vocal sounds, environmental sounds, etc.

2. Create a *resonating chamber,* similar to the soundbox of a guitar or Autoharp, by placing a sound maker of any kind on a box, wastebasket, or inverted drum. Place microphone inside the chamber and record the sound.

3. Organize a short composition of two sections (A B) using the *same* sound sources for both sections, but record one section with the *contact mike* technique, and the other with distance between the mike and the sound source.

4. See "Exploring Music with the Tape Recorder," SOM 5.

5. Listen to AUTOHARP SOUND PIECE by David Eddleman in SBM 3.

6. In *Etude Four* from *Eight Etudes and a Fantasy* by Carter (EM 5), duration, dynamics, and timbre give interest to this brief composition, which is based on one pitch (G).

ELABORATION *(PART II)*

1. Do similar experiments with other sound sources: musical instruments, environmental sounds, mouth sounds, sounds from classroom recordings, and so forth. Remember that deliberately distorted "everyday" sounds can provide very interesting raw materials for these tape compositions (or "sound pieces").

2. See "Working with Sounds" satellites in SBM 5 and 6.

BIBLIOGRAPHY

Dennis, Brian. *Experimental Music in Schools.* London: Oxford University Press, 1970. A short section of this imaginative and useful book is devoted to creative uses of the tape recorder.

Dwyer, Terence. *Composing with Tape Recorders* (Musique concrète for beginners). London: Oxford University Press, 1971. A very informative and helpful book; ideas ranging from the simplest applications of the tape recorder to challenging and sophisticated ones.

Ellis, Merrill. "Musique Concrète at Home, or How to Compose Electronic Music in Three Easy Lessons," *Music Educators Journal* 57, 9 (November, 1968), p. 33. One of the more practical articles in this special electronic music issue of this journal. (This issue is filled with good articles on the past, present, and future of electronic music.)

Kuchler, Leland P. "Musique Concrète and Aleatory — Two Ways to Recapture Interest," *Music Educators Journal* 59, 6 (February, 1973), p. 42. Interesting and useful ideas for creating, altering, notating, and organizing taped sounds.

Modugno, Anne D. "Electronic Creativity," *Today's Education,* 60, 3 (March, 1971), pp. 62–64. Many workable ideas for using the tape recorder creatively.

Paynter, John, and Peter Aston. *Sound and Silence* (Classroom Projects in Creative Music). Cambridge: Cambridge University Press, 1970. Good general descriptions of tape recorder techniques, as well as a number of specific compositional projects.

Schafer, R. Murray. *Creative Music Education.* New York: Schirmer Books, 1976, pp. 143–149. Describes decay, reverberation, and other aspects of sound.

Self, George. *New Sounds in Class.* London: Universal Editions, 1967.

These adjuncts to the basal music series provide a great deal of information and many creative ideas:

Crook, Elizabeth, *et al. Silver Burdett Music,* "Working with Sounds," levels 5 and 6, and "Sound: the Raw Material of Music," levels 7 and 8. Morristown, N.J.: Silver Burdett Company, 1974/5.

Marsh, Mary Val, *et al. Spectrum of Music,* "Sources of Musical Sounds" and "Electronic Music," for upper grade students. New York: The Macmillan Company, 1975.

D

Melody: a linear succession of pitches; the horizontal structure in music.

JANE, JANE
  Pitches in a tonal pattern can move by step.

ANCIENT CHINESE TEMPLE MUSIC
  Pitches in a tonal pattern can move by step.

Form: the shape, order, or design of a composition.

ALL AROUND THE KITCHEN: THE CLAM
  Repetition creates unity in games, poems, and songs.

Rhythm: all of the durations that occur in music.

A RAM SAM SAM (I)
  A melodic rhythm usually includes long and short sounds.

Form: the shape, order, or design of a composition.

LA VÍBORA
  Phrases in a melody can repeat.

CHINESE DANCE
  Paired phrases can contrast with each other.

*CONTRASTING MELODIC PHRASES (IMPROVISED)
  Paired phrases can contrast with each other.

Secure   Fairly secure   Insecure

After completing each model experience, decide how successfully you are able to identify, explain, or demonstrate the music learning that was the focus of the experience. Check the appropriate box.

*Group work-through experience

60

Music Learning	Pitches in a tonal pattern can move by step.
Musical Context	JANE, JANE (American folk song). SBM 4
Reading Objective	Optional:
Behavioral Objective	To identify, aurally and visually, pitches that move by steps; and to demonstrate that recognition by singing, playing, and using hand signs.
Grade	Lower
Materials	Recording: SBM 4, rec 9 Melody bells and mallet

Focusing Statement

AFTER YOU'VE HEARD THIS RECORDING, BE READY TO TELL ME THE NAME OF THE PERSON IN THE SONG.

Song notation, p. 227.

Play enough of the recording for students to discover the name and to gain an impression of the song.

YES! IT WAS JANE.
    Play the recording again, and encourage students to *sing* those "Jane, Jane" responses.

(Play verse 1 only.)

Discuss the pitches the students were singing. DID THE PITCHES OF "JANE, JANE" SEEM CLOSE TOGETHER, OR FAR APART? (close)
    Show the bells to the class and locate low D for them (if they are not already able to find it by themselves).
    Ask a student to locate another pitch "just next door" to it.

 (Help student to locate both C and E.)

Ask class to decide WHICH IS CORRECT: D TO E OR D TO C? (D-E) WHY? ("Jane, Jane" goes *up* in pitch.)

See Appendix for Curwen hand signs.

    Sing the song again, and show the students how to use the Curwen hand signs for so and la. Or, use *patsch*/clap to show the lower to higher pitch.

 Body movements

Summary

GOOD! YOUR BODY MOVEMENTS AND YOUR VOICES SHOWED ME YOU UNDER-
STOOD THOSE PITCHES WERE RIGHT NEXT TO EACH OTHER.

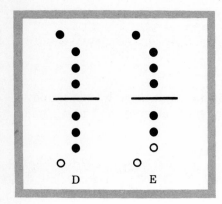

ANOTHER TIME

1. Play the melody bells on the "Jane, Jane" response. Move around
the room, giving several students an opportunity to play the D and E
bells. Bells may be held in a vertical position while you offer a mallet
to each student in turn.

2. Accompany *Jane, Jane* with your guitar, p. 227.

3. Play the responses on your recorder. See left margin.

4. Learn that these adjacent pitches (D-E) constitute the interval of
a *major second*. A major second is created by using two adjacent pitch
names (as in the alphabet), but there must be one chromatic pitch
name intervening. As: D-D#-E. On the staff, a major second moves
from a line to an adjacent space, or from a space to an adjacent line.
Practice writing major seconds on the staff below:

5. Tape-record *Jane, Jane* and make the tape available at a learning
station. Students will enjoy playing the responses on melody bells,
recorders, or guitars.

OTHER SONGS WITH STEPWISE MOVEMENT

CHORAL THEME by Beethoven, p. 264.

FLOWERS WON'T GROW. SBM 2

POOR BIRD, p. 278

ST. PAUL'S STEEPLE, p. 133

WHATEVER CAN THAT BE? MMYO 1 (D-E)

See also model experience *Ancient Chinese Temple Music,* p. 63.

> The *Exploring Music* book tells us this piece is performed in the style of Chinese temple music. Instruments include high-pitched metal bells, cymbals, drums, flute, and harp. The ancient Chinese developed metal instruments at a very early date because they were able to combine tin and copper to make bronze. This discovery did not occur in the West until much later.

Music Learning

Pitches in a tonal pattern can move by step.

Musical Context

ANCIENT CHINESE TEMPLE MUSIC. EM 6

Reading Objective

Behavioral Objective

To identify a tonal pattern that moves by step; and to demonstrate this recognition by playing the pitches on the melody bells and by raising hands when the pattern is heard in the recording.

Grade

Lower

Materials

Recording: EM 6, rec 11

Melody bells and two mallets

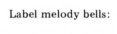
Label melody bells: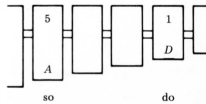

Teachers will elect to use either numbers, syllables, or pitch names, and will adjust lesson accordingly.

Focusing Statement

A system of number notation used by many Chinese musicians:

3̇   upper
2̇

8 or 1̇ ⎫
7   ⎪
6   ⎪
5   ⎬ "main" octave
4   ⎪
           ⎪
2   ⎪
1   ⎪
7   ⎭
6̣   lower
5̣

Hold the melody bells so all students can see them. IF THIS IS 1 (point to it), WHERE IS 2? (on the E to the right).

 AND IF THIS IS 5̣? WHERE IS 6̣? (on the B to the right).

 NOW LET'S FIND SOMEONE WHO CAN PLAY WHAT I'M WRITING ON THE BOARD:
 1 2 1 – 1 2 1 –
 D E D   D E D   (Write this chart on the board, or use staff
 do re do   do re do   notation, as above.)
WHO IS READY TO PLAY THIS? (select a student)

 Play.

GOOD! DID YOU SKIP ANY PITCHES, OR DID YOU PLAY BARS THAT WERE RIGHT NEXT TO EACH OTHER? (adjacent or stepwise)

 Play again, if students show any uncertainty that the pitches move by step.

NOW WE NEED ANOTHER PLAYER FOR THIS:

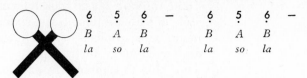

DID THAT PART SKIP AROUND, OR WERE ITS PITCHES CLOSE TOGETHER? (they move by step)

AND WHAT DO THESE MEAN? (Add repeat signs to numbers on the chalkboard, so that it looks like this:)

YES, THEY MEAN TO <u>REPEAT</u>. PLAYERS, LET'S TRY IT. NUMBER ONE PLAYER BEGINS, FOLLOWED BY THE SECOND PLAYER.

 (First student, then second student; repeat)

WHO ELSE CAN PLAY THIS BRIEF PASSAGE? Select pairs of students to play, as long as interest remains high.

Longer sections are heard, with this brief bridge passage between them:

NOW WE'RE GOING TO LISTEN FOR THESE PATTERNS IN ANCIENT MUSIC FROM CHINA. IT FORMS THE <u>BRIDGE</u> IN THE MIDDLE OF THE MUSIC. RAISE YOUR HAND WHEN YOU HEAR IT.

Recording

(The bridge is heard only once; there is a long A section before the bridge.)

Summary

Observe the degree of student success. Discuss the patterns once more, and how THE PITCHES MOVE BY STEPS, AND DO NOT SKIP AROUND.

Teachers will find most students quite entranced by the sounds of the Chinese instruments heard in the recording. A class of fourth graders in San Francisco actually ignored the excitement of two fire engines to continue listening!

ANOTHER TIME

1. Listen to the last half of this composition, and discover the series of phrases introduced by a solo instrument, then echoed by the full orchestra.

2. Examine photos of Chinese instruments in NDM 4:91 and in *Music Educators Journal,* 59, 2 (October, 1972), p. 65.

OTHER MUSIC WITH STEPWISE MELODIES

ALLAH HU (India). SBM 5 (This music is also included in model experience *Lechu Niraneno Arlayim Shova*, p. 205.)

AUBADE from *Le Cid Ballet Suite* by Massenet. EM 6

BARCAROLLE from *Tales of Hoffman* by Offenbach. AIM 3 (I); DMT 5; NDM 1.

LAMMAN BADA YATATHANNA (Middle East). NDM 6

PRINCE OF DENMARK MARCH by Clarke. EM 2

SAORA WEDDING SONG. SBM 5

Also see "Other Music" and "Other Songs," following model experiences *Five Angels,* p. 81, *Pianists,* p. 86, *Jane, Jane,* p. 62, and *St. Paul's Steeple,* p. 131.

BIBLIOGRAPHY

Dietz, Betty W. and Thomas Choonbai Park. *Folk Songs of China, Japan, Korea.* New York: John Day, 1964. Songs and recordings, as well as cultural information and pronunciation guides.

Marks, Robert W., "Music and Musical Instruments of Ancient China," *Musical Quarterly,* 18, 4 (October, 1932), p. 594. A literate discussion of the bell chime, the stone bell, and the reed mouth organ, with photos and drawings.

Picken, Laurence. "Chinese Music," in *Readings in Ethnomusicology,* ed. David P. McAllester. New York: Johnson Reprint Corp., 1971, p. 336. This interesting article has been reprinted from *The New Oxford History of Music.* The descriptions and sketches of musical instruments are fascinating; especially that of the sonorous stone bells! A well-written, informative article.

Music Learning	Repetition creates unity in games, poems and songs.
Musical Context	ALL AROUND THE KITCHEN (Black American play song). SBM 1 THE CLAM (Poem by Shelley Silverstein). SBM 2
Reading Objective	Game rhythm pattern:
Behavioral Objective	To identify aurally a rhythm pattern, a melodic phrase, and a word phrase that are repeated; and to demonstrate that recognition by repeating those phrases with voices and hand clapping.
Grade	Lower
Materials	Recording: SBM 1, rec 1 Poem: in SBM 2:187 (TE) Students should have experience with the echo game as used in the model experience SCOTLAND'S BURNING, p. 33, before proceeding to this experience.
Focusing Statement	LISTEN AND WATCH MY CLAPPING. AM I CLAPPING MANY <u>DIFFERENT</u> PATTERNS, OR AM I CLAPPING THE <u>SAME</u> PATTERNS OVER AND OVER? Clap game pattern six or more times. (Make each repetition identical.)

[*ta   ta   ti · ti   ta*]

Informal notation may be used:

When the students have identified the pattern, have them repeat it with you several times. Then write it on the board.

Clap game phrase.   (teacher and students)

LET'S USE THAT RHYTHM PATTERN FOR A GAME. WE'LL ALL CLAP THAT PATTERN ONCE TOGETHER. THEN, LET ME SNAP FOUR BEATS BEFORE WE REPEAT THE PATTERN.

Clap   (Alternate the game pattern with *four steady beats* several times.)

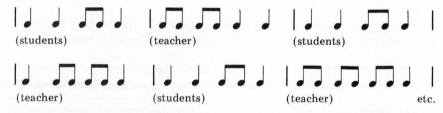

To make the game more challenging, create a simple rhythm pattern to fill the *teacher's* four beats. Direct students always to repeat their same pattern. Remind them that you will be doing something different!

Clap   (Begin with the game pattern from above, and then fill in the alternating four beats with various simple patterns, as follows.)

(students)   (teacher)   (students)

(teacher)   (students)   (teacher)   etc.

Compliment students if they are successful in repeating their rhythm pattern over and over. HERE'S A POEM THAT USES WORDS OVER AND OVER. After you have read several lines of the poem, gesture for students to join you on the repeated word phrase.

Read *The Clam* and stress the repeated word phrase, "It's all the same to the clam."

Discuss the rest of the words in the poem, and read again if interest is high.

GAMES USE REPEATED PATTERNS AND POEMS USE REPEATED PATTERNS. HERE'S A SONG WITH A TONAL PATTERN THAT REPEATS.

Summary

Play song only once.   Question students about the repeated pattern ("Cock-a-doodle-doodle-doo").

Repeat the words with students and invite them to sing the words with the recording.

LET'S TRY SOME MOVEMENTS THIS TIME. DURING THE INTRODUCTION, FIND A SPACE IN WHICH TO MOVE. DO WHAT THE WORDS TELL YOU AND SING "COCK-A-DOODLE-DOODLE-DO."

 Body movements

Summary

REPEATED PATTERNS CAN CERTAINLY HOLD A GAME, A POEM, OR A SONG TOGETHER.

ANOTHER TIME

Play the responses ("cock-a-doodle-doodle-doo") on melody bells, pianos, recorders, and guitars.

ELABORATION

Explore repetition and pattern in objects in the classroom (fabrics, paintings, decorations, book covers). Several books have pictures that may be studied for "repeats": NDM 2:16; NDM 3:94, 146; SBM 2:188; SOM 4:45.

OTHER SONGS WITH REPEATED MELODIC PATTERNS

ATADWE. NDM 3

BUT YOU ARE MINE (poem). SBM 3:64

GOGO. MMYO 2

GRIZZLY BEAR, p. 38

HILL 'N GULLY. MMYO 5; SBM 3

I CLAP MY HANDS. SBM 2

JANE, JANE, p. 227

OLD MACDONALD. DMT 3; EM 1; SOM 2

OZIBANE! SBM 3

Black American Play Song
Arranged by James Rooker

Transcribed and adapted from the Library of Congress Field Recording AFS 88.

Music Learning	A melodic rhythm usually includes long and short sounds.

Musical Context

A RAM SAM SAM (I) (folk song from Morocco). DMT (EC); MMYO-Kg; SBM 1 and 3

Reading Objective

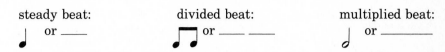

steady beat: ♩ or ____   divided beat: ♫ or ____ ____   multiplied beat: ♩ or ____

Behavioral Objective

To identify the steady beat (♩), the divided beat (♫), and the multiplied beat (♩) in a melodic rhythm; and to demonstrate that recognition in hand clapping and singing.

Grade

Upper

Materials

Recording: DMT (EC): MMYO Kg, rec 3; SBM 1, rec 8; SBM 3, rec 1
Small mallet
Optional (on chart or chalkboard)

Song notation, p. 233

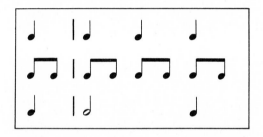

Focusing Statement

ECHO WHATEVER I CLAP. Use a moderately fast tempo.

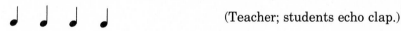

♩ ♩ ♩ ♩   (Teacher; students echo clap.)

As the clapping continues, add these words:

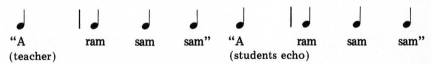

"A   ram   sam   sam"   "A   ram   sam   sam"
(teacher)   (students echo)

A ram sam sam =
ah RAHM sahm sahm

(Be sure to *clap four* times with the *four* syllables.)
Speculate on the dullness of a song that does nothing but move along in steady beats.

I'LL PLAY YOU A SONG THAT BEGINS WITH THE STEADY BEAT "A RAM SAM SAM." LISTEN FOR THE PART WE DID AND FOR SOME SHORTER SOUNDS WITH DIFFERENT WORDS.

 As voices begin in recording, *clap* quietly with students for the first eight beats. As the words "guli guli" begin, signal the clapping to stop so the shorter sounds (divided beats) will be heard.   (Play introduction and one verse only.)

Ask if the "guli guli" part was made up of sounds that were *longer* or *shorter* than the steady beats of "a ram sam sam." (shorter)

Rhythm syllables may also be used:

Spoken portions may always be sung.

LET'S PATSCH THESE SHORTER SOUNDS. (Alternate on left and right knees.)

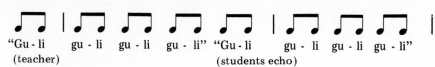

"Gu - li   gu - li   gu - li   gu - li"   "Gu - li   gu - li   gu - li   gu - li"
(teacher)   (students echo)

Repeat, if necessary.

Challenge students to sing as much of the song as possible as the recording plays. Remind them that both sets of words they echoed will be heard more than once.

(Play introduction and one verse. Teacher should be ready to give vocal help.)

Compliment their singing efforts, if appropriate!

Tell students that THE ONLY PART OF THE SONG LEFT TO LEARN IS:

a rafi = ah RAH-fee

"A   ra - fi,   a   ra - fi"   (teacher sing or speak)

Invite students to echo this part, using hand movements, such as: (teacher demonstrate, then have students echo).

Rhythm syllables:

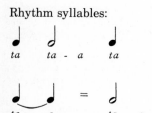

ta   ta - a   ta

ta - a   ta - a

"A   ra   fi"   (teacher first; students echo)

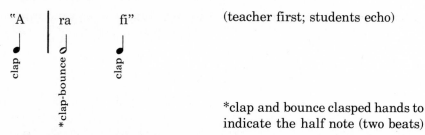

clap   *clap-bounce   clap

*clap and bounce clasped hands to indicate the half note (two beats)

NOW, LET'S SING THE ENTIRE SONG WHILE WE ALSO CLAP AND PATSCH THE MELODIC RHYTHM. YOU CAN DO IT!

Body rhythms (without recording)

Summary

A RAM SAM SAM HAS SEVERAL COMBINATIONS OF SHORT AND LONG SOUNDS. WHAT WERE THE SHORTEST? WHAT WERE THE LONGEST?

It might also be appropriate to discuss how each song has its own distinctive melodic rhythm; this helps us recognize and remember it.

ANOTHER TIME

1. Listen to *A Ram Sam Sam,* SBM 3:13, rec 1, to hear two versions (one monophonic, one with harmony.)

2. Assign three students three different percussion instruments. Assign one instrument to the steady beat, one to the divided beats,

and the third to the "a ra-fi" rhythm. Have them practice and then play the entire melodic rhythm as it occurs in the song. This may be either with or without the recording. This will lead very directly to model experience *A Ram Sam Sam* (II), p. 111, which utilizes tape recorder.

ELABORATION

1. Identify familiar melodies from their *melodic rhythms alone.* Clap or play the rhythms on a percussion instrument. See OTHER SONGS for ideas.

2. To contrast *melodic rhythm* with the *beat,* have students join hands to form two circles, one inside the other. First, have both circles "walk the beat." Then ask one circle to stand still and, while facing the moving ("beat") circle, clap the melodic rhythm. Use a familiar song, such as *Old MacDonald Had a Farm* or *This Old Man.*

3. See model experience *Polka,* p. 108.

OTHER SONGS FOR SIMILAR USE

ARE YOU SLEEPING? pp. 163, 259

JINGLE BELLS, p. 255

LOOBY LOO

SKIP TO MY LOU, pp. 176, 238

THIS OLD MAN, p. 283

(*Any* song with a distinctive combination of long and short durations in the melodic rhythm.)

BIBLIOGRAPHY

Choksy, Lois. *The Kodály Method: Comprehensive Music Education from Infant to Adult.* Englewood Cliffs, N.J.: Prentice-Hall, 1974. Detailed and valuable; includes rhythm syllables as used by Kodály in the Hungarian program. See also Appendix, p. 341.

Frey, Terry. "Cuisenaire Rods in the Music Class," *Music Educators Journal,* 63, 1 (September, 1976), p. 81. Ideas on how to make and use homemade wood blocks to study note durations.

Richards, Mary Helen. *Threshold to Music.* Belmont, Calif.: Fearon Publishers, Inc., 1964. Includes Richards' adaptation of the Kodály rhythm syllables used in this model experience.

See also Kidd, Eleanor, *Threshold to Music* (2nd ed.) Belmont, Calif.: Fearon Publishers, Inc., 1974.

Music Learning	Phrases in a melody can repeat.
Musical Context	LA VÍBORA ("lah VEE-bo-rah"; "The Sea Serpent"; Spanish-American folk song). MMYO 1
Behavioral Objective	To identify aurally that each phrase is identical in length and in melodic and rhythmic material; and to demonstrate that recognition in body rhythms and singing.
Grade	Lower
Materials	Recording, MMYO 1, rec 6

LISTEN TO THIS RECORDING, AND THEN TELL ME WHAT LANGUAGE WAS SUNG, SPANISH OR ENGLISH.

 (Play introduction and verse 1 *only*.)

After identifying that the song was sung in *Spanish,* explain that THE SONG IS ABOUT A SERPENT THAT LIVES IN THE SEA, A MAKE-BELIEVE MONSTER.

Sing the words of the first half of the phrase and have students repeat. Use Spanish or English words, whichever is more appropriate for your class.

Tune-up for singing: sound A on Autoharp (middle octave), bells, or recorder.

Inexperienced singers who have difficulty with the pitch may find that the key of F (tune-up on F) keeps the song within the range of most youngsters.

 Teacher:
"Serpent, serpent of the sea,"
Students:
Serpent, serpent of the sea,

Do the same with the second half of the phrase:

 Teacher:
"You must all pass under me!"
Students:
You must all pass under me!

Repeat the phrase, if necessary.

Sing the phrase *without pause* and have students *echo,* also without pause. Repeat until most are comfortable singing the phrase.

Mention that THIS PHRASE REPEATS AND REPEATS THROUGHOUT THE SONG, BUT WITH DIFFERENT WORDS. WE'LL LEARN THE REST OF THE WORDS LATER.

Arrange pairs of students around room. Have partners take hands, facing.

As everyone sings "Serpent, serpent of the sea" once, teacher and one student demonstrate by lifting joined hands to BUILD A TALL BRIDGE. Stop on the word "sea" and keep joined hands high. As everyone sings "You must all pass under me," BRING THE BRIDGE DOWN. Demonstrate with your partner.

Have all pairs of students repeat the action just demonstrated *while singing.*

 Body movement (Lift on first half of phrase, lower on second.)

Repeat the above, but ask students to "FREEZE" (arms lifted) on the word *sea*. While arms are up, ask IS THIS A GOOD PLACE TO STOP? (No, because it feels and sounds unfinished.) Have all sing and complete the phrase with "You must all pass under me."

 Body movement (Lift on first half of phrase, "freeze," then lower on second.)

Using recording, have all pairs repeat body movements throughout the playing of the recording, *without singing*.

SEE IF YOU CAN STAY RIGHT WITH THE MUSIC WITHOUT SINGING. IT TAKES GOOD LISTENING. BEGIN MOVING WHEN YOU HEAR THE <u>VOICES</u> ON THE RECORDING.

Body movement (Use all or part of recording.)

Summary

COULD YOU LIFT YOUR ARMS WITHOUT BRINGING THEM DOWN AGAIN? (Presumably, no.) THE TWO PARTS OF THE PHRASE NEED EACH OTHER. THEY ARE LIKE TWO HALVES THAT MAKE A WHAT? (Whole)

Have individuals return to their seats while singing the melody. SEE HOW MANY REPETITIONS OF THAT PHRASE IT TAKES FOR YOU TO GET BACK TO YOUR SEAT. MOVE RIGHT WITH YOUR SINGING.

ANOTHER TIME

Having already learned the simple melody of *La Víbora*, students will quickly learn the words. Begin with Spanish or English, whichever is most appropriate for your class.

ELABORATION

See model experience *Chinese Dance*, p. 74, and *Contrasting Melodic Phrases*, p. 77.

OTHER MUSIC FOR SIMILAR USE

LONG JOHN. MMYO 6 (phrases of equal length; *response* phrases are identical to *call* phrases, melodically and rhythmically.)

OLD TEXAS. EM 4; SBM 4; SOM 3

SPRINGFIELD MOUNTAIN. MMYO 3

BIBLIOGRAPHY

Wheeler, Lawrence, and Lois Raebeck. *Orff and Kodaly Adapted for the Elementary School.* Dubuque, Iowa: Wm. C. Brown Co., 1972, pp. 95–102. Many suggestions for developing phrase building using clapping and chanting.

LA VÍBORA (The Sea Serpent)

Spanish-American Folk Song
English Words by Margaret Marks
Arranged by Cameron McGraw

Music Learning	Paired phrases can contrast with each other.
Musical Context	CHINESE DANCE from *The Nutcracker Suite* by Peter Ilich Tchaikovsky ("chai-KOFF-skee") (Russian, 1840–1893). BOL 58; DMT 3; EM 2; NDM 1; SBM 2
Behavioral Objective	To identify a pattern aurally; and to demonstrate this recognition, first, by creating and clapping a contrasting pattern of the same length and, second, by raising hands or cards during each phrase heard in a composition.
Grade	Lower/Upper

Materials	Recording: BOL 58; DMT 3; EM 2, rec 8; NDM 1; SBM 2, rec 5

A 4 in. × 4 in. square of paper for each student, one color for half the class and another color for the other half

Before proceeding with this experience, students should have explored echo clapping. (See model experience *Scotland's Burning,* p. 33.)

Focusing Statement

REPEAT THIS RHYTHM AFTER ME!

Teacher might clap:

Students echo:

Rhythm syllables (ta, ti, etc.) may be verbalized along with the patterns.

Continue creating four-beat patterns. Avoid breaks between teacher's pattern and students' response.

GOOD! THIS TIME, LET'S BE DIFFERENT. INSTEAD OF YOUR REPEATING EXACTLY WHAT I CLAP, WHY NOT ANSWER WITH SOMETHING DIFFERENT?

Teacher may clap the *same* rhythm each time.

Clap

(Select several students to improvise contrasting patterns. Clap a four-beat rhythm. Students should create a response of the same length to follow yours. It is helpful to mark the students' four-beat pattern in the air, with your hand, to assist them.)

Encourage students to clap *something.* No one can create an "incorrect" response.

All students might wish to improvise now. Students can take turns creating patterns that contrast with yours. Move from student to student without breaking rhythmic flow. Be aware of individual differences in creating patterns for each student (simplifying, etc.).

GREAT! YOUR PATTERNS REALLY CONTRASTED WITH MINE. I KNOW A MUSICAL COMPOSITION WITH CONTRASTING MELODIES THAT "TAKE TURNS," AS WE TOOK TURNS CLAPPING.

Divide the class into two groups. Ask one group to raise hands when the first melodic phrase is heard. The other group will raise hands when the second phrase is heard. These paired phrases will alternate throughout. (See phrase analysis at end of this experience.)

I'LL HELP YOU GET STARTED AFTER THE INTRODUCTION.

(Indicate one or two of the paired phrases. Signal students not to raise hands during *coda,* which follows the sixth pair of phrases.)

Distribute cards of one color to one group and the other color to the other group.

Many students enjoy moving their cards to the beat of the music.

Encourage students to raise their cards at the appropriate times during another listening. Remind them of the introduction and the coda. Ask some students in each group to count the phrases *their* group responds to. (There are six of each, but don't tell them!)

(Raise cards to indicate phrases.)

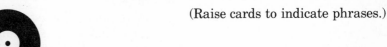

Discuss the answers from each group concerning the number of phrases heard. Conclude with a final listening, asking several students to place the colored cards, in phrase order, in chalk tray. Write *introduction* and *coda* on opposite sides of chalkboard, with room between for the twelve cards.

(See card order below.)

After several listenings, students might detect that the *b* phrases are always the same, but the *a* phrases vary. The third and fourth *a*'s differ slightly from the others.

Introduction □ ■ □ ■ □ ■ □ ■ □ ■ □ ■ Coda
(a b a b a* b a* b a b a b)

Summary

HOW MANY PAIRS OF CONTRASTING PHRASES DID WE HEAR IN THIS MUSIC? (6) DID ANYONE RECOGNIZE THE MUSIC? IT'S THE <u>CHINESE DANCE</u> FROM THE <u>NUTCRACKER SUITE</u>.

ANOTHER TIME

Discuss the orchestral instruments used in *Chinese Dance.* Choose high-pitched (triangle, finger cymbals, etc.) and low-pitched (large drums, etc.) percussion instruments; invite students to play the higher-pitched ones for the *a* phrases and the lower-pitched ones for the *b* phrases.

ELABORATION

1. Pairs of students can create percussion compositions based on this concept of paired, contrasting phrases.

2. See model experience *Contrasting Melodic Phrases,* p. 77, for specific ideas for creating melodic phrases based on the pentatonic scale.

Gottschalk (1829–1869) was an important American piano virtuoso, born of Creole-Jewish parents.

3. *Bamboula* by Louis Gottschalk is a piano composition that offers further experience with paired phrases *and* sectional form.

Bamboula is based on *Sweet Potatoes,* a Black play song that is said to have derived from the bamboula dance, popular with Black Americans in 19th century New Orleans.

Gottschalk also uses *Sweet Potatoes* in his "Grand Walkaround" from *Cakewalk Ballet Suite*, AIM 5, V.

Prepare students for listening to *Bamboula* (EM 5) by teaching them to sing *Sweet Potatoes* (EM 5). Note the two similar phrases that make up the song. These paired phrases comprise each A section of *Bamboula*. The 8-measure song (A section) is heard seven times in *Bamboula*.

Cut seven large construction paper triangles (A section), four circles (B section), and four squares (C section.) As the music plays, place the shapes on the chalktray, one at a time, to illustrate the design of *Bamboula*. The design is:

Intro. ▲ ▲ ▲ ▲ B B C C ▲ ▲ B B C C ▲

(Remember that each A is the length of the song: two phrases or eight measures.)

Have individual students place shapes during subsequent listenings or have all students prepare small versions of the shapes (15 pieces) so that all can lay out the design on their desk tops as they listen.

For less experienced classes consider dividing the class into three groups. Provide each group with paper squares of a different color (red for A, blue for B, yellow for C, perhaps.) Have the groups raise their colors as their sections are heard on the recording.

OTHER MUSIC WITH PAIRED CONTRASTING PHRASES

MARCH from *The Nutcracker Suite* by Tchaikovsky. BOL 58; DMT 3; EM 2

BIBLIOGRAPHY FOR YOUNG PEOPLE

Wheeler, Opal. *Peter Tchaikovsky* (1953) and *Peter Tchaikovsky and the Nutcracker Ballet* (1959). New York: Dutton.

BIBLIOGRAPHY

Doll, Edna and Mary Jarman Nelson. *Rhythms Today!* Morristown, N.J.: Silver Burdett Co., 1965, p. 173. Similar ideas are described for a "conversation game" using voices and melody instruments.

Doyle, John G., "Gottschalk: Nationalist Composer, Native Virtuoso," *Music Educators Journal,* December 1969, Vol. 56, No. 4, p. 25. An evocative article emphasizing folk influences upon this composer whose adult years spanned the mid-nineteenth century. *Bamboula* is mentioned, along with other compositions which "recapture the vision of a lost past."

Piper, Richard M., and David M. Shoemaker. "Formative Evaluation of a Kindergarten Music Program Based on Behavioral Objectives," *Journal of Research in Music Education,* 21, No. 2, Summer, 1973, p. 145. One of the few studies to investigate children's perception of form, it suggests that paired phrases are easy to understand.

WORK-THROUGH EXPERIENCE

Music Learning

> Paired phrases can contrast with each other.

Reading Objective

Contrasting Melodic Phrases (Improvised)

ta   ti ti   ta   ta   ta   ta   ta - a

and melodic notation (see step 10 below)

Behavioral Objective

To read and clap a rhythmic phrase; to create and play a melody added to this rhythmic phrase; to improvise and play a contrasting phrase that will complement the first phrase.

Grade

Materials

Resonator or melody bells (one for each student, or two students share a set) (Pianos may also be used.)

Tape recorder, microphone and tape

Pencils for each student

Model experience *Chinese Dance,* p. 74, could effectively precede this experience.

One student might tap the steady beat (ta = ♩) while the rest of the group tries the pattern.

1. Students should place bell sets on their laps or on desks.

2. First, try reading and clapping this rhythmic pattern:

3. Now, read and clap this pattern:

4. Put the patterns together, and clap them consecutively, like this:

Repeat the phrase until most of the group feels comfortable clapping it.

5. To add melody to this rhythmic phrase, use the black bells of your melody instrument. Each student should experiment with playing the rhythmic phrase (just clapped) on a single bell, or on several of them.

After allowing some time for experimentation, play your phrases for each other.

The black bells (and keys) have two letter spellings.

6. Now play this phrase on your bells:

Individually, play this for one another.

Remember it is impossible to improvise an "incorrect" phrase.

7. Select one student to play the phrase designated in step 6 above. This phrase will serve as the *question* phrase.

Every student should improvise a contrasting phrase to complement the *question* phrase. This improvised phrase will serve as an *answer*. Any of the black bells may be used, and they may be used in any order.

(Playing will always be in the order of: *question* phrase, followed by improvised *answer* phrase.)

8. Continue to improvise contrasting phrases. Ask a different student to play the *question* phrase (from step 6 above) while others, *one at a time,* create an *answer* phrase to pair with it. Try to make the *answer* phrase the same length (eight beats) as the *question* phrase.

Tape-record this improvisation.

9. Play back, and evaluate the improvisation.

10. Notate the *question* phrase (from step 6) on the staff below. Write *sharp* (♯) notation on staff no. 1, and *flat* (♭) notation on staff no. 2.

The first and last pitches are given.

11. For what grade level would this experience be appropriate? What prior experience would be necessary? Fill in the grade *you* suggest in the box at the beginning of this model experience.

BIBLIOGRAPHY

Mehr, Norma. "Improvising with Resonator Bells," from *The Idea Bank, Music Educators Journal,* 63, 1 (September, 1976), p. 84. Similar ideas for improvising melodic phrases on resonator bells.

Nichols, Elizabeth. *Orff Instrument Source Book,* I. Morristown, N.J.: Silver Burdett Co., 1970, p. 8. Ideas for improvising melodic phrases in singing, with hand signs, and with melody instruments.

Orff, Carl, and Gunild Keetman. *Orff-Schulwerk. Music for Children,* I, *Pentatonic,* English adaptation by Doreen Hall and Arnold Walter. Mainz: B. Schott's Sohne, 1950, p. 85. Six melodic phrase-building examples presented.

E

Melody: a linear succession of pitches; the horizontal structure in music.

FIVE ANGELS
Pitches in a tonal pattern can move by stepping up.

PIANISTS
Pitches in a melody can move by stepping up or down.

THIS OLD MAN
A song usually ends on the tonal center (tonic).

Form: the shape, order, or design of a musical composition.

GOOD MORNING, BLUES
Each phrase in "12-bar" blues consists of four measures (16 beats).

Rhythm: all of the durations that occur in music.

WE ARE GOING DOWN THE NUMBERS
Steady beats can be grouped in twos (duple meter).

ELEPHANT
Steady beats can be grouped in threes (triple meter).

After completing each model experience, decide how successfully you are able to identify, explain, or demonstrate the music learning that was the focus of the experience. Check the appropriate box.

Secure
Fairly secure
Insecure

Music Learning

Pitches in a tonal pattern can move by stepping up.

Musical Context

FIVE ANGELS (German folk song). MMYO 1

Reading Objective

(optional)

C   D   E   F   G
(*do   re   mi   fa   so*)

Behavioral Objective

To identify aurally and visually five pitches moving up; and to demonstrate this recognition by playing, singing, and counting the number of times the pattern is heard in the song.

Grade

Lower

Materials

Recording: MMYO 1 rec 3

Student's book, MMYO 1:24

Flannelboard with felt letters: C D E F G

Resonator bells: C D E F G (from lower end of set)

Model experiences *John the Rabbit,* p. 28, and *Grizzly Bear,* p. 36, should precede this experience.

Focusing Statement

Teacher may elect to present bells in scrambled order. More experienced classes may be able to arrange the bells in order by listening to the pitch of each bell.

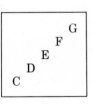

Hold up the C, D, E, F, and G resonator bells. WE NEED FIVE PEOPLE TO PLAY THESE BELLS.

Distribute bells to students. Arrange in ascending order by letter names or by sound, and have students play them in order.

DID THE PITCHES GO UP OR DOWN? (up)

Ask bell players to identify the letter written on their bell. Place the five letters on the flannelboard in ascending pitch-level arrangement (see margin).

(Use a staff-lined flannelboard and notes if students have had prior experience with the staff.) NOW, HERE'S A JOB FOR EVERYONE. LISTEN TO THIS SONG ABOUT SOME ANGELS, AND SEE HOW MANY TIMES YOU HEAR THE BELL PART WE JUST PLAYED.

Students might need to hear the pattern played on bells once again.

(As recording plays, point to the pattern on the flannelboard each of the five times it is heard.)

FIVE IS RIGHT. AND THERE WERE FIVE ANGELS IN THE SONG, TOO.

Discuss the jobs the angels were doing. The pictures in the pupil's book might help the discussion.

Choose some students to sing the first angel's part, another group to sing the second angel's part, etc. Review the words for each and sing the pattern with the bells.

Curwen hand signs may be used here.

First angel: "The first one lights the fire"
Second angel: "The second one butters the bread"
Third angel: "The third one pours the milk"
Fourth angel: "The fourth one sets the table"
Fifth angel: "The fifth one whispers softly"
Teacher: "Come, Sleepyhead, hop out of bed!"

WE'RE READY TO SING OUR PARTS WITH THE RECORDING. I'LL SIGNAL EACH GROUP WHEN IT'S TIME FOR YOU TO SING.

Summary

ALL FIVE GROUPS DID A FINE JOB SINGING THOSE SAME FIVE PITCHES THAT MOVED HOW? <u>UP</u> IS RIGHT!

ANOTHER TIME

1. When children are familiar with all the words, dramatize while singing.

2. Students can play the five note pattern on the melody bells, recorders, or piano.

3. College students might play these pitches on guitar.

a. Although they look equidistant, they are *not*. The E and the F are in adjacent frets; the others are not. (See the chromatic scale in the Guitar Instructor, p. 244)

b. When pitches (as E and F) are in adjacent frets they are called *half steps*.

c. When one fret is skipped between pitches, a *whole step* occurs. In this example, from C to D is a whole step.

```
      D
  (C♯)
C
```

d. Use this tablature to play the pitches shown above. The top lines represent the strings *closest to your feet*. Play in the same rhythm as the words. (Perhaps you can play and sing along with the song recording.)

ti   ti ti ti ti ta

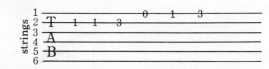

ELABORATION

1. Model experience *Pianists,* p. 84, would be a good follow-up to *Five Angels.*

2. See "Crayon Activities" 16 and 21, in SBM (EC) for practice with upward *and* downward direction.

OTHER SONGS WITH A BRIEF SCALE PATTERN

ADAM HAD SEVEN SONS. MMYO 1 (first phrase: D E F♯ G A)

COME AND SING TOGETHER. SOM 6 (D E F G A in D minor)

HEY HO, HEY LO. SBM 3 (descending A G F E D pattern used at conclusion of each of three phrases, D minor)

MY DREYDL. SBM (EC) (descending G F E D C pattern used twice)

SING A LITTLE SONG. SBM (EC) (D E F♯ G A)

THE ALPHABET by Mozart. SOM 4 (E F♯ G♯ A B, in E major)

BIBLIOGRAPHY

Debban, Betty. "The Direct Link in Reading Readiness," *Music Educators Journal,* 63, 5, (January, 1977), p. 42. An article focusing on the link between readiness to read music and successful reading of traditional notation.

Groff, Patrick. "Reading Music Affects Reading Language: Says Who?" *Music Educators Journal,* 63, 5 (January, 1977), p. 37. An article questioning reports that music and language reading are closely related.

Zinar, Ruth. "Reading Language and Reading Music: Is There a Connection?" *Music Educators Journal,* 62, 7 (March, 1976), p. 70. A fine article reporting the findings of many research studies on the correlation between language reading and music reading.

FIVE ANGELS

English Words by Adina Williamson
German Folk Song

Music Learning	Pitches in a melody can move by stepping up or down.
Musical Context	PIANISTS from *Carnival of the Animals* by Camille Saint-Saëns ("sa[n] saw[n]s") (French, 1836-1921). BOL 51; EM 2
Reading Objective	Optional (See "Another Time.")
Behavioral Objective	To identify, aurally and visually, melodies that step up and down; and to demonstrate that recognition by playing the melody bells and by raising colored cards.
Grade	Lower/Upper
Materials	Recording: BOL 51; EM 2, rec 8 (Be sure to set the needle down on the correct band!) Melody bells and three mallets Pegboard, about 2 ft. × 2 ft. Golf tees (24) selected by color, so as to have: 7 yellow 9 blue 8 white Construction paper squares—enough for each student to use *one* color: yellow for one-third of the class blue for one-third of the class white for one-third of the class

Focusing Statement

TODAY WE'RE GOING TO LISTEN TO SOME MELODIES THAT MOVE UP AND DOWN THE SCALE. Set up the tees on the pegboard as shown below. (This might be done by the teacher prior to lesson, or by students during lesson.)

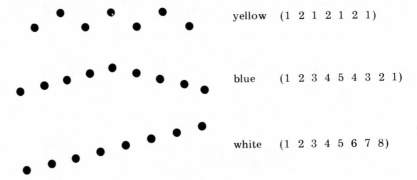

yellow (1 2 1 2 1 2 1)

blue (1 2 3 4 5 4 3 2 1)

white (1 2 3 4 5 6 7 8)

If the tees are being set up in class, be sure to note these understandings:

THE WHITE ROW MOVES UP, <u>BY STEP</u>, NOT BY SKIP.

THE BLUE ROW MOVES UP <u>BY STEP</u>, THEN DOWN <u>BY STEP</u>.

THE YELLOW ROW MOVES BACK-AND-FORTH, <u>BY STEP</u>.

C will be used as the tonal center for each. (C = 1 or "do")

Teachers may elect to add numbers, pitch names, or syllables to this lesson. For inexperienced children, bells may be held vertically, so all may see.

Curwen hand signs might be used.

Select a student to PLAY THE "WHITE MELODY" ON THE BELLS. Help the player to decide whether to begin on low C or high C. (Low C, because the melody moves up)

Place bells so others can see what is played.
C D E F G A B C
1 2 3 4 5 6 7 8/1
do re mi fa so la ti do

NOW WE'LL DISTRIBUTE WHITE CARDS TO USE WHEN THAT MELODY IS HEARD IN OUR RECORDING. Instruct students to lay cards on their desks until asked to use them.

WHO CAN PLAY THE BLUE ROW? Continue the process above, until the blue and the yellow row have been played, and the blue and yellow cards distributed.

(blue row:
C D E F G F E D C)
1 2 3 4 5 4 3 2 1
do re mi fa so fa mi re do

(yellow row:
C D C D C D C)
1 2 1 2 1 2 1
do re do etc.

Send bell players to a part of the room where they cannot be seen. Ask them to play their melodies, one at a time, and ask the class, RAISE YOUR COLORED CARDS AT THE RIGHT TIME.

(As each melody is played, identify it, verify the correct response, and go on to the next melody.)

Comment on the degree of success of the listeners.

AND THESE SAME MELODIES ARE IN A PIECE OF MUSIC ABOUT PIANISTS. I'LL PLAY IT, AND SEE IF YOU CAN HEAR YOUR MELODIES.

BUT IT'S DIFFICULT, BECAUSE THE MELODIES MOVE SO QUICKLY! LET'S TRY IT.

A few perceptive students may notice simultaneous ascending and descending scales:

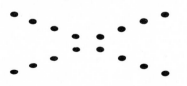

(Melodies occur in this order: yellow, blue, white. This is repeated four times.)

Replay the recording as long as interest remains high.

Summary

WHO CAN SUMMARIZE WHAT WE'VE LEARNED ABOUT THE DIRECTION OF THESE THREE MELODIES?
DID THEY MOVE BY STEP OR BY SKIP? (step)

ANOTHER TIME

Listen to the composition on other days, and learn to read the melodies from staff notation:

ELABORATION

1. See listening games in SBM 1, in which students are to identify ascending and descending melodies played on songbells.

2. To evaluate perception of upward and downward melodic movement, use SBM (EC) "Crayon Activities" 16 (page 88) and 21 (page 127). See also these "What Do You Hear?" charts:

> SBM 1:20, rec 1, and 1:81, rec 5
>
> SBM 2:23, rec 1, and 2:119, rec 5
>
> SBM 4:36, rec 2

SONGS WITH PROMINENT SCALEWISE MOVEMENT

ALL THE LITTLE BIRDS. SBM (EC)

BALL GOES ROUN'. SBM 1

BYM' BYE. EM 2; SBM 2

CHORAL THEME by Beethoven, p. 264

THE DEATH OF MR. FLY. SBM 1

GATATUMBA. SBM 1

HEY HO, HEY LO. SBM 3

HOLLA HI, HOLLA HO. SOM 6

JOHNNY ON THE WOODPILE. DMT 1

LET THERE BE PEACE ON EARTH. SOM 5

MICHIE BANJO. NDM 4

ROUND THE BAY OF MEXICO. NDM 4

SING A LITTLE SONG. SBM (EC)

SUO GAN. DMT 1; SBM 1

TWO WINGS. EM 5

WE SHALL OVERCOME. SOM 6

Stepwise melodies are also used in these model experiences: *Ancient Chinese Temple Music*, p. 63, *Five Angels*, p. 81, and *St. Paul's Steeple*, p. 131.

BIBLIOGRAPHY

Neidlinger, Robert J., "A study in teaching musical style and form to elementary school children," reviewed by Marilyn P. Zimmerman in *Council for Research in Music Education*, 18 (Fall, 1969), p. 39. A different, inventive use of a pegboard is described.

Music Learning	A song usually ends on the tonal center (tonic).
Musical Context	THIS OLD MAN. American game song, p. 283*

Optional: Tonic (D)

Behavioral Objective	To identify aurally the tonal center at the end of a song, and to demonstrate that recognition by playing a resonator bell as the song ends, and by rejecting incorrect alternatives to the final pitch.
Grade	Lower
Materials	Resonator bells D E F♯ G A B

Teacher should learn to play the ending of the song on resonator bells: "This old man came rolling home." See song notation, p. 283.

*Song notation in key of F in CMCM 1B; EM 1; MMYO 2; SBM 1

Focusing Statement

Vocal tune-up: A

AT YOUR HOUSE, IS THERE ONE ROOM IN WHICH YOU USUALLY REST? Discuss briefly. Decide that this room is usually the bedroom, and that the end of the day is the occasion for the longest rest time.

MELODIES CAN HAVE A "RESTING PLACE," TOO. Review *This Old Man* and ask students to RAISE YOUR HAND WHEN YOU THINK WE HAVE REACHED THE "RESTING PLACE" OF THE SONG.

The term *tonic* may be substituted throughout for *tonal center*.

Use staff notation for D, if desired.

YES! THE LAST NOTE IS THE "RESTING PLACE." WE CALL THAT NOTE THE TONAL CENTER. Ask students WHAT WAS THE LAST WORD OF THE SONG? ("home")

LET'S PLAY THAT NOTE ON THE BELLS. Set out the D bell and select a student to play it.

AS WE SING THIS OLD MAN, LET'S SEE IF OUR BELL PLAYER CAN JOIN IN WITH US WHEN WE REACH THE TONAL CENTER. WHO REMEMBERS WHICH WORD WE SING ON THE TONAL CENTER? ("home") HERE WE GO!

Allow other students to take turns playing the D tonal center as several verses are sung.

HERE'S AN EXPERIMENT: LET'S CHANGE TO A <u>DIFFERENT</u> BELL ON THAT LAST WORD. Teacher should now place these bells in order: E F♯ G A and B. *Remove* the D bell. Show the students the D bell, telling them the tonal center is now missing.

Ask a student to select A DIFFERENT BELL TO PLAY ON THE WORD "HOME." AND KEEP IT A SECRET UNTIL IT'S TIME TO PLAY! Student should stand beside the teacher.

NOW, LET'S SEE IF THAT DIFFERENT BELL STILL SOUNDS LIKE OUR "RESTING PLACE" OR TONAL CENTER.

Teacher plays "this old man came rolling," then student adds new pitch on "home."

Summary

DID THAT SOUND FINISHED? (no)

DOES THAT MEAN THAT THERE IS A PARTICULAR TONE THIS SONG SHOULD END ON? (yes) To "prove" it, let students try one or two other pitches. Then replace the D bell and culminate the experience by singing the song and playing the D bell as the tonal center. Select a student to play the D bell by asking WHO REMEMBERS WHAT WE CALL THE "RESTING PLACE" IN A SONG? Choose a student who answers "tonal center."

ANOTHER TIME

See Glossary.

1. Discover the final cadence ("rolling home") and play all three pitches on the bells.

2. Use these "arm signals" (variations on the Curwen hand signs) along with the tonal center (do) or with the final cadence (mi re do):

 mi   *re*   *do*

3. Older students may wish to read key signatures to locate the tonal center of these commonly used major keys:

OTHER SONGS FOR SIMILAR USE

BIBLIOGRAPHY

Richards, Mary Helen. *The Music Language,* 2 vols. Portola Valley, Calif.: Richards Institute of Music Education and Research, 1974. The author makes extensive use of "arm signs."

_____ . *Threshold to Music.* Belmont, Calif.: Fearon Publishers, 1964. 2nd ed. by Eleanor Kidd, 1974.

Music Learning	Each phrase in "12-bar" blues consists of four measures (16 beats).
Musical Context	GOOD MORNING, BLUES by Huddie Ledbetter ("Leadbelly") (Black American, 1888–1949). MMYO 6, EM 5
Behavioral Objective	To identify aurally and visually the two parts of the three 16-beat phrases; and to demonstrate this recognition by using two different body rhythms and/or percussion instruments.
Grade	Upper
Materials	Recording: MMYO 6, rec 8; EM 5, rec 4 Woodblock Tambourine

Each phrase in the diagram below represents a four-bar (16-beat) phrase of "12-bar" blues. The first half (eight beats) of the phrase is usually vocally active and the second half of the phrase is usually "filled in" by instrumental improvisation.

Draw this diagram on chalkboard prior to beginning the experience.

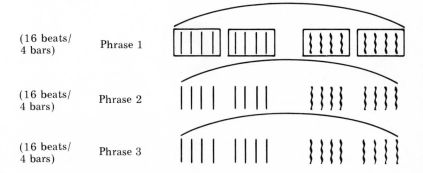

(16 beats/ 4 bars) Phrase 1

(16 beats/ 4 bars) Phrase 2

(16 beats/ 4 bars) Phrase 3

Focusing Statement

Note that each vertical mark, straight or wavy, represents one steady beat. Ask students to COUNT THE NUMBER OF STEADY BEATS IN EACH PHRASE. (16) Each half consists of eight beats.

Have all students tap steady beats (16 per phrase) with pencils on the edges of their desks as you play one chorus (verse) of the recording.

 (Point to steady beats in diagram on board as students tap.)

Divide class into three groups. One group will be responsible for tapping the 16-beat phrases, as above. A second group will *clap* the first eight beats and the third group will sound the second eight beats by *snapping* fingers.

Practice one phrase with all three groups: one group *clapping* eight beats, one group *snapping* eight beats, and one group *tapping* all sixteen.

Lead them through phrase 1 once. ONE, TWO, READY, GO:

Body rhythms (phrase 1 only)   Do your best to establish the same tempo as on the recording.)

(As there is no pause between the two halves of a blues phrase, each group should quietly respond to the sound of the other group. In case of difficulty, have the inactive group "mark time" with hands, silently, while the active group is making its sounds.)

Do the entire chart with the recording. Have students *begin* their sounds *when the singing begins on the recording.* Point to each beat on the chart as the instruments play one entire *chorus* before the singing begins. Encourage singing.

Body   (play instrumental *chorus* and
rhythms   first *sung chorus* only)

Lyrics are easy. Encourage singing early in process. See songbooks for lyrics and notation, if necessary.

When students are ready, play all *choruses* (verses) of the recording, adding singing and two percussion instruments. One student will play eight beats on woodblock and one will play the other eight beats on the tambourine. Invite the rest of the students to keep the beat in any *quiet* manner they choose.

WAIT FOR THE SINGING TO BEGIN YOUR SOUNDS.

(During last four beats of instrumental *chorus,* say ONE, TWO, READY, GO, signalling all to begin, except tambourine.)

Body
rhythms

Summary

Discuss performance of class and understanding of the above processes. Comment on: (1) each phrase being four measures (bars) long; (2) three phrases multiplied by four bars = "12-bar" blues; (3) the way the two halves of each phrase balance each other; and (4) the typical instrumental improvisation on the second half of each phrase.

ANOTHER TIME

1. More inventive rhythms can be utilized during this experience. For example, a four-beat rhythm pattern may be sounded twice during the first half and a different four-beat pattern sounded twice during the second half of the phrase.

2. Encourage students to identify the instruments featured in the recording of *Good Morning, Blues.* Allow students to experiment with percussion instruments of various tone colors.

3. Listen to Leadbelly's own recording of *Good Morning Blues* in *Negro Folk Songs for Young People,* Folkways FC 7533.

ELABORATION

1. Individual students may listen to blues recordings in the library or in their own collections to identify other examples of 12-bar blues.

2. See model experience *Joe Turner Blues,* p. 158.

OTHER 12-BAR BLUES

CITY BLUES. NDM 5

GUT BUCKET BLUES. SBM 6, rec 8

JOE TURNER BLUES, p. 158.

Listen to PORCUPINE ROCK for its blues influence. SBM 6, rec 7

ST. LOUIS BLUES. SOM 5

SHORTY GEORGE BLUES (instrumental only). MMYO 6

TILL THAT DAY BLUES. SBM 6

12-BAR BLUES IMPROVISATION. SBM 6, rec 6

BIBLIOGRAPHY FOR YOUNG PEOPLE

Surge, Frank. *Singers of the Blues.* Minneapolis: Lerner, 1969. Upper grades; includes all the "greats"; highly recommended.

BIBLIOGRAPHY

Jones, LeRoi. *Blues People: Negro Music in White America.* New York: William Morrow, 1963.

Oliver, Paul. *Savannah Syncopators: African Retentions in the Blues.* New York: Stein and Day, 1970.

Music Learning	Steady beats may be grouped in twos (duple meter).
Musical Context	WE ARE GOING DOWN THE NUMBERS (song from Nigeria, as sung by E. Ikpe). MMYO 1
Reading Objective	Beat groupings: 
Behavioral Objective	To visually and aurally identify beat groupings in two and to demonstrate that recognition through body rhythms and in a stick game.
Grade	Lower
Materials	Recording: MMYO 1, rec 2 Rhythm sticks (six or more pairs)
Song notation, p. 268	Write material from "Reading Objective" on chalkboard or use this informal notation: 

Focusing Statement

Point to the two examples of beat groupings on the board.
WHICH EXAMPLE, NUMBER 1 OR NUMBER 2, SHOWS BEATS GROUPED INTO SETS OF TWO? (No. 1)

Direct the students' attention to the visual difference in the two examples; demonstrate that difference in body rhythms.
LET'S TRY SOME STEADY BEATS IN SETS OF TWO.

      Body rhythms   (LAP, clap, LAP, clap, etc.)

Continue until most students are comfortable with the twos. Then, students should try the same motions *facing a partner*.
OUR SETS OF TWO WILL FIT NICELY WITH A SONG FROM AFRICA. WHEN THE SINGING BEGINS, YOU AND YOUR PARTNER BEGIN.

  Body rhythms   (Repeat until students seem comfortable with the motions.)

NOW WE CAN TRY A STICK GAME WITH THIS SONG!
Choose two students to sit cross-legged on floor, facing each other. Each should hold two sticks vertically.
The pattern for the game is:

Beat 1: hit own sticks on floor

Beat 2: hit own sticks together

Try these motions first *before* trying with the music.

Sticks

When students are ready, try the game with the song. BEGIN THE GAME WHEN THE SINGING BEGINS ON THE RECORDING.

 Sticks

Add other students to the stick game. Some classes may be ready to sing the song, too.

 Sticks

Summary

STICK GAMES ARE A GOOD WAY TO SHOW STEADY BEATS IN SETS OF TWO.

ANOTHER TIME

1. Well-coordinated partners might try hitting their laps on beat 1, and their partner's *right* palm (as in pat-a-cake) on beat 2. These motions may then be transferred to sticks.

2. Try the stick-*passing* game suggested for *We Are Going Down the Numbers,* MMYO 1, Teacher's Edition.

ELABORATION

Do stick games to the selections listed below and discover *both* duple-beat (2) and triple-beat (3) groupings.

OTHER SONGS FOR SIMILAR USE

● *Songs with beat groupings in twos*

A RAM SAM SAM, p. 233
DRILL DANCE (Samoa). CMCM 3A; MMYO 6
HAND GAME SONG. SBM 4
HAWAIIAN BOAT SONG. CMCM 2A; EM 3
MARCHING TO PRETORIA. CMCM 1B; MMYO 2 and 3; NDM 3; SBM 3
PASS THE SHOE. EM 1 (Shoe Game); SBM (EC)
SASA ABEREWA (Africa). SBM 4 (hand-clapping game)
STICK GAME. CMCM 3A
THIS OLD MAN, p. 283
ZIGY, ZIGY, ZA by Gilberto. SBM 5 (stone-passing game)
ZUM GALI GALI, p. 287, EM 4; NDM 3

● *Songs with beat groupings in threes*

See model experience *Elephant:* "Other Music," p. 97.

● *Beat groupings in twos and threes*

DIPIDU. DMT 1 and 2; SBM 1 and 2; SOM 2

MINEIRA DE MINAS. SBM 5

MY NIPA HUT. SBM 2

MY WAGON. SOM 4

ORION. SBM 6

TON MOULIN. DMT (EC); MMYO 3; SBM 1 (A B A form, with A sections in three and B section in four)

Listen to PIECE IN TWO METERS by Kingsley. SBM 3

BIBLIOGRAPHY

Jones, Russell L. "The Development of the Child's Conception of Meter in Music," *Journal of Research in Music Education*, 24, 3 (Fall, 1976), pp. 142–154. Results of this research study seem to indicate that the meter concept develops after about age 9½.

Music Learning	Steady beats can be grouped in threes (triple meter).
Musical Context	ELEPHANT from *Carnival of the Animals* by Camille Saint-Saëns ("sa[n] saw[n]s") (French, 1835–1921). AIM 1, II; BOL 51; EM 2; SOM 1
Reading Objective	See cards below. 
Behavioral Objective	To identify aurally beat groupings in three; and to demonstrate that recognition in body rhythms.
Grade	Upper
Materials	Recording: AIM 1, II; BOL 51; EM 2, rec 8; SOM 1, rec 7

Four cards as shown below. |
| *Focusing Statement* | WATCH MY CLAPPING, AND SEE IF YOU CAN DISCOVER ANY KIND OF BEAT GROUPING.

Body rhythms (Teacher claps a series of unaccented, even beats so there is *no discernible grouping*.)

Discuss why no grouping was apparent and tell students HERE ARE SOME WAYS THAT GROUPS OF <u>THREE STEADY BEATS</u> MIGHT BE INDICATED.

Display cards: |

1.  2.

3. 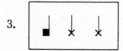 4.

Select individual students to demonstrate each card, using body rhythms.

If students are ready, discuss each type of accent shown on the cards.

1. Loud-soft-soft (dynamic) accent
2. Rest-snap-snap (dynamic accent using silence).
3. Clap-snap-snap (timbre accent)
4. Low-high-high (pitch accent, suggested here by spatial location)

Direct attention to the piano accompaniment.

AS WE LISTEN TO THIS RECORDING, LOCATE THE STEADY BEATS, AND TRY TO DETERMINE THE GROUPINGS.

Choose a performance of *Elephant* that maintains a steady tempo.

 (ELEPHANT. Play excerpt.)

DID YOU GET AN IDEA OF WHAT THE GROUPINGS WERE? Ask for group responses or demonstration. SHOW ME THE GROUPING YOU HEARD.

Body rhythms

(Elicit ideas from more than one student before correct response is identified.)

Decide that THE GROUPINGS WERE SUGGESTED BY LOCATION (low-high-high relationship of pitches), ALTERNATING WITH SILENCE OR REST (rest-beat-beat in accompaniment).

Replay the composition as long as interest remains high, asking students to DO A VARIETY OF BODY RHYTHMS SHOWING THE BEAT GROUPINGS (Lap-clap-clap, etc.).

 Body rhythms

Discuss the title *Elephant* given this music by the composer. He apparently thought this was humorous because an elephant would hardly dance a waltz!

Summary

Review HOW ARE STEADY BEATS GROUPED IN A WALTZ? (3 — triple meter)

ANOTHER TIME

Create a stick game in threes, similar to that suggested in the model experience *We Are Going down the Numbers*, p. 92.

ELABORATION

1. Learn the conducting pattern for triple meter.
2. Create a game, using meter signature flash cards:
   As student or teacher flashes each card, students respond with appropriate body rhythms.

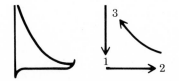

2	3	4
4	4	4

3. Invent symbols and perform them, grouping sounds into metric units by *accent*.

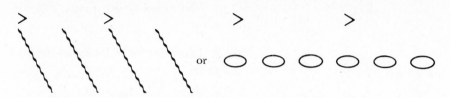

4. To evaluate perception of duple and triple meter, provide a tape of the following selections for students to use, on their own, at individual learning stations:

1. ALLEGRO DECISO from *Water Music Suite* by Handel. EM 5; NDM 5; SBM 6

2. DANCE OF THE SUGAR PLUM FAIRY from *The Nutcracker Suite* by Tchaikovsky. BOL 58; EM 2; NDM 1

3. WALTZ from *Suite No. 2 for Small Orchestra* by Stravinsky. EM 2; NDM 2; SBM 2; SOM 3

Prepare a worksheet for each student, offering the following choices:

1	2	3
TWOS $\frac{2}{4}$ THREES $\frac{3}{4}$	TWOS $\frac{2}{4}$ THREES $\frac{3}{4}$	TWOS $\frac{2}{4}$ THREES $\frac{3}{4}$

5. To evaluate perception of duple and triple meter, use these "What Do You Hear?" charts:

SBM 1:59, rec 4; SBM 1:105, rec 6

SBM 2:78, rec 4; SBM 2:161, rec 7

SBM 3:43, rec 3

SBM 4:49, rec 3; SBM 4:133, rec 9

6. See model experience *Samiotissa*, p. 202, for an example of asymmetric beat groupings.

7. Review conducting patterns in duple, triple, and quadruple meters:

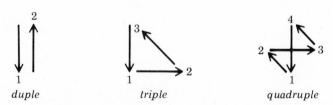

Physical movements may look more like this:

OTHER MUSIC

● *Music in triple meter*

THE BLUE DANUBE by Strauss. SOM 6

CARILLON from *L'Arlesienne Suite No. 2* by Bizet. EM 4

MINUET from *Royal Fireworks Music* by Handel. MMYO 4

MINUET from *Symphony No. 40* by Mozart. DMT 1

VARIATIONS ON A THEME BY SATIE by Blood Sweat and Tears. NDM 6

WALTZ IN C♯ MINOR by Chopin. EM 3

Nearly any composition titled "waltz" or "minuet" should be evaluated for use in similar experiences.

● *Music in duple or quadruple meter*

GAVOTTE from *Classical Symphony* by Prokofiev. NDM 4

MARCH from *Suite No. 2 for Small Orchestra* by Stravinsky. EM 2; NDM 2; SBM 2

MARCH FOR BRASSES by Goldman. DMT 1

SONATA IN C MAJOR by Mozart. NDM 6

STARS AND STRIPES FOREVER by Sousa. DMT 3; EM 5; NDM 5

TREPAK from *The Nutcracker Suite* by Tchaikovsky. BOL 58; EM 2; NDM 1

Nearly any composition titled "march" may be considered for use.

Answers:
(1) threes
(2) twos
(3) threes

F

Expressive qualities: those qualities (dynamics, tempo, timbre) which, combined with other musical elements give a composition its unique musical identity.

HAIKU SOUND PIECE
> Each instrument has a characteristic timbre which, combined with others, contributes to a composition's unique identity.

Form: the shape, order, or design of a musical composition.

CLAP YOUR HANDS
> Sections of a song can contrast with each other (A B).

Melody: a linear succession of pitches; the horizontal structure in music.

*SOUND PIECE 7
> Octave displacement and change of duration can be produced electronically.

Rhythm: all of the durations that occur in music.

POLKA
> A melodic rhythm usually includes long and short sounds.

Form: the shape, order, or design of a musical composition.

A RAM SAM SAM (II)
> Sections of a composition can contrast with one another and sections can be repeated (A B A).

CARILLON
> Sections of a composition can contrast with one another and sections can be repeated (A B A).

SCRATCH, SCRATCH, etc.
> Sections of a song can contrast with one another and sections of a song can repeat (A B, A B A).

After completing each model experience, decide how successfully you are able to identify, explain, or demonstrate the music learning that was the focus of the experience. Check the appropriate box.

Secure   Fairly secure   Insecure

*Group work-through experience

98

> Haiku is a three-line form of nature poetry which has been popular for centuries in Japan.

Music Learning

> Each instrument has a characteristic timbre which, combined with others, contributes to a composition's unique identity.

Musical Context

HAIKU SOUND PIECE

Behavioral Objective

To create an original composition by choosing and playing percussion instruments in combination with a haiku poem.

Grade

Upper

Materials

Assorted percussion instruments—claves, maracas, drums, melody bells, notched sticks, and so forth.

Or, use homemade instruments (see "Bibliography").

Chart of poem and design (See below.)

Focusing Statement

THE WORDS YOU SEE ON THE CHART ARE A HAIKU POEM. Read the poem with the class, and discuss any unfamiliar words or ideas.

Tell the students that the "design" is a visualization of the sounds that might accompany this haiku poem:

Poem from *The Way of Haiku;* original verses in English by J. W. Hackett. Tokyo-New York: Japan Publications, Inc., © 1968.

> These barnacled rocks,
>   Just uncovered by the tide . . .
>   How busy they sound!

LET'S LOOK AT THE "DESIGN" ON THE CHART. WHAT KIND OF SOUND IS SUGGESTED BY THE LINES AND DOTS?

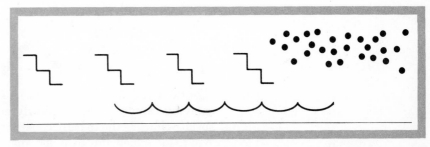

These barnacled rocks, just uncovered by the tide . . . how busy they sound!

Ideas which follow must be considered merely as possible outcomes. Each class will create an entirely original sound piece.

Discuss the "design" in relation to the assortment of instruments available. Decide how the timbre of any particular instrument might be suitable for expressing one part of the "design." Explore sounds:

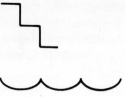

Suggests levels: in music, *pitch* levels might well be indicated. Consider using a xylophone-type instrument.

Suggests an "up-and-down" sound that is continuous. Decide which instrument might produce such a sound. Try a glissando on the Autoharp or bells, sand blocks, notched sticks, and so forth.

———— suggests a continuum, but it does not require a sound. It represents the "time line" along which the sounds move.

Suggests sounds that are short, and not sustained. Ideas might include castanets, sticks, high-pitched drums, temple blocks, and so forth.

Distribute the instruments to selected students. Choose a student to read the poem, being sure to PAUSE AT THE PUNCTUATION MARKS, and to read expressively.

Poem

Add the instruments. Refer to the "design" and decide approximately WHEN WILL EACH INSTRUMENT BEGIN? DO THEY ALL ENTER AT THE SAME TIME? (no) DO THEY END AT THE SAME TIME? (no)

Poem

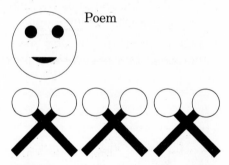

Evaluate the effort in terms of its expressiveness. Are the instruments playing rapidly enough? Slowly enough? Do they enter at the appropriate time? Is the texture constant, or does it vary? (It should probably vary, for added interest. All instruments should *not* play the entire time.)

Experiment as often as necessary to obtain the desired effect.

Poem

Summary

Conclude by discussing how each instrument—both singly, and in combination with others—has a distinctive timbre which adds expressiveness to the composition.

Many of these ideas can be developed by individuals or small groups.

ANOTHER TIME

1. Create your sound piece out of the *words* of the poem by repeating them, using dynamic emphasis, and create texture by varying the number of different parts to be performed simultaneously. Listen to the sound piece in SBM 4:103, which does this very thing, using a haiku poem.

2. Use nontraditional sound sources to create a composition with a haiku poem. Try using paper, metal or glass objects, combs, wastebaskets, and other unconventional resources. Or make your own instruments. (See Bibliography.)

3. Use body or mouth sounds. All sorts of smacking, popping, and "whooshing" sounds are useful. The sound piece in SBM 6:12 suggests many similar ideas.

4. Using a tape recorder, manipulate previously recorded sounds into an expressive composition. Read the poem along with the recorded sounds, which might include surf, dripping water, wind, birdsong, and other sounds of nature. For many ideas, see *Sound Experiments with Tape Recorder,* pp. 35, 105, 111, 128, and 164.

ELABORATION

1. Listen to (and sing) *Two Haiku* by Diemer in NDM 6. Improvise a rhythmic accompaniment, as suggested. See the sound piece in SBM 5:56 for some ideas on combining sounds.

2. For your composition, use a longer Chinese poem, in NDM 5, by Tu Fu; in MMYO 6, by Liu Tsung-Yuan, Wang Wei, and Meng Hao-Jan; or, in SBM 6, by Tu Fu.

3. Notate your composition, using nontraditional notation. Look at these for ideas:

SBM 6:13 and 6:44 (graph paper)

SBM 4:103 (contemporary notation for rhythm, pitch, dynamics)

SBM 4:13 (graph)

See also the Kaplan article in "Bibliography," below.

4. Create a composition which will be an artistic response to a series of paintings. Strongly contrasting painters such as Jackson Pollock and Piet Mondrian might spur creative endeavors.

5. Hear IMPROVISATION FOR STICKS, STONES, CANS, AND BONES by Greg Polski. SOM 2. Pictures and score are included.

OTHER HAIKU POEMS

NDM 4: poems by Basho and Issa

NDM 5: poems by Onitsura and Jōsō

NDM 6: poems by Basho and Rokwa

Use one of these haiku poems by J. W. Hackett:

Searching on the wind,
the hawk's cry . . .
is the shape of its beak.

A leaf on the stream
sinks slowly through the current
to the deepest pool.

Crow pecks into the sand,
swallows what he finds, then
shudders all over.

In its traditional three-line form, the haiku poem consisted of 17 syllables, composed in a 5–7–5 arrangement. With masters such as Basho, the haiku became an art of Zen Buddhism and was highly esteemed by the Japanese. Today, haiku are written in many languages, and the form is popular throughout the world. Although the traditional form has occasionally been modified, haiku poetry retains its characteristic spirit of naturalness, simplicity, and directness.

BIBLIOGRAPHY

Hackett, J. W. *Bug Haiku*. Tokyo: Japan Publications, Inc., 1968.

———. *Haiku Poetry,* 4 vols. Tokyo: Japan Publications, Inc., 1968.

Kaplan, Don. "The Joys of Noise, Part I," *Music Educators Journal,* 62, 6 (February, 1976), p. 37.

Marsh, Mary Val. "Setting Haiku to Music," in *Explore and Discover Music.* New York: The Macmillan Company, 1970, pp. 78–84. Use of xylophones.

Schafer, R. Murray. *Creative Music Education.* New York: Schirmer Books, 1976, p. 202. Suggestions for using haiku in choral improvisations which emphasize texture and contour.

BIBLIOGRAPHY FOR HOMEMADE INSTRUMENTS

Hofsinde, Robert. *Indian Music Makers.* New York: William Morrow and Company, 1967.

Mandell, Muriel, and Robert E. Wood. *Make Your Own Musical Instrument.* New York: Sterling, 1959.

Morales, Humbert. *Latin American Rhythm Instruments.* New York: H. Adler Publishers Corp., 1954.

Weidemann, Charles C. *Music in Sticks and Stones; How to Construct and Play Simple Instruments.* New York: Exposition Press, 1967.

Weil, Lisl. *Things That Go Bang.* New York: McGraw-Hill Book Company, 1969. Ideas for making nontraditional instruments.

Music Learning	Sections of a song can contrast with each other. (A B)
Musical Context	CLAP YOUR HANDS (American folk song). CMCM 1A and 1B; DMT (EC): MMYO 1 and 2; NDM Beg., 1 and 2; SBM 1
Behavioral Objective	To identify aurally the song's two contrasting sections (A and B); and to demonstrate this recognition by responding with contrasting body rhythms and by placing contrasting shapes on a flannelboard.
Grade	Lower
Materials	Recording: MMYO 1, rec 1; MMYO 2, rec 2; SBM 1, rec 3 (or others from "Musical Context" references above) Flannelboard and two shapes (one △ and one ☐)

Focusing Statement

LET'S PLAY A "SIMON SAYS" GAME WITHOUT WORDS! Explain to students that you will make some body sounds. They are to do them *with* you.

> Body rhythms   (Teacher explores, class follows: tap head, shoulders; clap hands; *patsch;* stamp feet.)

Vary game, using changes in tempo (fast and slow) and dynamics (loud and soft).

GREAT LISTENING AND WATCHING! LISTEN TO A SONG THAT WILL SUGGEST A BODY SOUND. DO WHAT THE WORDS TELL YOU.

 Clap *(first verse only)*

Now, invite students to try *two* body sounds. Clap on the parts where the words tell you, and *patsch* on the "la" words.

Observe how many students are able to change motions at the beginning of the second section.

 Body rhythms   (*Play first verse only;* fade out recording.)

Ask students how many different actions they did for this latest playing of *Clap Your Hands.* (2) Ask if they repeated either of them. (No)

Summary

YOU DID TWO DIFFERENT ACTIONS FOR THE TWO DIFFERENT SECTIONS OF THE SONG.

Point to flannelboard with shapes. Choose two students. Each will place a shape on the flannelboard as the song is played. One shape should be placed at the *beginning* of the *clapping* part of the song (after introduction). The second should be placed when the "la" part begins. Most students will be ready to sing the words of the first section of the song ("clap, clap").

Second section is not within the vocal range of many children.

 first verse only

 Body rhythms
Placing shapes

WHAT WAS THE DIFFERENCE BETWEEN THE FIRST SECTION OF THE SONG AND THE SECOND? The different words will be noted. Also, point out how the melody of the second section is both different and higher than the first.

Repeat, choosing different students to place the shapes. Encourage students to sing the first section. More verses may be attempted as long as students understand that the additional verses are *repeats* of the form of the first verse.

 Body rhythms and shape placement

Summary

YOU DID A SUPER JOB, SHOWING THE DIFFERENCE BETWEEN THOSE TWO SECTIONS OF THE SONG.

ELABORATION

1. Create your own action piece in two sections. One section might use finger-snapping as the action. Another section might use marching. A leader for each section should be responsible for the starting and concluding.

2. See model experience *Scratch, Scratch,* p. 116.

OTHER SONGS WITH TWO CONTRASTING (A B) SECTIONS

BIG-EYE RABBIT. SBM 1

BOIL THEM CABBAGE DOWN. SBM 3

DAYENU. SBM 4

FLOATING DOWN THE RIVER. SBM (EC)

MARCHING TO PRETORIA. CMCM 1B; DMT 2; EM 4; MMYO 2 and 3; NDM 3; SBM 3

MISTER RABBIT. CMCM 2A; MMYO 1; SBM 1

OLD JOE CLARK (variant of CLAP YOUR HANDS). EM 5; MMYO 6; SBM 2 and 3; SOM 5

RIG-A-JIG-JIG. CMCM 2B; EM 2; MMYO Kg, 1 and 2; SOM Kg

ROLL AN' ROCK, p. 120

BIBLIOGRAPHY

Wheeler, Lawrence, and Lois Raebeck. *Orff and Kodaly Adapted for the Elementary School.* Dubuque, Iowa: Wm. C. Brown Co., 1972, pp. 1–9. Similar ideas to the "Simon Says" game are presented (called "tempo-dynamic clapping").

CLAP YOUR HANDS

American Folk Song

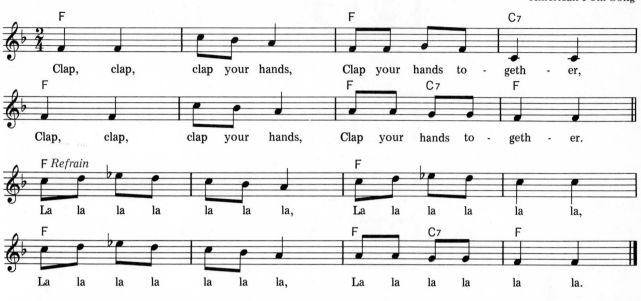

Clap, clap, clap your hands, Clap your hands to - geth - er,

Clap, clap, clap your hands, Clap your hands to - geth - er.

Refrain

La la la la la la la, La la la la la la,

La la la la la la la, La la la la la la.

WORK-THROUGH EXPERIENCE

Music Learning	Octave displacement and change of duration can be produced electronically.

SOUND EXPERIMENT WITH TAPE RECORDER: PITCH AND DURATION

Musical Context	SOUND PIECE 7 by Joyce Reimer ("REE-muhr") (contemporary American). SBM 4
Behavioral Objective	To record sounds of melody bells and Autoharp, and to play back these recorded sounds at 7½ i.p.s. and at 3¾ i.p.s., observing the differing pitch and duration.
Grade	Upper
Materials	Reel-to-reel tape recorder
	Microphone
	Recording tape (clean)
	Melody bells and mallet (or resonator bells)
	Autoharp
	Recording: *Sound Piece 7,* SBM 4, rec 8

i.p.s. = inches per second, the rate at which the tape travels past the record or playback head

1. Select one person to handle each piece of the equipment.

2. Set the tape recorder speed at 7½ i.p.s.

3. Put the machine in *record* mode.

4. Tape-record one person playing randomly and rapidly on the bells for about five seconds. This can be timed precisely, if you wish, by using a watch with a sweep second hand.

7½

5. Play the sound back, at the *same* (7½ i.p.s.) speed.

7½

6. How long will these five seconds of sound last if played back at 3¾ i.p.s. instead of 7½ i.p.s.? Try it and see. (Also see left margin.)

3¾

7. In step 6, did you notice an alteration of *pitch* as well as duration? Play the segment again at 3¾ i.p.s. and notice that change of pitch.

3¾

See Glossary.

8. This *octave displacement* (one octave lower) may be "proved" by this experiment:

a. play C²-D²-E² (upper register of bells) and record at 7½ i.p.s.

7½

b. play this recording at 3¾, and *at the same time* play C¹-D¹-E¹ on the bells (the lower register).

3¾

(Most school tape recorders run at only two speeds: 7½ and 3¾ i.p.s. If your tape recorder has an additional speed, it is probably 1⅞ i.p.s. In this case you can record sounds at 3¾ and play them back at either a *slower* [1⅞ i.p.s.] or a *faster* [7½ i.p.s.] speed.)

9. Assuming that your tape recorder has but two speeds, how can you achieve the *opposite* of the lengthened duration and lower pitch experiment from steps 4–7 above? (See left margin.)

10. Now try recording at 3¾ and playing back at 7½ i.p.s. This time, bounce a bell mallet all over the Autoharp strings without pressing any chord buttons. (You may choose to record a specific amount of sound. Remember that ten seconds of recorded sound will play back for only five seconds if the speed is increased.)

3¾

12. Listen to the recorded sound at the original speed of 3¾ i.p.s.

3¾

13. Listen to the same sound at 7½ i.p.s.

7½

Summary

Answers:

9. Record at 3¾ i.p.s., playback at 7½ i.p.s.

14. half as long; lower by one octave

14. Formulate answers to these questions:

When music recorded at 3¾ i.p.s. is played at 7½ i.p.s. the *duration* of the pitches is _____.

When music recorded at 7½ i.p.s. is played at 3¾ i.p.s. the *pitch* is _____ by _____. (See left margin.)

15. Play the recording of *Sound Piece 7,* in which composer Joyce Reimer uses piano sounds, altered by speed change and other interesting tape techniques. (The piano sounds, as *originally* recorded, are heard on the record before the composition is played.) If possible, use the score in SBM 4, pp. 190–191, to see how the composer has visualized her ideas.

ELABORATION

1. Follow this experiment with model experience *Greeting Prelude* p. 171.

2. Invent your own tape techniques to use in association with model experience *Haiku Sound Piece,* p. 99.

3. Students in the elementary classroom will need time to discover that certain recorded sounds become more interesting when played back at a faster speed, and others at a slower speed.

Encourage them to utilize a wide variety of sound sources, such as environmental sounds, mouth sounds, standard instruments used nontraditionally, and so forth.

4. See "Working with Sounds" satellites in SBM 5 and 6.

5. See *Sound Piece 2*, SBM 4, where students are given instructions on how to create a tape piece, *by chance,* by utilizing changes of tempo (speed).

6. See "Compose Your Own Electronic Music," EM 6, following *Three Synchronisms* by Davidovsky.

7. See "Style: New Music . . . ," *Dawn Figures* by Reimer, SBM 6, rec 5.

8. Listen to *Sonic Contours* by Ussachevsky, a tape composition, EM 1.

9. Listen to *Sound Patterns* by Oliveros, SBM 2.

10. See SOM 6 for creative ideas utilizing tape recorder speed change.

BIBLIOGRAPHY

See "Bibliography," p. 59.

Music Learning

A melodic rhythm usually includes long and short sounds.

Musical Context

POLKA from *Suite No. 2 for Small Orchestra* by Igor Stravinsky ("strah-VIHN-skee") (Russian–American, 1882–1971). EM 2; NDM 2; SOM 3

Reading Objective

(optional)

Behavioral Objective

To identify aurally the beat and divisions of the beat in a melodic rhythm heard in an orchestral composition; and to demonstrate that recognition in body rhythms.

Grade

Upper

Materials

Recording: EM 2, rec 7; NDM 2, rec 8; SOM 3, rec 8

Focusing Statement

PATSCH WITH ME. (*Slow* tempo.)

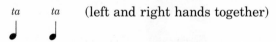

Class continues until signalled to stop.

Have students snap fingers high over their heads once.
READY GO:

snap (once)

NOW, TRY CLAPPING TWO TO A BEAT:

Rhythm syllables can be used with all notation.

NOW, FOUR TO A BEAT:

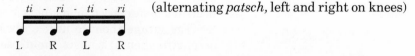

(alternating *patsch,* left and right on knees)

THAT'S PRETTY FAST! BETTER TRY IT AGAIN!

Repeat *patsch.*

Challenge class to do this combination, after you demonstrate it:

ti - ri - ti - ri	*ti - ti*	*ti - ti*
L R L R	clap - clap	clap - clap
1	2	3

Repeat, with students. Once only.

THERE'S ONE FINAL MOTION TO ADD, THE OVERHEAD SNAP. ADDED TO WHAT WE JUST DID, IT WORKS LIKE THIS:

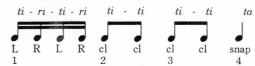

ti - ri - ti - ri	*ti - ti*	*ti - ti*	*ta*
L R L R	cl cl	cl cl	snap
1	2	3	4

Have class perform this same rhythm pattern once, *pause* while you count four beats, then do the pattern again.

Body rhythms:	body rhythm pattern	1-2-3-4	body rhythm pattern	1-2-3-4 etc.

SOME OF YOU ARE GOOD ENOUGH TO BE IN THE ORCHESTRA THAT PLAYS THAT RHYTHM! Play first part of *Polka* recording and direct students' attention to the rhythm just learned.

Invite students to try the rhythm with the recording. REMEMBER THE FOUR-BEAT BREAKS BETWEEN OUR PATTERNS. I'LL GET YOU STARTED AFTER THE SHORT (six-beat) INTRODUCTION:

Body Rhythms}	six-beat *intro.*	Rhythm pattern	four beats

(this sounds five times)

Summary

STRAVINSKY'S MUSIC CERTAINLY IS MORE INTERESTING BECAUSE OF THE WAYS HE COMBINES SHORTER AND LONGER SOUNDS IN THE RHYTHM OF THE MELODY.

ANOTHER TIME

1. Provide a tape of *Polka* for students to use at a learning station. Provide students with rhythmic notation, or ask them to create their own, using popsicle sticks, arranged in this rhythm:

 etc.

2. Encourage students to follow the notation as they listen and do body rhythms.

ELABORATION

1. See "Reading Rhythm" satellites, SBM 5 and 6.

2. Use the following music for an evaluative experience with upper-grade students:

> CHESTER from *New England Triptych* by Schuman. (American, b. 1910). BOL 75; EM 5
>
> GERMAN DANCE ("Sleighride") by Mozart ("MOE-tsart") (Austrian, 1756–1791). DMT 4; EM 3
>
> MARCH from *The Nutcracker Suite* by Peter Ilich Tchaikovsky ("chai-KOF-skee") (Russian, 1840–1893). BOL 58; DMT 3; EM 2

Prepare a worksheet for each student, using the material illustrated below. In item one, first "speak" each line of notation, using rhythm syllables. Play the recording so that students can make their choices. Then replay the selection if necessary to reinforce the understanding. Proceed in a similar manner with items two and three.

CHESTER:

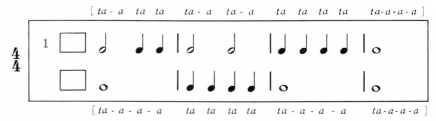

GERMAN DANCE:

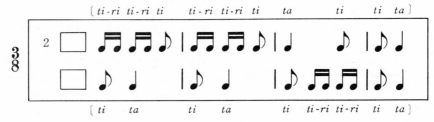

MARCH:

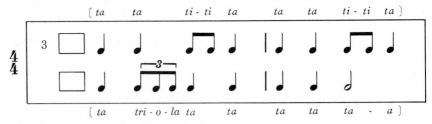

OTHER MUSIC WITH DISTINCT RHYTHM PATTERNS

CUM-MA-LA BE-STAY. SMB 6

FINALE from *H. M. S. Pinafore* by Gilbert and Sullivan. SOM 6

I AM THE CAPTAIN OF THE PINAFORE from *H. M. S. Pinafore* by Gilbert and Sullivan. SOM 6

LISTEN TO THE WATCHMAN'S CRY. SOM 6

MELCHIOR AND BALTHAZAR. SBM 1

SWEETHEART OUT A-HUNTING. SBM 2

TO SEE SWAINSON. SOM 4

See also model experience *Kangaroo:* "Other Music," p. 44.

It is important that students begin to put their new tape recorder sounds and techniques into some form, since they quickly become bored with the randomness of unstructured sounds. This experience assumes that *A Ram Sam Sam* is well known by the students. (See end of this experience for other songs that may be substituted for *A Ram Sam Sam.*)

Music Learning

Sections of a composition can contrast with one another and sections can be repeated (A B A).

Musical Context

A RAM SAM SAM (II) (Folk song from Morocco). DMT (EC); MMYO Kg; SBM 1

Behavioral Objective

To play and record a melodic rhythm, and to identify and select the contrasting section that results when the tape is replayed at different speeds.

Grade

Upper

Materials

Two-speed reel-to-reel tape recorder

Recording tape

Double bongos and Chinese temple blocks (or two woodblocks of different pitches)

Precede this experience by model experience *Sound Piece 7*, p. 105.

Focusing Statement

Song notation, p. 233.

Lead class in singing *A Ram Sam Sam* and accompany the singing by clapping the melodic rhythm (word rhythm). CLAP EVERY SOUND (syllable) YOU SING. THERE'LL BE A LOT OF CLAPPING WHEN YOU GET TO THE "GULI GULI GULI" PART.

Establish pitch by singing or playing C–F. Establish tempo by saying: ONE, READY, SING:

 and Clap

Clap or tap the melodic rhythm again. DON'T SING THIS TIME. JUST "MOUTH" THE WORDS, SO THAT I CAN READ YOUR LIPS.

 Clap and "mouth" words.

Choose a student to play the first half of the melodic rhythm on the bongos. Player will play:

A   ram   sam   sam,   a   ram   sam   sam,   Gu - li

gu - li   gu - li   gu - li   gu - li   ram   sam   sam.

Encourage drummer to use both heads of the bongos to add variety to the sound. If drummer "mouths" the words, it will be easier to stop at the right place in the song.

Choose another student to play the remainder of the melodic rhythm on the woodblocks. Remind player to pay close attention to the *longer* sounds of "ra" in "a-RA-fi."

A   ra - fi,   a   ra - fi,   Gu - li

gu - li   gu - li   gu - li   gu - li   ram   sam   sam.

Next, have drummer and woodblock player play entire melodic rhythm, uninterrupted. Suggest that woodblock player "think" the drummer's part, in order to keep the flow of the rhythm going.

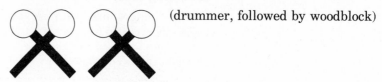

(drummer, followed by woodblock)

With tape recorder set at 3¾ i.p.s., record the melodic rhythm, drums followed by woodblocks.

(Record at 3¾.)

Rewind and play tape back at same speed, 3¾.

(Play back.)

Explain that you are going to play the tape again, this time at the faster speed, 7½ i.p.s.

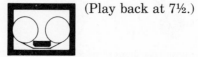

(Play back at 7½.)

Record this segment and the following ones *in immediate succession* on the tape. The eventual tape composition will have no "gaps" in it if you tape the three sections closely together.

Have drummer and woodblock player pass their instruments on to two other players. Practice the same melodic rhythm routine once, then record at the *faster speed* (7½) and play back at the *slower speed* (3¾).

(record 7½)   (play back 3¾)

THAT PLAYBACK TOOK TWICE AS LONG AS THE ORIGINAL. AND THE PITCHES WERE LOWER, JUST AS THEY WERE IN THE SOUND EXPERIMENT WE DID THE OTHER DAY.

IF WE USE OUR FIRST RECORDED VERSION OF A RAM SAM SAM AS THE A SECTION OF A COMPOSITION AND THE SLOWER ONE AS THE B SECTION, HOW COULD WE EASILY TURN OUR TAPE COMPOSITION INTO A B A FORM? (Discuss. Students may suggest that the melodic rhythm be recorded again at 3¾, as in the beginning, and played back at 7½. This will make the final section identical to the first A.)

 (record 3¾)

The A B A "composition" is now ready to be played back. The simplest way is to play the entire recording at 7½. In this case, the A sections will sound faster and higher than the original recording and the B section will sound just as it did when recorded.

Discuss how this experience resulted in a tape composition with a section that repeated (A) and a contrasting section (B). HOW WAS THE CONTRAST ACHIEVED? (speed change)

NOTE: For greater contrast and interest, play the tape as follows:

1. Play first A at 7½.

2. As first A ends, change speed to 3¾ (for upcoming B).

3. As B ends, change speed back to 7½ for final A.

This playback routine will alter each of the original sections: the A sections will sound faster and higher than the original and the B section will sound slower and lower than the original.

Summary

Some tape recorder speeds can be changed while the tape is running. Otherwise, stop recorder, change speed, and start again, *as quickly as possible*.

ANOTHER TIME

Listen to two versions of *A Ram Sam Sam* in SBM 3, rec 1. One is *monophonic*, the other with harmony.

ELABORATION

1. This model experience can be repeated, using different melodic rhythms. *This Old Man* and *Are You Sleeping?* have well-known, interesting melodic rhythms that will work well.

2. See *Sound Piece 1* in SBM (EC), rec 1. Students listen to the recording and improvise their own B section in the middle of the piece.

BIBLIOGRAPHY

See "Bibliography," p. 59.

> This model experience describes one technique which aids listeners in identifying and remembering the A section when it recurs in an extended composition.

Music Learning

> Sections of a composition can contrast with one another and sections can be repeated (A B A).

Musical Context

CARILLON from *L'Arlesienne Suite No. 1* by Georges Bizet ("bee-ZAY") (French, 1838–1875). BOL 78; EM 4; SOM 4.

Reading Objective

Behavioral Objective

To identify the ostinato heard in the A section; and to demonstrate that recognition by playing the ostinato and by raising hands when it is heard in the recording.

Grade

Upper

Materials

Recording: EM 4, rec 9, BOL 78; or SOM 4, rec 8

Resonator bells E, F♯ and G♯ (or melody bells)

Hold E and G♯ bells side by side, so all students can see.

Focusing Statement

WHO CAN TELL US WHICH OF THESE WILL SOUND LOWER? (the E bell) WHY? (It is a longer bar.)

Write this on the chalkboard (or on chart paper);

(These notes are deliberately spaced widely; see below.)

1-2-3 = do-re-mi. Curwen hand signs may be used.

Identify the lower pitch (E) and the higher pitch (G♯). Label each. Also put number *1* under the E (or use syllables).

NOW WE'LL ADD ANOTHER PITCH IN BETWEEN. Add F♯. WHAT SHALL WE NUMBER THESE? Point to F♯ and G♯. YES, 2 AND 3 BECAUSE THEY ARE "NEXT-DOOR NEIGHBORS."

Identify these by pitch names: F♯ and G♯. Complete the notation on chalkboard so that it looks like this:

Before playing the bells, consider writing all possible combinations of 1-2-3 (3-1-2, 2-1-3, etc.)

NOW, LET'S PLAY SOME PATTERNS USING THESE THREE PITCHES. I'LL WRITE EACH AS WE PLAY IT. Or, provide students with staff paper and ask them to write the notation.

Several students play a three-pitch pattern:

Focus on the G♯-E-F♯ (3-1-2) pattern (see "Reading Objective"). Ask one student to play this pattern over and over. Encourage a tempo approximating that of the recording. Player should not pause between repetitions of pattern, but should maintain a steady beat rhythm.

As student plays, place needle on recording, with volume on its lowest setting. Gradually increase volume so the recording may be heard along with the bell player. (Assist player in adjusting to playing with recording, if necessary.) Play 60 to 90 seconds of recording.

WHEN A MELODIC PATTERN IS REPEATED OVER AND OVER, AS IT IS IN THIS PIECE, IT'S CALLED AN OSTINATO.

See Glossary.

(Play the first third of the composition. Some well-coordinated students will want to play the bells along with the recording.)

. . . .

With some classes, this may be enough for one day.

A carillon consists of bells hung in a tower, played manually or mechanically.

Find another student to play the 3-1-2 *ostinato*. AS WE LISTEN AGAIN, YOU'LL DISCOVER THIS COMPOSITION CARILLON IS RATHER LONG. SEE IF YOU CAN BE VERY CAREFUL LISTENERS: RAISE YOUR HANDS WHEN YOU HEAR OUR BELL PATTERN AT THE BEGINNING AND NEAR THE END.

(Play *entire* composition. The form is A B A, with the *ostinato* occurring during the A sections.)

As the recording plays, draw (or have students draw) one of these shapes on the chalkboard as each section begins:

▲   ●   ▲
(as A   (as B   (as *final*
begins)   begins)   A begins)

Summary

HOW DO THESE SHAPES SHOW THE DESIGN OF <u>CARILLON</u>? Determine that the ostinato is heard in the first and last sections, and that it is *not* heard in the contrasting middle section. Place the letters A B A *inside the shapes,* if desired. As B ends, some students will hear suggestions of the forthcoming, final A.

ANOTHER TIME

See Glossary.

1. Invent movement ideas for the B section. It is in compound meter ($\frac{6}{8}$). Long scarves may be used to elicit flowing movement. (See the CHINESE RIBBON DANCE in *Rhythms Today!* for some excellent ideas.) The A sections might suggest a different movement activity.

2. Provide a tape recording of CARILLON so students can listen on their own at a single cassette player with headphones. Provide melody bells for playing along with the recording.

OTHER MUSIC IN A B A FORM

ALLEGRO DECISO from *Water Music Suite* by Handel. EM 5; NDM 5; SBM 6
CIRCUS MUSIC from *The Red Pony* by Copland. AIM 3, I; EM 1; SOM 3
DANCE OF THE MIRLITONS from *The Nutcracker Suite* by Tchaikovsky. AIM 1, II; BOL 58; EM 2; NDM 1
DANCE OF THE SUGAR PLUM FAIRY from *The Nutcracker Suite* by Tchaikovsky. AIM 1, II; BOL 58; EM 2; NDM 1
FOSSILS from *Carnival of the Animals* by Saint-Saëns. BOL 51; EM 2
GAVOTTE from *Classical Symphony* by Prokofiev. BOL 73; NDM 4; SBM 6
LAIDERONETTE, EMPRESS OF THE PAGODAS from *Mother Goose Suite* by Ravel. BOL 57; DMT 2
MINUET from *Symphony No. 94* by Haydn. BOL 63; EM 3
PRELUDE NO. 2 by Gershwin. EM 5, MMYO 2
PROVENCE from *Suite Française* by Milhaud. DMT 1
RUN, RUN from *Memories of Childhood* by Pinto. BOL 68; DMT (EC)

Music Learning

Sections of a song can contrast with one another, and sections of a song can repeat (A B, A B A).

Musical Context

SCRATCH, SCRATCH by Harry Belafonte and Irving Burgess. SBM 3 and 4
LITTLE DAVID, PLAY ON YOUR HARP (Black spiritual). NDM 6; SBM 3, SOM 6
ROLL AN' ROCK (Black spiritual). SBM 3

Behavioral Objective

To identify aurally the contrasting and repeated sections of a song; and to demonstrate this recognition by circling corresponding letters on a worksheet.

Grade

Lower and upper

Materials

Recordings: SCRATCH, SCRATCH SBM 3, rec 5; SBM 4, rec 1
LITTLE DAVID . . . NDM 6, rec 2; SBM 3, rec 4; SOM 6, rec 3
ROLL AN' ROCK SBM 3, rec 4

Tambourine and guiro

Worksheet for each student (See below.)

Songbooks: NDM 6; SBM 3; SBM 4; SOM 6

This evaluative experience should be preceded by experiences such as *Clap Your Hands* and *Carillon*.

Teacher should practice with the recordings and follow songs in books, in order to stop the recording when each song has been heard once.

Focusing Statement

CAN YOU REMEMBER A SONG THAT HAS TWO DIFFERENT SECTIONS? (CLAP YOUR HANDS or other familiar song) Write A B on chalkboard.

Sing the song, pointing out the sections on the board.

HOW ABOUT MUSIC THAT HAS THREE SECTIONS IN WHICH THE FIRST SECTION REPEATS? (THE ELEPHANT [Palmer], SHOO FLY, or other familiar song) Write A B A on chalkboard.

Sing song, point out sections.

Distribute the worksheets. Instruct students that they will listen to three songs. They should *circle* the letters that match the form of each song.

1.	A B	A B A
2.	A B	A B A
3.	A B	A B A

HERE'S NUMBER ONE. THE SONG IS SCRATCH, SCRATCH. LISTEN BEFORE YOU DECIDE WHICH SET OF LETTERS SHOWS THE FORM OF THIS SONG.

Play song one time *only*.

NOW, FOR NUMBER TWO, LITTLE DAVID, PLAY ON YOUR HARP.

Play song one time *only*.

HERE'S THE LAST ONE, NUMBER THREE. IT'S CALLED ROLL AN' ROCK.

Play song *one* time only.

Check answers by playing each song again. Elicit active involvement in this evaluation. Suggestions follow.

LET'S CHECK OUR ANSWERS. WHEN YOU HEAR THE SECOND SECTION OF NUMBER ONE, FILL IN THE SILENCES BY CLAPPING THIS PATTERN:

 (This will heighten the contrast between A and B.)

 Clap   (Play first verse *only*.)

THAT ANSWER WAS A B. Repeat the song, pointing out the two sections. To heighten the contrast, students might like to fill in the silences of B with the *guiro* (notched gourd with scraper.)

IN NUMBER TWO, THE WORDS FOR THE A SECTION ARE "LITTLE DAVID, PLAY ON YOUR HARP, HALLELU." LET'S SING THOSE WORDS WHENEVER WE HEAR THEM.

 Play song one time *only*.

WHERE DID WE SING OUR WORDS, AT THE BEGINNING? (yes) AND AT THE END? (yes) WAS THERE SOMETHING DIFFERENT IN BETWEEN? (yes) THIS SONG IS IN A B A FORM. Sing again, if appropriate.

FINALLY, ROLL AN' ROCK. WHEN YOU HEAR THE SECOND SECTION OF THIS SONG, CLAP YOUR HANDS TO THE BEAT.

 Clap   (Play the song *one* time.)

GOOD! THIS SONG IS A B. Song may be repeated with tambourine added to the B section.

Summary

LISTENING FOR SECTIONS OF A SONG THAT ARE DIFFERENT AND THOSE THAT ARE THE SAME IS REALLY HARD WORK! MAYBE YOU CAN THINK OF OTHER SONGS THAT FIT THE A B AND A B A DESIGNS.

ELABORATION

For evaluating recognition of form, use the "What Do You Hear?" charts from SBM: SBM 1:41, rec 3; SBM 3:61–62, rec 4; SBM 4:71, rec 4; SBM 5:57, rec 2; SBM 6:137, rec 6

OTHER SONGS WITH CONTRASTING AND REPEATED SECTIONS A B A

ALL HID. SBM 3

BROTHER RABBIT. SBM (EC)

CONSIDER YOURSELF, from *Oliver.* EM 6

THE ELEPHANT. SBM 1

GET ON BOARD. EM 3; NDM 3

HEY, BETTY MARTIN. CMCM 1A; MMYO 1

IT'S A SMALL WORLD. EM 4

SWING LOW, SWEET CHARIOT. CMCM 1A; NDM 4

TON MOULIN. DMT (EC); MMYO 3; SBM 1

For songs with contrasting sections (A B), see p. 104.

LITTLE DAVID, PLAY ON YOUR HARP

Black Spiritual

ROLL AN' ROCK

Black Spiritual

G

Harmony: the simultaneous sounding of two or more pitches; the vertical structure in music.

*ARE YOU SLEEPING? (I)
  Polyphonic texture can be created by vertically combining phrases of a round.

THE GHOST OF TOM
  A phrase of a round can serve as an ostinato to accompany the entire melody.

*STRING QUARTET NO. 4
  An ostinato can be created electronically.

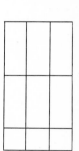

Melody: a linear succession of pitches; the horizontal structure in music.

ST. PAUL'S STEEPLE
  Pitches in a melody can move stepwise through a scale.

*HOLD ON
  Pitches in a melody can move through chord tones.

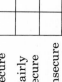

After completing each model experience, decide how successfully you are able to identify, explain, or demonstrate the music learning that was the focus of the experience. Check the appropriate box.

Secure Fairly secure Insecure

*Group work-through experience

121

WORK-THROUGH EXPERIENCE

Music Learning

> Polyphonic texture can be created by vertically combining phrases of a round.

Musical Context

ARE YOU SLEEPING? (I) (French round, "Frère Jacques"). CMCM 1A and 2A; DMT 1 and 2; EM 3; MMYO 3; NDM 2 and 3; SOM 2

Reading Objective

Reading blank notation and/or writing notation for one phrase of the melody (see step 2 below).

Behavioral Objective

Grade

Materials

Four sets of bells, preferably resonator bells (but can be done with only two sets)
Tape recorder
Microphone
Tape

1. Select one person to operate the tape recorder.

With only two sets of bells, assign two players to each set.

2. Four individuals should be selected to play the song below. Each player will need one set of melody bells, and should learn to play only *one* phrase of the song.

At first, play from the blank notation on the left.

♪ (eighth note)

♩ (quarter note)

♩ (half note)

3. Now, write musical notation for *one* phrase, in the staff on the right. (Each person should select a phrase to write, even those who are not playing the bells.)

(To check the accuracy of your work, see p. 259.)

4. When the four players are ready, play the phrases in order.

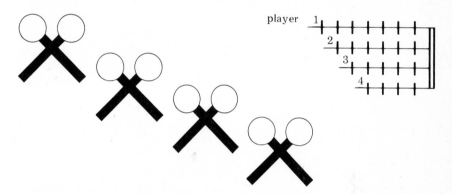

5. Now try creating the effect of a *round* by "stacking" the four phrases. Start with player number one and have the other players join in one by one. Each player will repeat the phrase several times. The "stacking" might be visualized as follows:

Summary

6. Note the interesting *texture* of this performance. Repeat step 5 and tape-record the performance, so that players can evaluate their playing.

7. Those who are not playing could try singing along with the bell players. Begin singing with the first player, and sing the song *once*. Strike the F bell separately and hum the tone for a vocal tune-up.

8. Select different bell players and repeat the playing and singing.

See Glossary

9. Write the musical term for the texture created by combining melodic fragments: _____

(See beginning of the model experience for correct term.)

10. What grade level would be appropriate when using this experience with children? Would the students need any specific background? What changes would be necessary in this learning sequence? Write the level *you* believe appropriate in the box on the top of p. 122. (See suggestion in margin at end of model experience.)

11. Formulate a behavioral objective statement for the grade level you have determined. Write it in the box provided on p. 122. (See suggestion in margin at end of model experience.)

ANOTHER TIME

See Glossary

1. Sing the song. Instead of using four players to accompany it, use only *one* player at a time. Thus the one phrase, played over and over again as an accompaniment, becomes an *ostinato*. At different times, use each of the four phrases as an ostinato.

2. Find players who can play the *entire* song. Then, play the song as a *round*. Players begin when player one reaches phrases 2, 3, and 4, as indicated in notation. Tape-record for evaluation.

3. Play the song on your pianos, recorders, and guitars.

ELABORATION

Behavioral Objective
To read, write, and play the four phrases of a round; and to perform these four phrases simultaneously on bells.

Grade
Upper

Follow this experience with model experience *Voiles,* p. 188, and *Are You Sleeping?* (II), p. 161.

OTHER SONGS USABLE IN THE SAME MANNER

GOD BLESS ALL. DMT 4; NDM 4

GOOD NEWS. SBM 6

LOVELY EVENING, p. 267

MAKE NEW FRIENDS. DMT 3; EM 4; MMYO 4; NDM 3

MORNING. SOM 5

MORNING IS COME. SBM 2

SING AND REJOICE. NDM 3

BIBLIOGRAPHY

Doll, Edna, and Mary Jarman Nelson. *Rhythms Today!* Morristown, N.J.: Silver Burdett Co., 1965, p. 167. How to use *Are You Sleeping?* with a body pantomine for each different phrase.

Schubert, Inez, and Lucille Wood. *The Craft of Music Teaching.* Morristown, N.J.: Silver Burdett Co., 1976, p. 1. Many ideas for using *Are You Sleeping?* with children: how to create variations based on the song; presentation of Mahler's *Symphony No. 1,* which uses this familiar melody in a minor key.

Music Learning	A phrase of a round can serve as an ostinato to accompany the entire melody.

Musical Context   THE GHOST OF TOM. EM 6

Reading Objective

Behavioral Objective   To sing, read, and play a phrase of a round; and to use this phrase as an ostinato.

Grade   Upper

Materials   Resonator bells, D E F♯ G A B and mallet
Songbooks for each student: EM 6
Recording: EM 6, rec 7

Ostinato = ah-stih-NAH-toe   Recordings of rounds often sound very complex at first hearing. Singing a phrase as an *ostinato* (while recording is playing) often works well to achieve immediate involvement.

Focusing Statement   With songbooks open, have students FOLLOW THE NOTES OVER THE WORDS, "WOULDN'T IT BE CHILLY WITH NO SKIN ON," AS I SING THEM. (Or play the phrase on a melody instrument.)

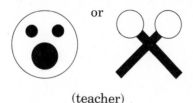

(Sing or play first phrase at least twice.)

(teacher)

See Glossary   Explain that YOU ARE TO BEGIN SINGING THE OSTINATO ("wouldn't it be . . .") WHEN GIVEN A SIGNAL. Use the recording this time.

Begin singing *ostinato* as the instruments play it at end of introduction; continue singing ostinato until singers on recording finish the four-part *round. Fade* recording *before final section begins,* as it is not a round.

Choose a student to play the ostinato just sung. Write the phrase on the chalkboard in staff notation (see "Reading Objective" above) or in this "blank" notation:

```
  BB
    AA
      GG
        F♯
          E       E
            D
```

Remind bell player to START WITH THE HIGHEST PITCH (B) ON THE RIGHT. Suggest that he or she practice the ostinato a few times while the rest of the class goes on to something else.

 (Student practices quietly, alone)

Help the class learn to sing another ostinato: the first phrase. Again, as they follow the notes in their songbooks, sing (or play) the phrase "Have you seen the ghost of Tom."

 (Teacher sings)

Repeat, and ask the class to JOIN IN SINGING THIS NEW PHRASE SEVERAL TIMES, WITHOUT STOPPING.

 (Teacher and students sing, "Have you seen . . .")

The bell player who has been rehearsing should now join you. As the first ostinato ("wouldn't it . . .") is played several times, without interruption, the class should add the "new" ostinato ("Have you . . .").

  Allow first ostinato to be heard *twice,* then add second (sung) ostinato.

"wouldn't it . . ." "Have you . . ."

Play the recording again, adding it to what has been rehearsed above.
 BELL PLAYER: BEGIN WHEN YOU HEAR THE WORDS "WOULDN'T IT BE CHILLY" FOR THE FIRST TIME. I'LL SIGNAL THE SINGERS WHEN TO JOIN.

 After bell player is well established, signal singers to begin. Continue through *round* section of recording. Fade before final section, as before.

Summary   AN EASY WAY TO LEARN A ROUND OR CANON IS TO TAKE A PHRASE AND USE IT AS AN <u>OSTINATO</u>. THAT WAY, WE DON'T HAVE TO WAIT UNTIL WE'VE LEARNED THE WHOLE SONG TO ENJOY IT!

ANOTHER TIME

1. After students have learned the entire song, encourage them to transform it into a percussion round. They may choose a different tone color for each phrase. "Hallowe'en-ish" sounds would be appropriate. Each player should sound the *melodic rhythm* (word rhythm) of one phrase. (Four phrases = four players) The effect of a round is achieved by stacking the ostinati until all four are sounding simultaneously, as follows:

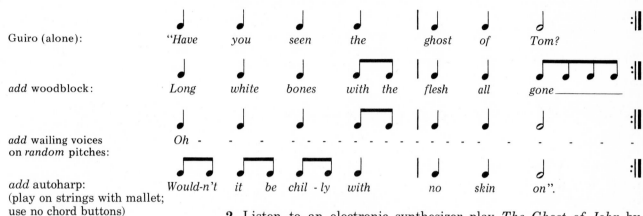

Guiro (alone):   *"Have   you   seen   the   ghost   of   Tom?*

add woodblock: *Long   white   bones   with the   flesh   all   gone_____*

add wailing voices on *random* pitches: *Oh - - - - - - - - - - - - -*

add autoharp: (play on strings with mallet; use no chord buttons)   *Would-n't   it   be   chil - ly   with   no   skin   on".*

2. Listen to an electronic synthesizer play *The Ghost of John* by Grubb in SBM 3:46, rec 3.

3. See also model experience *Voiles,* "Elaboration," p. 188.

ELABORATION

Listen to recordings of compositions with easily recognizable ostinati. See p. 130.

OTHER ROUNDS FOR SIMILAR USE

MY DAME HAD A LAME, TAME CRANE. SBM 4

RALLY SONG. SBM 4

See "Other Songs," p. 124.

GHOST OF TOM

Traditional Round

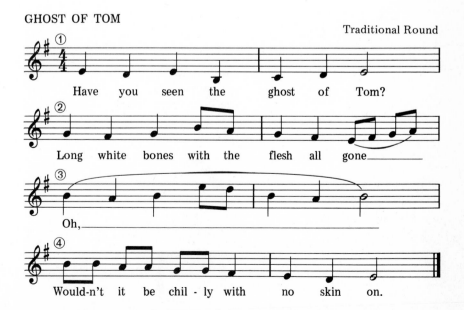

WORK-THROUGH EXPERIENCE

Music Learning

An ostinato can be created electronically.

Musical Context

SOUND EXPERIMENT WITH TAPE RECORDER: TAPE LOOP
STRING QUARTET NO. 4, second movement, by Henry Cowell (American, 1897–1965). SOM 5

Behavioral Objective

To create, perform, and tape-record a sequence of sounds; to form the tape into a loop (ostinato); to use this ostinato as an accompaniment to another sound sequence.

Grade

Upper

Materials

Recording: SOM 5, rec 8

Reel-to-reel tape recorder

Recording tape (clean)

Microphone

Splicing tape (do not use substitutes!)

Scissors (or splicing block and razor blade)

Selection of percussion instruments (sustaining and nonsustaining sounds)

Chalkboard and chalk; or chart paper and felt-tip pen

Read "Splicing Recording Tape" (Appendix, p. 347) before attempting this model experience.

Sample:

—————   x yz z xx z y x   —————

1. Designate individuals to manipulate the equipment listed above.

2. On a horizontal line randomly place several X's, Y's, and Z's. (See left margin for example.)

3. Have three students each choose a percussion instrument. Select instruments that will produce sounds of short duration (sticks, drums, guiro) and assign one player to the X, another to the Y, and another to the Z.

4. Players will play the sequence of sounds (one sound for each letter) as a fourth student moves a pointer across the line. Pointer should move smoothly. The entire sequence should take about five seconds to play. Note the spacing of the sounds and the *silences* that occur where there are *no letters* on the line.

 Practice sequence once or twice.

i.p.s. = inches per second.

5. Now set the tape recorder speed at 3¾ i.p.s. and record the sound sequence from step 4 above.

3¾

6. Play back the sound sequence at 3¾ i.p.s.

3¾

7. Play back the sound sequence at 7½ i.p.s.

7½

8. The section of tape on which the sound sequence is recorded should now be cut from the reel.

You will have a piece about 18 in. long. Splice the tape into a loop. *Be sure to place the splicing tape on the shiny side of the tape.*

The sound sequence will be heard over and over again as an ostinato. See Glossary.

9. Anticipate what will happen when the loop is placed on the tape recorder and allowed to play indefinitely (see left margin).

10. Play the loop, first at 7½ i.p.s. and then at 3¾ i.p.s.

7½   3¾

NOTE: If you do not hear any sounds, the loop has been placed in the tape recorder wrong edge up. Simply lift the loop and replace it with the opposite edge up.

Also, be sure to *hold a pencil or smooth stick vertically inside the loose end of the loop in order to produce moderate tension.* Otherwise, the loop may be "eaten" by the machine and may damage the recorder!

11. The next step is to produce another sequence of sound to add interest to the *ostinato* (loop). Have three students choose three different percussion instruments that produce sounds of *longer duration* to contrast with the short sounds already on the loop. (Consider triangle, gong, finger cymbals, long scrapes on the guiro.)

See Glossary for definition of "decay." See also *Oven Grill Concerto.* p. 55

12. Practice the sound sequence (of step 2) using these *new* instrumental sounds. Note how these sounds overlap because of their slow *decay.*

13. Play the original loop and perform the new sound sequence along with it. Continue as long as you wish, but consider giving more variety to the new, added part.

Play it forward or backward.
Play it at different tempos.
Play it, leaving out one of the sounds (or, leaving out a different one on each repetition).

Try producing shorter sounds by *damping* each instrument after it is struck.

See Glossary.

14. Play recording of Cowell's string quartet movement. The melody is played by the first violin and the cello plays a *pedal point*. Focus on the parts being played by the second violin and the viola. (The unusual tone quality you will hear is achieved as they play *col lengo*, i.e., by striking the strings with the wooden part of the bow.)

Summary

15. In your own words, define *ostinato* and *tape loop*.

ANOTHER TIME

If two tape recorders are available, the second sound sequence in the model experience above (step 11) can also be recorded. This will enable students to evaluate their tape composition and to further manipulate their sound sequences with volume control and speed changes.

ELABORATION

1. Place two or more ostinati on tape loops and play them simultaneously on two or more tape recorders. Use speed change and volume control for greater variety.

2. See model experience *Voiles*, p. 188.

3. See also "My Name Is" by Reich in SBM 5:234–236 for *many* ideas for creating and combining tape loops.

4. See information on making a tape loop in SBM 5:105 and SBM 6:232.

5. See "Working with Sounds" satellites in SBM 5 and 6.

6. Encourage students to bring unusual "sound makers" from home, outdoors, and different areas of the school. Sounds outside the classroom can be collected on tape, using portable tape recorders.

OTHER MUSIC WITH EASILY RECOGNIZABLE OSTINATI

ARABIAN DANCE from *The Nutcracker Suite* by Tchaikovsky, BOL 58, DMT 3, EM 2, NDM 1

BUMBLEBEES SIP HONEY (Balinese), SOM 5

CARILLON by Bizet, BOL 78, EM 4

DANZON from *Fancy Free* by Bernstein, BOL 74

FERRIS WHEEL by Donovan, NDM 6 (long ostinato in bass instruments)

HANDE, HANDE (African story song), SBM 5

OSTINATOS from *Tabu-Tabuhan* by Colin McPhee, SOM 5

BIBLIOGRAPHY

See "Bibliography," p. 59.

Music Learning	Pitches in a melody can move stepwise through a scale.

Musical Context ST. PAUL'S STEEPLE (English folk song). NDM 2

Reading Objective Optional (See notation on p. 133.)

Behavioral Objective To identify aurally the stepwise movement of a major scale; and to demonstrate that recognition by singing and by playing melody bells.

Grade Upper

Materials Resonator bells: C D E F G A B C
Eight mallets
Melody bells for teacher (optional)
Songbooks for each student. NDM 2:122.

The teacher should play the eight pitches of the C-major scale, asking the students to listen.

 Teacher plays: C D E F G A B C

Focusing Statement

WHO KNOWS THE MUSICAL TERM FOR A SERIES OF PITCHES, PLAYED ONE AT A TIME, IN ORDER, AS I DID? (a scale; a major scale in this instance)

IF I "SCRAMBLE" THE PITCHES IN THE SCALE, I WONDER IF YOU CAN PUT THEM IN ORDER, USING YOUR EARS?

Discourage students who want to arrange bells in order by reading pitch names on bells! Put tape over pitch names.

Distribute the eight bells (*withhold* the mallets) in random order, directing students to form a row at the front of the room. Ask them to remain in random order.

Give each player a mallet. Ask the students to play their bells, one at a time, beginning with the person on the *left*.

 Eight players   The pitches will be out of order.

Discuss the fact that these are not stepwise, as they should be, but that they skip around.

This "living scale" technique will take some time, but the experience of arranging pitches *by sound* will be valuable.

Begin again with the player on the left, and have each person play until the *lowest* bell (C) is located. Ask the class to RAISE YOUR HAND WHEN YOU HEAR THE BELL WHICH SHOULD BE IN THE LOWEST POSITION IN THE SCALE.

 Eight players

When the C bell is identified, *put that player in the number one position at the left end of the row.*

Repeat the above process until all eight bells are in order. (NOTE: For less experienced classes, try this: sound C, followed by the next bell in the row. If this is not the correct bell (D), repeat C, followed by the *third* bell in the row. Continue this process until the adjacent D is heard and placed next to C. Proceed similarly through the scale.)

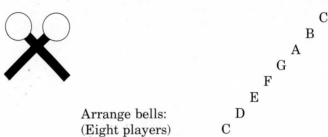

Arrange bells:
(Eight players)

```
                          C
                        B
                      A
                    G
                  F
                E
       D
   C
```

When scale is finally in order, play the *ascending* scale. Note the fact that the lowest and highest bells have the same pitch names (C and C.)

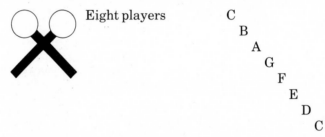

Eight players

Play the *descending* scale. Note the seven different pitch names.

Eight players

```
          C
            B
              A
                G
                  F
                    E
                      D
                        C
```

Help the class to remember that the scale they have just organized moves *stepwise*.

Tell the class you are going to sing (or play) a song that uses this descending scale pattern. WHEN YOU HEAR A SCALE, SHOW WITH YOUR HAND THE DIRECTION OF THE PITCHES.

Teacher may play melody on bells or use recording.

Some classes may wish to identify *whole* and *half* steps in major scale, using syllables or this ladder diagram:

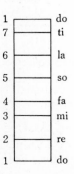

1	do
7	ti
6	la
5	so
4	fa
3	mi
2	re
1	do

or   Body movements

(teacher)

Distribute song books and discuss the text of the song. Locate the ascending and descending scales and have students "frame them," using their index fingers.

ST. PAUL'S STEEPLE

English Folk Song

Numerals indicate fingerings for piano.

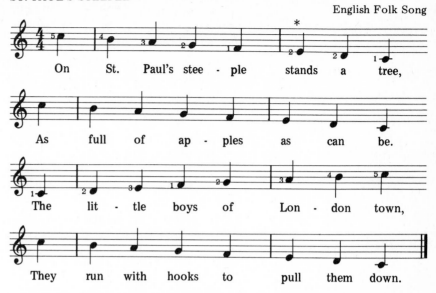

On St. Paul's stee - ple stands a tree,

As full of ap - ples as can be.

The lit - tle boys of Lon - don town,

They run with hooks to pull them down.

LET'S SEE IF THE BELL PLAYERS CAN PLAY ALONG WITH THE SCALES IN OUR SONG. Sing song at a slow tempo at first, with bell players striking each scale tone in turn, and the rest of the class singing the song as shown in their songbooks.

(If necessary, assist bell players by pointing to each player at the appropriate time.)

Bell players may have difficulty playing the ascending scale, since it occurs just once. Remind student playing the *low C bell* to play *twice* (on the words "be" and "The.")

Sing and play until the class can work rather independently. If appropriate, select a different group of bell players. The song will sound more "bell-like" when sung and played at a fairly quick tempo.

Encourage the class to sing and play independently, but be ready to give assistance when needed.

Summary

WHO CAN TELL US HOW THE SCALE IN OUR SONG MOVED, BY SKIP OR BY STEP? (by step) Review the pitch names, and note that the lowest and highest pitches have the same name.

ELABORATION

1. To expand understanding of scales, experiment with tuned bottles or glasses. See MMYO 1:74 and MMYO 2:52, plus several references under "Bibliography," below.

2. Create a "flower-pot scale" by suspending clay pots of graduated sizes from a sturdy rod. Use small rope with the end knotted inside the pot, strung and tied to the rod. Strike gently with a rubber mallet.

3. Flatten one end of a soda straw and snip off the "corners" with scissors (⌒). Pinch the straw between your lips, "buzzing" into it to create a musical pitch. As you continue to blow, use scissors to snip off segments of the straw. Discover what happens to the pitch!

OTHER SCALE SONGS
● *Songs with major scales*

AUTUMN LEAVES. NDM 1 (Key of C)

DO-RE-MI from *The Sound of Music.* NDM 3, rec 6 (no score). (Key of A♭, modulating to A major.)

JOHNNY MORGAN. SOM 5 (Key of C)

JOY TO THE WORLD. MMYO 6 (Key of D)

MA BELLA BIMBA. DMT 6 (Key of B♭) (Also see *Bella Bimba,* SBM 3 (Key of G).

PUSSY WILLOW. CMCM 1A (Key of C)

SING! SING! SING! SOM 6 (Key of C)

WHY DO BELLS FOR CHRISTMAS RING? NDM 1 (Keys of D major and D minor)

See model experience FIVE ANGELS: "Other Songs," p. 83.

A variant of ST. PAUL'S STEEPLE may be found in SOM 3 (Key of C).

● *Songs with minor scales*

ALL THE PRETTY LITTLE HORSES. CMCM 1A (natural minor scale on E)

AUTUMN. DMT 3 (harmonic minor scale on D)

HAVE YOU SEEN A CHILD? from *Amahl and the Night Visitors* by Menotti. SOM 5 (harmonic minor scales on F and A)

BIBLIOGRAPHY
Johnston, Thomas F. "How to Make a Tsonga Xylophone," *Music Educators Journal,* 63, 3 (November, 1976), p. 38. A marvelously informative article for the adventurous student who has access to a few basic tools. For those interested in African instruments, this article is a must!

Kettlekamp, Larry. *Flutes, Whistles and Reeds.* New York: William Morrow, 1962. Upper grade history, along with instructions on how to make simple flutes.

———. *Singing Strings.* New York: William Morrow, 1958. Upper grades; descriptions of several stringed instruments; how to make simple stringed instruments.

(The children's section of your local library will include many books of this kind.)

WORK-THROUGH EXPERIENCE

Music Learning

Pitches in a melody can move through chord tones.

Musical Context — HOLD ON (American folk song). MMYO 3; SBM 4

Reading Objective — See steps 5, 8, and 10 below.

Behavioral Objective — To identify visually the pitches D-F-A as melody and as a chord; and to demonstrate that recognition by playing each on the melody bells, and by singing.

Grade

Upper

Materials

Recording: MMYO 3, rec 5; or SBM 4, rec 5

Melody or resonator bells

Three bell mallets

Hold On is based on the D harmonic minor scale (see Appendix):

D
C♯
B♭
A
G
F
E
D

1. Select an individual to manage the recording and the phonograph.

2. Distribute as many sets of bells as are available.

3. Look at the "step scale" below. Play a series of pitches that are *adjacent*. Decide if this is *stepwise* or *skipwise* movement. (See left margin, p. 137.)

 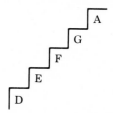

4. Next play a series of pitches that move by *skip* (that are not adjacent).

5. Play from the notation below. Are the tones moving by skip or by step?

Song notation, p. 262.

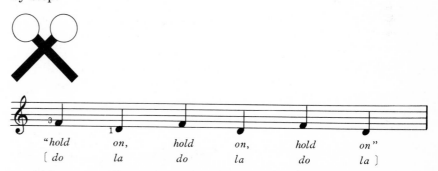

"hold	on,	hold	on,	hold	on"
[do	la	do	la	do	la]

6. Sing the words as you play step 5 again. Note that D and F are three steps (or pitch names) apart. This interval is called a *third*. (What pitch is skipped between D and F?)

7. Now listen for these words and this melody in a recording of *Hold On,* and sing along. If the recording and the bells are in tune, play *and* sing.

Curwen hand signs: use *la-do-mi* for this minor chord.

8. Perhaps you noticed that each phrase began with these pitches:

d min. chord
(broken)

What is the interval from F to A? Play these pitches. Notice that a *third* moves from a *space* to the next *space*, in this case. (Otherwise, thirds move from a *line* to the next *line*.)

9. Listen to the recording again, and join in singing (and playing) the pattern from step 8 when you hear these words:

"When you plow . . .
"Can't plow straight . . .
"Keep your hand . . ."

Don't forget also to sing the "hold on, hold on, hold on" that ends the verse and the refrain.

10. Try this experiment: play D, F, and A simultaneously, with one player using three mallets.

In the D-minor chord, D is the root, or "strongest" chord tone. See model experience *Joe Turner Blues,* p. 158.

D min. chord

A chord is formed, using thirds.

11. What were you playing in step 8 above, *melody* or a *chord?*

12. What were you playing in step 10?

13. Will a chord "fit" a melody which uses pitches identical to those in the chord? Try just the verse, with bell players sounding the chord (step 10), and singers singing the words from step 9 above.

Summary

The chord "fits" the melody because both use the same pitches, D, F, and A.

ANOTHER TIME

1. Encourage students to practice playing the entire *verse* melody on bells, piano, and recorder. The only pitch needed, in addition to D, F, and A, is G.

A₇ chord *will* fit the C♯ portion of refrain.

2. Try a more complicated chord and melody experiment with the refrain of HOLD ON. At the beginning of the refrain, a C♯ is sung in the melody. Will the D-minor chord "fit" that portion of the melody containing the C♯? Try it. Then answer "why" or "why not." (C♯ is not in the D-minor chord.)

3. Suggest that individuals and small groups experiment with using the Autoharp, guitar, or piano to accompany HOLD ON.

ELABORATION

1. Draw chords above the root tones given below. Discover and name the *root,* the *third,* and the *fifth.*

Notice the line-line-line or space-space-space relationship in each chord.

2. As an individual plays *minor* chords on the Autoharp, either hum the chord tones, sing 1-3-5, or sing la-do-mi.

OTHER SONGS WITH STRONGLY CHORDAL MELODIES
● *Songs with minor melodies*
HANUKAH TIME. SOM 2

OLD HOUSE. MMYO 2

SHAKE HANDS, MARY. SBM 2

● *Songs with major melodies*
BOW, BELINDA, p. 176

CHIAPENECAS. CMCM 1A

EL COQUI. EM 2 (*The Frog.* SOM 2)

KUM BAH YAH, p. 269

MICHAEL, ROW THE BOAT ASHORE. MMYO 3

MY HOME'S IN MONTANA. SOM 5

PAW PAW PATCH. DMT 3

REVEILLE. CMCM 3A

SANDY LAND, p. 234

SKIP TO MY LOU, pp. 176, 238

TAPS. CMCM 3A

Answers:

3. by step
4. by skip
6. E has been skipped
8. a third
11. a melody
12. a chord
13. it will "fit"

H

Form: the shape, order, or design of a composition.

ALA DAL'ONA
Phrase length reflects stylistic and cultural traditions in folk songs.

Expressive qualities: those qualities (dynamics, tempo, timbre) which, combined with other musical elements, give a composition its unique musical identity.

*WOMAN'S WEDDING SONG, etc.
Instruments can be grouped according to their vibrating material (membranophones, idiophones, chordophones, aerophones).

Rhythm: all of the durations that occur in music.

SING HALLELU
Short and long sounds in a tonal pattern can be grouped to create syncopation.

JIN-GO-LO-BA
Different rhythm patterns can sound simultaneously within a composition (polyrhythms).

WAR DANCE SONG, etc.
Music can suggest the presence or absence of steady beats and can include rhythm patterns.

After completing each model experience, decide how successfully you are able to identify, explain, or demonstrate the music learning that was the focus of the experience. Check the appropriate box.

Secure   Fairly secure   Insecure

*Group work-through experience

138

Music Learning	Phrase length reflects stylistic and cultural traditions in folk song.
Musical Context	ALA DAL'ONA (melody from the Middle East). NDM 4
Reading Objective	Beats (♩) or melodic rhythm (See below.)
Behavioral Objective	To identify aurally and visually the six steady beats in a phrase; and to demonstrate that recognition by circling the beats in the melody, by clapping, and moving to the six-beat phrase.
Grade	Upper
Materials	Recording: NDM 4, rec 8 Songbooks: NDM 4 Notation of melody on chalkboard or chart

Focusing Statement

WHO CAN GUESS THE PART OF THE WORLD WHERE THIS MUSIC ORIGINATED? Suggest possible areas, if appropriate.

 (Play 40–60 seconds)

This is an extremely popular melody from the Middle East and is heard in several countries. Students may respond to the vocal tone quality and to the instrumentation: a flute *(nay)* and a zither-like instrument *(kanoon.)*

   AS WE LISTEN AGAIN, FIND THE STEADY BEAT AND SHOW IT IN SOME QUIET WAY. (Tap fingertips, mark beat in air, etc.)

 Body movements

HERE IS THE NOTATION OF THAT MELODY. Use songbooks or put notation on chart or chalkboard so all can see. CAN ANYONE DECIDE, FROM THE METER SIGNATURE, THE VALUE OF THE BEAT? (The bottom number, 4, represents a quarter note.)

Decide what durations each beat includes. Proceed to identify note values, and decide on the equivalents for one beat (♩). They are:

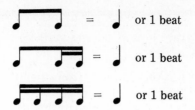

CIRCLE EACH GROUP OF NOTES THAT EQUALS ONE QUARTER NOTE (♩).

(See notation below.) Students can take turns at the chalkboard doing this.

Clap all or part of this melodic rhythm if class is fairly experienced.

Teacher may point to the beat notes below the melody while the recording is playing and students are listening and watching.

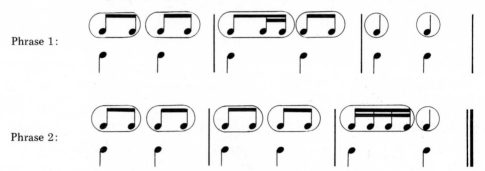

Phrase 1:

Phrase 2:

THIS MELODY IS REPEATED OVER AND OVER AGAIN IN THE RECORDING. TRY TO SHOW ME WHEN YOU HEAR THE SONG <u>BEGIN</u> EACH TIME. TRY TO CLAP THAT BEGINNING BEAT.

(Play about 90 seconds.)

Optional step; for use only if students have difficulty.

Observe how successful the students are in locating the beginning of this melody. Ask, IN A WHOLE CAN THERE BE PARTS OR HALVES? (Yes) IN THE SAME WAY, A WHOLE SONG CAN HAVE MORE THAN ONE PART (OR PHRASE). THIS SONG HAS TWO PHRASES, ALMOST LIKE TWO HALVES.

AS WE LISTEN AGAIN, TRY TO COUNT THE STEADY BEATS AND DECIDE <u>HOW MANY BEATS ARE IN THE ENTIRE SONG</u>, AND HOW MANY IN EACH "HALF" (or PHRASE).

Clap (Play as much as necessary)

As performed on the recording, *Ala Dal'ona* is a two-phrase song. See Bibliography.

DID ANYONE COUNT THE NUMBER OF BEATS IN THE SONG? YES. THERE WERE 12 BEATS IN THE ENTIRE SONG. IF YOU COUNT THE CIRCLES WE DREW AROUND THE NOTE GROUPINGS, YOU'LL SEE THERE ARE 12 OF THEM.

Try to elicit the understanding that each circled beat might include several melody notes moving faster than the beat.

HOW MANY PHRASES OR "HALVES" WERE THERE IN THE SONG? (There were two six-beat phrases.) Discuss the fact that the 12-beat song is composed of two six-beat phrases.

Repeat the listening and clapping.

   Body rhythms

Summary

Conclude by noting that MANY OF THE SONGS WE KNOW USE FOUR-BEAT (or eight-beat) PHRASES, BUT THIS IS NOT UNIVERSAL. Ask students to think of familiar songs using four- or eight-beat phrases. (*Clap Your Hands, The Frog and the Mouse, All Around the Kitchen,* etc.) Other cultures do not necessarily think about music in the same way we do. This is reflected in the differing tone qualities and in the six-beat phrases.

For some groups, this may be enough work for one day.

. . . .

NOW LET'S PUT THOSE SIX BEATS "INTO OUR FEET." In Greece and Turkey they do a fast sailor's dance called *Hasapikos* ("hah-SAH-pee-kohss"). It may be a very ancient dance, and is danced in many versions.

Hasapikos is a line or circle dance without partners. Hands are on neighbors' shoulders. Dancers move counterclockwise.

Arrange your students according to the space in your room. It is important that the students be able to see steps demonstrated by the teacher, and that the teacher be able to move freely among the students as they learn.

This dance became familiar through the film *Zorba, the Greek.*

Demonstrate the dance in the correct tempo.

   (teacher)

PUT YOUR WEIGHT ON YOUR LEFT FOOT. STEP WITH THE RIGHT, STEP IN FRONT WITH THE LEFT, AND STEP AGAIN WITH THE RIGHT.
   TRY IT. Use this "rhythmic and verbal cue":

   "right cross, right"

Be sure students find enough room to move in. Try to see students, and locate those having difficulty. Quietly demonstrate the pattern in front of those needing help.
   NOW WE'RE READY TO FINISH. YOU FINISHED THE FIRST PART ON YOUR RIGHT FOOT. NEXT, SWING YOUR LEFT LEG OVER IN FRONT OF YOUR RIGHT FOOT. (Don't touch the floor with left foot.) BRING IT BACK, STEP ON IT, AND SWING THE RIGHT LEG IN FRONT.
   LET'S TRY THAT WITH THIS CUE:

   "right swing, left swing"

READY, GO:

   ("right swing, left swing")

If students seem ready, arrange them into circles of up to ten students. Arms are on neighbors' shoulders, with arms fairly straight.

NOW TRY THE ENTIRE SIX-BEAT PATTERN. BEGIN WITH YOUR WEIGHT ON YOUR LEFT FOOT.

*"Dip" (bend the knees) on this second beat.

 "right, cross, right, swing, left, swing"
　　　　　　　*

Do slowly several times. Increase dance tempo to that of the recording when students can coordinate movements.

Put the dance with the recording as soon as possible. (If there is not room for all students to dance, some might play percussion instruments to emphasize the phrase-lengths: finger cymbals for one phrase, tambourine for the other, for instance.)

 Dance

(Play *no more than half* the band on the recording, because the piece changes to four-beat phrases. Fade out recording at appropriate time.)

Summary

Conclude by summarizing that THIS MUSIC USED A SIX-BEAT PHRASE AND THE DANCE STEP FIT THAT PHRASE EXACTLY.

ANOTHER TIME

1. Add a *drone* (D and A) accompaniment. Learn to play *Ala Dal'Ona* on piano, melody bells, recorder or guitar.

2. For several exciting variations on *Hasapikos* see Mynatt, Constance V. and Bernard D. Kaiman, *Folk Dancing for Students and Teachers,* Dubuque, Iowa: Wm. C. Brown Co., 1968.

ELABORATION

1. Learn the Israeli *hora,* which uses a similar dance pattern. See excellent directions in *Rhythms Today!* by Edna Doll and Mary Jarman Nelson. The *hora* with a six-beat dance pattern is often done to music with a four-beat phrase. Students who have already learned the *hasapikos* may be able to detect this difference. See also, MMYO 5 or 6 and SBM 6:242.

2. Look at "Music of the Middle East" sections in NDM 4, 5, and 6 (includes photographs) and in SBM 6.

3. Follow this model experience with *Samiotissa,* p. 142, and discover music with groups of seven beats.

4. Locate other dances by checking the index of "Dances" in the basal music texts; see the "Respond Through Movement" satellites in SBM 5 and 6.

OTHER MUSIC

THE BIRCH TREE. MMYO 5 (six-beat phrases)

FIESTA TIME. SOM 6 (six-beat phrases)

GERAKINA. MMYO 6 (seven-beat phrases)

SPRING HAS COME by Brahms. MMYO 5 (six-beat phrases)

THE TAMBOURINE. SOM 5 (five-beat phrases)

WORK-THROUGH EXPERIENCE

Music Learning

> Instruments can be grouped according to their vibrating material (membranophones, idiophones, chordophones, aerophones).

Musical Context

WOMAN'S WEDDING SONG (Afghanistan). SBM 6

IDIOPHONE SOLO. Africa (Liberia: Kpelle people). SBM 3

RAGA YAMAN (India). SBM 5

BAIRO (Japan). NDM 5

Behavioral Objective

Grade

Upper

Materials

Recordings:

WOMAN'S WEDDING SONG—SBM 6, rec 1

IDIOPHONE SOLO—SBM 3, rec 2 (p. 31, TE)

RAGA YAMAN—SBM 5, rec 6

BAIRO—NDM 5, rec 9

Worksheet for each student (See step 7, next page.)

1. Designate individuals to manage the phonograph, recordings, and answers.

2. Ethnomusicologists have developed descriptive categories for instruments which are especially appropriate in studying non-Western music. The categories are based on *the material that creates the vibrations we perceive as sound.*

Japanese Gaguku Ensemble

● CHORDOPHONES—	● AEROPHONES—
violin zither piano etc.	flute trumpet Baroque recorder etc.
● MEMBRANOPHONES— (Vibrating membrane) drums with skin heads	● IDIOPHONES— (Basic vibrating material is *not stretched.*) xylophones rattles
● ELECTROPHONES— (Vibrations created by electrical impulses) electronic organs	log "drums" etc.

mehm-BRAN-uh-fone

3. *Membranophones* generate tone by a vibrating membrane. A skin-head drum is an example of a membranophone.

AIR-uh-fone

4. The sound of an *aerophone* is created by the vibrating column of air. Flutes, oboes, and trumpets are examples of aerophones.

KORD-uh-fone

5. *Chordophones* produce sound through a vibrating string. The harp, the violin, and the zither are chordophones.

IH-dee-uh-fone

6. *Idiophones* produce sound, but without the basic vibrating material being stretched. Castanets, rattles, and xylophones are three examples from a multitude of idiophones.

Electrical impulses generate the sound in electrophones.

7. Look at the worksheet below. As you hear each selection, circle the term which is appropriate. Verify the correct answers either

1	2	3	4
Membranophone *Aerophone* *Chordophone* *Idiophone*	*Membranophone* *Aerophone* *Chordophone* *Idiophone*	*Membranophone* *Aerophone* *Chordophone* *Idiophone*	*Membranophone* *Aerophone* *Chordophone* *Idiophone*

after each selection is played, or after hearing all four selections. (See p. 145 for answers.)

SBM 6 indicates that two women sing about the new gold jewelry of the bride.

8. WOMAN'S WEDDING SONG. (use box 1)

This instrument originated in Africa and is most frequently used by a singer to accompany his own voice.

9. IDIOPHONE SOLO. (use box 2)

RAH-gah YAH-mahn

10. RAGA YAMAN. Listen to the introduction only, and stop the recording when the drums *(tabla)* begin. (use box 3)

buy-row

Gagaku is the broad designation for ancient Japanese music.

(Bairo is a dance form of *gagaku* called *bugaku*.)

11. BAIRO. This is an example of *Gagaku* (literally "elegant music"). (use box 4)

12. Discuss and replay any selections if appropriate. Formulate a behavioral objective for this experience and write it in the box at the beginning of the model experience. For the authors' ideas, see the left margin.

ELABORATION

1. Listen to "Folk Instrument Collage" in SBM 6:16, rec 1.
2. Listen to *Introduction to Indian Music,* NDM 6.

OTHER MUSIC

Behavioral Objective

To identify aurally four instrumental groups and demonstrate this recognition by circling the appropriate word on a worksheet.

Answers

8. membranophone (drum). Leg bells may also be heard.
9. idiophone (thumb piano). The *sansa, kalimba, mbira, likembe* are all names for this instrument: plucked flexible tongues of wood or metal fastened over a box or gourd resonator.
10. chordophone *(sitar)*. This instrument from India includes 5 melody strings, 2 drone strings, and 13 strings which vibrate sympathetically along with all the others.
11. *aerophones* dominate, though two drums are heard at the beginning, and strings enter late in this excerpt. Oboe-like instruments *(hichiriki)*, flutes *(komabue)* and "mouth organs" *(sho)* are heard in *Bairo.*

● *Membranophones*

AFRICAN DRUMS. NDM 5

MUSIC OF THE DAN (West Africa). NDM 4

AFRICAN MUSIC, NDM 2, and AFRICAN MUSIC (West Africa, Cameroons). NDM 4

SONG FOR THE HAJ (Near East). SBM 6

● *Idiophones*

MUSINGASUIGA YAKARA EGALE (East Africa, Uganda). NDM 5 (xylophones)

HANDE, HANDE (Africa). SBM 5 (thumb piano)

MUSIC OF MEXICAN INDIANS (no. 3). SBM 6 (log "drum")

MBIRA MUSIC OF RHODESIA (thumb piano). Recording from the University of Washington Press, Seattle.

● *Chordophones*

VARIATIONS ON SAKURA (Japan). EM 4; NDM 3 (koto); SBM 5, rec 3

PERSIAN CLASSICAL SONG WITH VIOLIN. SBM 6

● *Aerophones*

INDIAN FOLK MUSIC (India). NDM 5

MUSIC OF THE MEXICAN INDIANS (no. 1). SBM 6 (triple flute)

TURKISH OBOE AND DRUM DANCE TUNE. SBM 6

IMPERIAL COURT MUSIC OF JAPAN. Lyrichord LL ST7126.

BIBLIOGRAPHY

Edwards, Walford I. "Africa," *Music Educators Journal,* 56, 1 (September 1969), p. 63. An informative article which includes an excellent description of idiophones.

Malm, William P. "Central and Southern Asia," and "Moslem Africa and the Near East," in *Music Cultures of the Pacific, the Near East, and Asia,* 2nd ed., Englewood Cliffs, N.J.: Prentice-Hall, Inc., 1977. A lucid introduction to these complex musical cultures by an eminent musicologist.

———. *Japanese Music and Musical Instruments.* Rutland, Vt.: Charles E. Tuttle Co., 1959. Technical, but beautifully written and illustrated.

"Music in World Cultures" issue of *Music Educators Journal,* 59, 2 (October, 1972). An excellent source of photographs of non-Western musicians. (See also the articles on Asian music by Menon, p. 40, and by Yamaguchi, p. 30. Both are valuable to the general reader.)

Discovering the Music of India, 1969. An excellent film from BFA Educational Media, 2211 Michigan Avenue, Santa Monica, Calif., 90404.

Music Learning	Short and long sounds in a tonal pattern can be grouped to create syncopation.

Musical Context   SING HALLELU. Black spiritual. SBM 1

Reading Objective   1   2

Behavioral Objective   To identify aurally and visually the long and short sounds in a tonal pattern; and to demonstrate this recognition by singing, clapping, speaking, and playing the pattern.

Grade   Upper

Materials   Recording: SBM 1, rec 9 (or teacher's ability to sing the song)

Patterns from "Reading Objective," written on chalkboard or paper chart

---

Focusing Statement   HAVE A LOOK AT THESE TWO PATTERNS AND <u>THINK</u> HOW THEY MIGHT SOUND.

NOW, I'LL CLAP ONE OF THE PATTERNS. YOU DECIDE WHICH ONE I'M CLAPPING.

Song notation, p. 261   Clap pattern 1

I'LL REPEAT THAT.

Clap pattern 1

WHICH ONE? (1) YES. LET'S ALL CLAP THAT SEVERAL TIMES. ONE, TWO, READY, GO:

Kodaly syllables are:

Clap   (Repeat three or four times, until claps are accurate and well coordinated.)

syn - co - pay

or

ti   ta   ti

WITH RHYTHM SYLLABLES, THAT WOULD BE "TA TI-TI TA-A." (Write syllables under notes of pattern 1.)

LET'S CLAP <u>AND</u> USE RHYTHM SYLLABLES A COUPLE OF TIMES.
Body rhythms   (Clap and speak syllables; repeat
                                          for accuracy.)

PATTERN 2 LOOKS QUITE DIFFERENT, DOESN'T IT? IT SOUNDS <u>VERY</u>
DIFFERENT. LET'S REARRANGE THOSE <u>SAME</u> LONG AND SHORT SOUNDS
FROM PATTERN 1. Write rhythm syllables under notes of pattern 2,
eliciting student help in matching syllable to note

Permit more experienced classes
to "sound out" this pattern for
themselves.

LET'S SPEAK AND CLAP PATTERN 2. REMEMBER, THE FIRST "TI" IS
SHORT, SO MOVE QUICKLY TO THE STEADY BEAT, "TA," LIKE THIS: "TI TA
TI TA-A." ONE, TWO, READY, GO:

Clap and speak syllables.   (Repeat for accuracy.)

Teacher may sing song instead of
using recording.

GOOD. I HAVE A SONG RECORDING IN WHICH YOU'LL HEAR THE WORDS
"SING HALLELU" SEVERAL TIMES. DECIDE, AS YOU LISTEN, WHETHER
THOSE WORDS ARE SUNG TO THE RHYTHM OF PATTERN 1 OR PATTERN 2.
AS SOON AS YOU'VE DECIDED, START SINGING THOSE WORDS WITH THE
RECORDING.

(Play all or part of recording; encourage students to sing after
first verse.)

Summary

See Glossary.

PATTERN 2 FITS THE STYLE OF THAT SONG VERY WELL. THE WAY THOSE
LONG AND SHORT SOUNDS ARE COMBINED IN "SING HALLELU" CREATES
SYNCOPATION. (Discuss further, if appropriate.)

ANOTHER TIME

1. Sing with the recording, asking students to listen and discover
whether the "sing hallelu" patterns are repeated on higher or lower
pitch levels. Sing one or two verses, adding the *calls,* if possible.
Elicit that each successive pattern is lower than the preceding one.
Provide resonator bells, A, G, F, and D, for students to play the four
patterns of each verse.

2. Tape-record song for students to use at a learning station. Provide
notation of the four *responses* and bells on which to play them.

ELABORATION

1. Discover syncopated patterns in favorite songs and play them on
classroom instruments. Spirituals and calypso songs often include
such patterns.

2. Listen to the syncopation in GOLLIWOG'S CAKE WALK by Debussy,
SBM 4:98, rec 6.

3. Create a composition, using the rhythm patterns suggested for
SOUND PIECE 1, SBM 5:16.

4. To evaluate aural perception of syncopation, use "What Do You
Hear?" in SBM 4:93, rec 6.

5. Perform CLAPPING MUSIC FOR TWO PERFORMERS, SBM 6:224.

OTHER SONGS WITH SYNCOPATED PATTERNS

See variants of SING HALLELU in CMCM 1B and EM 1.

ARTSA ALINU. SBM 6; SOM 4

CHE CHE KOOLAY. SBM 2 and 3

DO LORD. NDM 5

DOWN BY THE RIVER. DMT 5

EPO I TAI TAI E. SBM (EC)

GOIN' DOWN THE ROAD. SOM 4

HALLELOO. DMT 1 and 3

HEY LILEY, LILEY OH. SBM (EC)

KUMA ECHA. SOM 6

LI'L LIZA JANE. DMT 3

NOAH. SBM 4

NOBODY'S BUSINESS. SBM 3

SEE, CAN'T YOU JUMP FOR JOY. SBM 4

WAKE ME. SBM 2

BIBLIOGRAPHY FOR YOUNG PEOPLE

Hughes, Langston, *Famous Negro Music Makers.* New York: Dodd Mead, 1955. Upper grades.

Johns, Altona T. *Play Songs of the Deep South.* New York: Associated Publishers, 1944.

Whiting, Helen Adele. *Negro Art, Music and Rhyme, Book II.* New York: Associated Publishers, 1967. For lower-grade children to read; illustrated.

BIBLIOGRAPHY

Rublowsky, John. *Black Music in America.* New York: Basic Books, 1976. A brief introduction for the generalist.

Still, William Grant. "The Negro Musician in America," *Music Educators Journal,* 56, 5 (January, 1970), p. 100.

Music Learning	Different rhythm patterns can sound simultaneously within a composition (polyrhythms).
Musical Context	JIN-GO-LO-BA by Michael Olatunji ("oh-lah-TOON-jee"). EM 4
Reading Objective	Optional (Experienced classes may notate their rhythm patterns.)
Behavioral Objective	To create rhythm patterns; and to perform them simultaneously, utilizing body sounds or percussion instruments.
Grade	Upper.
Materials	Recording: EM 4, rec 9; *Olatunji! Drums of Passion,* Columbia CS 8210 Optional: percussion instruments of varied tone colors suggestive of African instruments (drums, rattles, sticks, etc.) Precede this work with model experiences *Bingo,* p. 48, and *Sing Hallelu,* p. 146.

Focusing Statement

AS WE LISTEN TO <u>JIN-GO-LO-BA</u>, QUIETLY TAP OR CLAP A SHORT RHYTHM PATTERN THAT YOU HEAR, OR CREATE ONE THAT YOU FEEL FITS THE COMPOSITION.

Olatunji based this composition on the drum rhythms of West Africa.

 Body rhythms

(Some students will be able to sing along with *Jin-Go-Lo-Ba.* See "Another Time.")

The deeper-pitched *iya-ilu* ("YAI-loo"), or "mother drum," functions as the lead drum.

Discuss the Olatunji composition: DID YOU HEAR RECURRING RHYTHM PATTERNS? WAS THERE A "LEAD" INSTRUMENT UNIFYING THE OTHERS? (yes) WERE THE PLAYERS HOLDING TO THE SAME BEAT OR PULSE? (yes)

Now try experimenting with rhythm patterns, using different body sounds. Invent your own body sounds, or try some of these:

*Do this authentic African body percussion gently!

Body sounds {
handclapping with cupped palms, with flat palms, or with rigid fingers;

strike shoulders, knees, thighs;

while humming, tap Adam's apple* with the side of the forefinger;

mouth sounds, such as clacking tongue, popping lips, humming, or grunting;

foot stomping, sliding, or tapping.

Have individual students demonstrate their patterns. As they do so, discuss and decide which patterns show combinations of long and short sounds *(rhythm patterns)* and which show steady, even beats. Inexperienced students may need encouragement to develop their own rhythm patterns.

Divide the class into small groups of four or five students. Place groups in different parts of the classroom.

"Layering" these repeated patterns (rhythmic ostinati) results in polyrhythm.

NOW USE THE BODY SOUND YOU LIKE BEST FOR A RHYTHM PATTERN. TRY TO COMBINE YOUR PATTERNS INTO AN ENSEMBLE. SELECT ONE PERSON IN YOUR GROUP TO ACT AS LEADER. Stress simultaneous sounding of patterns.

Body rhythms

Teacher should move from group to group, encouraging efforts and offering assistance.

AS WE LISTEN TO EACH GROUP, SEE IF WE HEAR A VARIETY OF PATTERNS AND SOUNDS. These may include:

● Body rhythms

● high-pitched
low-pitched
sustained
short

● pitched
non-pitched
vocal
body

Summary

Also help students decide WHICH ARE PATTERNS AND WHICH ARE STEADY BEATS. A rhythm pattern is a combination of short and long sounds, and is a unit which is repeated. YOU COMBINED YOUR RHYTHM PATTERNS INTO A COMPOSITION.

Play *Jin-Go-Lo-Ba* again. Discuss briefly any new perceptions.

ANOTHER TIME

1. Sing this tonal pattern when you hear it in the recording:

"*Jin - go - lo,   jin - go - ba*"

2. Notate patterns created by students. Use blank (informal) notation or standard musical notation.

ELABORATION

1. Listen to a narrated demonstration of the *iya-ilu* playing three different patterns, on EM 6, rec 12, band 1E.

2. Learn how the *dundun* drum "speaks" rhythmic and tonal patterns. Hear EM 4, *Yoruba Drumming.*

3. Listen to the changing patterns in *Frekoba* by Olatunji, EM 4.

4. Study "Rhythm Patterns to Study and Play," SBM 6:8; "Drum Language in India," NDM 4; and, "Rhythm Patterns" (Africa) in NDM 5.

5. Accompany familiar songs with rhythm patterns played on percussion instruments. For ideas see model experience *Jamaica Farewell:* "Other Songs," p. 198.

OTHER MUSIC WITH DISTINCTIVE RHYTHM PATTERNS

(AFRICAN) DRUM MUSIC (Bantu). NDM 4

AI A LA O PELE (Hawaii). SBM 4. Also included in model experience *War Dance Song,* p. 151, which focuses on rhythm patterns.

AKIWOWO-CHANT TO THE TRAINMAN by Olatunji. NDM (EC).

ALLAH HU (India). SBM 5

KALANGA DANCE (Africa). SBM 5

MUSINGASIUGA YAKARA EGALE (Africa). NDM 5

SAMA VEDIC CHANT (India). SBM 5

SOUNDS OF AFRICA. NDM 4, rec 7 (side 2, band 3)

TURKISH OBOE AND DRUM DANCE. SBM 6

WOMAN'S WEDDING SONG (Near East). SBM 6

An excerpt of JIN-GO-LO-BA is included in SBM 2.

BIBLIOGRAPHY

Dietz, Betty W., and Michael Babatunde Olatunji. *Musical Instruments of Africa.* New York: John Day, 1965. The excellent photographs and text will be of interest to upper grade students and teachers. Many ideas for body percussion are described.*

Emery, Lynn. *Black Dance in the United States, 1619–1970.* Palo Alto, Calif.: National Press, 1972.

Fox, Sidney, Barbara Reeder Lundquist, and James A. Standifer, *The World of Popular Music: Afro-American,* teacher's edition. Chicago, Ill.: Follett Publishing Company, 1974. An outstanding resource for the generalist.

Marsh, Mary Val. "An Exploration in Percussion," *Music Educators Journal,* 48, 6 (June–July, 1962), p. 37. Using percussion creatively, to explore form, rhythm, notation, and simpler principles of composition.

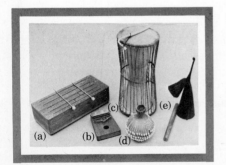

RHYTHM INSTRUMENTS: (a) slit drum, (b) sansa, (c) donno, (d) axatse, (e) gankogui.

*The African *donno* (pressure drum), *axatse* (gourd rattle), and *gankogui* (metal double bell) are now available from Rhythm Band, Inc., P.O. Box 126, Ft. Worth, Texas 76101.

Music Learning	Music can suggest the presence or absence of steady beats and can include rhythm patterns.

Musical Context

WAR DANCE SONG (Salish: American Indian). SBM 5

AI A LA O PELE (Hawaii). SBM 4

SAMA VEDIC CHANT (India). SBM 5

CHITIRUANO TRIBAL DANCE SONG, *Samandoze-Iwe* (Africa) SBM 2

Behavioral Objective

To identify aurally a steady beat, no beat, and rhythm patterns in four musical selections; and to demonstrate that recognition by circling the appropriate word on a worksheet.

Grade

Upper

Materials

Recordings:

WAR DANCE SONG — SBM 5, rec 5

AI A LA O PELE — SBM 4, rec 9; *Lahaina's Fabulous Emma Sharpe,* Tradewinds Records (P.O. Box 8294, Honolulu)

SAMA VEDIC CHANT — SBM, rec 6

CHITIRUANO . . . — SBM 2, rec 5

Worksheet for each student (boxed material below)

Large world map

Prior to this experience, students must have worked with these rhythm concepts. (See model experiences *Bingo,* p. 48, and *Sing Hallelu,* p. 146.) This experience is designed to measure rhythm understandings.

Review students' knowledge of steady beats and rhythm patterns by clapping, singing, or playing.

Distribute worksheets. As students examine them, call their attention to the four cultures whose music will be played. Note that the world map will be used to locate the areas producing these styles of music.

1 *American Indian*	2 *Hawaii*	3 *India*	4 *Africa*
NO BEAT STEADY BEAT	NO BEAT PATTERNS STEADY BEAT	NO BEAT STEADY BEAT PATTERNS	NO BEAT STEADY BEAT PATTERNS

Focusing Statement

Instruct students to LISTEN FOR THE RHYTHMS IN EACH MUSICAL SELECTION. CIRCLE THE WORD OR WORDS YOU DECIDE ON: NO BEAT, STEADY BEAT, OR PATTERNS.

Answers at end of lesson.

Selection 1:   WAR-DANCE SONG (play about 40 seconds)

At powwows, which are primarily social, women often sing with the men, using strident voices.

DID YOU NOTICE THAT THE SINGERS WERE AMERICAN INDIAN MEN AND WOMEN? Drums and leg bells are also heard.

Choose a student to locate northwestern Montana on the map. Explain that this is the home of these Salish ("SAY-lish") (Flathead) singers. Announce the second selection, music from Hawaii. MARK BOX TWO, "NO BEAT," "STEADY BEAT" OR "PATTERNS."

A traditional chant about *Pele,* the fire goddess; accompanied by *ipu* (gourd "drum") which plays changing patterns throughout.

AI A LA O PELE (Play 40–60 seconds.)

Choose a student to locate the Hawaiian Islands on the map. Prepare students for selection 3 by mentioning that MUSIC IS VERY OFTEN USED IN WORSHIP. THIS MUSIC, FROM INDIA, IS A RELIGIOUS CHANT OR SONG.

SBM 5 tells us this is an example of the earliest type of religious chant sung by nomadic shepherds.

SAMA VEDIC CHANT (play 40–60 seconds)

Select a student to locate India on the map.

THE FINAL SELECTION, 4, IS FROM AFRICA. IN THIS, YOU WILL HEAR TWO RHYTHMS. BE READY TO CIRCLE <u>TWO</u> ANSWERS IN COLUMN FOUR.

African rhythms can be extremely complex and varied.

CHITIRUANO TRIBAL DANCE SONG (play entire selection)

THAT'S A GOOD EXAMPLE OF HOW COMPLICATED AFRICAN RHYTHMS CAN SOUND.

Choose a student to locate the African continent on the map.

NOW WE'LL LISTEN TO EACH SELECTION AGAIN, AND CHECK FOR CORRECT ANSWERS. (See margin, p. 153.)

replay

Summary

Discuss students' understanding of music with and without steady beats, and the fact that rhythm patterns (of long and short sounds) function within the framework of steady beats, as in the African and Hawaiian examples.

ANOTHER TIME

Provide a tape recording of this model experience for use at an individual learning station.

OTHER MUSIC FOR SIMILAR USE

● *Music with a steady beat*

Much music fits into this category. Selections listed here highlight a single instrument playing a steady, "one-beat" rhythm.

CHEROKEE STOMP DANCE (American Indian). SBM 3

CORN GRINDING SONG (Navaho Indian). EM 3

NAVAHO NIGHT CHANT SONG (American Indian). SBM 3 and 5

SILVERSMITH SONG (Navaho: American Indian). EM 3

● *Music with no steady beat*

BAIRO (Japanese court music). NDM 5, rec 5

PERSIAN CLASSICAL SONG (Near East). SBM 6

RAGA YAMAN (India). SBM 5 (use only first half)

● *Music with distinctive rhythm patterns*

ALLAH HU (India). SBM 5

E MANONO LA EA (Hawaii). CMCM 1A

KALANGA DANCE (Africa). SBM 5

LAMMAN BADA YATATHANNA (Near East). SDM 6

WOMEN'S WEDDING SONG (Afghanistan). SBM 6

HAWAIIAN CHANT, HULA, AND MUSIC. Folkways FW 8750.

BIBLIOGRAPHY

Bernice Bishop Museum. *Musical Instruments of Hawaii.* Thirty slides and tape, available from the Department of Anthropology, Bishop Museum, P.O. Box 6037, Honolulu, Hawaii.

Gillett, Dorothy K. "Hawaiian Music for Hawaii's Children," *Music Educators Journal,* 59, 2 (October, 1972), p. 73. Includes a chant composed in the indigenous style that is easy enough for children to learn.

Malm, William P. "Australia and the Pacific Islands," in *Music Cultures of the Pacific, The Near East, and Asia* (2nd ed.). Englewood Cliffs, N.J.: Prentice-Hall, Inc., 1977. An excellent introduction to the music of this vast area, and to its functional qualities for the people who use it.

Rhodes, Willard. "Acculturation in North American Indian Music," in *Acculturation in the Americas,* ed. Sol Tax. Chicago: University of Chicago Press, 1952, p. 127. A look at the changing nature of American Indian music by an important investigator.

Answers:

1. steady beat
2. patterns and steady beat
3. no beat
4. steady beat and patterns

I

Form: the shape, order, or design of a musical composition.

VIENNESE MUSICAL CLOCK
    The initial section of a composition may alternate with contrasting sections (rondo).

Harmony: the simultaneous sounding of two or more pitches; the vertical structure in music.

JOE TURNER BLUES
    Chord roots can serve as a song accompaniment.

*ARE YOU SLEEPING? (II)
    Melodies based on differing scales can be combined (polytonality).

*IMPROVISATION FOR SOLO PERFORMER AND
FIVE TAPE RECORDERS
    Aleatoric composition can be created electronically.

Melody: a linear succession of pitches; the horizontal structure in music.

MINKA
    A tonal pattern can be restated, beginning on different pitches. (sequence)

After completing each model experience, decide how successfully you are able to identify, explain, or demonstrate the music learning that was the focus of the experience. Check the appropriate box.

Secure Fairly secure Insecure

*Group work-through experience

154

Music Learning	The initial section of a composition can alternate with contrasting sections (rondo).
Musical Context	VIENNESE MUSICAL CLOCK from Háry János Suite by Zoltán Kodály ("KOH-dye") (Hungarian, 1882–1967). AIM 2; BOL 81; EM 4; NDM 4
Behavioral Objective	To identify aurally the recurrence of the first section, A, as it alternates with contrasting sections B, C, and D; and to demonstrate this recognition by placing like and differing objects in the correct order.
Grade	Upper
Materials	Recording: AIM 2, Vol I; BOL 81; EM 4, rec 10; NDM 4, rec 7
	Objects: four oranges and three different fruits (or any objects available, four identical and three contrasting, as kitchen utensils, flowers, figurines, etc.).

Focusing Statement

MANY ORCHESTRAL PIECES ARE LONGER THAN THE SONGS WE SING. I BROUGHT THESE PIECES OF FRUIT TO HELP YOU LISTEN MORE CAREFULLY TO A RECORDING, AND TO REMEMBER WHAT YOU HEAR.

As music plays, place fruit, one at a time, where all students may see. The order is:

Intro.　A　B　A　C　A　D　A　Coda

apple　lemon　apple　grapefruit　apple　orange　apple

(Introduction and coda are very brief.)
*(Don't place C object too soon!)

Students may be responding to instrumental timbre. If so, lead them to discover the identical *melodies* in the A sections and the differing melodies in the other sections.

Ask students to count the number of apples they see. (4) Encourage them to verbalize that there are four because similar music was heard four times. Students should also be able to explain that each different fruit represents a different section of the music heard.

WHEN ONE SECTION RETURNS OFTEN AND ALTERNATES WITH DIFFERENT SECTIONS, THE DESIGN IS CALLED RONDO. Select a student to set out the fruit this time. Lay them in order (not scrambled) for student to lift into full view at the correct times.

Allow several students to demonstrate their listening skills.

Summary

WHAT IS THE MUSICAL DESIGN CALLED WHEN ONE SECTION KEEPS RETURNING AND ALTERNATING WITH DIFFERENT SECTIONS? *(Rondo)*

ANOTHER TIME

1. Students may be interested in knowing that in this composition, Kodály is using music to describe the moving and changing figures on a large mechanical clock in Vienna. (See AIM 2, I, EM 4, and NDM 4 teacher's editions, for additional information.)

2. Study the notated musical themes of the *Háry János Suite* in DMT6.

3. Provide a tape of *Viennese Musical Clock* for use at a single tape recorder equipped with earphones. Individuals may listen and arrange objects on their own.

ELABORATION

1. Small groups can *improvise* rondos. An initial "section" (A) can be created and performed with percussion instruments or body sounds.
   Example:

Three individuals might then improvise three contrasting rhythmic ideas (B, C, and D) for the rondo.
   Examples:

The entire group should perform A, and individuals should play the B, C, and D "sections." Tape-record this *improvised rhythmic rondo* for students to hear and evaluate.

2. Create a rhythmic rondo based on the melodic rhythms of familiar songs:

   a. Sing and clap the melodic rhythms of four well-known songs, such as THIS OLD MAN, LONDON BRIDGE, SKIP TO MY LOU, and ARE YOU SLEEPING? (Be sure to clap every word syllable!)

   b. Clap the four melodic rhythms *without singing*. Think the words as you do.

   c. Choose four percussion instruments of contrasting tone colors (drum, wood block, sandpaper blocks, tambourine, etc.). Decide which instrument is to be played for each melodic rhythm. Have four students play the four rhythms.

   d. Suggest that the four melodic rhythms be organized into a *rondo*. Review the rondo design by writing on the board: A B A C A D A. Elicit from students the distinguishing characteristic of rondo design (contrasting sections between recurring identical sections).

   e. Have students select one of the melodic rhythms for each section of their rondo.

Rondos need not be based on *four* different ideas. For instance, *three* will suffice: A B A C A.

See model experience *A Ram Sam Sam* (II), p. 111, and Splicing Tape, p. 347.

f. Prepare to perform the rondo by reminding students that the sections should follow each other without hesitation. Also, note that section A will end, as well as begin, the rondo.

3. Create a *tape rondo.* Plan and record several contrasting sound sequences. Record as many "performances" of A as you will eventually need. Each section should be several seconds long. Splice the taped sections together in rondo form. Play the tape and decide if speed changes and volume control will add variety to the rondo.

OTHER MUSIC IN RONDO FORM

ALLEGRO from *Quartet in C Minor,* Op. 18, No. 4, by Beethoven. MMYO 5

THE ALLIGATOR AND THE 'COON from *Acadian Songs and Dances* by Thomson. AIM 3, vol. 2; EM 5

CASTILLANE from *Le Cid Ballet Suite* by Massenet. EM 6

QUARTET IN C MAJOR, OP. 33, NO. 2, fourth movement, by Haydn. SOM 5

GIGUE EN RONDEAU by Rameau. SBM 6:140, rec 6 (Call Chart No. 7)

HINEY MA TOV. NDM 5 (song in rondo form)

PERCUSSION RONDO by Mitchell. SOM 3

RONDO by Ernst (electronic). SOM 6

FRENCH HORN CONCERTO NO. 4, third movement, by Mozart. SOM 4

VIOLIN CONCERTO IN D MAJOR, Op. 61, third movement, by Beethoven. EM 4

BIBLIOGRAPHY

Esselstrom, Michael J. "Listening Comes Alive in the Classroom," *Music Educators Journal,* 57, 8 (April, 1971), p. 44. "Live" concerts presented in association with techniques similar to those used in this model experience.

Hollander, Fred M., and Patricia D. Juhrs. "Orff Schulwerk, an Effective Treatment Tool with Autistic Children," *Journal of Music Therapy,* vol. 11 (Spring 1974), p. 1. Report on a carefully designed project which made extensive use of rondo form.

Marsh, Mary Val. *Explore and Discover Music.* New York: The Macmillan Co., 1970, p. 172. "Rondo Fiesta," for percussion instruments, is composed by a group of fourth, fifth, and sixth grade students in a Beverly Hills, California, summer program. See also p. 166.

O'Brien, James P. "Let's Not Only Get Their Attention . . ." *Music Educators Journal,* 59, 4 (December, 1972), p. 28. Clever ideas to motivate a lesson, while still relating these "tricks" to the objective.

Orff, Carl, and Gunild Keetman. *Orff-Schulwerk, Music for Children, I, Pentatonic.* English adaptation by Doreen Hall and Arnold Walter. Mainz: B. Schott Söhne, 1950, pp. 86–87 (rhythmic rondos) and pp. 88–90 (melodic rondos).

Music Learning	Chord roots can serve as a song accompaniment.

Musical Context   JOE TURNER BLUES (American blues). CMCM 3C; MMYO 6

Behavioral Objective   To identify aurally and visually the letter names of the chords C (I), F (IV), and G_7 (V_7); to sing and play these pitches as an accompaniment to the song.

Grade   Upper

Materials   Recording: MMYO 6 or CMCM 3C
Autoharp
Resonator bells C, F, and G (from lower range of set)
Three mallets
Chord chart (write on chalkboard, or make a reusable paper chart):

Play four steady beats per box (box represents one bar or measure of music).

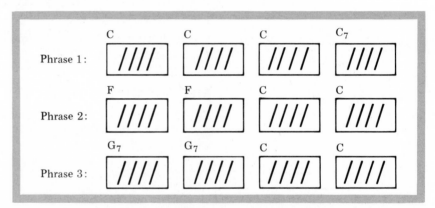

Some experience with *two* chord songs, using Autoharp, should precede this lesson. See model experience *Good Morning Blues*, p. 89.

Before beginning, be certain that bells and Autoharp are in tune with each other *and* with your record player. If not, use only bells and Autoharp, and tune the Autoharp to the bells.

Focusing Statement   As you play the recording for the first time, ask the students to LISTEN FOR REPETITION IN THE LYRICS. SING ALONG, AS SOON AS YOU ARE ABLE.

 (Introduction and two verses)

Discuss. Students will have noted that THE FIRST LINE OF EACH VERSE IS SUNG TWICE, AND THE THIRD LINE IS DIFFERENT. THIS OFTEN HAPPENS IN "12-BAR" BLUES. Also note that IN JOE TURNER BLUES THE SAME THIRD LINE OF TEXT IS USED IN EVERY VERSE.

Song notation, p. 243.   Play first verse again, skipping most of the introduction. Encourage students to sing along, as you begin using the chord chart, pointing to each BEAT. Four steady beats are represented by each box.

Distribute C, F, and G bells to three students.

PLAY FOUR STEADY BEATS FOR EACH MEASURE (or BOX), AS THE CHART INDICATES. Explain that THE BELLS BEING PLAYED INDICATE THE LETTER NAME OF EACH CHORD.

As a rehearsal, point to one of the boxes as the bell player plays the four steady beats. Do this with all three chords and all three players.

These letter names are called chord *roots*.

SINGERS, LET'S SING THAT SAME BELL PITCH AS THEY PLAY. USE THIS PATTERN (write on board, if necessary):

This is similar to *scat singing* in jazz.

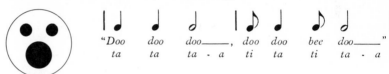

(teacher)

Practice the pattern above, along with the bell players. All will be participating.

("Doo bee doo")

EVERYONE IS PERFORMING THE CHORD ROOTS OF THE C, F, AND G₇ ("G-SEVEN") CHORDS.

Using recording, set needle down about in the middle of the introduction.

C major scale

C	
B	
A	
G = 5 (V)	*G · b · d*
F = 4 (IV)	*F · a · c*
E	
D	
C = 1 (I)	*C · e · g*

(Chord roots; play as many verses as seem profitable.)

C, F, and G₇ are primary chords in the key of C major.

Summary

Conclude that THE BELL PART AND THE SINGING OF CHORD ROOTS FIT AS AN ACCOMPANIMENT BECAUSE THE LETTER NAMES PERFORMED ARE THE "STRONGEST" TONES OF EACH CHORD.

ANOTHER TIME

1. Individual students can prepare chord root accompaniments on cello, ukulele, or even guitar.

2. Students can prepare a chordal accompaniment using Autoharp, piano (see p. 265), and guitar (see p. 243.)

Many students will be able to harmonize "by ear."
○ root
● third or fifth, or seventh of chord

3. If singers are able, learn some vocal chording so that their "scat" singing can be done in parts:

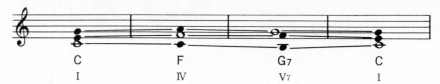

C   F   G7   C
I   IV   V7   I

ELABORATION

1. Individual students may use the chord pattern to create their own blues songs. The chords, when strummed, will support their voices as they create blues melodies.

Consider topics such as pets, family, friends, home, ecology, or events at school. In 12-bar blues, the text of the first two phrases is the same. The third phrase sometimes includes this same text, but expands on it with additional words.

OTHER "12-BAR" BLUES

THE CITY BLUES. NDM 5

NEW YORK CITY. SOM 6

ORIGINAL TALKING BLUES. SOM 6

SHORTY GEORGE. MMYO 6

See model experience GOOD MORNING BLUES: "Other Songs," p. 91

BIBLIOGRAPHY FOR YOUNG PEOPLE

Hughes, Langston. *First Book of Jazz.* New York: Franklin Watts, 1955. Upper grades; jazz history, relating to Louis Armstrong's career.

BIBLIOGRAPHY

Finkelstein, Sidney. *Jazz: A People's Music.* New York: Citadel Press, 1948. A fascinating book by a brilliant and knowledgeable writer.

Genovese, Eugene D. *Roll, Jordan, Roll: The World the Slaves Made.* New York: Pantheon Books, a division of Random House, Inc., 1974. A monumental interpretation of slavery, vivid in its detail and compassion, and wide-ranging in its scope. A stimulating landmark in the literature about Black Americans.

WORK-THROUGH EXPERIENCE

Music Learning

┌───┐
│   │
│   │
└───┘

Musical Context

ARE YOU SLEEPING? (II) (French round, "Frère Jacques"). CMCM 1A and 2A; DMT 1 and 2; EM 3; MMYO 3; NDM 2 and 3; SOM 2 and 3

Reading Objective

Writing pitch names of the D-major scale
Writing notation for ARE YOU SLEEPING? in D major

Behavioral Objective

┌───┐
│   │
│   │
└───┘

Grade

┌───┐
│   │
└───┘

Materials

Two or more sets of bells, preferably resonator bells

Two mallets

Tape recorder and tape

Notation chart from model experience *Are You Sleeping?* (I)

This experience must be preceded by *Are You Sleeping?* (I), including playing the song as a round, as suggested in "Another Time," p. 124.

1. Select one person to manipulate the tape recorder and tape.

Song notation, p. 259

2. One person or several persons should review and prepare to play the entire song *Are You Sleeping?* on the melody bells. As you play from the chart of notation, note that it is based on the F-major scale.

See Glossary.

3. One or more persons should prepare to play *Are You Sleeping?* on bells, *transposed* to the key of D major. If your group is able, transpose the song yourselves. (A transposed version is included at the conclusion of this work-through experience.)

First, write the pitch names for the D-major scale. To determine the correct pitches, either locate them "by ear," or determine the whole and half-step arrangement:

⌣ = whole step
v = half step

___ ___ ___ ___ ___ ___ ___ ___
  ⌣   ⌣   v   ⌣   ⌣   ⌣   v

Now write the transposed notation for *Are You Sleeping?* on the staff below. The first and last pitches are given.

4. The person(s) playing the song in F major should now play for the group.

The person(s) playing the song in D major should next play for the entire group.

5. *Both* players now perform in the two keys *at the same time!* (Another person should signal both players when to begin.) Play simultaneously and at the same tempo.

Summary

See Glossary.

6. Discuss the resultant sound of a song played in two different keys simultaneously. Contemporary composers often combine different scales. The term for this is *polytonality*.

7. Try performing the song as a round. Let the F-major player begin. The D-major player starts after eight beats.

8. This time, tape-record your performance of this *polytonality*.

9. Play the tape and discuss the results.

10. Discuss the *music learning(s)* developed in this experience. Formulate a statement and write it in the box provided at the top of the preceding page. (An acceptable statement is shown in the left margin near the end of this model experience.)

11. Write a *behavioral objective* statement for this experience. Write it in the box provided. (See acceptable statement near end of this experience.)

12. For what grade level would this experience be appropriate? What prior experience would be necessary? Would any alterations be required in this learning sequence? Write the grade level in the box provided. (See left margin near end of this experience.)

See Glossary.

ANOTHER TIME

Add an Autoharp *drone* in another key. Press the A$_7$ and A minor buttons *simultaneously.* Strum twice per measure (every two beats.) Work out an arrangement using all three parts: bells in F, bells in D, and Autoharp *drone* in A. Tape and evaluate.

Suggestions:

Music Learning

Melodies based on differing scales can be combined (polytonality).

Behavioral Objective

To transpose, read, and perform a familiar song in a new key; to perform a song in two different keys simultaneously.

Grade

Upper

ELABORATION

1. Transpose other simple songs (such as *Scotland's Burning,* p. 283) and those listed in model experience *Are You Sleeping?* (I), p. 124. Then play in two keys for a similar experience in polytonality.

2. Students may *sing* a song based on a specific scale and accompany the singing with an Autoharp in a *different* key. Use keys three or more steps apart. Be sure to tape these experiences so all students may hear the results.

3. View the film *Canon* (National Film Board of Canada, 1964).

OTHER POLYTONAL MUSIC FOR LISTENING

BLACK AND WHITE from *Sketches in Color* by Starer. SBM 6

FRÈRE JACQUES, arranged for piano by David Ward-Steinman. SOM 3 and 5. You will hear some contemporary harmonies accompanying this familiar song.

LA PUERTA DEL VINO, from *Preludes,* Book II, by Debussy. MMYO 5

PUTNAM'S CAMP and REDDING, CONNECTICUT from *Three Places in New England* by Charles Ives. BOL 75; EM 5

BIBLIOGRAPHY

Knuth, Alice M., and William E. Knuth. *Basic Resources for Learning Music.* (2nd ed.) Belmont, Calif.: Wadsworth Publishing Co., Inc., 1973, p. 223. An experiment combining two familiar songs in different keys, and singing and playing them simultaneously.

Marsh, Mary Val. *Explore and Discover Music.* New York: Macmillan Publishing Company, Inc., 1970, p. 143. Ideas are presented for working with polytonality and bitonality in a fifth-grade class.

Nye, Robert, and Meg Peterson. *Teaching Music With the Autoharp.* Union, N.J.: Music Education Group, 1973, p. 60. An idea similar to this model experience is developed for using Autoharp accompaniment in a different key while singing a familiar melody.

ARE YOU SLEEPING? , transposed to *D* major:

WORK-THROUGH EXPERIENCE

Music Learning	Aleatoric compositions can be created electronically.

SOUND EXPERIMENT WITH TAPE RECORDER: TAPE DELAY

Musical Context　IMPROVISATION FOR SOLO PERFORMER AND FIVE TAPE RECORDERS by Georg Polski. SOM 5

Behavioral Objective　To create, perform, and record a sound sequence on one tape recorder while a second tape recorder plays back the recorded sounds; to identify aurally the aleatoric "layering" that results.

Grade　Upper

Materials

Two matching (or very similar) reel-to-reel tape recorders

Recording tape (clean)

One microphone

Selection of percussion instruments (some wood sounds, some metal sounds)

Recording: SOM 5, rec 7

Precede this experience with model experience *String Quartet No. 4,* p. 128.

Tape delay technique involves recording sound on tape recorder 1. This sound is played back almost instantly from tape recorder 2. The playback sounds from the second recorder feed back into the recording microphone of the first and join any "live" sounds still being recorded. The sounds multiply and "re-multiply" as long as the process is continued.

1. Five individuals should prepare to manage the two tape recorders, the tape, the microphone, and the percussion instruments.

2. Place the two tape recorders about 3 ft. apart, at the same height (opposite ends of a large table). Place the recorders so that the tape will run *unobstructed* from tape recorder 1 to tape recorder 2, as in the diagram below.

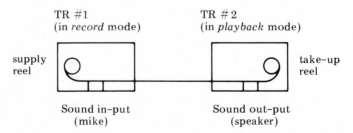

TR #1　　　　　　　　TR #2
(in *record* mode)　　　(in *playback* mode)

supply reel　　　　　　　　　　　　　　take-up reel

Sound in-put　　　　　Sound out-put
(mike)　　　　　　　　(speaker)

3. Run the tape from supply spindle of recorder 1 through the record-playback heads of *both* machines, and attach the tape to the take-up reel of recorder 2. Place both volume controls at a fairly high level and adjust later, if desired.

Sample score:

  Y   ZZX   YX   Z   YY   X
──────────────────────────────

4. Be sure both recorders are set to run at the *same speed.*

5. Plan a sound sequence similar to the one you created for *String Quartet No. 4,* (or see left margin).

   —three students might choose three instruments to play: the X, the Y, and the Z. It might be interesting to choose sounds all of similar timbre, such as "wood" sounds: claves, temple blocks, wood blocks.

6. Play through the sound sequence after deciding on an approximate time for one playing (as, 10–15 seconds).

This sound sequence will serve as the *planned* portion of an aleatoric composition.

7. Plan for several repetitions of the XYZ sequence, as you will want to continue feeding sounds into the tape recorder. Variety will be interesting. Use your own ideas, or assign a group for each of these:

   spoken sounds

   metal sounds

   body sounds

   sounds from objects in the room (that can be brought close to the microphone)

8. Practice these sound sequences, and make any quick adjustments you believe will make them more interesting. But keep it simple and brief!

   Remember to move smoothly through each sound sequence and *allow for silences* where there are no letters.

If you use *stereo* tape recorders (with two mikes), direct one mike toward the "live" sounds and the other toward recorder 2, the playback machine.

9. Prepare to record by having the two individuals managing the tape recorders start them *simultaneously,* but with recorder 1 in *record* mode and recorder 2 in *playback* mode. As soon as the tape is moving, begin the sound sequence.

10. On a pre-determined signal, stop feeding "live" sounds into recorder 1. Remain silent, and listen to what happens as only the playback sounds are fed into the microphone! (Both tape recorders remain *on.*)

Summary

11. Discuss the *chance* "layering" that results when *all* recorded sounds, both *"live"* and *playback,* are accumulated on the tape. You will notice that distortion of the sounds will become extreme.

12. Play recording of the aleatoric composition *Improvisation for Solo Performer and Five Tape Recorders.* Notice how many trombonists you *seem* to hear, even though this composition is performed by a *soloist.* Compare this to what you have done in this experience. Discuss what might have been planned and what was left to chance in this composition.

ANOTHER TIME

This model experience can be altered slightly to create a *canon:*

5 seconds × 3¾ inches-per-second = 18¾ inches apart.

1. Place the two tape recorders so that the *record* and *playback heads* are *exactly* 18¾ inches (five seconds) apart.

2. Set both recorders at 3¾ i.p.s.; thread tape from recorder 1 to recorder 2, as in step 2 of the model experience.

3. Plan and practice two contrasting sound sequences (A and B), each exactly five seconds long.

4. Prepare to record, as in step 9 of the model experience.

Total recording time: 20 seconds

5. When recorders are running, record the sound sequences, *without interruption, two complete times* (A B A B). Stop both tape recorders *immediately* (and simultaneously).

6. Rewind the tape and play it back on just *one* tape recorder. Focus your listening on the accumulation of the five-second sequences ("stacking"). The diagram below shows that the final 20-second *canon* will have four sequences sounding simultaneously in the final five seconds:

	5″	10″	15″	20″
Recorder 1 (live)	A	B	A	B
		+	+	+
Recorder 2 (playback)		A	AB	ABA

ELABORATION

1. Listen to Otto Luening discuss and play his composition *Fantasy in Space.* It is composed entirely of electronically manipulated flute sounds. *Listening to the Composer Otto Luening,* MMYO 6.

2. Encourage students in your classroom to experiment with *any* recordable sounds they wish. A favorite poem or quotation (or song) could make a very interesting composition using the *tape delay* technique.

3. "What Do You Hear?" in SBM 4:159 deals with *texture.*

4. See "Experiencing the Arts: Multi-Media," SBM 6:25.

BIBLIOGRAPHY

Schafer, R. Murray. *Creative Music Education.* New York: Schirmer Books, 1976, pp. 64–65. Good definitions and exercises concerning texture.
See "Bibliography," p. 59.

Music Learning	A tonal pattern can be restated, beginning on different pitches (sequence).
Musical Context	MINKA (Russian folk song). MMYO 6
Reading Objective	
Behavioral Objective	To identify aurally and visually tonal patterns that repeat, beginning on different pitches; and to demonstrate this recognition by singing and playing the tonal patterns.
Grade	Upper
Materials	Resonator bells F♯, G, A, and B♭
	Four bell mallets
	Recording: MMYO 6, rec 5
	Allow experienced students to read notation above and to select correct resonator bells for this experience.

Song notation, p. 288.

Portions of text in parentheses have a different melodic contour.

Copy the following on the chalkboard:

G	G	G	G	G	
"Said	the	cos - sack	to	the	maiden"

F♯	F♯	F♯	F♯	F♯	
"Love,	my	heart	is	hea - vy	la - den"

G	G	G	G	G	
"Du - ty	calls	so	I'm	afraid,	en - (chantress we must part.")

B♭	B♭	B♭	B♭	B♭	
"I	be - seech	you	fair - est	Minka"	

A	A	A	A	A	
"Wait	for	me,	I	hate	to think an -"

G	G	G	G	G	
"oth - er	man	might	come and	tinker	(with your faithful heart.")

Give the F♯, G, A, and B♭ bells to four students.

Focusing Statement

Pattern may also be clapped.

$\flat$ = *ti*

FIND THE NAME OF YOUR BELL ON THE CHALKBOARD.

Instruct bell players to play their pitches five times (as you point to each part), in this rhythm:

Give each bell player a turn.

(four players)

Ask class to notice what happens to the *shape* of the melody (trace lines above lyrics) *after* each group of *repeated tones*. (There is a rise and fall at the end of each phrase.)

Play the song recording to give all students an introduction to the complete melody.

Bell players should listen for the places where they will be playing (later) and others should listen to the shape of each phrase. Teacher may point to help students follow phrases.

(Fade after one verse)

Use bells with recording *only* if they are in tune with each other.

Challenge bell players and singers to join the recording this time. Bell players should sing rhythmically to help them keep up with the tempo of the recording.

(One verse)

If playing the bells in this fast tempo is too difficult, eliminate the step above and continue the bell playing with the class singing at a suitable tempo.

Summary

WHEN YOU HEAR THE SAME MELODY AGAIN AND AGAIN, BUT BEGINNING ON HIGHER OR LOWER PITCHES, IT IS CALLED SEQUENCE. THE MINKA MELODY STARTS ON HOW MANY DIFFERENT PITCHES? (Call attention to chalkboard material.) FOUR. (F♯, G, A, and B♭.)

ANOTHER TIME

1. With a little practice, students can expand their bell parts by adding the three descending pitches that follow each set of repeated pitches. The repeated G is followed by B♭-A-G; the repeated F♯ is followed by A-G-F♯, etc. (See song notation, p. 288.)

2. Later, students can be challenged to learn the notes ending the two sections of MINKA:

Some students will be able to put all the melodic fragments together and play the entire melody.

3. To dramatize the musical interest created by *melodic sequence,* try singing the first three phrases of *Minka,* starting each phrase on the *same* pitch. Have a student help by playing the five repeated pitches on G at the start of each phrase. Follow this with a quick review of the same three phrases, starting as in the actual song, on G, F♯, and G, respectively.

OTHER MUSIC USING MELODIC SEQUENCE

CASTILLANE from *Le Cid Ballet Suite* by Massenet. EM 6

EVENING BELLS. DMT 3 (phrases 2 and 3)

EV'RYBODY LOVES SATURDAY NIGHT. SOM 4

KHUKHABARA, p. 285

LOVELY EVENING, p. 000 and EM 4

MARCHING TO PRETORIA. DMT 2; MMYO 3

SHOO FLY, p. 229

SKIP TO MY LOU, pp. 176, 283

THREE BLIND MICE, p. 254

WHERE IS JOHN? EM 4

WHO'LL DANCE WITH MARY? MMYO 5

J

Melody: a linear succession of pitches; the horizontal structure in music.

*GREETING PRELUDE
Composers can alter melodies by displacing the pitches one or more octaves.

Harmony: the simultaneous sounding of two or more pitches; the vertical structure in music.

BOW, BELINDA; SKIP TO MY LOU
Two melodies that use the same chords at the same time can be performed simultaneously.

Melody: a linear succession of pitches; the horizontal structure in music.

CORN GRINDING SONG
A melody can exhibit a distinctive contour as it moves up or down or repeats.

GAMBANGAN
A single melody can serve as the basis for an entire composition.

Rhythm: all of the durations that occur in music.

SYMPHONY NO. 94
The rhythm of a melody can be varied when the melody is repeated.

After completing each model experience, decide how successfully you are able to identify, explain, or demonstrate the music learning that was the focus of the experience. Check the appropriate box.

Secure Fairly secure Insecure

*Group work-through experience

WORK-THROUGH EXPERIENCE

Music Learning	Composers can alter melodies by displacing the pitches one or more octaves.
Musical Context	GREETING PRELUDE by Igor Stravinsky ("strah-VIHN-skee") (Russian-American, 1882–1971). EM 1; MMYO 6; NDM 6; SOM 3 and 5
Reading Objective	Melodic contour. See step 3 below.
Behavioral Objective	
Grade	
Materials	Recording: EM 1, rec 9; MMYO 6, rec 6; NDM 6, rec 3; or SOM 5, rec 8 Four sets of resonator bells and four mallets Two colored pencils for each student Tape recorder, microphone, and a *clean* tape

1. Select one person to operate the tape recorder, a second person to manage the phonograph, and a third to locate recordings and book.

2. Listen to *Greeting Prelude* and identify the familiar song on which it is based.

3. Four players can perform this familiar song. Each player needs one set of resonator bells. Look at the staves below and assign one phrase to each player.

 Players should: determine pitches to be used; remove bells from their sets and place them in front of themselves; perform entire melody, one player at a time.

(If you read staff notation, please don't reveal the name of this tune prior to step 2!)

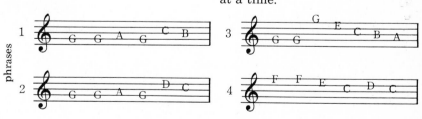

4. With a colored pencil, connect the pitches of each phrase (in step 3 above). Notice how most of the pitches are close together. Also notice which phrase has a leap. When the notes are close together, you can see how smooth and flowing the melody line is.

5. Discuss what made Stravinsky's version of this song *different* from ours. To focus on the differences, have the first two players perform their phrases, and then immediately play the beginning of *Greeting Prelude* to hear Stravinsky's version of these same two phrases. Try to describe the differences as precisely as possible.

6. To explore *one* way Stravinsky varied this familiar song, each bell player should substitute one or two (no more) pitches in each phrase. For example, player 1 could use a higher or lower G. (You will discover that a higher G is the only option available.) Place that higher G in front of you, and put the other G back in the box.

Octave displacement.

Each player should now substitute at least *one* bell. Then play the new version created by these substitutions.

Tape the performance so that players can evaluate their performance.

7. Using the different-colored pencil, write these substituted pitches in their proper position (higher or lower) on the staff. (Use staff in step 3.)

Connect these new pitches to those that remain unchanged. Are all the pitches close together now? Presumably, some pitches will be farther apart, thus creating a melody line (contour) that is jagged and leaping.

Summary

This displacement of pitches is one technique Stravinsky used to vary the melody.

8. Discuss, in your own words, the music learning developed in this experience. Compare your perceptions with those noted in the "Music learning" box at the beginning of this experience.

9. If you were to use this with children, what grade level would be appropriate? What background would be necessary? What alterations would be needed in the sequence here? Write your decision in the box provided at the beginning of this model experience. (Compare your judgment with that of the authors. See left margin near end of model experience.)

10. Formulate a *behavioral objective,* and write it in the box provided. Do this individually or as a group. (See left margin, next page.)

Behavioral Objective:

To identify aurally *Happy Birthday* in a different version and to play that melody on bells; to substitute pitches in that melody in order to create a new version, and to play that new version on melody bells.

Grade:

Upper

ANOTHER TIME

1. Try substituting other pitches to create another version of *Happy Birthday.* Perform and tape-record the new version.

2. Hear Stravinsky describe and discuss *Greeting Prelude* on the recording in MMYO 6, rec 6, "Listening to the Composer."

3. Play this melody on your guitar, piano, or recorder.

ELABORATION

1. Try the pitch-displacement ideas with other simple and familiar songs. Discover how many different versions are possible. This might be an interesting project for individual students.

2. In *Frère Jacques,* arranged by David Ward-Steinman, SOM 3 and 5, rec 8, you will hear pitch displacement.

3. Listen to composer Harry Partch's use of *Happy Birthday* in his composition *Afro-Chinese Minuet,* SOM 5, rec 8. (See also *Plectra and Percussion Dances,* Gate 5 Records.)

4. See "Pitch Displacement" in NDM 6.

5. Try the octave displacement experiment based on *Streets of Laredo* in SOM 5:154.

BIBLIOGRAPHY FOR YOUNG PEOPLE

Burch, Gladys, and John Wolcott. *Modern Composers for Young People.* New York: Dodd, Mead, 1941. Upper grades.

Posell, Elsa Z. *Russian Composers.* Boston: Houghton Mifflin, 1967. Upper grades.

BIBLIOGRAPHY

Landon, Joseph W. "Strategies for Opening the Traditional Classroom," *Music Educators Journal,* 60, 8 (April, 1974), p. 64. Octave displacement is the focus for a sample *Learning Activity Package* (LAP).

Marsh, Mary Val. *Explore and Discover Music.* New York: Macmillan Publishing Co., Inc., 1970, pp. 138–142. Describe ideas for working with pitch displacement, with specific reference to *Greeting Prelude* and *Afro-Chinese Minuet* as used with a summer school class of 8- to 12-year-olds.

Teacher's editions of EM 1, NDM 6, and SOM 5 also provide additional information on pitch displacement and *Greeting Prelude.*

Music Learning

> Two melodies that use the same chords at the same time can be performed simultaneously.

Musical Context

BOW, BELINDA (American singing game). CMCM 1B; MMYO 2; NDM (EC)

SKIP TO MY LOU (American singing game). CMCM 1A; DMT (EC), 2 and 3; MMYO 1 and 4; SBM 1; SOM 4

Behavioral Objective

To demonstrate perception that melodies with identical chord patterns are compatible, by reading and playing the chords on Autoharps and singing two songs simultaneously.

Grade

Upper

Materials

Autoharp(s)

Chord chart (see left margin below)

Model experience *Skip to My Lou,* p. 14, should precede this experience. Students should be able to sing both *Skip to My Lou* and *Bow, Belinda.*

Focusing Statement

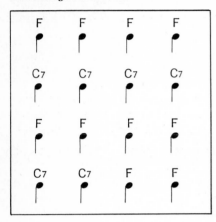

Display the chord chart. WE NEED SOME AUTOHARP PLAYERS TO ACCOMPANY US AS WE SING SKIP TO MY LOU. Select players. Use the first line of chords for an introduction. Pluck the middle-octave A string for the starting pitch.

 (Start Autoharp players by saying, ONE, TWO, READY, STRUM.)

LET'S TRY ANOTHER SONG WE KNOW WITH THESE SAME CHORDS! DO YOU REMEMBER BOW, BELINDA?

Change Autoharp players, if you wish. Instruct students that they will play the chart exactly as before, but this time the words and melody of *Bow, Belinda* will be sung. Pluck the middle-octave F string for the starting pitch.

THOSE CHORDS CERTAINLY WORKED FOR BOW, BELINDA, AS WELL AS SKIP TO MY LOU.

LET'S SING BOTH SONGS TOGETHER. Choose one group for SKIP TO MY LOU and another for BOW, BELINDA.

If two Autoharps are available, use one for each group.

Each group should practice separately, with the Autoharp.

 (each group practice separately)

WE'RE READY TO TRY BOTH GROUPS TOGETHER. AUTOHARP PLAYERS, PLAY THE INTRODUCTION, THEN BOTH GROUPS SING.

Call out ONE, TWO, READY, STRUM, to start the Autoharp players.

Discuss meaning of *partner* in other contexts.

THOSE TWO SONGS FIT TOGETHER VERY NICELY. THEY'RE CALLED PARTNER SONGS.

Sing the songs several times to coordinate the two partner songs better.

Summary

WHAT WAS THE SAME ABOUT THE SONGS THAT MADE THEM FIT SO WELL? Students will certainly observe that the accompanying chords were the same. Comment to students that WHEN TWO SONG MELODIES USE THE SAME CHORDS AT THE SAME TIME, THEY CAN BE PERFORMED TOGETHER.

"kwoad-LIH-bet"

Quodlibet is the term often used to identify two or more melodies that can be performed simultaneously.

ANOTHER TIME

1. Using two sheets of tissue paper, trace just the *note heads* and *bar lines* of the two song notations. When one sheet is laid on top of the other, the chord pitches that sound simultaneously can be seen.

2. Identify the notes in the first measure of each song. Write these pitches on the staff:

Sing the pitches one at a time. Then, sing them simultaneously, as a *chord.* This will emphasize that two melodies moving through the same chord tones at the same time may be performed simultaneously.

3. Substitute *Sandy Land* for either *Bow, Belinda* or *Skip to My Lou.* Notice the identical chord patterns.

ELABORATION

1. Choose two other songs which may be paired as a quodlibet (partner songs) and use them in a similar way. See lists below.

OTHER SONGS PAIRABLE AS QUODLIBETS

ANGEL BAND and SWING LOW, SWEET CHARIOT. NDM 4

EVENING and MORNING (rounds). SOM 5

GOODBYE, OLD PAINT and SWEET BETSY FROM PIKE. MMYO 2 and 4; NDM 4

I BELONG TO THIS BAND. SBM 4 (sing verse and refrain simultaneously)

NOW LET ME FLY and EZEKIEL SAW THE WHEEL. MMYO 4

SMALL WORLD. EM 4 (sing verse and refrain simultaneously)

THERE'S WORK TO BE DONE and NO NEED TO HURRY. NDM 5

TZENA. MMYO 5 (sing verse and refrain simultaneously)

BIBLIOGRAPHY

Beckman, Frederick. *Partner Songs* and *More Partner Songs*. Boston: Ginn & Co., 1958 and 1962. Collections of songs to be sung as quodlibets.

BOW, BELINDA

American Singing Game

Bow, bow, bow, Be-lin-da; Bow, bow, bow, Be-lin-da; Bow, bow, bow, Be-lin-da; You're the one my dar-ling.

SKIP TO MY LOU

American Singing Game

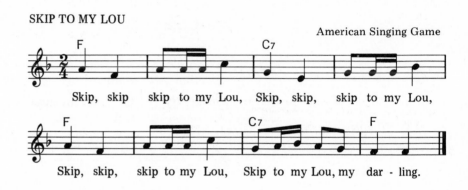

Skip, skip skip to my Lou, Skip, skip, skip to my Lou, Skip, skip, skip to my Lou, Skip to my Lou, my dar-ling.

American Indians do not sing many work songs. Groups harvesting corn or acorns did develop songs to accompany grinding. This Navaho song from Arizona is sung by a woman, accompanied by a steady drum beat. It was not unusual, however, for a Navaho man to sing grinding songs *for* the women as they worked.

Music Learning

A melody can exhibit a distinctive contour as it moves up or down or repeats.

Musical Context

CORN GRINDING SONG. Navaho Indian. EM 3

Behavioral Objective

To identify aurally the repeated pitches and the pitches that move up and down in a melody; and to demonstrate that recognition by tracing the contour of the melody as it is heard.

Grade

Upper

Materials

Recording: EM 3, rec 7; *Music of the Sioux and Navaho,* Folkways FE 4401.

Worksheet for each student, showing a line drawing of the melodic contour (see p. 178).

Draw "practice contour" on chalkboard (see below).

Distribute worksheets to students.

Focusing Statement

Navaho melodies often move through 1-3-5-6 of the scale, using an up-and-down contour.

LOOK AT THE LINE ACROSS YOUR PAPER. IS IT LEVEL, OR DOES IT ALSO MOVE UP AND DOWN? (Up and down, as well as level.)

WE'RE GOING TO LISTEN TO AN AMERICAN INDIAN MELODY THAT ALSO MOVES UP AND DOWN, AND STAYS THE SAME: JUST LIKE THE LINE.

Direct students' attention to the short segment of melodic contour on the chalkboard:

("Practice contour")

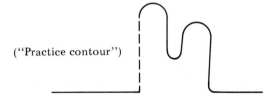

AS WE LISTEN FOR PRACTICE, MOVE YOUR ARM FROM LOW TO HIGH TO SHOW THE "UPS AND DOWNS."

DO YOU SEE THE DOTTED LINE? THAT MEANS TO MOVE UP VERY QUICKLY AND LEAP JUST AS THE SINGER'S VOICE DOES. HERE WE GO. Teacher traces contour on board as students trace in air.

 Play *only* first 22 beats of the song. (NOTE: "practice contour" ends with repeated pitches.)

THAT WAS TRICKY, WASN'T IT! LET'S PRACTICE AGAIN.

Stress correct labeling of high, low, and repeated tones.

Try at least once again, until most students understand the quick melodic movement from low to high, indicated by the dotted line.

Now prepare to play the entire recording.

PUT YOUR PENCIL DOWN ABOVE THE WORDS "BEGIN HERE" AND TRACE THE LOW AND HIGH TONES AS YOU HEAR THEM. TRY NOT TO TRACE TOO QUICKLY ON THE HORIZONTAL LINE REPRESENTING THE REPEATED PITCHES. Teachers *must* move throughout the class, to observe the degree of student success.

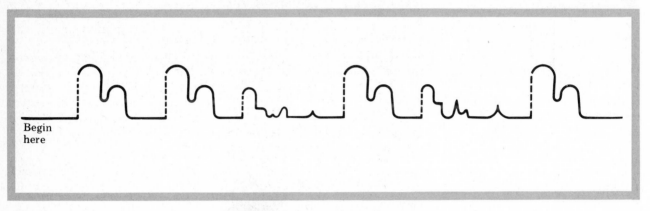

Begin
here

(Play entire recording.)

DID ANYONE FINISH TOO SOON? WHY? (They drew too quickly or slowly, not really listening for the high and low tones.)

Remind students, if necessary, about the function of the dotted line. LET'S TRY AGAIN.

By now, several students may be humming or singing the melody.

(Play entire recording. Students will enjoy hearing the music several times.)

Summary

LOOK AT YOUR CONTOUR DRAWING OF THE MELODY. HOW OFTEN DOES THE MELODY LEAP TO ITS HIGHEST POINT? (four) WHAT HAPPENS THE REST OF THE TIME? (Melody remains on the same, repeated tone. Some students will notice the two sections where the contour leaps to a "mid-point.")

DID YOU HEAR THE SINGER "KEEP TIME" WITH HER VOICE ON THOSE REPEATED TONES? TRY SINGING "HAY-YEA-YEA-YEA" FOR FOUR BEATS. ("Push" the breath on each *yea*.)

Vocal pulsation and nasality are typical of *Navaho* singing style.

"Rainbow tracing" is fun; use a different color on each hearing.

THIS IS HOW NAVAHO INDIANS IN ARIZONA SOUND WHEN THEY SING. LET'S FOLLOW THE MELODIC CONTOUR ONE FINAL TIME, AND LISTEN TO THIS "BEATING IN TIME" WITH THE VOICE.

ANOTHER TIME

Provide students with tape, recorder, headphones, and worksheet, so that they may work independently.

ELABORATION

1. View the excellent film *Discovering American Indian Music,* BFA Educational Media, 1971, 2211 Michigan Ave., Santa Monica, Calif. 90404. Dances, outfits, and songs of several groups are seen in this fine color film; includes a Navaho corn-grinding song.

2. Utilize these "What do you hear?" charts to measure perception of melodic direction:

SMB 1:20, rec 1, and 1:81, rec 5

SBM 2:23, rec 1, and 2:119, rec 5

SBM 3:32, rec 3

SBM 4:35, rec 2 (nos. 3, 4, 5)

3. See also "Crayon Activity" 16, SBM (EC):88

The text of the song used in this experience is not described in EM 3. It is a combination of *vocables* and Navaho language. (*Vocables* are comparable to "tra la la.")

4. Draw contour lines, and then speak them, using words or *vocables*.

5. Prepare a ditto master of a *familiar* melody, so that students can trace the melodic contour by drawing a continuous line to connect each note.

6. Listen to *Corn-Grinding Song* from Venezuela in NDM 5.

OTHER MUSIC FOR SIMILAR USE

INDIAN FOLK MUSIC (India; men and drum). NDM 5
NAVAHO NIGHT CHANT (American Indian). SBM 3, rec 4; SBM 5, rec 5
SAMA VEDIC CHANT (India; voices) SBM 5, rec 6
SILVERSMITH SONG (Navaho man, anvil). EM 3
SIOUX RABBIT DANCE (boy, drum). SBM 3, rec 4
WOMAN'S WEDDING SONG (Afghanistan). SBM 6, rec 1

BIBLIOGRAPHY FOR YOUNG PEOPLE

Hofmann, Charles. *American Indians Sing.* New York: John Day Co., 1967. Upper grades. An excellent survey, this book helps the reader understand the amazing vitality of oral literature, dance, and music in Indian life, past and present.

Hofsinde, Robert. *Indian Music Makers.* New York: William Morrow, 1967. "Graywolf" has written this book for upper grade students, describing the uses of music in Indian life, and also how to make several Indian instruments.

BIBLIOGRAPHY

Ballard, Louis. "Put American Indian Music in the Classroom," *Music Educators Journal,* 56, 7 (March, 1970), p. 38. Somewhat technical discussion of song style and vocal techniques, by an Indian educator and composer.

Lomax, Alan. "Song Structure and Social Structure," in *Readings in Ethnomusicology,* ed. David P. McAllester. New York: Johnson Reprint Corp., 1971, p. 227. Description of a monumental study by Lomax which attempts to understand what folk song is, and what it says. Fascinating summaries of what his cantrometric coding system has revealed about Amerindian and Negro African music, oriental bards, and musical acculturation; also an illuminating comparison of Pygmy-Bushman and European song style. Don't miss this!

Johnson, Charlotte. "Navaho Corn Grinding Songs," *Ethnomusicology,* 8, 2 pp. 102–120. A very informative article on the uses and texts of these songs.

Malm, William P. "Preparing the Music Teacher for Handling the Music of Non-Western Traditions," in *International Seminar on Teacher Education in Music,* ed. Marguerite Hood. U.S.O.E.: 1966, p. 194. The author, an ethnomusicologist, describes the ease with which his young daughter learned the traditional Japanese vocal style while the family lived in Japan.

See also "Bibliography," p. 24; and "Bibliography," p. 153.

Pronunciation guide:

gamelan - GAH-muh-lahn
anklung = AHN-klung
gupek   = goo-PEK
kempur = kehm-POOR

> The *gamelan* (percussion orchestra) from South Bali adds musical brilliance to village festivals. This *gamelan anklung* includes the small two headed drum (the *gupek,* beat with the hands), medium-sized gong *(kempur),* the tuned bamboo tube rattle *(anklung),* and metallophones with keys suspended over bamboo resonating tubes.
>
> The drums set the tempo in this piece, and the gong marks each phrase (difficult to hear in this recording), bamboo rattles shade each note, and the high-pitched metallophones elaborate upon the basic melody that is played by the low-pitched metallophones.
>
> It is this *low,* sustained melody that is the focus of this model experience. This basic melody is called the principal melody or nuclear theme. Many layers of elaboration are constructed around it (mostly above it) by the other instruments. *Gambangan* is divided into six "sections."

Music Learning

> A single melody can serve as the basis for an entire composition.

Musical Context

GAMBANGAN ("gahm-BAHNG-ahn") (from Bali). EM 6

Reading Objective

F♯, G♯, A♯ and C♯

Behavioral Objective

To identify aurally the basic melody of a composition, and to demonstrate that recognition by playing the melody and by raising hands when the melody is heard.

Grade

Upper

Materials

Recording: EM 6, rec 12; or *Indonesian Music from New Guinea, Moluccas, Borneo, Bali and Java* (Columbia KL 210; out of print but available in many libraries.)
Resonator bells and mallet (use two sets, if available)

Focusing Statement

LET'S LEARN TO PLAY A MELODY ON HIGH-PITCHED INSTRUMENTS, AND LATER WE'LL LISTEN TO IT.

Help students to locate F♯, G♯, A♯ and C♯ bars from the resonator bells. Place them on a table top or desk, evenly spaced, to approximate the keys on the metallophones used in *Gambangan.*

These pitches only approximate those heard on the Balinese instruments.

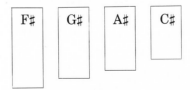

* is sometimes replaced by A♯-F♯ played quickly.

Write this on the chalkboard: F♯ A♯ C♯ A♯ F♯ A♯ C♯ F♯[*]
WHO IS ABLE TO PLAY THIS MELODY IN A SLOW, <u>STEADY</u> RHYTHM?
Select a student.

THAT WAS ONLY HALF A MELODY. HERE IS THE CONCLUSION. Write on the chalkboard:
(F♯ A♯ C♯ A♯ F♯ A♯ C♯ F♯) A♯ C♯ A♯ G♯ A♯ G♯
WE NEED ANOTHER PLAYER. (Select)
GOOD. NOW, TRY JOINING THE TWO PARTS.

(The same two students play the first part, then the second part.)

For more information about Bali, see Bibliography.

Teacher should practice, so as to be able to point to pitches in the notation as recording plays.

Gambangan is a recently developed form of composition making use of traditional gambang (cremation rite) melodies. This gambangan is played by a folk gamelan; it would not be notated.

1–2 3–4 5–6

slow fast slow

Summary

THIS MELODY IS USED SIX TIMES IN A COMPOSITION FROM BALI. THE LAST TIME IT IS PLAYED, IT ENDS LIKE THIS: C♯ A♯ F♯ (Write on chalkboard. Refer to complete representation below.)

I'LL HELP YOU LISTEN FOR THIS RECURRING MELODY IN THE RECORDING WE'RE GOING TO HEAR.

THE MELODY IS PLAYED ON THE LOW-PITCHED XYLOPHONE. RAISE YOUR HAND EACH TIME YOU HEAR THE MELODY BEGIN.

Replay recording as long as interest remains high. Most students will be quite fascinated by the tonal effects of this music, but will need many opportunities to listen.

ONE MELODY WAS HEARD OVER AND OVER AGAIN IN THIS GAMELAN MUSIC. Review how many times the melody was heard and that it was played on the low-pitched xylophone (only the drum sounded lower). Some students may also hear the many layers of melody produced by different instruments elaborating on this slow-moving, low-pitched melody.

The pitch labelled F♯ sounds on the recording *between* F and F♯. Third presentation of the theme (slow). Dots represent pulsations that can be felt.

The principal melody (read every pitch as a sharp: F♯, A♯, etc.)
F...A. ..C...A. ..F..A. ..C..F. ..A..C. ..A..G. ..A..G----
F....A. .C....A. .F....A. .C....F. .A....C. .A....G. .A.....G---
On the last (sixth) presentation, the theme is shortened:
F....A..C....A..F...A..C....F...C...A...F

ANOTHER TIME

1. Provide students with a tape recording of *Gambangan*. Perhaps they can learn to point to the cipher notation as they listen for the principal melody.

2. Learn to play the principal melody on a low-pitched metallophone. Because Balinese tuning differs from ours, the melody can only be approximated.

OTHER MUSIC

There are almost no recordings from Java or Bali included in the basal music series. You may wish to locate these commercial recordings. .

EXOTIC SOUNDS OF BALI. Columbia ML 4618

THE JASMINE ISLE. Nonesuch 72031

GAMELAN MUSIC OF BALI. Lyrichord LLST 7179

MUSIC OF THE VENERABLE DARK CLOUD. Institute of Ethnomusicology, U.C.L.A.: includes booklet with a valuable commentary and analysis by Mantle Hood and Hardja Susilo.

BIBLIOGRAPHY

The material in "Gambangan" has been reviewed for accuracy by Dr. William M. Anderson, School of Music, Kent State University.

Anderson, William M. *Teaching Asian Musics in Elementary and Secondary Schools: An Introduction to the Musics of India and Indonesia.* Adrian, Michigan: The Leland Press (Box 301), 1975. An outstanding source of information, materials, and resources for the teacher.

Hood, Mantle. *The Ethnomusicologist.* New York: McGraw Hill Book Co., 1971. "Introduction." A vivid comparison of the place of music and arts in the culture of Bali and in our own.

May, Elizabeth, and Mantle Hood. "Javanese Music for American Children," *Music Educators Journal* (April–May, 1962), p. 38. A "must" article! Describes a music-making experiment by elementary grade children, using authentic Javanese instruments.

McPhee, Colin, "Children and Music in Bali" in *Childhood in Contemporary Culture,* Margaret Mead and Martha Wolfenstein, eds., Chicago: Chicago University Press, 1955. Those interested in Orff Schulwerk will find this fascinating.

A Club of Small Men. New York: The John Day Company, 1948. A charming tale of a boys musical club in Bali.

Susilo, Hardja. "Musics of Southeast Asia," *Music Educators Journal,* 59, 2 (October, 1972), p. 35. For the general reader. Many fine photographs are also found in this special *Music in World Cultures* issue of the journal.

Music Learning	The rhythm of a melody can be varied when the melody is repeated.
Musical Context	SYMPHONY NO. 94 ("Surprise"), second movement, by Joseph Haydn ("HY-dn") (Austrian, 1732–1809). BOL 62; EM 2; SOM 6
Reading Objective	♩ and ♪ (See notation below.)
Behavioral Objective	To identify aurally the melodic rhythm of the theme; and to demonstrate this recognition by blinking a flashlight in that rhythm as rhythmic variations are heard.
Grade	Upper
Materials	Recording: BOL 62; EM 2, rec 7; SOM 6, rec 8 Flashlight Notation below, on chalkboard or chart.

Darken the room. Play the first 16 beats of the recording while you manipulate a flashlight so that the *melodic rhythm* "plays" or "bounces" on the ceiling. This will introduce the A theme of the composition.

Focusing Statement

WATCH MY FLASHLIGHT AS IT "PLAYS" THE MELODIC RHYTHM OF THE MAIN THEME. (Use the rhythm of the notation below.)

 Flashlight (teacher)   (Play first 16 beats of recording.)

To use flashlight, hold in one hand and strike it lightly on the other, or use a flashlight with a pushbutton.

Rhythm syllables may be used here:

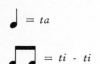

♩ = *ta*

♫ = *ti - ti*

A theme:

Using the rhythmic notation above, students should practice by clapping or tapping lightly. Then choose a student to manipulate the flashlight in time with the melodic rhythm in the recording. Play this main theme (16 beats) several times. Allow several students to use the flashlight. The class will then become familiar enough with the melodic rhythm and the theme.

Select a student to manage the phonograph.

 Flashlight   (Play *only* the first 16 beats.)

Choose one "player" to play the entire 32 beats (A theme twice).

Haydn is supposed to have remarked that this would cause the ladies to scream!

See "Bibliography for Young People" at end of this model experience.

Thus, students will hear the very loud chord that concludes this section and gives the symphony its popular name.

 Flashlight (Play until loud chord. Other students hum melody or sing rhythm syllables.)

I THINK YOU ARE ALL FAMILIAR WITH HAYDN'S THEME. NEXT, WE NEED TO HEAR HOW HE VARIED THE RHYTHM WHEN HE USED IT THROUGHOUT THE ENTIRE COMPOSITION.

· ·

For some classes, this may be enough work for one day.

Now, play the entire theme and variations. Give the flashlight to five different students, *one at a time*. To avoid stopping the recording, the teacher should take the flashlight when one student has finished a variation, and give it to the next student. The design of the movement is outlined below. While the rhythm of the theme is varied, encourage students to PLAY THE ORIGINAL RHYTHM. DO <u>NOT</u> FLASH THE B THEME. This will demonstrate that they can *conserve* that rhythm, and should be even better able to identify a rhythmic variation.

For B theme notation, see p. 186.
See Glossary.

Statement of A theme (32 beats), followed by B theme (32 beats)

Variation 1 (32 beats) with no rhythmic change; B theme (32 beats); the violins play a decorative countermelody above the theme.

 Variation 2 (32 beats) with no rhythmic change, though the last eight beats are varied melodically; B theme (32 beats). The theme shifts into minor and is played *fortissimo*.

Variation 3 (32 beats) ♪♪♪♪ replaces ♩ ♩ on first 16 beats, but not on repeat; B theme (32 beats). This variation, in a new rhythm, returns to a major key.

Variation 4 (32 beats); on the repeat ♩. ♪ replaces ♩ ♩; B theme (32 beats) is a new melody. Dynamics, register, orchestration, and accompaniment all change.

Coda includes brief statement of original rhythm, using new harmonies.

Summary

One entire playing may be enough for inexperienced classes. Summarize the listening by eliciting the information that HAYDN VARIED THE RHYTHM OF HIS ORIGINAL THEME. Discuss specific rhythmic variations with more experienced students.

ANOTHER TIME

Select two students to use two flashlights. Each will play eight beats of the 16-beat theme (8 + 8), which comprises the *musical period*. A different-colored cellophane might be placed over each flashlight.

ELABORATION

1. Use these Call Charts to provide experience in hearing theme and variation form:

SBM 3:108, rec 7 (*Sonate for Viola d'Amore and Viola* by Stamitz); SBM 5:69, rec 3 (*Theme and Variations on a Burgundian Theme, Pat-a-pan,* by Gerrish); SBM 6:138, rec 6 *(The Harmonious Blacksmith* by Handel); SBM 6:152, rec 7 (*Symphony No. 3,* third movement, by Beethoven).

2. Create rhythmic variations on familiar songs.

3. See "Varying a Musical Idea" (using *Yankee Doodle*), SOM 6:142

OTHER THEMES AND VARIATIONS SUITABLE FOR STUDY

CHESTER from *New England Triptych* by Schuman. MMYO 5, rec 3; EM 5

ENGLAND'S CAROL ("God Rest Ye Merry, Gentlemen") by The Modern Jazz Quartet. SOM 6

VARIATIONS ON A NEGRO FOLK SONG by Schmidt. SOM 4

VARIATIONS ON "AH, VOUS DIRAI-JE, MAMAN" ("Twinkle, Twinkle") by Mozart. MMYO 1 (excerpts) and 6 (complete); SOM 3

VARIATIONS ON "AMERICA" by Ives. NDM 4; SBM 1 (excerpts)

VARIATIONS ON "POP! GOES THE WEASEL" by Caillet. SOM 4, AIM 4, Vol. 1

VARIATIONS ON "SAKURA." EM 4; NDM 3; SBM 5, rec 3

BIBLIOGRAPHY FOR YOUNG PEOPLE

Burch, Gladys, and John Wolcott. *Famous Composers for Young People.* New York: Dodd, Mead, 1939. Upper grades.

Mirsky, Reba Paeff. *Haydn.* Chicago, Ill.: Follett, 1963. Upper grades.

Wheeler, Opal, and Sybil Deucher. *Joseph Haydn: The Merry Little Peasant.* New York: Dutton, n.d. Upper grades.

BIBLIOGRAPHY

Zimmerman, Marilyn P. "Percept and Concept: Implications of Piaget," *Music Educators Journal,* 56, 6 (February, 1970), p. 49. A valuable article which notes that rhythm pattern can be difficult for children to *conserve,* and urges teachers to work with such difficult materials and concepts.

B theme:

K

Melody: a linear succession of pitches; the horizontal structure in music.

*VOILES
   Melodies can be altered by replaying them in scales that reflect differing pitch relationships (major to whole-tone scale).

MINUET
   The twelve tones of a chromatic scale can be re-arranged in a composition (tone-row music).

Harmony: the simultaneous sounding of two or more pitches; the vertical structure in music.

JAMAICA FAREWELL
   Chord tones can be played one after another as a song accompaniment.

Melody: a linear succession of pitches; the horizontal structure in music.

*TUTU MARAMBA
   A melody can be varied by changing it from minor to major mode.

Rhythm: all of the durations that occur in music.

*SAMIOTISSA
   Duple and triple groupings of beats can alternate (asymmetric meter).

Melody; harmony: a linear succession of pitches (the horizontal structure in music); the simultaneous sounding of two or more pitches (the vertical structure in music).

*LECHU NIRANENO ARLAYIM SHOVA, ET AL.
   Musical texture results from the combining of melodic and harmonic elements (monophonic, polyphonic, and homophonic styles).

After completing each model experience, decide how successfully you are able to identify, explain or demonstrate the music learning that was the focus of the experience. Check the appropriate box.

*Group work-through experience

Secure
Fairly secure
Insecure

187

WORK-THROUGH EXPERIENCE

Music Learning

> Melodies can be altered by replaying them in scales that reflect differing pitch relationships (major to whole-tone scale).

Musical Context

VOILES (vwahl) by Claude Debussy ("deh-buu-SEE") (French, 1862–1918). EM 6; MMYO 5

Reading Objective

Writing accidentals to change B♭, C, and D to B♮, C♯, and D♯

Behavioral Objective

To substitute pitches B, C♯, and D♯ for B♭, C, and D in the melody of *Are You Sleeping?* and play the newly arranged song on resonator bells; to identify aurally and to describe verbally the similarities of whole-tone scale, tempo, dynamics, and timbre between the performance of the song and the composition by Debussy.

Grade

Materials

Recording: EM 6, rec 10; or MMYO 5, rec 5

Notation chart from model experience *Are You Sleeping?* (I), p. 122

Four sets of bells, preferably resonator bells (but can be done with two sets)

This experience *must* be preceded by model experience *Are You Sleeping?* (I), p. 122. (Song notation, p. 259)

---

1. Select one person to handle the phonograph and recording, and another the bells and book.

2. Four individuals should prepare to play the four phrases of *Are You Sleeping?* as developed in the model experience mentioned above. Rehearse each phrase separately, and then "stack" the phrases.

3. The arrangement you have just played is based on the F-major scale. Now, to give the song a more contemporary sound, use a *whole-tone scale.* You will need to substitute some pitches. Write the changes on the staff below.

    Pitches F, G, and A remain the same. Then:

    B♭ becomes B♮

    C becomes C♯

    D becomes D♯

To check your notation of the whole-tone scale, see end of the model experience.

F major scale   Whole-tone scale

4. Bell players should make these same changes in their bell parts.

5. Using these different bells, play through the song. Take turns, playing one phrase at a time. (*Do not stack* the phrases.)

6. Next, play *Are You Sleeping?* with all the parts *stacked.* Play *softly,* in a *slow* tempo. Each player does the two-measure phrase *four* times, then stops. At the end of this performance, everyone must be absolutely silent while the recording of *Voiles* begins.

To manage this, just before the last player finishes, set the needle on the recording with the volume control at its *lowest* level. Then gradually increase the volume so that the recording seems to "grow out of" the bell performance:

 As bells finish, they will fade into recording.

 (Increase volume to level desired.)

Grade: Upper

Whole-tone scale:

Notice how each tone is one whole step apart.

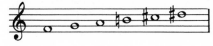

7. Discuss the similarities you heard between your playing and the Debussy piano music. Then fill in the following portion of the behavioral objective statement:

To identify aurally, and to describe verbally the similarities of scale, _____ , _____ , and _____ between the performance of *Are You Sleeping?* and Debussy's *Voiles.* (To check your accuracy, refer to the beginning of this model experience under "Behavioral objective.")

8. For what grade level would this experience be appropriate? What prior experience would be necessary? Would any changes be required in the learning sequence you have just experienced? Fill in the grade level you suggest in the box at the beginning of this experience.

ANOTHER TIME

1. Follow this with model experience *Are You Sleeping?* (II), p. 161.

2. Examine the realistic and impressionistic sea pictures on pp. 140–141, MMYO 5. How do these pictures relate to your playing and to *Voiles?* Which picture would better be compared with the *original Are You Sleeping?* (based on F-major scale)?

ELABORATION

1. Listen to other examples of impressionistic music (Ravel, Debussy); examine impressionistic paintings (Monet, Manet, Renoir). See BOL 70.

2. Experiment by changing other songs to a whole-tone context:

THE BIRD'S SONG. SBM 1

GOD BLESS ALL. DMT 4; NDM 4

LADY COME, p. 259 and SBM 2

MAKE NEW FRIENDS. DMT 3; EM 4; MMYO 4; NDM 3

MORNING. SOM 5

OTHER WHOLE-TONE MUSIC

REFLETS DANS L'EAU ("Reflections in the Water") by Debussy. DMT 5 (Notation for whole-tone theme is included.)

BIBLIOGRAPHY FOR YOUNG PEOPLE

Brower, Harriette. *Story Lives of Master Musicians.* Frederick A. Stokes Co.

Burch, Gladys, and John Wolcott. *Famous Composers for Young People.* New York: Dodd Mead and Co., 1941.

Harvey, Harry B. *Claude of France.* Lothrop and Co.

Music Learning	The 12 tones of a chromatic scale can be rearranged in a composition (tone-row music).
Musical Context	MINUET from *Suite for Piano,* op. 25, by Arnold Schoenberg ("SHURN-behrg") (Austrian-American, 1874–1951). MMYO 6
Reading Objective (optional)	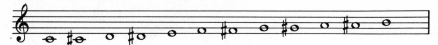
Behavioral Objective	To identify aurally, first, the stepwise movement (connected) of the 12 tones of a chromatic scale, then, the skipping movement (disconnected) that results when the 12 tones are rearranged into a 12-tone row, and to demonstrate these recognitions by describing the aural perceptions and by creating an improvisation on the tone row.
Grade	Upper
Materials	Recording: MMYO 6, rec 2 Resonator bells 13 bell mallets

Song notation, p. 283.

Teacher should practice playing the melodic rhythm of *This Old Man* on the 12-tone row before presenting this lesson.

Focusing Statement

I NEED 13 VOLUNTEERS. Line up 13 students side by side, facing the class. Give each a mallet. To student at left end (as you face them), give the resonator bell for low C, to the next student C♯, and so on, until you have constructed a chromatic scale (see illustration 1 in margin).

Have students examine the letter names on their bells. IF YOU HAVE A BELL WITH TWO NAMES (C♯/D♭, etc.), TAKE ONE STEP BACKWARD. (See illustration 2 in margin; this positioning allows students to visualize the keyboard arrangement of a chromatic scale. Note black-key groupings of two keys and three keys.)

Instruct bell players to play each bell in turn, starting with low C. A CERTAIN KIND OF SCALE WILL SOUND. IT IS A SCALE THAT MANY OF YOU HAVE DISCOVERED WHILE EXPERIMENTING WITH THE PIANO.

1. C C♯ D D♯ E F F♯ G G♯ A A♯ B C

2 black   3 black

2. C ⌐C♯ D D♯⌐ E F ⌐F♯ G G♯ A A♯⌐ B C

   (ascending scale)

Before discussing the sound, have players play the descending scale, starting with high C this time.

 (descending scale)

Discuss how THIS SOUND IS CREATED BY PLAYING EVERY PITCH BETWEEN THE TWO C's (or within any other octave) IN ASCENDING OR DESCENDING STEPWISE ORDER. Note the "connected" sound.

ONE WAY 20TH-CENTURY COMPOSERS HAVE FOUND TO CREATE A NEW KIND OF MUSIC IS TO REARRANGE THE CHROMATIC-SCALE PITCHES SO THAT THE PITCHES DON'T SEEM "CONNECTED," THE WAY THEY DO IN MOST SCALES WE KNOW.

Chromatic scale and 12-tone row can be visualized on pegboard. See model experience *Pianists*, p. 84.

THIS REARRANGEMENT CAN BE CALLED A 12-TONE ROW. BUT WE HAVE 13 BELLS. WHICH ONE DO YOU THINK WE WILL ELIMINATE? (One C, the higher one, to avoid any duplication of pitch names)

Number the remaining twelve bell players 1–12, from left (C) to right (B). Rearrange them by having them form a new line as you call out the *new order*. Announce slowly as they re-form the line:

Do *not* announce by pitch names.

Say: 2   12   7   6   9   10   1   3   11   5   4   8
      (C♯   B   F♯   F   G♯   A   C   D   A♯   E   D♯   G)

Ask all to listen to the new arrangement and decide if the pitches seem *connected* (conjunct or stepwise movement) or *disconnected* (disjunct or skipping movement):

 (If necessary, point to each player, in order to maintain a moderate tempo.)

Discuss stepwise movement of the chromatic scale versus the skipping pitch movement of this *12-tone row*.

(At this point, consider replacing the original 12 players with 12 new ones.)

Choose a student to direct those playing the tone row. Have student point to each player in turn. A rhythm pattern, such as the one below, will make the row sound more interesting.

 [*ti - ti   ta*]

Comment on the added interest of the rhythm pattern.

Teacher should play the tone row this time, noting that YOU WILL BE PLAYING THE RHYTHM OF A VERY FAMILIAR SONG. SEE IF YOU CAN FIGURE OUT WHAT SONG THE RHYTHM COMES FROM.

Have bell players move into a tight semicircle and hold bells in front of them, so that you can strike the bells easily. (They will not need their mallets from this point on.)

(teacher)

Before hearing their answers, play again to give all students a chance to determine the song on which the new "composition" is based.

Discuss. If no one recognized *This Old Man,* identify it for them. Play once more as all students quietly whisper the lyrics, in rhythm.

 (teacher)   (students chant)

For contrast, have class sing *This Old Man,* in the usual way, based on a *major* scale, rather than on a 12-tone row.

Establish pitch for singing by playing B-G♯-B from the bells in the row.

 (Sing one verse, unaccompanied.)

Discuss contrasts, particularly the connected *(conjunct)* sounds versus the disconnected *(disjunct)* sounds.

Choose one student to improvise on the tone row. DO YOUR "COMPOSITION" DIFFERENTLY FROM MINE. PLAY EACH SYLLABLE OF THIS OLD MAN, BUT DON'T USE THE RHYTHM WE KNOW. INSTEAD, SHORTEN SOME OF THE SYLLABLES AND LENGTHEN OTHERS. ADD SILENCES ANY-WHERE YOU LIKE. (See margin.)

THIS (silence) OLD-MAN-HE (silence) PLAYED (silence) ONE-HE-PLAYED-KNICK (silence) KNACK-ON-HIS (silence) KNEE, etc.

THE ONLY RULE TO FOLLOW THIS TIME IS THE RULE THAT SOME COM-POSERS HAVE FOLLOWED: USE THE ENTIRE ROW, THEN COME BACK TO THE BEGINNING AND REUSE THE ROW AS MANY TIMES AS YOU NEED TO FINISH.

YOUR COMPOSITION WON'T BE TOO LONG IF YOU PLAY THROUGH THE SYLLABLES OF THIS OLD MAN JUST ONCE.

 (student)

Summary

COMPOSERS ARE ALWAYS LOOKING FOR NEW WAYS TO ORGANIZE SOUNDS TO EXPRESS THEIR IDEAS. ONE WAY IS TO REARRANGE THE 12 TONES OF A CHROMATIC SCALE INTO A 12-TONE ROW.

AS YOU LISTEN TO A PIANO COMPOSITION BASED ON A TONE ROW, SEE HOW IT RESEMBLES WHAT WE'VE BEEN DOING TODAY.

   MINUET

Encourage students to verbalize their understandings of this music (disjunct, silences, "spareness" of sound).

ELABORATION

1. Individuals or small groups may create their own pieces by laying out a tone row of bells and working from the ideas below. First, establish the rule that a tone in the row, once used, may not be reused *until all 11 others have been used.* Students may think of ideas similar to those below.

> a. Use the row in *retrograde* (right to left, instead of left to right.)
>
> b. Play *every other* bell from left to right; return to play the ones skipped.
>
> c. Using two mallets, one player may play two adjacent bells simultaneously, progress to the next two, and so on.
>
> d. With bell row on a table, place two players on *opposite sides.* Each player will play from left to right (contrary motion). Take care to avoid mallet collisions. (Players might start at different times, for a *canonic* effect, or they might play at different tempos.)
>
> e. Use your imagination!

2. Encourage students to examine the tone row on which Schoenberg based his MINUET. See MMYO 6.

3. Listen to recordings and examine visual materials related to tone rows:

> DUALISMS NO. 1 by Eddleman, SBM 5
>
> DUALISMS NO. 2 by Eddleman, SBM 6

4. See SOUND PIECE 3, SBM 6:92, where instructions are provided on how to create and play your own *atonal* composition, using melody bells.

5. Listen to THREE PIANO PIECES by Schoenberg, NDM 6

6. See ROWS ARE STRANGE by Maves, NDM 6

OTHER TONE-ROW MUSIC

PARTING OF THE WAYS by Schoenberg. SOM 6
PRELUDE from *In Memoriam Dylan Thomas* by Stravinsky. EM 6
SYMPHONY NO. 3, first movement, by Riegger. NDM 6
TONE ROADS NO. 3 by Ives. EM 6
VIOLIN CONCERTO, first movement, by Berg. NDM 4

See Glossary.

BIBLIOGRAPHY

Fowler, Charles B. "The Misrepresentation of Music," in *Perspectives in Music Education: Source Book,* III, ed. Bonnie Kowall. Washington, D.C.: Music Educators National Conference, 1966, p. 289. An eloquent and persuasive article which urges music educators to utilize music which truly represents the world of music, including contemporary composers.

Holderried, Elizabeth Swist. "Creativity in My Classroom," *Music Educators Journal,* 55, 7 (March, 1969), p. 37.

Larsen, Ronald L. "Levels of Conceptual Development in Melodic Permutation Concepts Based on Piaget's Theory," *Journal of Research in Music Education,* 21, 3 (Fall, 1973), pp. 256–263. Third-, fifth-, and seventh-grade students manipulated the resonator bells in problems that included retrograde, inversion, etc. Technical; valuable.

Music using oil drums is a very special phenomenon which originated in the West Indies. After World War II, the steel drum (called *pan*) was developed from discarded oil drums, using a principle of construction unknown in any other instrument. They are played in ensembles which may include the *ping-pong* (soprano), *alto pan, guitar pan* (tenor), and *bass pan*. *Jamaica Farewell* is often played on steel drums in the West Indies.

Music Learning

Chord tones can be played one after another as a song accompaniment.

Musical Context

JAMAICA FAREWELL by Irving Burgess. NDM 6

Behavioral Objective

To identify, aurally and visually, chords with rearranged tones; and to demonstrate that recognition by playing those tones as an improvised accompaniment to a song.

Grade

Upper

Materials

Resonator bells and six mallets

Sketch of steel drum (see below) on chalkboard or reusable paper chart

Autoharp (for teacher)

Song notation, p. 241

Be sure students are able to sing JAMAICA FAREWELL.

Display chart or chalkboard sketch of prepared oil drum.

Focusing Statement

TO PREPARE AN OIL DRUM FOR PLAYING, WEST INDIANS CUT OFF THE BOTTOM OF A 55-GALLON OIL DRUM AND DIVIDE THE TOP INTO SECTIONS RESEMBLING A TURTLE'S SHELL.

Note that each section of the drum compares to one key on a piano or one resonator bell.

Similar to the *guitar pan:*

Lines are actually rows of tiny dents, made with the point of a nail.

Use high or low resonator bells, as indicated.

(To play in key of F, substitute B♭ for B.)

Roman numerals represent the *scale degrees* on which the chords are built.

As you write pitch names on the design, have one or two students set up resonator bells on a small table. Place D bell diagonally in center. Then place others around it, following the design on the board.

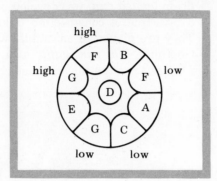

Use colored yarn (three colors) to separate the chord groups. Notice that C (*) is shared by two players (two chords).

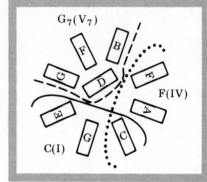

Assign three students, each with one mallet, to find one bell each: C, F, and G. THESE ARE THE <u>ROOTS</u> OF THE THREE CHORDS WE NEED TO ACCOMPANY <u>JAMAICA FAREWELL</u>.

Write on board: C   F   G₇   C
                     (I)   (IV)   (V₇)   (I)

Have bell players play four steady beats for each chord symbol, in the given order. Corresponding Autoharp chords, strummed by teacher, may help bell players.

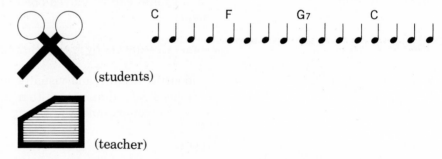

Next, add singers. Have chord root pattern played once as an introduction and repeat continuously as accompaniment to singing.

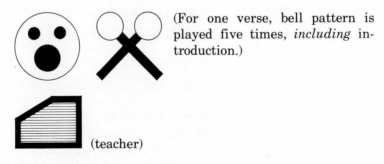

(For one verse, bell pattern is played five times, *including* introduction.)

More experienced classes may be called upon to build chords: C-e-g, F-a-c, G-b-d-f.

Add more pitches, as follows, to chord *roots* already on board:

		f		(Use small letters to distinguish
g	c	d	g	added pitches from chord *roots*.)
e	a	b	e	
C	F	G	C	
(I)	(IV)	(V₇)	(I)	

Give each player a second mallet. Each player will now handle a different chord of three or four tones. Encourage them to experiment by moving freely and quickly among the bells making up each chord.

IT DOESN'T MATTER IN WHAT ORDER YOU PLAY THE BELLS IN YOUR BROKEN CHORD. Remind them that THERE IS ONLY ONE FOUR-BEAT SPAN TO BE FILLED FOR EACH CHORD SYMBOL.

Note that the C- and F-chord players will be sharing the C bell, since this pitch is common to both those chords. (See diagram above.)

Guitar players: see p. 240 for an accompaniment to *Jamaica Farewell*.

(teacher)

Support this experimentation by strumming the harmonic progression on the Autoharp, calling out chord names as they occur.

Repeat above procedure, if desired.

Combine the bell players' "steel drum accompaniment" with Autoharp and singing, using one complete harmonic pattern as an introduction.

Summary

CHORD TONES CAN BE REARRANGED AND USED IN MANY WAYS TO MAKE ACCOMPANIMENTS INTERESTING. If appropriate, review the patterns of broken chords or arpeggios discovered by students.

ANOTHER TIME

1. Using Latin-type percussion instruments (or good homemade substitutes), create rhythm patterns to accompany *Jamaica Farewell*. (For some ideas, see the Courlander articles under "Bibliography," below.)

ELABORATION

1. View the excellent film *Music from Oil Drums,* 1956, by Peter Seeger, a Folkways film.

2. Read the information on steel drums in EM 6 and MMYO 6.

3. Listen to THE MUSIC OF TRINIDAD, National Geographic recording no. 3297 (1971) of steel bands.

4. Hear YELLOW BIRD in EM 6, played by the Barbados Steel Band.

5. Obtain the 16-page pamphlet *Story of the Steel Band* (Trinidad and Tobago Tourist Board). It is available free of charge from the Trinidad and Tobago Tourism and Trade Center, Suite 701, 200 S.E. First St., Miami, Florida, 33131.

/ = play the chord for an additional beat.

OTHER SONGS

● *Songs for similar use*

GUANTANAMERA. EM 5 (transpose up a major second to: G / A₇ / D / C /)

HEY LIDEE. NDM 2 (use this progression three times: C / / G₇ / / / C)

I LOVE THE MOUNTAINS. CMCM 3B (Use D / B min. / G / A₇ /)

LIMBO LIKE ME. NDM 6 (C / F C / / G₇ C)

LINSTEAD MARKET. MMYO 6; NDM 4 (C, F, G₇ chords, as indicated)

TINGA LAYO. EM 3 (F / C / G₇ / C /)

TZENA, TZENA. MMYO 5 and 6 (C / F / G₇ / C /)

WATER COME A ME EYE. EM 6; SBM 5 (D / / / A₇ / D /)

Many rounds are suitable because each phrase of a round is based on a specific harmonic progression.

BIBLIOGRAPHY

Carpentier, Alejo. "The Angel of the Maracas," *Music Educators Journal,* 61, 9 (May, 1975), p. 43. A brief history, with photos, of New World music and its composers. For the general reader.

Courlander, Harold. "Musical Instruments of Cuba," *Musical Quarterly,* 28, 2 (April, 1942), p. 227.

———. "Musical Instruments of Haiti," *Musical Quarterly,* 27, 3 (July, 1941), p. 371. An oversized *sansa* (thumb piano), played while held between the knees, is only one of the instruments described in this informative article. Photos are included.

Lewis, Olive. "Biddy Biddy, Folk Music of Jamaica," *Music Educators Journal,* 63, 1 (September, 1976), p. 38. Many songs for young people are notated.

Seeger, Peter. "The Steel Drum: A New Folk Instrument," *Journal of American Folklore,* 71, (January–March, 1958), p. 52. Detailed instructions for making steel drums.

Waterman, Richard. "African Influences on Music of the Americas," in *Acculturation in the Americas,* ed. Sol Tax. Chicago: University of Chicago Press, 1952, p. 213. A valuable summary for the generalist.

WORK-THROUGH EXPERIENCE

Music Learning

> A melody can be varied by changing it from minor to major mode.

Musical Context

TUTÚ MARAMBA (folk song from Brazil). SBM 5 (too-TOO mah-rahm-bah)

Reading Objective

See step 1 below.

Behavioral Objective

To identify aurally a melodic fragment and parts of a song played in both major and minor modes, and to demonstrate recognition of mode by circling *major* or *minor* on a worksheet.

Grade

Materials

Recording: SBM 5, rec 2

Bells (resonator or melody)

Three bell mallets

Tutú Maramba is based on two parallel scales, G major and G minor (harmonic):

G major	G minor
G	G
F♯	F♯
E	E♭
D	D
C	C
B	B♭
A	A
G	G

See song notation, p. 201.

Prior to beginning this experience, select individuals to:

> play melodic fragments *I* and *II* (see step 1 below);

> manage the phonograph and recording, and rehearse the "cues" indicated in step 6 below.

1. *Tutú Maramba* is a song in which these two melodic fragments are heard several times. When the song is played in *G minor,* fragment 1 will be heard, and when in *G major,* fragment 2. Listen to each fragment, played on the bells until you are acquainted with the *major* and *minor* sounds.

minor   *major*

2. The difference in the two fragments is in the overall range they encompass: the minor version embraces D to B♭ and the major version goes a half-step further, to B♮. This diagram may help you to understand the intervallic distances. (The pitches used in the melodic fragment are starred.)

See Glossary: "interval"

G	A♭	A♮	B♭	B♮

is enharmonically the same as:

G	G♯	A	A♯	B

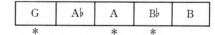

minor:

D		G	A♭	A	B♭	B
*		*		*	*	

major:

D		G	A♭	A	B♭	B
*		*		*		*

You will perceive the major fragment as spanning a greater distance than the minor. This is, in fact, the case: *B♮ is a half step higher than B♭.*

3. Discuss step 2 in other contexts: major and minor athletic leagues and other major and minor relationships.

4. Practice labeling the fragments *major* or *minor* as the bell players play their melodies for you. Bell players should plan the order in which they will play four examples.

As the four examples are played, circle your answer below:

1. MAJOR   MINOR   3. MAJOR   MINOR
2. MAJOR   MINOR   4. MAJOR   MINOR

5. Check correct answers as examples are replayed.

Repeat step 4, if appropriate.

6. Now play the recording of *Tutú Maramba*. The record manager should follow the "cues" below, calling out each number slightly before each phrase ends.

Call "1" as the introduction ends
Call "2" after the words "frighten you away"
Call "3" after ". . . cruel wings"
Call "4" after ". . . find you sleeping"
Call "5" after ". . . the morning light"
Call "6" after ". . . frighten you away"

Mark your answers on the chart below. You may want to play the selection more than once.

1. MAJOR   MINOR

2. MAJOR   MINOR

3. MAJOR   MINOR

4. MAJOR   MINOR

5. MAJOR   MINOR

6. MAJOR   MINOR

More experienced students may hear the tonality shift from major to minor or minor to major elsewhere in song. This experience focuses only on the sections that begin with these two melodic fragments.

7. Check answers (see left margin) as you replay the recording.

8. For what grade level would this experience be appropriate? What prior experiences would be necessary for success?

Summary

ANOTHER TIME

Answers for step 7:

1, 2, 5, 6 are minor; 3, 4 are major.

Encourage students to prepare an Autoharp accompaniment for *Tutú Maramba*. Note that all of the song, except the third section, is in *G minor*.

TUTÚ MARAMBA

Folk Song from Brazil
English Words by Julia W. Bingham

Tu - tú Ma - ram - ba, ___ stop scratch-ing at my door. ___

The mas - ter is home, He will fright - en you a - way. ___

Tu - tú Ma - ram - ba, ___ don't come here an - y more; ___

My child must be safe in his sleep, in his play. ___

Loud-ly ring - ing bells will drive a - way all e - vil things,

Things that lurk in dusk - y holes or dart on cru - el wings. ___

A - ran - ha Ta - tan - ha, A - ran - ha Ta - tan - ha,

If Tu - tú should come back, he must sure - ly find you sleep - ing.

A - ran - ha Ta - tan - ha, A - ran - ha Ta - tan - ha,

All night by your bed I my watch will be keep - ing.

Soft - ly sound the eve - ning bells that mark the com - ing night;

Na - ture sinks to peace - ful rest un - til the morn - ing light. ___

ELABORATION

1. Change the following melodies from major to minor by lowering the third scale degree by one half-step:

THE BIRD'S SONG. SBM 1

GO TELL AUNT RHODY, pp. 255, 281

GOD BLESS ALL. DMT 4; NDM 4

LADY COME, p. 259, SBM 2

MAKE NEW FRIENDS. DMT 3; EM 4; MMYO 4; NDM 3

MORNING. SOM 5

WHEN THE SAINTS, p. 256

NOTE: When the *sixth* degree appears in a melody it must also be lowered one half-step. An example is KUM BA YA, p. 269.

2. Use these "Call Charts" to develop experience in listening for tonality: SBM 5:127, rec 1 (*Waltz* by Schubert) and *Songs in Major or Minor*, SBM 6:77, rec 4.

3. Use these "What Do You Hear?" charts to evaluate perception of tonality: SBM 4:150, rec 10; SBM 6:83, rec 4 (all include major, minor, and atonal).

BIBLIOGRAPHY

Zimmerman, Marilyn P., and Lee Sechrest, "Brief Focused Instruction and Musical Concepts," *Journal of Research in Music Education,* 28, 1 (Spring, 1970), p. 25. This study indicated that *mode* is a difficult concept for children to grasp. Training on this concept is desirable.

WORK-THROUGH EXPERIENCE

Music Learning	Duple and triple groupings of beats can alternate (asymmetric meter).

Musical Context SAMIOTISSA ("sahm-YOH-tih-sah") (Greek folk song). SBM 5

Reading Objective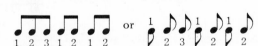

Behavioral Objective To identify aurally the alternation of groups of three and two steady beats; and to demonstrate that recognition in body rhythms and drumming.

Grade Upper

Materials Recording: SBM 5, rec 3

Double bongos (or other drum)

---

1. *Patsch* in *threes.* Use *left* hand on *left* thigh for "1" and *right* hand on *right* thigh for "2-3." Do several sets without stopping. (Someone may need to establish steady beat and start the group.)
Patsch (threes).

2. *Patsch* several sets in *twos;* again using *left* hand for accented "1" and right hand for "2."

　　Patsch (twos).

3. Alternate patschen in twos and threes, as follows:

You may wish to use this rhythmic/verbal cue:
　　LEFT right right, LEFT right right
　　LEFT right right, LEFT *ready change*
　　LEFT right, LEFT right, LEFT right, *ready change,*
　　LEFT right right, etc.
Patsch (four sets each of threes, then twos).

4. Now alternate in *this* manner:

Four sets of three, four sets of two, etc.

 etc. (3 + 2 + 2)

Patsch.

5. Repeat the above at a slightly faster tempo. Try to *patsch* the weak beats *quietly* and *stress* the strong "1" beats.

　　Patsch (as above: faster tempo).

6. Transfer the pattern in step 5 to the bongos or other drum. Start the movement on the thighs (if desired) and then transfer it, *without stopping,* onto the drum head.

　　As before, *left* hand should play the accented "1" (on the larger, lower drum) and the right hand should sound the weaker beats (on the smaller, higher drum).

 etc.

Listen for the tambourine as it is struck on each "1."

7. As soon as this seems fairly secure, play the recording of *Samiotissa.* Try to fit the 3 + 2 + 2 pattern to the recording. (See left margin below for aid.)

Patsch. etc.

8. Repeat step 7 until most students feel comfortable.

9. Alternating meters (threes and twos) make the rhythm of a piece seem "imbalanced" because we are accustomed to hearing music that is *consistently* in twos or threes. This should add to the evidence that each culture thinks about music in a different way.

Summary

10. Decide how many eighth notes (♪) would be contained in the pattern above (in steps 6 and 7).

If that were written as a meter signature, how would it appear? (See "Reading Objective" to verify your answer.)

ANOTHER TIME

In the classroom, make the recording of *Samiotissa* available (along with a drum) so students can refine their perception of asymmetric meter.

ELABORATION

Sa - mio - tis-sa, Sa - mio - tis-sa,
 <u>1</u> 2 3 <u>1</u> 2 <u>1</u>2 <u>1</u> 2 3 <u>1</u> 2<u>1</u>2

1. A typical Greek dance step is described in SBM 5:81. It involves stepping only on the accented "1's" of $\frac{7}{8}$ meter: <u>1</u> 2 3 <u>1</u> 2 <u>1</u> 2.

2. You may try to learn that dance in SBM, or an even simpler "grapevine step" described below. Move counterclockwise in a circle, arms in shoulder position. Step only on the accents (1's) as follows:

1—2—3	1—2	1—2	1—2—3	1—2	1—2
step **RIGHT**	left steps behind right	step **RIGHT**	left steps *in front* of right	step **RIGHT**	left behind right

Invent a "rhythmic/verbal cue" to aid in learning this dance. A suggestion might be: (begin with weight on *left*)

<u>1</u>23	<u>1</u>2	<u>1</u>2	<u>1</u>23	<u>1</u>2	<u>1</u>2
STEP,	back,	STEP,	front,	STEP,	back
	*		*		*

repetition is:

*Notice how these alternate.

<u>1</u>23	<u>1</u>2	<u>1</u>2	<u>1</u>23	<u>1</u>2	<u>1</u>2	
STEP,	*front,*	STEP,	*back,*	STEP,	front,	etc.
	*					

OTHER MUSIC WITH ASYMMETRIC BEAT GROUPINGS

ALBANIAN WEDDING SONG. MMYO 6

BLUE RONDO A LA TURK by Brubeck. SOM 4 (written in $\frac{9}{8}$ meter, but grouped as follows:
    A section: every four measures (36 beats) is grouped
    2 + 2 + 3 (3 times) = 27 beats } 36 beats
    3 + 3 + 3 (once)   = 9 beats }
    The B section is clearly in $\frac{4}{4}$ meter, and the A section returns to end the piece.

BULGARIAN FOLK MELODY. NDM 6

GERAKINA. MMYO 6 ($\frac{7}{8}$ meter)

HIPPOPOTAMUS. NDM 4

RAGA YAMAN. SBM 5

SEARCHING FOR LAMBS. SBM 4 ($\frac{5}{4}$ meter)

SIX DANCES IN BULGARIAN RHYTHM by Bartók. NDM 6

TAKE FIVE by Brubeck. SOM 6

TUNIS NEFTA by Ibert. MMYO 4 (bass part helps locate accents)

UNSQUARE DANCE by Brubeck. EM 4

WAKE UP NOW. SOM 4 ($\frac{5}{8}$ meter)

WALTZ by Russell. SOM 6 (*not* in triple meter!)

BIBLIOGRAPHY

Mynatt, Constance V., and Bernard D. Kaiman. *Folk Dancing.* Dubuque, Iowa: Wm. C. Brown Co., 1975, pp. 33, 58, and 59.

WORK-THROUGH EXPERIENCE

Music Learning

> Musical texture results from the combining of melodic and harmonic elements (monophonic, polyphonic, and homophonic styles).

Musical Context

LECHU NIRANENO ARLAYIM SHOVA (Hebrew chant). NDM 5

SIX CANONIC SONATAS, No. 1, third movement by Georg Phillipp Telemann ("TELL-uh-mahn") (German, 1681–1767). SBM 6

PRAISE THE LORD (Moravian hymn) by J. C. Bechler. MMYO 5

Behavioral Objective

To identify aurally a melody heard alone; two melodies moving simultaneously; and a melody and harmony moving in the same rhythm; and to demonstrate these recognitions by marking the appropriate drawing on a worksheet.

Grade

Upper

Materials

Recordings:

   LECHU NIRANENO . . . NDM 5, rec 10

   THIRD MOVEMENT — SBM 6, rec 6

   PRAISE THE LORD — MMYO 5, rec 3

   Worksheet for each student (see below)

---

1. Select one person to manage the record player and recordings.

2. Many writers refer to the fabric or texture of music. This can be a useful analogy. In music, the melodic (horizontal) and the harmonic (vertical) elements can be combined in many ways. In the worksheet below, you will see drawings suggesting three different musical textures.

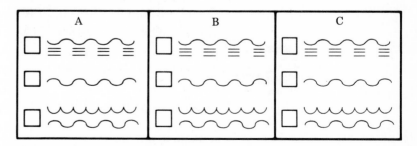

See Glossary.

3. Monophonic texture is represented by the single line. A melody performed without harmonic accompaniment is called *monophonic music.*

4. Polyphonic texture is represented by the bottom drawing, which suggests two independent melodies. *Polyphonic music* may consist of *many* independent parts (melodies).

5. *Homophonic* texture is depicted in the top drawing. A melody is heard at the "top" of the musical texture, with supporting tones (harmonies) under it. These lower tones may form chords, moving in a rhythm complementary to, but not detracting from, the melody.

6. Play each selection to identify its texture. Mark the appropriate drawing and verify the correct answer after each selection is played. (See left margin for answers.)

7. LECHU NIRANENO ARLAYIM SHOVA (use box A)

8. THIRD MOVEMENT (use box B)

9. PRAISE THE LORD (use box C)

10. Discuss and replay selections if appropriate. Try to formulate descriptions of these musical textures in your own words. Can you think of other arts in which texture is an important element?

11. For what grade level would this experience be appropriate? What background would be necessary?

ELABORATION

1. Look at "Identification of Musical Textures" in NDM 6:144.

2. Use the "Call Chart" 13 in SBM 3:144, rec 8, on texture.

3. See "Call Chart" 4 in SBM 6:98, rec 4 (polyphonic and homophonic styles, using Alleluia from Bernstein's *Mass.*

4. See *Ahrirang* (Korean folk song) and the photographic representation of all three textures in SBM 6:102-3.

5. Use "What Do You Hear?" chart 6, on texture in SBM 6:106, rec 5.

6. Provide a tape and worksheet of this kind of experience for use at an individual learning station.

OTHER MUSIC

● *Monophonic music*

ALLELUIA (Gregorian chant). NDM 5

SAMA VEDIC CHANT (India). SBM 5

O COME, O COME, EMMANUEL. SOM 6 (see song notation, p. 284)

Many other examples may be found.

● *Homophonic music*

CHESTER. MMYO 5

ETERNAL FATHER, STRONG TO SAVE. MMYO 5

THE GREAT GATE OF KIEV from *Pictures at an Exhibition* by Moussorgsky. BOL 82

Many hymns and hymn-style arrangements.

● *Homophonic music in a melody-with-accompaniment style*

DANCE OF THE SUGAR PLUM FAIRY from the *Nutcracker Suite* by Tchaikovsky. AIM 1 (II) BOL 58

BYDLO from *Pictures at an Exhibition* by Moussorgsky. AIM 2; BOL 82 (Ox-Cart)

TRAUMEREI by Schumann. BOL 63

ARABIAN DANCE and DANCE OF THE TOY FLUTES from *Nutcracker Suite* by Tchaikovsky. BOL 58; DMT 3; EM 2

● *Polyphonic music*

LITTLE FUGUE IN G MINOR by J.S. Bach. AIM 6; BOL 86

CANON FOR STRING QUARTET by Schoenberg. EM 5

CANZON À 12 IN ECHO by Gabrieli. EM 5

CANZONA NO. 2 FOR BRASS AND ORGAN by Gabrieli. EM 3; BOL 86

ORGAN FUGUE IN G MINOR by J.S. Bach. NDM 5

Other rounds, canons, and fugues may be used.

Answers to steps 6, 7, and 8:

6. A — monophonic (tenor voice)
7. B — polyphonic (Baroque recorders)
8. C — homophonic (brass instruments)

BIBLIOGRAPHY FOR YOUNG PEOPLE

Britten, Benjamin, and Imogen Holst. *Wonderful World of Music.* New York: Doubleday and Co., 1968.

SECTION TWO

Playing Instruments

The Autoharp Instructor

The Autoharp program offers beginning experiences playing the Autoharp. These experiences focus on learning to accompany melodies for classroom singing. Proceed through the program at your own pace. Note the factual labeling of music learnings and materials in the left margins.

Songs (in order of study)

- ARE YOU SLEEPING? (words only)
- THE FARMER IN THE DELL (words only)
- MISTER FROG WENT A-COURTIN'
- SHALOM, CHAVERIM
- HEY, HO! NOBODY HOME
- OH, SUSANNA
- TOM DOOLEY (words only)

Music Theory

- Steady beat
- Duple. triple, and quadruple meters
- Drones
- Primary chords (I, IV, V_7)
- Transposition
- Keys of *F major, C major, G major,* and *D minor*

Skills and Techniques

- Steady beat strums
- Mallet playing on strings
- Drones
- "Waltz" strum
- "Banjo effect"

A *chord* is three or more tones sounding together.

Autoharp and *ChromAharP* are trademark names for instruments designed for playing simple chords to accompany melodies. Chords can be produced by pressing buttons on the bars down firmly with the left hand and strumming across the strings with the right hand. The Autoharp player determines the chord needed ("by ear" or from notation), finds that chord bar, depresses it, and strums the chord. Because it is easy to play, the Autoharp is frequently used in the classroom, both by teacher and student.

Chord roots are the strongest tones of each chord.

There are two sizes of Autoharp manufactured—the 12-chord-bar model and the 15-chord-bar model. The letter names on the chord bars identify the chord roots. A diagram of the bar arrangements of the 12-chord and 15-chord Autoharps follows:

Autoharp accompaniments can be played in the keys of C, F, and G major on a 12-chord-bar Autoharp and the additional major keys of B♭ and D on a 15-bar model. Accompaniments can be played in the minor keys of A, D, and G on both models.

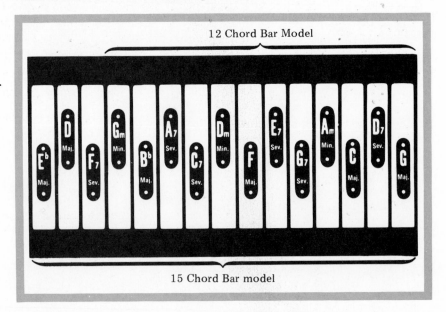

PLAYING POSITION

Place the Autoharp on your lap or on a table in front of you with the longest side near you. Rest your left hand on the chord buttons. Your right hand will strum across the strings. You can use a pick or use the fingernail of your index finger. Strumming is usually to the left of the chord bars in a crossover fashion, but beginners may more comfortably strum to the right of the chord bars. When you strum, start near your body and swing your hand outward across the strings.

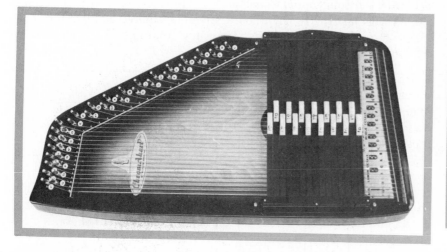
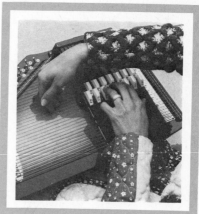

1
F-major chord

Notice that the *lower-pitched* strings are near the longer side and the *higher-pitched* are near the shorter side.

Examine the staff notation of Autoharp strings on p. 219.

Musical notation for *Are You Sleeping?* is on p. 259.

Pick the F string in the middle range of the Autoharp, if you need help with the starting pitch for singing.
/ = steady beat
F = First steady beat

● *Ready, Set, Go!* Place your left index finger on the F-major button and press it down firmly. Rest your other fingers on the neighboring buttons. Cross your right hand over and strum three or four times across the strings, remembering to swing your hand outward away from your body.

● Strum across the strings *without* pressing down a chord bar. Notice that *all* the strings sound! By pressing buttons on the chord bars, you damp certain strings. Those remaining strings, which sound, are the desired pitches for specific chords.

● While holding the F-major button down again, pick each string on the Autoharp. Discover which specific strings are sounding when the F-major chord bar is pressed down. The letter name for each string also appears on the Autoharp. Locate the names and write the letter names of the strings sounding for the F-major chord:

—— —— ——

● Strum steady beats continuously while you sing the song *Are You Sleeping?* The F-major chord will work for the entire song. Strum four times before you sing; think to yourself, "one, two, ready sing."

ARE YOU SLEEPING? French Round

F   /   /   /   /   /   /   /
Are you sleeping, Are you sleeping, Brother John, Brother John,
/   /   /   /
Morning bells are ringing, Morning bells are ringing,
/   /   /   /
Ding, dong, ding! Ding, dong, ding!

● Use the F-major chord to accompany the song *The Farmer in the Dell.* Strum a few times before you begin singing. Pick the C string in the middle range to locate the starting pitch for this song.

THE FARMER IN THE DELL   English Folk Song

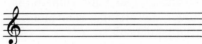

F   /   /   /

The farmer in the dell, the farmer in the dell,

/   /   /   /

Hi ho the derry o! The farmer in the dell.

● Locate the song *Lady, Come,* p. 259. This song may also be accompanied with just the F-major chord. Listen to the recording of the song (SBM 2), and learn the words. Then, try singing and strumming on the Autoharp.

2
C-major chord

● Locate the C-major button, and press it down firmly with your left index finger. Discover which strings are sounding when the C-major button is pressed down. Write the three different letter names for those strings here:

   ____   ____   ____

● Accompany the songs *Row, Row, Row, Your Boat* (p. 253) and *Three Blind Mice* (p. 254) with the C-major chord. (The starting pitch for "Row" is C—pick the string (C) in the middle range. Pick the E string in the middle range to locate the starting pitch for "Three.")

3
G-major chord

● Find the G-major button, and press it down firmly with your left index finger. Discover which strings are sounding for the G-major chord. Write the pitch names on the staff.

Refer to the grand staff (p. 272) if you need help with the pitch names.

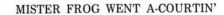

● Listen to the recording of the song *Mister Frog Went A-Courtin'* (MMYO 2). Learn to sing the song. Quietly strum the G-major chord as you listen and sing.

MISTER FROG WENT A-COURTIN'
                                                    American Folk Song

1. Mis-ter Frog went a-court-in' and he did ride, Um - hm! Um -

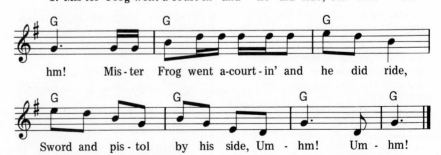

hm!   Mis-ter Frog went a-court-in' and he did ride,

Sword and pis-tol by his side, Um - hm! Um - hm!

2.   He said, "Miss Mouse, are you within?"
      "Oh yes, Sir, here I sit and spin."

3.   He took Miss Mouse upon his knee,
      And he said, "Miss Mouse, will you marry me?"

4.   Oh, where will the wedding supper be?
      Away down yonder in a hollow tree.

● Try singing the song, and strumming the accompaniment without the recording.

4
D-minor chord
mallet playing

● Locate the D-minor chord, press it down, and strum. What strings sound in the D-minor chord? Write the pitches on the staff below.

Accompany the song *Shalom, Chaverim* with the D-minor chord. Listen to a recording of the song (EM 5) if you are not familiar with the melody and words. Quietly strum the D-minor chord as you listen and sing. When you are able, sing and strum without the recording.

SHALOM, CHAVERIM

Israeli Round

● An interesting accompaniment for *Shalom, Chaverim* can be created by bouncing mallets (wood or rubber) on the Autoharp strings. While holding the D-minor chord button down, scrub or bounce lightly two or three mallets on the strings.

● Use the mallet playing to accompany *Shalom, Chaverim*. Ask a friend to strum a steady beat to the right of the chord bars on the same Autoharp, while you bounce the mallets to the left.

● Try some other songs that might be especially suited for the mallet-type Autoharp accompaniment:

ZUM GALI GALI. p. 287

ALA DAL'ONA. p. 139 (sing "la" throughout)

TUTÚ MARAMBA. p. 201

5

G-D drone

When two chord buttons with the same letter names are pressed simultaneously, the middle note of the chord does not sound.

● Press both the G-major button and the G-minor button down. Strum and listen to the sound. You should notice by picking the strings that *only two tones* are sounding: the G and the D. These two tones sounded together and repeated may serve as a *drone* accompaniment for the song *Hey, Ho! Nobody Home.*

● Try this accompaniment with a song. If you are not familiar with *Hey, Ho! Nobody Home,* listen to a recording of the song (MMYO 6). Learn to sing it, and practice strumming the steady beats. Try without the record as soon as possible.

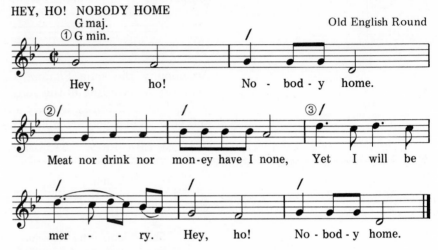

HEY, HO! NOBODY HOME

Old English Round

Hey, ho! No-bod-y home.
Meat nor drink nor mon-ey have I none, Yet I will be
mer - - ry. Hey, ho! No-bod-y home.

● Try some other songs with the G-D drone:

SCOTLAND'S BURNING. p. 283

MISTER FROG WENT A-COURTIN'. p. 212

ZUM GALI GALI. p. 287

6

key of
F major

F, C₇
chords

Play an introduction of four strums on the F-major chord before you begin singing.

● Now play using *two chords.* Put your left index finger on the F-major chord button. Then, place your middle finger on the button to the left: the C_7 chord. Alternate between the two chords several times, remembering to keep the buttons pressed down firmly until you are ready to change chords.

● Play the two chords in this order:

F / / C_7 / / / F
F / / C_7 / / F /

● You've just played the chordal accompaniment for the *refrain* of *Shoo, Fly.* Find the song notation on p. 229. Look at the progression of these chords in the *verse* part. Listen to the recording (MMYO 2) and learn to sing the song. Practice changing chords silently as you listen and sing. Try without the recording as soon as possible.

● Practice other songs which use the F and C_7 chords:

THE WIND BLEW EAST. p. 14

CLAP YOUR HANDS. p. 105

SWEET POTATOES. p. 287

A RAM SAM SAM. p. 233

7
key of F major
F, B♭ chords	"waltz strum"

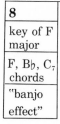

F major scale	F	>		
	E	>		
	D			
	C	5	(V)	
	B♭	4	(IV)	
	A	>		
	G			
	F	1	(I)	

Steady beats may be grouped in three. (triple meter)

♩ ♩ ♩ = **3** or **3**
                ♩   **4**

● The F-major chord (built on the first degree of the F-major scale) and the C₇ chord (built on the fifth degree of the F-major scale) are the two chords most often needed to accompany a song in the key of F major. The B♭ chord is the other chord often used to accompany a song in F major. Place your ring finger on B♭, the chord built on the fourth degree of the F-major scale.

● Alternate between the F and B♭ chords. These chords will allow you to accompany the song *Lovely Evening,* p. 267. Try playing one strum per measure.

● Next, try a "waltz strum" to accompany *Lovely Evening.* This strum is especially suitable for songs with beat groupings of three. Sweep the lower, thicker strings once, then, the higher strings twice (=low, high, high). Strum three times in each *measure* of *Lovely Evening,* using the low-high-high positions.

● Use the "waltz strum" for these songs:

BLOW THE MAN DOWN. MMYO 5

CLEMENTINE. MMYO 4, SBM 5

DOWN IN THE VALLEY. EM 5, MMYO 3, NDM 2, SBM 5

OLD PAINT. p. 281

ON TOP OF OLD SMOKY. EM 5, MMYO 4 & 5

SILENT NIGHT. p. 231 (Key of B♭; use 15-bar autoharp)

STREETS OF LAREDO. EM 6

THE CUCKOO. CMCM 3A, EM 4

8
key of F major
F, B♭, C₇ chords
"banjo effect"

Primary chords are the chords built on the:

first step of scale—I
fourth step of scale—IV
fifth step of scale—V

● Let's use three chords: F, B♭, and C₇. The fingering for these chords will be:

F — index finger

B♭ — ring finger

C₇ — middle finger

These three chords are the primary chords in the key of F major.

● Use these three chords to accompany the song OH, SUSANNA. You'll find that you only need to use the B♭ chord once. Listen to the MMYO 2 recording and learn to sing the song. Practice changing chords silently. Then, sing and strum the steady beats without the recording. (Disregard the strum marks above the notation for now.)

Notice the beat groupings of two in *Oh, Susanna.* (duple meter).

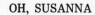

OH, SUSANNA

Words & Music by Stephen Foster

I— came from Al - a - ba-ma, With my ban-jo on my knee,

I'm— going to Loui - si - an-a, My true love for to see;

It — rained all night the day I left, The weath - er it was dry;

The— sun so hot I froze to death; Su - san-na, don't you cry.

Refrain

Oh, Su - san - na, Oh, don't you cry for me,

I've— come from Al - a - ba-ma, With my ban-jo on my knee.

● *Oh, Susanna* might sound especially interesting with an Autoharp accompaniment that creates a "banjo effect." Strum to the *right* of the chord bars, and strum in a rhythm that is *faster than the beat.* (♫) Use a flat pick, and strum four times per measure. Alternate between the lower and middle registers (low, middle, low, middle,), as indicated by strum marks.

● Try other songs using the "banjo effect":

DIXIE. MMYO 5

MICHIE BANJO. MMYO 3

I'VE BEEN WORKING ON THE RAILROAD. MMYO 3

POLLY-WOLLY-DOODLE. MMYO 3

BOATMEN'S DANCE. MMYO 6

9
key of C major
C, F, G₇ chords

C-major scale

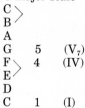

C ⟩
B /
A
G   5   (V₇)
F ⟩ 4   (IV)
E /
D
C   1   (I)

Notice the beat groupings of four in *Tom Dooley.*

♩ ♩ ♩ ♩ = **4/♩** or **4/4**

● Find the three primary chords for the key of C major. The fingering is:

    I — index finger
    IV — ring finger
    V₇ — middle finger

Write the letter names of these three chords below. Check the C-major scale in the margin for help.

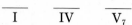

   I   IV   V₇

● Accompany the song *Tom Dooley* with the C and G₇ chords. Pick the G string for the starting pitch. Play four strums on the C-major chord for an introduction.

TOM DOOLEY   American Folk Song

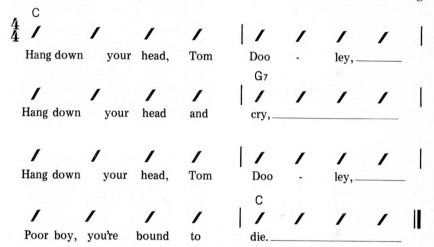

● Use the C and G₇ chords to accompany these songs:

    GO TELL AUNT RHODY. p. 255
    JINGLE BELLS. p. 255
    LOVE SOMEBODY. p. 256
    ROW, ROW, ROW YOUR BOAT. p. 253
    THREE BLIND MICE. p. 254
    SKIP TO MY LOU, p. 176

● Use the C and F chords to accompany KOOKABURRA, p. 285.

● Use the C, F and G₇ chords to accompany:

    BATTLE HYMN OF THE REPUBLIC. p. 281
    KUM BA YA. p. 269
    WHEN THE SAINTS GO MARCHING IN. p. 256
    JAMAICA FAREWELL. p. 241

10

key of G major

G, D₇ chords

trans-position

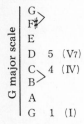

G major scale

G
F♯
E
D   5   (V₇)
C   4   (IV)
B
A
G   1   (I)

● Perhaps singing *Tom Dooley* in the key of C major required you to sing *too* low. Try accompanying the song instead in G major. Find the chord that you will play with your index finger (I) and the chord that you will play with your middle finger (V₇). Refer to the G-major scale in the margin. Write the letter names of these two chords:

_____   _____   (key of G major)
  I   V₇

● Examine the *Tom Dooley* chord chart. Substitute the G-major chord for the C chord and the D₇ for the G₇. You have now transposed *Tom Dooley* from C major to G major. Sing and strum the chords in this new key. Your starting pitch will be D.

● Use the G and D₇ chords to accompany the songs:

     GO TELL AUNT RHODY. p. 281

     FAIS DO DO. p. 278

     BINGO. p. 49

     SANDY LAND. p. 234

     DOWN IN THE VALLEY. MMYO 3

     HUSH, LITTLE BABY. SBM 2

● Use the G, C, and D₇ chords for these songs:

     AMAZING GRACE. p. 236

     THIS LAND IS YOUR LAND. MMYO 3 & 5

11

key of D minor

D-minor, G-minor, A₇ chords

D minor scale

D
C(♯)
B♭
A   5   (V₇)
G   4   (IV)
F
E
D   1   (I)

● Locate the three primary chords in the key of D minor. Write the letter names of the chords below; use the D-minor scale in the margin, if you need help.

_____   _____   _____   (key of D minor)
  I   IV   V₇

● Accompany the song *Hold On* with these three chords. Examine the musical notation and words on p. 262. Listen to the recording (SBM 4) until you are able to sing and play the chords for *Hold On*. Strum two times per measure.

● Use the D-minor, G-minor, and A₇ chords to accompany the *Hanukah* song on p. 289. Sing on "la" or other neutral syllable.

12

four or more chords

● You're ready to try songs that use more than three chords. Find the song *The Frog and the Mouse* on p. 289. This song is in D minor but uses an additional chord. Strum two times per measure. Use the EM 3 recording if you need help learning the song.

● Locate *Minka* on p. 288. This song is in the key of G minor. Try one strum per measure. Use the MMYO 6 recording to learn the words and practice the strumming.

● *Tutú Maramba*, p. 201, will give you practice with the chords in G major and G minor. Strum two times per measure. Use the recording (SBM 6) to learn the song, and practice the strumming.

● *Joe Turner Blues,* on p. 243, will give you an opportunity to play the "blues" chord progression in C major. Strum two times per measure. Practice with the MMYO 6 recording to learn the song and strumming.

● Try songs in any of the basal text elementary school series. Chords are usually indicated for those songs that may be accompanied on the Autoharp.

13
tuning the Autoharp

● All the teacher's editions of the SBM series EC−6 include a page of clear instructions entitled *Tuning the Autoharp.*

● A recording entitled *Tuning Your Autoharp* (Oscar Schmidt-International, Inc., Garden State Rd., Union, N. J. 07083) is available to assist in tuning.

● Consult the tuning sections in the books specified below.

BIBLIOGRAPHY

John, Robert W. and Charles H. Douglas. *Playing Social and Recreational Instruments.* Englewood Cliffs, N.J.: Prentice-Hall, Inc., 1972. Information on tuning is given on pp. 29–33.

Nye, Robert E., and Meg Peterson. *Teaching Music with the Autoharp.* Union, N.J.: Music Education Group, 1973.

Peterson, Meg. *The Many Ways to Play the Autoharp,* 2 vols. Union, N.J.: Oscar Schmidt-International Inc., 1966.

Winslow, Robert W., and Leon Dallin. *Music Skills for Classroom Teachers.* Dubuque, Iowa: Wm. C. Brown Co., 1971, p. 170. (Tuning information on p. 171.)

Musical notation of the register and range of the Autoharp

The Guitar Instructor

This program in folk guitar offers opportunities for learning chords and right hand techniques. It uses songs appropriate for children, in keys suitable for children's voices. Each unit focuses on one song and introduces chords or right-hand techniques (or both). Beginning players and those with previous experience will benefit from study of every unit, learning new songs, music theory, and right-hand techniques. Each unit ends with a list of familiar songs (from the basal music series) which make use of either the same chords or the same right-hand techniques that were studied in the unit. These additional songs will provide beginning players with more practice and allow experienced players to expand their repertoire.

Songs

- JOHN THE RABBIT (words only)
- LOVELY EVENING (words only)
- JANE, JANE
- SHOO, FLY
- SILENT NIGHT
- A RAM SAM SAM
- SANDY LAND
- AMAZING GRACE
- SKIP TO MY LOU
- JAMAICA FAREWELL
- TOM DOOLEY (words only)
- JOE TURNER BLUES

Music Theory

- Major and minor chords (thirds)
- Chord root, third, fifth, seventh
- Triple, compound, quadruple meter
- Tonal center
- Chromatic scale
- Scale
- I, V_7 chords
- Half steps
- Triad seventh chord
- Syncopation

Skills and Techniques

- Chords (in order of study): E minor, E major, A major, D major, A_7, E_7, B_7, G major, D_7, C major, G major, G_7, F (small bar)
- Right-hand techniques: brush, root, scratch, arpeggio, plucking, bass run, alternate bass, syncopated, hammer-on, mute.
- Tuning
- Vocal tune-up
- Use of capo
- Transposition

Also: chord charts, ukulele chord charts, ideas for finger-picking, hammer-on, bass runs

The Guitar

The guitar and the lute originated in Asia. Guitar-like instruments have a nearly flat back, and the lute has a round back. The guitar began to be widely played in late-17th-century Europe. This increase in popularity reflected the efforts of amateurs to match the artistry of the prestigious (and more accomplished) lutenists. Indigenous guitars may still be heard in South America, Asia, and Russia, but the modern guitar is one of the most widely used instruments in folk and popular music throughout the world.

Because electronic amplification of guitars is commonplace today, the nonamplified instrument is often referred to as the acoustic guitar. The advantages of amplification include control of tone quality, sustaining power, and widely variable levels of volume. In a group including several amplified guitars, each instrument functions in a different musical role, with one or more serving as the lead.

SELECTING A GUITAR

The *classical guitar* is a lightly built instrument with a mellow tone. Strings are nylon, though the three bass strings are wrapped with steel. Because these nylon strings are easier on the fingers, the classical guitar is often recommended for beginners.

The *flat-top guitar* has a narrower neck than the classical guitar and is strung with steel strings. They have a bright, lively sound. Individuals with very large hands and thick fingers may have difficulty using the flat-top guitar. Beginners should use light-gauge strings for ease in playing.

Check the quality of a guitar by looking for tight joints and an unwarped neck and fingerboard. Strings should not buzz or rattle. Ask someone to play the instrument, being sure it is correctly tuned. Assuming you have competent help, buy as expensive an instrument as you can afford (and a hard case to carry it in). A cheap guitar will be difficult to play.

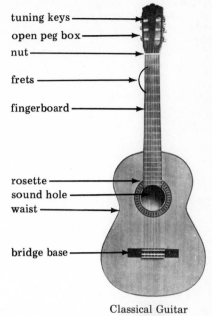

tuning keys
open peg box
nut
frets
fingerboard
rosette
sound hole
waist
bridge base

Classical Guitar

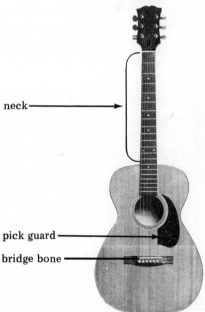

neck

pick guard
bridge bone

Flat-top Guitar

PLAYING POSITION

Hold the guitar with the neck at an upward angle. Folk guitarists usually hold the instrument at about a 15-degree angle (upward) from the floor. Do *not* allow the neck to drop below a horizontal position, even though you may see many popular performers doing this. Your ability to perform many finger-picking styles will be hampered if you do this, because the reach of the fingers will be restricted.

Keep the face of the guitar in a nearly vertical position, close to the body. In place of the footstool used by classical guitarists, folk performers usually cross the right leg over the left and place the waist of the guitar on the right thigh. The right-hand forearm rests on the edge of the guitar, just above the bridge.

ARM AND HAND POSITIONS

In general, keep the left-hand palm away from the neck of the guitar. If you clamp the hand tightly around the neck, you will inhibit the maximum reach for the fingers. Fingers of the left hand should be arched, and the wrist is dropped. "Pinch" the neck between the thumb and second finger of this hand.

The right-hand position varies. It is a good practice to keep the thumb extended toward the tuning keys of the guitar. The wrist will bow out slightly. Fingernails of both hands need extend no farther than the pads of the fingers.

TUNING

Only a few beginners are able to tune accurately, so it may be best to ask a friend or your instructor to take over this important task initially.

The first skill required is the ability to compare the sound of two guitar strings and decide if they are sounding the same pitch. It can be helpful to tune your guitar to that of a friend. Tuning methods which compare the sound of a guitar to the differing timbre of a piano or pitch pipe seem of little help to beginners. Some persons find they can tune a guitar string to a vocal hum. A tuning fork helps others.

While tuning, twist the tuning key with the left hand while you *continuously pluck* that same string with the right-hand thumb. You will hear the pitch going up or down. This will help when you use the system of *relative tuning*. Follow these steps:

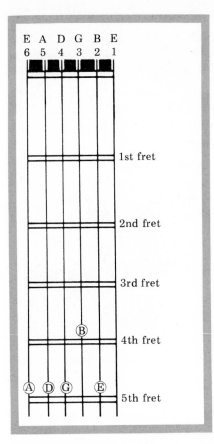

Relative tuning

(See conclusion of the Guitar
Instructor for tuning to piano.)

● Tune the bass E string.

● With the second finger (left hand), fret that same E string at the *fifth* fret (see right). Match the next A string to that pitch.

● Fret the A string at the *fifth* fret. Match the next D string to that pitch.

● Fret the D string at the *fifth* fret. Match the next G string to that pitch.

● Fret the G string at the *fourth* fret. Match the next B string to that pitch.

● Fret the B string at the *fifth* fret. Match the next E string to that pitch.

● Play an E-minor or E-major chord to check your tuning.

Some individuals reverse the steps in relative tuning.

Many times, it is easier to tune a string that is much lower than it should be. If a string is difficult to tune, try *lowering* it below the required pitch, and gradually bringing it up.

GETTING READY TO PLAY

● Obtain an elastic *capo* for a 12-string guitar. The 12-string capo will be somewhat stronger than the six-string capo. A metal capo may also be used.

● Memorize the pitch names and numbers of the guitar strings:

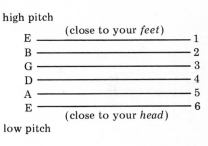

high pitch

	(close to your *feet*)	
E		1
B		2
G		3
D		4
A		5
E		6
	(close to your *head*)	

low pitch

● Learn the finger numbers or designations for each hand:

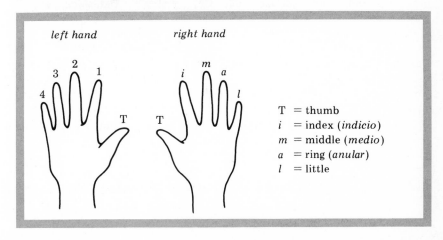

T = thumb
i = index (*indicio*)
m = middle (*medio*)
a = ring (*anular*)
l = little

1
E minor E major
brush
major, minor

JOHN THE RABBIT. *John the Rabbit* is used in a model experience of the same title. Notation may be found in the *Piano Instructor*, p. 266. The song recording is found in MMYO-Kg, rec 6 and SBM 2, rec 9.

● Study the chord frame and photographs for the E-minor and E-major chords. Notice that when the fingers are already in the E-minor position, only the first finger needs to be added in order to play the E-major chord.

E minor

E major

● Practice changing between these two chords. With the right hand, brush the thumb from low pitch (close to your head), to high pitch.

● Examine the song text below. Note that the E-major chord begins on ". . . if I live, Oh, yes!" and continues to the end. Now sing and play the song, using the recording if necessary. The arrows indicate a *steady beat brush* of the right hand thumb.

Vocal tune-up: high E°

voice

E° = high E string, open (not fretted)

● To begin *John the Rabbit* it will be helpful first to "tune up" your voice. Pluck the highest E string and hum that pitch. Quickly hold the E-minor chord position, brush two steady beats for an introduction, and begin singing.

JOHN THE RABBIT

American Folk Song
Collected by John W. Work

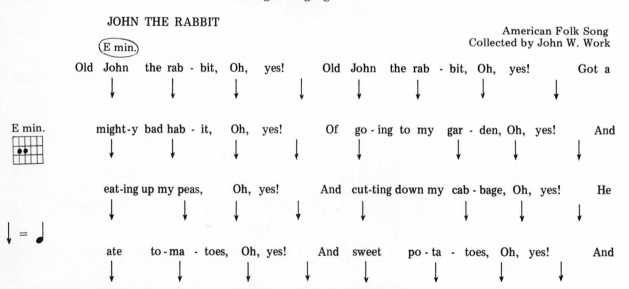

E maj.

(E maj.)	if	I	live,	Oh,	yes!	To	see	next	fall,	Oh,	yes!
↓	↓			↓		↓		↓		↓	↓

	I	won't	plant,	Oh,	yes!	A	gar	-	den at	all!
	↓		↓	↓		↓			↓	↓

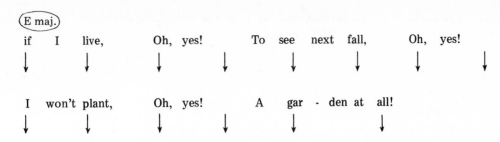

- The E-minor and E-major chords sound similar partly because they share the same *root,* E.

- The difference in sound is produced, on the guitar, by the use of the index finger. The E-minor chord does *not* use the index finger; as a result, the open G string sounds.

- The E-major chord *does* use the index finger. It is placed in the first fret (on the G string) to produce the pitch G♯ (G-sharp).

- This is the only difference between the two chords.

- The terms *major* and *minor* (greater and lesser) which are used to describe this difference refer to the distance between the root (E) and the G or G♯:

$$\text{Major}\ \left.\begin{matrix}\text{G♯}\\\text{G}\\\text{F♯}\\\text{F}\\\text{E}\end{matrix}\right\}\ \begin{matrix}\text{third}\\\ \\\ \\\text{root}\end{matrix} \qquad \text{Minor}\ \left.\begin{matrix}\text{G}\\\text{F♯}\\\text{F}\\\text{E}\end{matrix}\right\}\ \begin{matrix}\text{third}\\\ \\\text{root}\end{matrix}$$

- Other songs which can be accompanied throughout by either the E-minor or E-major chord:

> ARE YOU SLEEPING? p. 259. Substitute the E-major chord for the F-major. Tune up by plucking the high E string (E°).

> SHALOM, CHAVERIM. p. 213. Use E minor in place of D minor. Tune up by plucking the B string (B°).

> SKIN AND BONES. p. 278. Use E minor. Tune up on high E°.

> ZUM GALI GALI. p. 287. Use E minor in place of G minor. Tune up on high E°.

2
E, A
triple meter
tonal center

LOVELY EVENING. Song notation, p. 267.

- Examine the chord frame for the A-major chord. Notice that all three fingers are placed within the same fret.

A maj.

	1	2	3

R

- The root (or strongest chord tone) is labeled "R" below the chord frame. Using the right-hand thumb, pluck this A string, then *rest the thumb on the adjacent* string below. *Without lifting,* brush down the remaining four strings. Quickly bring the thumb up again and brush the remaining four strings once more.

- The sound will be "thumb-brush-brush," for triple meter in *Lovely Evening.*

E maj.

R

- Review the chord frame for E major. Locate the root on the bass E string (string 6). Pluck the root, as above, and brush the remaining strings twice.

- Practice alternating between the E-major and A-major chords.

T_6 = thumb plucks E string

T_5 = thumb plucks A string

T ↓ ↓ = ♩ ♩ ♩
triple meter

LOVELY EVENING

Traditional Round

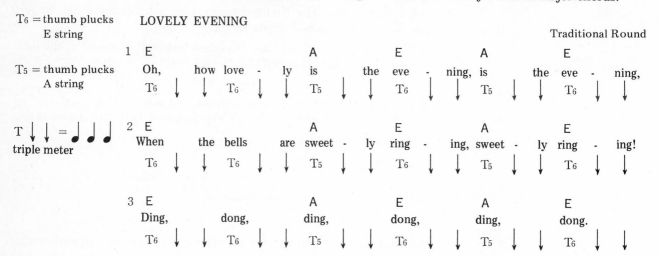

1 E   A   E   A   E
   Oh,   how love - ly is   the eve - ning, is   the eve - ning,
   T₆   ↓   ↓ T₆   ↓   ↓ T₅   ↓   ↓ T₆   ↓   ↓ T₅   ↓   ↓ T₆   ↓   ↓

2 E   A   E   A   E
   When   the bells   are sweet - ly ring - ing, sweet - ly ring - ing!
   T₆   ↓   ↓ T₆   ↓   ↓ T₅   ↓   ↓ T₆   ↓   ↓ T₅   ↓   ↓ T₆   ↓   ↓

3 E   A   E   A   E
   Ding,   dong,   ding,   dong,   ding,   dong.
   T₆   ↓   ↓ T₆   ↓   ↓ T₅   ↓   ↓ T₆   ↓   ↓ T₅   ↓   ↓ T₆   ↓   ↓

E (sounds F)   A (sounds B♭)

R   R

*When no other designation follows a chord name (as, "minor"), the chord is a *major* chord.

**Not every melody begins on the tonal center, but nearly all will *end* on it.

- To begin singing *Lovely Evening,* tune up by plucking and humming the pitch of the first or highest E string.

- To play *Lovely Evening* along with a piano player (using F and B♭ chords), try the *capo.*

When the capo is placed across the first fret, the strings are shortened (see right). The guitar player still plays the E-major and A-major chords, but they will sound *higher.*

Finger the E* and A chords just as before.

- Though two different chords are used in LOVELY EVENING, the song began and ended on the E-major chord. (In this song, the melody also began and ended on E.**

The *tonal center* of the *Lovely Evening* melody is E. Therefore, the song is said to be "in the key of E." The chord which uses E for its *root* is called the *tonic* or I ("one") chord.

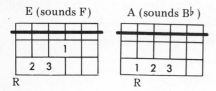

3
E minor
thumb-scratch
root chromatic scale

E minor

R

JANE, JANE. Recording: SMB 4, rec 9 (also used in a model experience).

- Review the E-minor chord, and locate the *root* of this tonic (I) chord.

Pluck this root with the thumb, so that it rings out as a single pitch.

Now, using the index and middle fingers, *scratch downward*. This will produce a bright, lively sound. Alternate between the thumb and the scratch. During this scratch, the wrist rotates.

- Listen to the song recording and play along.

Pay careful attention to the guitar strum, as noted below the song words. The thumb often plays while the voice is resting ( ). A good, solid thumb stroke helps to emphasize this syncopation.

JANE, JANE

American Folk Song

2. Hey, hey, Jane, Jane,
   My Lordy, Lord, Jane, Jane,
   I'm a-gonna buy, Jane, Jane,
   Three hunting dogs, Jane, Jane,
   One a-for to run, Jane, Jane,
   One a-for to shout, Jane, Jane,
   One to talk to, Jane, Jane,
   When I go out, Jane, Jane.

3. Hey, hey, . . .
   My Lordy, Lord, . . .
   I'm a-gonna buy, . . .
   Three muley cows, . . .
   One a-for to milk, . . .
   One to plough my corn, . . .
   One a-for to pray, . . .
   On Christmas morn, . . .

4. Hey, hey, . . .
   My Lordy, Lord, . . .
   I'm a-gonna buy, . . .
   Three little blue birds, . . .
   One a-for to weep, . . .
   One a-for to mourn, . . .
   One a-for to grieve, . . .
   When I am gone, . . .

Vocal tune-up:

guitar: E⁷ (sounds B)

voice

Seventh fret often indicated by a dot on the guitar neck.

● As soon as possible, sing *Jane, Jane* without the recording. To tune up for singing, place the left hand, first finger, on the high E string, *in the seventh fret. This will sound B,* the starting pitch (see below). Hold the E chord, then play two "sets" of the thumb-scratch as an introduction.

● Some individuals may be challenged to investigate the chromatic scale. Using the high E string, play it first *open,* then place the first finger in each consecutive fret until the seventh fret is reached. The pitches sounded will be:

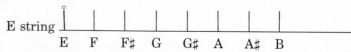

E string

E　F　F♯　G　G♯　A　A♯　B

At the conclusion of the Guitar Instructor there is a drawing of the entire range of pitches produced on the guitar. Study that drawing to learn how the chromatic scale progresses by adjacent *half steps.* Discover that between E-F and B-C there are no intervening sharp or flat names.

● Other songs using E *minor* or E *major* as the tonic (I) chord and suitable for the "thumb-scratch" strum:

HEY, HO! NOBODY HOME, p. 214. Tune up on high E°.

This substitution of chords is called *transposition* (see Glossary).

MISTER FROG WENT A-COURTIN', p. 212. For the G major chord, substitute the E-major chord, and use it throughout. Tune up on B°.

OLD HOUSE. MMYO 2. Use E minor throughout. Tune up on high E°.

'TATERS. SBM 3. Use E minor throughout. Tune up on E⁷.

4
D, A₇
scratch
scale
I, V₇

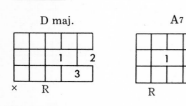

D maj.　　　A₇

×　　R　　　R

X = do not sound

SHOO, FLY

● Look at the D-major chord frame. Place the left hand fingers firmly just behind the fret. If the fretted strings produce a "buzz," you need to either press more firmly or move the fingers closer toward the fret.

● Examine the A₇ chord. (It is similar to the A major, and shares several pitches.)

● Locate the root of each chord. Use the same thumb-scratch as in *Jane, Jane.*

The D-major chord root is the D (T₄ in the notation for *Shoo, Fly* and the A₇ root is the A (T₅ in the notation).

Practice moving between these two chords, using the thumb-scratch.

T₄ ↓ = ♪♪

ti - ti

● Sing and play as soon as possible. The vocal tune-up is on high E, second fret (E²) (sounds F♯).

(If the song is unfamiliar, listen to the recording in MMYO 2, rec 4. It will be most difficult, however, to play along with the fast tempo. To play along with the recording, it is also necessary to place the capo in the third fret, and then to finger the D and A₇ chords.)

SHOO, FLY

American Game Song

Vocal tune-up: guitar: high E² (F♯)

voice

D.C. = return to the beginning and play to *Fine*.

= hold

● Look at *Shoo, Fly* and find the words "I belong to somebody." These words move through adjacent pitches:

Scala means "ladder" in Italian.

At this point, the melody is moving through the tones of a *scale*.

● The different tones used in *Shoo, Fly* may be arranged into a scale. Scales are usually presented in ascending order. Here is the complete major scale for *Shoo, Fly:*

Major scale: ∨ designates *half steps*. The other intervals are *whole* steps.

D	E	F♯	G	A	B	C♯	(D)	
		∨				∨		D major scale
1	2	3	4	5	6	7	(1)	
do	re	mi	fa	so	la	ti	(do)	

Beginning on the open D string play this scale "by ear."

The D-major chord (I) is located on the first scale degree (the tonal center). Can you locate the scale degree that serves as the root of the A₇ chord?

*dominant-seventh

**This substitution of chords is called *transposition*.

It is the fifth scale degree, so the chord is often labeled V_7 ("five-seven").*

● Other songs with only the I and V_7 chords (use the "thumb-scratch" strum):

BOW, BELINDA. See model experience, p. 176. Substitute D major or for F and A_7 for C_7.** Tune up on B^3 (sounds D).

CLAP YOUR HANDS. See model experience, p. 105. Substitute D major for F, and A_7 for C_7. Tune up on B^3.

GOOD NEWS, see p. 280. Transpose to D. Tune up on high E^2 (sounds F♯).

LONDON BRIDGE. Tune up on high E^5.

LOVE SOMEBODY, see p. 256. Transpose to D. Tune up on B^3.

MERRILY WE ROLL ALONG, see p. 279. Transpose to D. Tune-up is high E^2.

OLD PAINT, see p. 281. Transpose to D. Tune up on E^7 (sounds B). (Triple meter)

ROW, ROW, ROW YOUR BOAT, see p. 253. Tune up on B^3.

THE WIND BLEW EAST. See model experience. Transpose to D. Tune up on B^3.

| 5 |
| A, D, E_7 |
| arpeggio |
| triad |

SILENT NIGHT.   Recording: NDM 6, rec 6 (key of B♭).

● Study the chord frame for the E_7 chord. Locate and play the root.

● Hold the A chord, then rest the right-hand thumb on top of the A string.

Place the fingers of the right hand as follows:

—ring finger *(a)* just *under* the high E string;

—middle finger *(m)* just *under* the B string;

—index finger just *under* the G string.

● Without moving the thumb, snap each finger, one at a time, into the palm of the hand. Begin with index *(i)*, then middle *(m)*, then the ring *(a)*.

Each finger should remain in contact with the string until it is time to play.

E7

A maj.

D

● Next, pluck the thumb (root: A string), then play each string in turn: *i, m, a.*

Finally, create a six-beat pattern to fit *Silent Night* by allowing the middle and index fingers to play again at the end of the pattern:

T₅   *i*   *m*   *a*   *m*   *i*   This is an *arpeggio* strum.

● Practice this pattern several times. Try it with all three chords. No matter what the chord, *the index, middle, and ring fingers play the same three strings.*

However, the thumb strikes a different root for each chord. See the chord frames.

● As soon as possible, sing and play *Silent Night.*

● Study the E₇ chord frame; practice the arpeggio. It is notated as written in one of the sixth-grade basal music books. For the music to sound in the written key of B♭, the capo must be placed in the first fret.

● The vocal tune-up is high E°.

*When singing *Silent Night* with lower-grade children, capo in fret II or III. These keys are more appropriate for their higher voices.

SILENT NIGHT
Optional: capo in fret I to sound B♭

Words by Joseph Mohr
Music by Franz Grueber

● Some players may wish to enhance the accompaniment by playing the pattern *twice as fast* as suggested. It could be indicated as follows:

● The arpeggio strum sounds chord tones one at a time. Play the A-major chord slowly and listen to the tones. From low to high they are E, A, E, A, C♯, and E.

Notice there are only three different pitch names; the others are duplications. This grouping of tones is a *triad:* a specific type of chord sounding *three* different pitches.

Interval = a musical distance. See Glossary.

● The name of this chord is A. Because the root is A, the chord is "spelled" A-C♯-E (from the root up). From A to C♯ is the interval of a third (B is skipped). From C♯ to E is the interval of a third (D is skipped). Most chords are formed using intervals of a *third*.

● *Other songs suitable for the arpeggio strum:*

First decide whether the song requires patterns of four or six beats.

If there is a meter signature of 2/4 or 4/4, try a four-beat pattern.

If there is a meter signature of 3/4 or 6/8, try a six-beat pattern.

AMERICA, THE BEAUTIFUL. See p. 270. Substitute A major for C, D major for F, E_7 for G_7. Capo in fret I.

GO TELL AUNT RHODY. See p. 258.

HUSH, LITTLE BABY. See p. 290. Substitute D major for A, and A_7 for E_7.

KUM BAH YA. See p. 269. Substitute D major for C and A_7 for G_7. The G chord is also needed (in place of the F chord).

For more advanced players:

ALL THE PRETTY LITTLE HORSES. CMCM 1-A, EM 2. Use E minor, B_7.

GREEN GROW THE LAURELS. EM 6. Substitute D major for F, G major for B♭, A_7 for C_7, and E minor for G minor. Capo in fret I or II.

I KNOW WHERE I'M GOIN'. CMCM 3-A. Substitute E major for F, B_7 for C_7, A for B♭.

JOHNNY HAS GONE FOR A SOLDIER. EM 6. A minor, C major.

SCARBOROUGH FAIR. CMCM 3-A, MMYO 6, SBM 5. D minor, A minor, G, C, A, B♭, G minor.

STREETS OF LAREDO. EM 6. Substitute E major for F, B_7 for C_7, A major for G minor.

WILD MOUNTAIN THYME. SBM 6. Substitute D major for F, G major for B♭, and B minor (see chord chart for D minor).

WINDS OF MORNING. SBM 5. D, G, A_7.

6
E, B_7
thumb,
scratch-a

B_7

	1		
2	3		4

× R

A RAM SAM SAM. Recording: MMYO Kg, rec 3. (Also used in a model experience.)

● Examine the chord frame for B_7. Notice that string 6 is not sounded.

● Review the E-major chord.

When moving between these two chords, *do not lift the second finger of the left hand.*

This chord progression may require considerable practice. Remember to pluck the root separately, and scratch the remaining three or four strings with the first and second fingers.

E maj.

R

- Vary that strum slightly by doing this:
  - After the downward scratch by the first and second fingers.
  - Quickly scratch back up toward your head.

Rotate the wrist while doing this.

A verbal cue might be:

"thumb,   scratch - a"   *ta*   *ti - ti*

T   ↓   ↑   =   ♩   ♫

- As soon as possible, sing and play *A Ram Sam Sam.* To play along with the recording, it is necessary to capo in fret I. Play the E and B_7 chords as indicated, and they will sound one half step higher (F and C_7).

Vocal tune-up is B°.

A RAM SAM SAM

Folk Song from Morocco

E maj

R

B7

×R

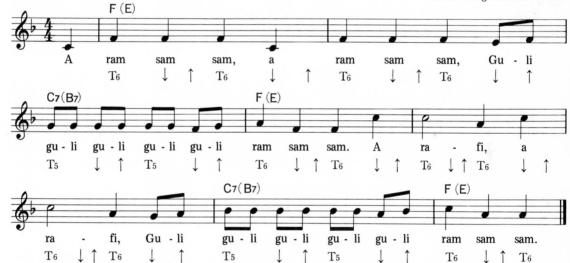

Pronunciation: ah RAHM sahm
sahm
GOO-lee
ah RAH-fee

- Other songs to chord "by ear" with the E and B_7 chords (all *begin* and *end* on the E chord):

  SKIP TO MY LOU.

  THIS OLD MAN.

  MARY HAD A LITTLE LAMB. EM 1

  DOWN BY THE STATION. EM 2

7
G, D_7
thumb-pluck
transposition

SANDY LAND   Recording: EM 3, rec 2.

You have just been playing the I and V_7 chords in the key of E major (E and B_7).

- Now look at the I and V_7 chords in G major. Finger the G-major chord. Locate the root.

- Do the same for the D_7 chord.

- Practice moving between these two chords. Pluck the root each time. Considerable practice may be necessary. The fourth finger is sure to seem weak at first!

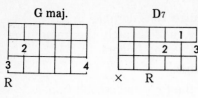

G maj.   D7

● Try a useful new strum, in which several strings are plucked simultaneously:

Finger the G-major chord.

Rest the right hand thumb on the bass E string.

Place the other fingers as follows:

—ring finger (*a*) just *under* the highest E string;

—middle finger (*m*) just under the B string;

—index finger (*i*) just under the G string.

Bunch the fingers together with the tips touching the strings.

Without moving the thumb from the E string, pull the other *fingers simultaneously up and into the palm* of the hand. The arm moves very little.

● Now, alternate between the thumb playing the root of the chord and the fingers plucking the three highest strings simultaneously. Try this verbal cue:

" thumb,   pluck,   thumb,   pluck" etc.

$$T \qquad {}^{a}_{m}_{i} \qquad T \qquad {}^{a}_{m}_{i} \qquad = \qquad ♩ \quad ♩ \quad ♩ \quad ♩$$

● Listen to *Sandy Land.* Learn to sing the song, and fit the chords to the music as indicated.

The vocal tune-up is E^7.

SANDY LAND

Folk Song from Oklahoma

1. Make my liv-ing in sand-y land, Make my liv-ing in sand-y land,

Make my liv-ing in sand-y land, La-dies, fare you well.

2. Raise my ta-ters in sand-y land,
3. Keep on dig-ging in sand-y land,

Make up your own verses!

● Other songs using G and D$_7$ (I or tonic; V$_7$, or dominant-seventh):

Chord these songs "by ear," using the G and D$_7$ chords. Every song will begin and end on the G chord. In unit 6, you played some of these same songs using E and B$_7$. Now, you will be *transposing* these songs from the key of E to the key of G.

DOWN IN THE VALLEY

THE FARMER IN THE DELL

LOOBY LOO

MARY HAD A LITTLE LAMB

SKIP TO MY LOU.

THIS OLD MAN.

TOM DOOLEY.

8
G, C, D$_7$
thumbpluck
bass run

AMAZING GRACE. Recording: SBM 6, rec 3. (Also listen to the *Amazing Grace Collage,* SBM 6, rec 3.)

In this song, you will use the I, IV, and V$_7$ chords in the key of G major: G, C, and D$_7$.

● Study the chord frame for C major. Locate the root, and practice this chord using the "thumb-pluck" strum just learned in *Sandy Land.* Because *Amazing Grace* is in triple meter, the strum must be varied to become "thumb, pluck, pluck."

● Review the D$_7$ chord. When going between the D$_7$ and C-major chords, *keep the first finger of the left hand down.* Practice this movement, using the strum suggested.

● Sing and play the song. Pluck every root, stressing the triple meter.

AMAZING GRACE

Early American Melody
Words by John Newell

Vocal tune-up: D°

1. A - maz - ing___ grace how sweet the sound,

That saved a___ wretch like me!___

I once___ was___ lost but now am___ found,

Was blind but___ now I see.___

2. 'Twas grace that taught my heart to fear,
   And grace my fears relieved;
   How precious did that grace appear,
   The hour I first believed!

3. Through many dangers, toils, and snares,
   I have already come;
   'Tis grace has brought me safe thus far,
   And grace will lead me home.

This song can be played in the key
of E. Make these changes:
G becomes E
C becomes A

4. The Lord has promised good to me,
   His word my hope secures;
   He will my shield and portion be
   As long as life endures.

• Shape notes grew out of a system of sight-singing widely used in America and England during the 17th and 18th centuries. These particular symbols were devised in 1802 and used throughout the rural South.

◢ = half note

◣ = quarter note

◢♪ = eighth note

A bass run often uses scale degrees 5-6-7-8.

do re mi fa so la ti do

Look at this interesting article by George H. Kyme: "An Experiment in Teaching Children to Read Music with Shape Notes" in the *Journal of Research in Music Education*, 8, 1 (Spring, 1960), p. 3.

• Now try a technique that adds interest to accompaniments: the *bass run*. This is a succession of individual pitches played on the bass strings. The run usually connects the root of one chord to the root of another.

For example, playing G-A-B-C connects the roots of the G-major and C-major chords.

To begin, hold the G-major chord, using the alternate fingering. Use the second finger to play notes on the second fret, and the third finger to play notes on the third fret. The run will be fingered:

$$E^3 \quad A^0 \quad A^2 \quad A^3$$

(pitches sounded) G   A   B   C
                   G   C
                   chord   chord

● Step-by-step directions:

Hold the G-major chord;

—Pluck the bass E string (E^3);

—Pluck the open A string;

—Place the second finger in the second fret of the A string and pluck it;

Hold the C-major chord, and pluck the A string (A^3).

Use this bass run between the G and C chords in *Amazing Grace* on the words "grace" and "lost."

● Some individuals may wish to try the following pattern between the D_7 and C-major chords. It may be used in AMAZING GRACE at the words "me" and "now."

fingering: D^0 E^0 E^2 E^3
(use base E)
pitches sounded   D   E   F♯   G
                  D_7 G
                  chord   chord

D_7 becomes B_7

● Several other frequently used bass runs may be found at the conclusion of the Guitar Instructor.

● Use bass runs as introductions, between sections of a song, and at the final cadence of a song.

● Other songs for bass runs in triple* meter:

DOWN IN THE VALLEY. SBM 5. G, D_7

GREEN GROW THE LAURELS. EM 6. Substitute D major for F, G major for B♭, A_7 for C_7, and E minor for G minor. Capo in fret I or II.

STREETS OF LAREDO. EM 6. Substitute E major for F, B_7 for C_7, and A major for G minor.

HAMMER SONG. SBM 5. D, G, A_7

THIS LAND IS YOUR LAND. MMYO 3 and 5. C, G, D_7.

Many songs composed by guitarists seem to suggest bass runs; country-and-western music has many good examples.

*To play bass runs in quadruple meter, insert a *scratch* between the first and second notes, as:

9
C, G₇
root, alternate

SKIP TO MY LOU.   (Also used in a model experience.)

● Look at the chord frame for the G₇ chord. When playing this and other G chords, keep the palm *away from the neck* of the guitar. The thumb should be positioned behind the fingers, about in the middle of the neck.

Practice moving between the G₇ and C-major chords. Pluck the root of each.

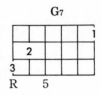

● Next, learn to play an *alternate bass*. The strings to be used are labeled "5" under the chord frames.

For the G₇ chord, alternate the right-hand thumb between the bass E and the D string (string 6 and string 4):

● The C-major alternate bass is somewhat more complicated. Finger the C chord. Pluck the root with your right-hand thumb.

Now *lift the left-hand third finger across to the bass E string.* Stay in the third fret for both. This is suggested by the ◯ in the chord frame.

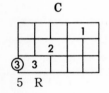

● Practice this movement. Your right-hand thumb will be alternating between the fifth and sixth strings: T₅ T₆

At the same time, the left-hand third finger alternates between those same two strings, in the third fret.

● At first, play and sing *Skip to My Lou* plucking the root and alternate bass, shown by the T symbols below. (The complete plucking pattern is described below.)

The vocal tune-up is high E°.

SKIP TO MY LOU

2. Little red wag - on, paint - ed blue,
3. Lost my part - ner, what'll I do?

ti - ri ti - ri

Four to one beat

Chords may use more than three pitches.

● The strumming pattern shown opposite is often called "Woody's lick" because it was used a great deal by the Oklahoma balladeer Woody Guthrie.

Simultaneously plucking the index (*i*), middle (*m*), and ring (*a*) fingers is already familiar through *Sandy Land* and *Amazing Grace*.

● The *arpeggio* is performed very rapidly. It might help to learn this rhythmic cue:

"thumb, pluck,   ti - ri, ti - ri"

C: T₅ $\frac{a}{m}$ T₆ *i m a*   =

Remember that the *i, m,* and *a* pluck the three highest-pitched strings (G, B, E).

As you sing and play SKIP TO MY LOU using "Woody's lick," play two "sets" as an introduction.

● The alternate bass may be explained in relation to chord roots. The C triad is spelled (by thirds) C-E-G. C is the root, E the third, and G the *fifth*. This fifth (labeled "5" under the chord frame) is the tone most commonly used in alternation with the root. This G is played on the bass E string, fret III.

The G₇ chord uses G-B-D-F. G is the root, B the third, D the fifth, and F the seventh. The root (G) usually alternates with the fifth (D). The fifth is sounded on open string D.

● Other songs suitable for this strum:

CLAP YOUR HANDS, p. 105. Transpose to E major.

OH, SUSANNA, p. 216. Transpose to E major.

HAMMER SONG. SBM 5. D, G, A₇

OLD BRASS WAGON. EM 2. G, D₇

POLLY WOLLY DOODLE. EM 4. Transpose to E major.

THE YELLOW ROSE OF TEXAS. NDM 4. G, C, D₇

● Square-dance tunes, play-party songs, and children's singing games may be accompanied by this strum. It's also good for country-and-western songs.

10
C, F, G₇
syncopated strum

small bar
F

×   R

JAMAICA FAREWELL.   Recording: NDM 6, rec 2. (Also used in a model experience).

● Look at the chord frame for the F-major chord. You will see that the first finger is used to cover *two* strings. When several strings are fretted at the same time, it is called *barring*. Fretting fewer than five strings is referred to as *small bar* or *half bar*. (Fretting five to six strings is called *great bar,* and requires considerable practice.) The F-major chord may be played using several barrings. The small bar is the easiest for beginning players.

The first finger covers the first and second strings. Fret close to the metal fret, to avoid a "buzz."

—Add the second finger, and avoid touching the intervening string.

—Add the third finger. Short fingernails are a must!

● If this seems very difficult at first, because of the pressure required, practice the technique at the fifth fret and the third fret.

● Practice this chord progression, which may be repeated throughout *Jamaica Farewell:*

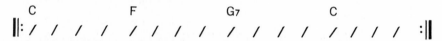

● As soon as possible, try the *syncopated strum.*

This rhythmic cue may help *before* you even begin playing:

All the right hand movements are played as a scratch, except the second, which is a *brush* of the thumb. This intensifies the syncopated sound.

sc = scratch
B = brush of thumb

● As soon as possible, learn to sing *Jamaica Farewell.* Use the recording at first, if necessary.

The vocal tune-up is high E³ (sounds G). Strum one unit of the chord progression (above) for an introduction and as an interlude between verses.

JAMAICA FAREWELL

Words and Music by
Irving Burgess

- Other songs to accompany with the syncopated strum:
  TINGA LAYO. EM 3. F, C, G₇ and C in that order. (A repeating pattern, as in JAMAICA FAREWELL.)

  GUANTANAMERA. EM 5. Transpose, using G, A₇, D, and C. (Also a repeating pattern.)

  JOHN B. SAILS. SBM 6. G, C, D₇.

  LIMBO LIKE ME. NDM 6. C, F, G₇.

  PAY ME MY MONEY DOWN. SBM 4, 5. C, F, G₇.

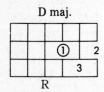

11

D, A₇

hammer-on

D maj.

R

T③ = hammer-on, string 3

A₇

R

*When singing *Tom Dooley* with upper-grade children, a higher key might be better. Experiment with the capo in fret I or II.

TOM DOOLEY.   The *hammer-on* is a useful device for adding rhythmic interest to an accompaniment. It is widely used in folk music.

● Look at the chord frame for D major, and hold that chord. The circled number indicates the left hand *first* finger.

— Lift that first finger.

— With the *right* hand thumb, pluck this open G string.

— Return the left hand first finger to the string, banging it down hard with a very quick motion. Two successive pitches (G-A) will be sounded.

Practice this several times.

● Now, work this into a strum.

Slowly alternate the thumb between the D and G string while holding the D-major chord:

— Thumb plucks D (string 4).
— Thumb plucks G (string 3).

As soon as this is "solid," insert a scratch between each thumb stroke:

T₄   ↓   T₃   ↓   =   ♩ ♩ ♩ ♩   (quadruple meter)

Continue strumming the pattern above, but begin to *speak:*

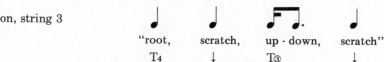

"root,   scratch,   up - down,   scratch"
T₄   ↓   T③   ↓

Gradually the left-hand first finger should begin to lift on the "up" and hammer quickly on the "down." **The right hand does not change** *its root, scratch rhythm.*

Give this some practice! Really hammer that first finger down hard.

● Discover that the A₇ chord also indicates a hammer-on by the first finger of the left hand. Practice this chord in the same way you practiced the D major. You will be hammering-on the D string (string 4).

Practice moving between these two chords.

● As soon as you can, sing and play along with *Tom Dooley.* Tune up for singing by plucking G² (sounds A).

Get the pattern going well as an introduction *before* the singing begins.

TOM DOOLEY

American Folk Song

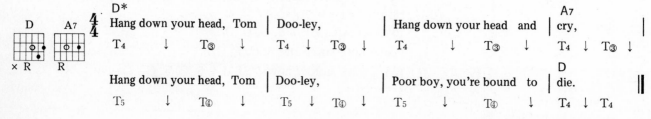

● A chart of commonly used hammer-on patterns will be found at the conclusion of the Guitar Instructor. Try them with songs in a quick tempo. Hammering-on seems to fit best with work songs, some blues, and many country-and-western tunes.

12
A, A$_7$, D$_7$ E$_7$
mute strum
seventh chords

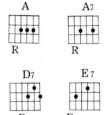

Vocal tune up is high E^3 (sounds G).

JOE TURNER BLUES.   Recording: MMYO 6, rec 8.

By looking at the notation for *Joe Turner Blues,* you can see that many seventh chords are played. The F$_7$ is a fairly difficult chord to play on the guitar. So it is desirable to *transpose* the song.

● It is easier to play in the key of A major. The chords required are A, A$_7$, D$_7$, and E$_7$. You are already familiar with all of these.

Review the chord frames for these chords.

● Learn a *mute strum* to accompany *Joe Turner Blues:*

—Scratch quickly down with all fingers (the strings will ring out).

—Follow through with the hand, extending the fingers, and,

—Place the flat of the palm across all six strings. This last motion will stop (or mute) the sound of the strings.

Practice this until it happens *so quickly* it sounds virtually like one movement. Add extra energy to get a solid, "gutsy" tone.

● To accompany *Joe Turner Blues,* alternate the mute with the root of the chord:

T$_4$ M↓   T$_4$ M↓

● Listen to the recording and sing and play as soon as you can!

Note that the pattern shown above equals *one measure.* The A-major chord sounds for three measures, but the A$_7$ for only one measure.

JOE TURNER BLUES

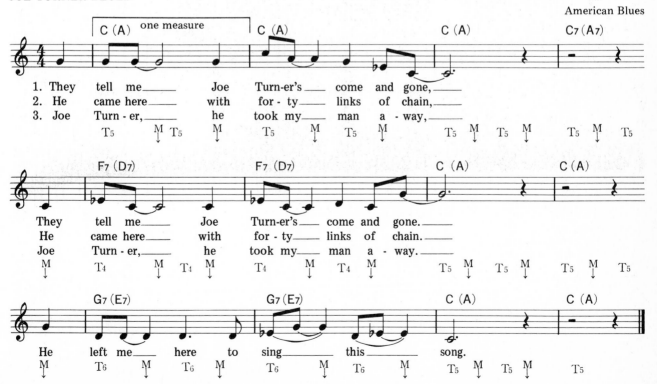

● For *Joe Turner Blues* to sound in the key of C, the capo must be placed in fret III. Unfortunately, this doesn't produce a very suitable timbre for blues. The key of A may be too low for the voices of upper-grade children.

A compromise might be to capo in fret I (sounds B♭) or fret II (sounds B). This still sounds "bluesy" on the guitar and would be better for most children's voices.

● The many *seventh chords* in *Joe Turner Blues* add additional "color."

Notice that the song begins on A major. This indicates a *triad* sounding three different pitches: A-C♯-E.

The A-major triad is followed by the A_7 chord using *four* different pitches: A-C♯-E-G. (Notice that both the A and A_7 are spelled using intervals of a third.) A is the root, C♯ the third, E the fifth, and G the seventh. This seventh is the only pitch not shared by the two chords.

The D_7 chord is spelled D-F♯-A-C.

The E_7 chord is spelled E-G♯-B-D.

● *Other songs to accompany with the mute strum:*

THE CITY BLUES. NDM 6. G, G_7, C, D_7. Tune up on E^3.

DRILL, YE TARRIERS. MMYO 5, NDM 5. No chords suggested. Transpose from C minor to D minor and use D minor, A_7. Tune up on B^3.

GOOD MORNING, BLUES. MMYO 6. Transpose from F to E, and use E, E_7, A_7, B_7. Tune up on B^0.

SINNER MAN. SBM 5, 6. D minor, C major, A minor. Tune up on G^2.

See the model experience *Joe Turner Blues* for ideas about how to create your own blues.

The notes produced by the strings of the guitar

	Open string	1st Fret	2nd Fret	3rd Fret	4th Fret	5th Fret	6th Fret	7th Fret	8th Fret	9th Fret	10th Fret	11th Fret	12th Fret
1st String	E	F	F♯/G♭	G	G♯/A♭	A	A♯/B♭	B	C	C♯/D♭	D	D♯/E♭	E
2nd String	B	C	C♯/D♭	D	D♯/E♭	E	F	F♯/G♭	G	G♯/A♭	A	A♯/B♭	B
3rd String	G	G♯/A♭	A	A♯/B♭	B	C	C♯/D♭	D	D♯/E♭	E	F	F♯/G♭	G
4th String	D	D♯/E♭	E	F	F♯/G♭	G	G♯/A♭	A	A♯/B♭	B	C	C♯/D♭	D
5th String	A	A♯/B♭	B	C	C♯/D♭	D	D♯/E♭	E	F	F♯/G♭	G	G♯/A♭	A
6th String	E	F	F♯/G♭	G	G♯/A♭	A	A♯/B♭	B	C	C♯/D♭	D	D♯/E♭	E

↑ NUT

Tuning to the piano

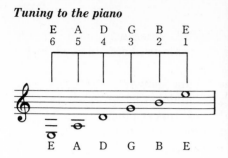

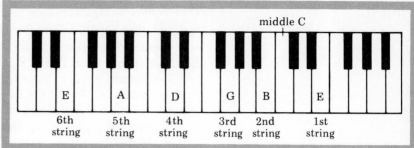

Guitar notation sounds one octave lower than written above.

Hammer-on

It is also effective to hammer-on an entire chord.

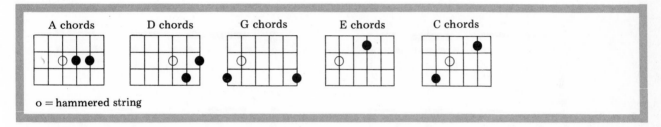

o = hammered string

Bass runs

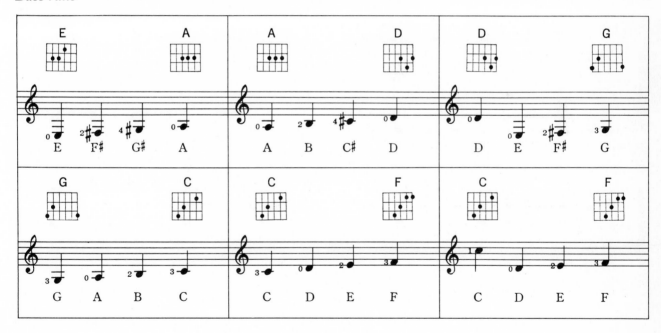

RIGHT-HAND STRUMS

Patterns given apply to the E-major chord. When using other chords with these strums, it will often be desirable to choose bass notes for the thumb other than T_6 and T_5.

T = Thumb	In all the strums shown,
i = index	the index (i), middle (m)
m = middle	and anular (a) fingers pluck
a = anular	the third, second, and first
l = little	strings, respectively.

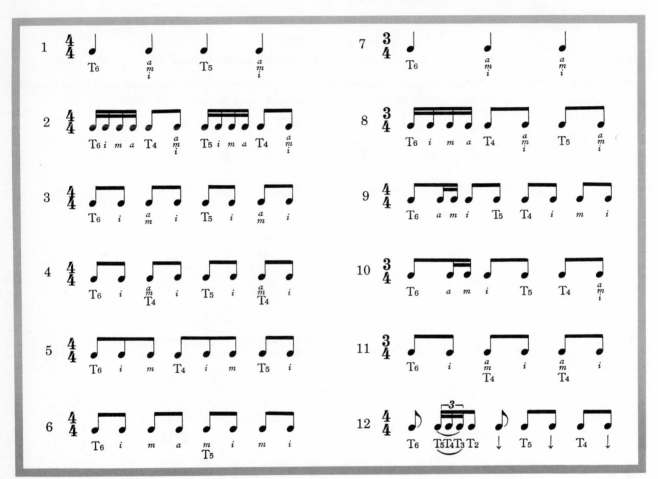

BIBLIOGRAPHY

Bay, Mel. Another guitar method series which proves of great value to many guitarists. Available at many stores.

D'Auberge, Alfred, and Morton Manus publish a comprehensive series of guitar instruction books. The first in the series will be *very* helpful to students who wish to learn to read music while they learn to play melodies and chords. Alfred Music Company, New York. Available at nearly every music store.

Noad, Frederick. This guitarist has published many excellent books which you will find at your library or bookstore.

Oak Publications has published many instructional methods including the *Folksinger's Guitar Guide* by Peter Seeger.

Snyder, Jerry. Another guitar player who has published many collections. *Basic Sing Book for Guitar* (volumes 1 and 2) is a real value, including melodies, words, and chords for almost 200 folk AND popular tunes. Hansen Music & Books, New York.

The primary chords (I, IV, V₇) for the basic guitar keys — *Ukelele*

Key	I chord	IV chord	V₇ chord	I chord IV chord V₇ chord
Key of C — Use C, F, G₇	C	F	G₇	C F G₇
Key of G — Use G, C, D₇	G	C	D₇	G C D₇
Key of D — Use D, G, A₇	D	G	A₇	
Key of A — Use A, D, E₇	A	D	E₇	
Key of E — Use E, A, B₇	E	A	B₇	
Key of F — Use F, B♭, C₇	F	B♭	C₇	F B♭ C₇
The three basic minor chords	Am	Dm	Em	Am Dm E₇ A₇

In chord charts, "m" is a common abbreviation for "minor."

*Tuning for ukulele: G-C-E-A (C tuning, low to high). When using D tuning (A-D-F♯-B), the fingerings shown will sound chords one whole step higher.

Baritone ukulele: tuned D-G-B-E, corresponding to the four highest-sounding strings of the guitar. Use guitar fingering for those strings, as shown in chord frames above.

Guitar Chords

R = Root *of the chord*
X = *string not to be played*
5 = Fifth *of the chord (alternate bass string)*
⌒ = *Bar (first finger lies flat across several strings).*
③ = *String position for left-hand finger when using alternate bass*

The Piano Instructor

This piano program offers beginning experiences at the keyboard. These experiences focus on learning to read and play simple melodies and accompaniments. A number of theoretical concepts of music are presented simultaneously with the playing experiences. Proceed through each unit at your own pace. For factual labeling of music learnings and materials note the information in the left margins.

Students with prior piano background may profitably review the skills and musical information in this program. Then, proceed to supplementary song sources for additional experiences.

Songs (in order of study)

- ROW, ROW, ROW YOUR BOAT
- THREE BLIND MICE
- GO TELL AUNT RHODY
- JINGLE BELLS
- WHEN THE SAINTS GO MARCHING IN
- LOVE SOMEBODY
- ARE YOU SLEEPING?
- LADY, COME
- SING HALLELU
- HOLD ON
- SKIN AND BONES
- CHORAL THEME (from Beethoven's *Ninth Symphony*)
- JOHN THE RABBIT
- LOVELY EVENING
- WE ARE GOING DOWN THE NUMBERS
- KUM BA YA
- THE FIRST NOEL
- AMERICA, THE BEAUTIFUL
- JOY TO THE WORLD

Music Theory

- Pitch notation in treble and bass clefs
- Chromatic (C), major (C, F, G) and minor (D, E) scales.
- Drones
- Chords and their inversions
- Duple, triple, quadruple and compound meters.
- Note durations and rest durations
- Ties

Skills and Techniques

- Five-finger positions
- Expanded hand position
- Crossover and crossunder fingerings
- Left-hand chord fingerings

INTRODUCTION

Pianofortes come in two basic shapes—the *upright* and the *grand*.

There are 88 keys—52 white and 36 black keys—on a standard-size piano.

The precise name for the instrument we call the piano is *pianoforte*. *Piano* is the Italian term for "soft," and *forte* is the Italian term for "loud." The name *pianoforte* refers to this keyboard instrument's potential for many degrees of loudness and softness. The earliest pianofortes were built about 1709, but the instrument was not used often until 1770.

PLAYING POSITION

At the piano, sit directly in front of the middle of the keyboard. The manufacturer's label may be used as a landmark on most pianos.

Sit far enough back from the keyboard so that your arms can move freely. Drop your arms down to your sides in a relaxed position. Your arms should hang loosely from the shoulders. Now, lift your hands to the keyboard, *keeping that same relaxed position.* Rest your fingers on the keys. Observe that your hands are slightly arched and your fingers are curved. At all times your fingers need to stay very close to the keys.

1
black keys
lower register

Pitches go *lower* when your fingers move to the left and *higher* as you move to the right.

● *Explore the black keys:* Locate a set of two black keys together. Play all of the groups of two black keys on your piano. Notice that the groups to the left are the lower pitched and the ones to the right are the higher pitched.

● Locate and play the sets of three black keys together.

● Play a *high* group of threes.

● Play a *low* group of twos.

● Find the following arrangement of twos and threes on the *lower* (left) part of the keyboard. Try playing with your left hand only those black keys marked with an "X." Just "walk" up and then down those marked keys. You'll be playing a "boogie bass"!

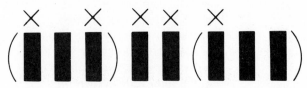

● Improvise other bass patterns with these lower black keys.

2
black keys
middle register

Combining the groups of two and three black keys produces one form of a *pentatonic scale.*

● Locate the set of two black keys directly in the middle of the keyboard. Find the set of three to the *right* and the set of two to the *right* of the threes. The black-key arrangement will look like the diagram below.

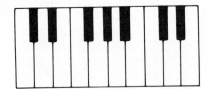

● You can play lots of songs "by ear" using these black keys! With your right hand, try the first part of *Mary Had a Little Lamb.* Start on the black key marked with an "X" and walk down the group of threes and back up. You'll have to play three times on the "X" key when you walk back up.

— = eighth note

$$\left(\begin{array}{c}♪\\ti\end{array}\right)$$

—— = quarter note

$$\left(\begin{array}{c}♩\\ta\end{array}\right)$$

You can play *Scotland's Burning*, too. Start with the first "X" at number 1. Play "Scotland's burning" (1) and repeat. Play number 2—"Look out" and repeat. Go to number 3—"Fire! Fire!" and repeat. Finally, play number 1 again for "Pour on water" and repeat.

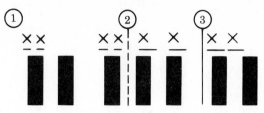

You can see why we need to read music! It's difficult to give directions for playing a song all in words and by marking keys.

● Create a melody of your own using these black keys.

● Try playing some of the following songs "by ear." The starting key(s) for each song are marked with an "X." You might try just the beginning of each tune.

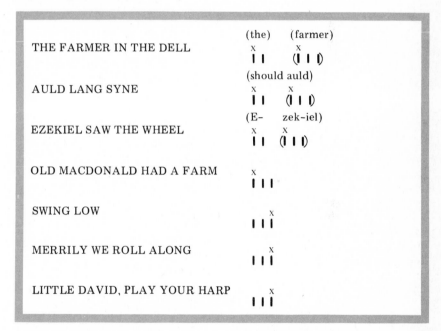

● Play the melody of *Scotland's Burning* with your right hand, and play the two keys marked below with your left hand (in the lower range). Play the two keys together in a steady rhythm to accompany the melody.

Two pitches sounded together and played throughout are called a *drone* accompaniment.

● Improvise in a boogie-woogie style with two other players. See the ideas presented in MMYO 6.

<table>
<tr><td>**3**
letter names
of white keys</td></tr>
</table>

Only the first seven letters of the alphabet (A B C D E F G) are used to name the 88 keys of the piano.

● In the middle of the keyboard, find the white key to the immediate left of the group of two black keys. Label this key C on this sample keyboard. This is "middle C."

● The pitch F is found to the left of each group of three black keys. Write F on this white key on the keyboard chart.

● Find all of the C's and F's on the piano. Play them.

● Can you find the white key to the immediate *right* of the two black keys? This pitch is E. The white key to the right of the three black keys is B. Add those pitches to the keyboard chart and play them on your piano.

● Decide what the letter names will be for the remaining white keys. Write the names on the chart. Notice how these pitches repeat up and down the entire keyboard.

● Become familiar with the names and location of the white keys. Start with the lowest white key on the keyboard and play up, saying the names as you play. Try starting with the highest white key and playing downward. Again, *say* the names of the keys as you play.

<table>
<tr><td>**4**
letter names
of black keys</td></tr>
</table>

Tones sounding the same pitch but written differently are called *enharmonics*.

● The black keys use the same letter names as the white keys, but with the addition of a ♯ (sharp) or ♭ (flat). Each black key's name is taken from the white key on either side of it. For example, find the black key between C and D. This black key is called either C♯ or D♭—the black keys have two letter spellings. Add C♯/D♭ to the keyboard chart.

● What are the two names for the black key between D and E? Between F and G? Between G and A? Between A and B? Add these names to the keyboard chart.

<table>
<tr><td>**5**
staff notation
for middle
register</td></tr>
</table>

Treble clef or G clef sign establishes the placement of G above middle C on the second line up. The right hand usually plays the notes in the treble clef.

● The seven white keys and the five black keys offer us a total of 12 different pitches with which to work. Examine the following staff to *see* where those pitches in the middle of the keyboard are notated.

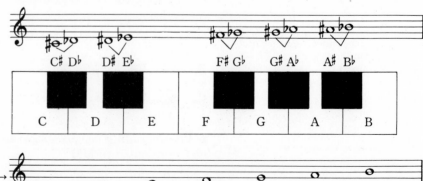

- Read from the above staff. Play up and down between C and B on the white keys, naming each key.

- Read, name, and play up and down between C♯ and A♯ on the black keys. Notice the two spellings for each black key.

A *chromatic scale* is a 12-tone scale with half steps between all adjacent tones.

- Play up and down using *every key between* C and B. You will be playing a *chromatic scale*. When you move from a white key like C to the next black key (C♯), this distance is referred to as a *half step*. Note that *no* black key comes in between E and F and B and C. These are "natural" half steps.

6

C-major,
5-finger
right hand

- Explore the C-major five-finger pattern: Locate middle C on the piano. That's the white key to the left of the group of two black keys in the *middle* of the keyboard. Put the thumb (1) of your right hand on middle C.

The *five-finger pattern* is a particular combination of half and whole steps. The five fingers cover the five consecutive degrees of the diatonic scale (see Glossary).

- Rest your index finger (2) on D; your middle finger (3) on E; your ring finger (4) on F; and your little finger (5) on G. Now you are in position to play the first five pitches of the C-major scale.

- Experiment playing these five notes—C-D-E-F-G—with the five-finger pattern.   1 2 3 4 5

- Try playing the beginning of the song *Row, Row, Row Your Boat*. You'll start on C. Try playing "by ear," then look at the informal notation that follows.

C̄   C̄   C̄   D̄   Ē   Ē   D̄   Ē   F̄   Ḡ

"Row, row, row your   boat, Gent - ly down the stream"

—— = 𝅘𝅥𝅭
    (ta - i)

—— = 𝅘𝅥
    (ta)

—— = 𝅘𝅥𝅮
    (ti)

- Did you notice how this part of the melody stepped up and down? Look at the musical notation for the first four measures of *Row, Row*. The numbers by the notes are the suggested fingerings. Try playing again, but this time read from the musical notation. Think three counts for each dotted quarter note (𝅘𝅥𝅭); two for each quarter

note (𝅘𝅥); and one for each eighth note (𝅘𝅥𝅮).

ROW, ROW, ROW YOUR BOAT

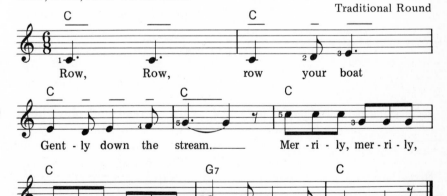

⁶⁄₈ or ⁶⁄♩ meter = 𝅘𝅥𝅮𝅘𝅥𝅮𝅘𝅥𝅮𝅘𝅥𝅮𝅘𝅥𝅮𝅘𝅥𝅮
                    1 2 3 4 5 6

𝅘𝅥𝅭 = 𝅘𝅥𝅮 𝅘𝅥𝅮 𝅘𝅥𝅮
(ta - i) *(ti - ti - ti)*

● Play the beginning of *Three Blind Mice*. The starting pitch is E. Try playing "by ear" first; then, examine the notation below.

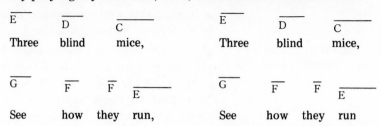

E̅	D̅	C̅		E̅	D̅	C̅
Three	blind	mice,		Three	blind	mice,

G̅	F̅	F̅		G̅	F̅	F̅
			E̅			E̅
See	how	they	run,	See	how	they	run

Did you notice how this part of the melody "stepped"? There was a big "skip" though from C to G. Repeat, but this time read and play from the first 8 measures of musical notation. Say or sing the names of the notes as you play.

THREE BLIND MICE

The arching line connecting two identical pitches is called a *tie*. To perform a tied note, strike the first note *only,* but hold through all five beats.

Observe the *tie* in *Row, Row.*

See model experience *Pianists*, p. 84.

Notice how these melodic fragments "step."

C, D, E, F, and G are the first five pitches of the C-major scale.

● Learn to read and play the first two melodies heard in *Pianists* from *Carnival of Animals* by Saint-Saëns. Write the letter names under the staff. Write the appropriate fingerings next to the notes.

● You're ready to try a *whole* song using the first five pitches in the *C-major* scale. *Go Tell Aunt Rhody* begins on E (finger 3). Try playing from the blank notation first; then try reading and playing from the staff notation.

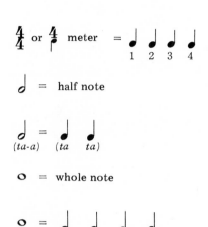

GO TELL AUNT RHODY

American Folk Song

Go tell Aunt Rho - dy, Go tell Aunt Rho - dy,

Go tell Aunt Rho - dy, The old grey goose is dead.

• Does the melody of *Go Tell Aunt Rhody* move mainly in steps or skips? Steps, it is! One big skip did occur (from C to G).

• Try the refrain of *Jingle Bells.* The beginning pitch is E (finger 3). Explore a little bit "by ear"; then try reading and playing from the musical notation.

JINGLE BELLS

Words and Music by
James Pierpont

Jin - gle bells, Jin - gle bells, Jin - gle all the way,

Oh, what fun it is to ride in a one - horse o - pen sleigh!

Jin - gle bells, Jin - gle bells, Jin - gle all the way,

Oh, what fun it is to ride in a one - horse o - pen sleigh!

• Rest your right hand on the five-finger pattern in C major. Take a close look at the distance between each of those notes. What is the distance between E and F? Do you recall what that distance was called when you played the *chromatic scale?* (A half step.)

One *whole step* consists of two half steps.

⌣ = whole
    step
∨ = half
    step

Look at the distance between C and D. This is called a *whole step* because another key (in this case, a black one) comes in between.

● Write the distance between D and E on this line.

● Is the distance from F to G a whole step or a half step?

● This specific whole and half step pattern is characteristic of the first five pitches of a major scale.

C   D   E ∨ F   G
1   2   3   4   5

● Play another song in C major. Read entirely from staff notation.

WHEN THE SAINTS GO MARCHING IN

Spiritual

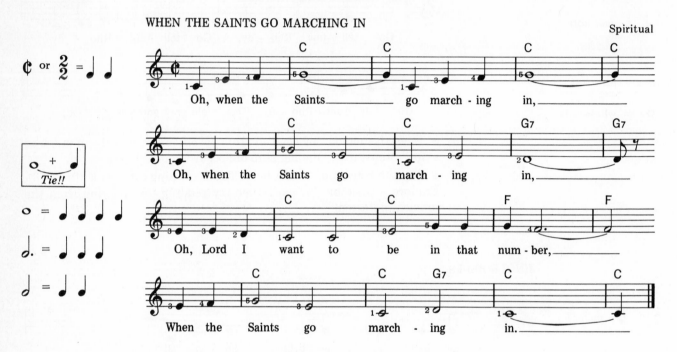

● Now, try *Love Somebody.*

LOVE SOMEBODY

American Folk Song

● Other songs using the pitches C, D, E, F, G are: verse of MARCHING TO PRETORIA, MMYO 2 and 3; HEY LIDEE, NDM 2, MY DREYDL, SBM (EC), AMBOS A DOS, SBM (EC).

7
C-major left-hand drone

Left-hand
fingering for
first five tones
in C major:
(G) 1 – thumb
(F) 2 – index
(E) 3 – middle
(D) 4 – ring
(C) 5 – little

● Put your little finger of your left hand on the nearest C to the left of middle C. Rest your left thumb on the G between the two C's. Play those two pitches together four times!

● Those two pitches sounded together will make a good left-hand accompaniment for *Row, Row*, p. 253. Play this C-G drone on the first beat of each measure while you sing the melody.

"Row, row, row your boat,   Gently down the stream"
G   G   G   G
C   C   C   C

● Ask a friend to play the right-hand melody while you play the left-hand part.

You can also play this drone accompaniment for the first part of *Three Blind Mice*, p. 254. Sing or play the melody and accompany with the C-G drone on the first beat of each measure.

"Three blind mice, three blind mice, ...
G   G   G   G
C   C   C   C

8
staff notation for lower register

Bass clef *or **F clef** sign establishes the placement of F below middle C on the fourth line up. The left hand usually plays the notes in the bass clef.*

● Examine the staff that follows to *see* where the pitches to the *left* of middle C are notated.

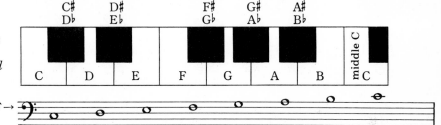

● Read from the above staff. Play up and down between C and B on the white keys, naming each key.

● Read, name, and play up and down the black keys between D♭ and B♭. Note again the two spellings for each black key.

● Play up and down the chromatic scale, starting on C. Remember, the chromatic scale uses every black and white key!

● Try playing the left-hand drone accompaniment while you play *Row, Row* and *Three Blind Mice* from the musical notation, pp. 253 and 254.

𝅗𝅥. = 𝅘𝅥. + 𝅘𝅥.

9
C-major left-hand chord roots

● Alternate between C and G with your left hand. Play two times on C and one time on G; then once again on C. Like this:

                    G
C   C   C

● C and G played in this order will provide a left-hand accompaniment for *Go Tell Aunt Rhody.* Try singing the melody while you play with your left hand.

Grand or great staff is the combination of a staff with treble clef and a staff with bass clef.

Go tell Aunt Rhody,   Go tell Aunt Rhody, ...

C   C   C
                              G

A *chord* is three or more tones sounding together.

● Here's the musical notation for *Go Tell Aunt Rhody.* Try reading and playing both parts. Notice that C and G are the chord roots for the C-major chord and the G-major chord.

GO TELL AUNT RHODY

American Folk Song

The letter names of the chords identify the chord roots.

g
e   = C Major Chord
C

d
b   = G Major Chord
G

Chord roots are the strongest tones of each chord.

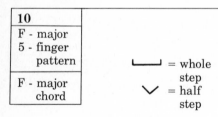

10
F - major 5 - finger pattern
F - major chord

⌐_⌐ = whole step

∨ = half step

● Move up the keyboard to F. Put your right thumb on the F to the right of middle C. If F is the first pitch in the F-major scale, can you decide what pitches will be the second, third, fourth, and fifth tones in F major?

● Recall the specific arrangement of whole and half steps in a major scale:

Now, put your index finger on the note a whole step up from F. That note is G.

● Now, place your middle finger on the key one *whole step* up from G. Write the first three notes of the F-major scale on the staff below.

● The distance from third tone (A) to the fourth tone in the major scale is a *half step.* Put your ring finger on this key; then add this pitch to the staff above.

● With your ring finger (4) on B♭, move up a *whole step,* and place your little finger (5) on the fifth tone in the *F-major* scale. Add this note to the notation above.

F, G, A, B♭, and C are the first five scale tones in F major.

● Play this pattern in F major, noticing that the only *half step* is between 3 and 4.

		F major scale
F	1 (8)	
E	7	
D	6	
C	5	
B♭	4	
A	3	
G	2	
F	1	

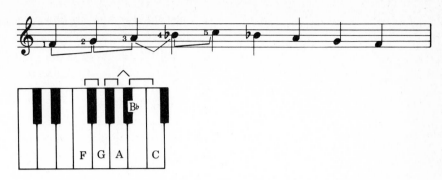

- Use the F-major five-finger pattern (F-G-A-B♭-C) for the first four measures of *Are You Sleeping?*

ARE YOU SLEEPING?

Traditional Round

Steady beats may be grouped in four (quadruple meter).

Are you sleep - ing? Are you sleep - ing? Bro - ther John? Bro - ther John?

Morn-ing bells are ring-ing, morn-ing bells are ring-ing, Ding, ding, dong, Ding, ding, dong.

- Here's an entire song using these pitches. It's the English folk song *Lady, Come.* Listen to a recording of the song in SBM 2.

LADY, COME

Folk Song from England

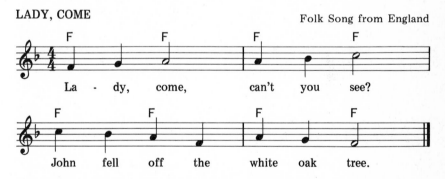

La - dy, come, can't you see?

John fell off the white oak tree.

A *chord* is three or more tones sounding together.

The chord's letter name indicates the *chord root*.

- When you feel comfortable playing the melody for *Lady, Come,* try a left-hand accompaniment. This song can be accompanied by an F-major chord (as can *Are You Sleeping?*).

- To construct an F-major chord, put the little finger (5) of your left hand on the chord root: F. Use the F below middle C. Place your middle finger on A and your thumb on middle C. Play these three pitches together and you will be playing the F-major chord. Did you notice that we skipped a scale tone in between each chord tone? This is how chords are built.

F major

● Play the F-major chord on the first beat of each measure ("La," "can't," "John," "white") to accompany *Lady, Come.*

● For other songs with the pitches F, G, A, B♭, C, locate *Merrily We Roll Along,* p. 279, *A La Volette,* MMYO 2, *Hop, Old Squirrel,* SBM 2, *Winter, Ade!* MMYO 2, *Old Woman,* CMCM 1A, *Whistle, Mary, Whistle,* CMCM 2A.

11
D - minor
5 - finger pattern
D - minor chord

● Place your right thumb (1) on the D to the right of middle C. Play D-E-F-G-A up and down in the five-finger pattern.

D　E　F　G　A　G　F　E　D

● Rest your fingers on D-E-F-G-A. Notice the *whole-step* distance between D and E.

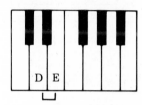

● Observe that a *half step* separates E and F. This is one of the natural half steps. (B and C is the other one!)

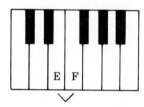

D, E, F, G, and A are the first five tones of the *D-minor scale.*

D minor scale	D	1	(8)
	C	7	
	B♭	6	
	A	5	
	G	4	
	F	3	
	E	2	
	D	1	

● F to G is another *whole* step, and G to A is also. This specific whole- and half-step arrangement is characteristic of the first five pitches of a *minor* scale.

D　E　F　G　A

● With your little finger (5) on A, play this rhythmic pattern:

syn - co - pa   *ta - a*

● Play this same rhythmic pattern on G (4), on F (3), and finally, on D (1).

(syn - co - pa   *ta - a*)

Steady beats can be grouped in twos (duple meter).

Use circled fingerings on the "Chorus" parts when you are ready to play the entire song later.

● These syncopated patterns on A, G, F, and D are the "Chorus" part in the song *Sing Hallelu.*

● Listen to a recording of the song in SBM 1. Try reading and playing just the "Chorus" part from the musical notation. Think or sing the "Solo" part. Later, you'll come back and play the entire song.

SING HALLELU

Black Spiritual from South Carolina

● Create a melody of your own using the D-E-F-G-A pitches. As you improvise, try to remember your more interesting melodies and write them down.

● Try these tonal patterns:

● These tonal patterns are all part of the song *Hold On.* Listen to a recording of the song in SBM 4. Try reading and playing the verse of *Hold On.*

HOLD ON

American Folk Song

D min.

A7

3. Keep on plowin' and don't you tire,
   Ev'ry row goes higher and higher.
   Keep your hand on that plow,
   Hold on, hold on, hold on.
   (Refrain)

4. If that plow stays in your hand,
   Head you straight for the promised land.
   Keep your hand on that plow,
   Hold on, hold on, hold on.
   (Refrain)

On the piano, melodies are often played with the right hand and chords with the left.

• Play the D-minor chord as a left hand accompaniment to the verse of *Hold On.* To construct a D-minor chord, put your little finger (5) on the chord root—D. Use the D below middle C. Place your middle finger on F and your thumb on A. Play these pitches together on the first beat of each measure.

12

E-minor
5-finger
pattern
drone

Note that you'll need to extend the index finger slightly to strike the F♯.

E minor scale		
E	1 (8)	
D	7	
C	6	>
B	5	
A	4	
G	3	>
F♯	2	
E	1	

For "pickup" note, see *anacrusis* in Glossary.

• Place your right thumb on the E just above middle C. The finger pattern for the first five tones of the *E-minor* scale is E-F♯-G-A-B. Notice the *whole-, half-, whole-, whole-step* arrangement again in this minor-scale pattern.

• Play each note of the pattern, going up and down!

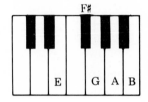

• Here's the folk melody *Skin and Bones.* It uses only E, G, A, and B of the E-minor scale. Listen to a recording of the song in MMYO 3. Notice the ⁶⁄₈ meter and the "pickup" note at the beginning. This accounts for the presence of only five beats in the final measure.

SKIN AND BONES

Folk Song from Kentucky
Collected by Jean Ritchie

There was an old wo-man all skin and bones, Oo!_____

A drone accompaniment is usually constructed by sounding the first and fifth tones of a scale.

• Locate E and B below middle C. Play these two notes together with your left hand as a drone accompaniment for *Skin and Bones.*

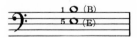

• Read and play from the musical notation.

• Create a melody of your own using the same pitches used in *Skin and Bones:* E, G, A, and B. Try adding the E-B drone as a left-hand accompaniment to your melody.

<table>
<tr><td>

13

G-major
5-finger
pattern

G and D₇
chords

</td></tr>
</table>

• Can you build the five-finger pattern in G major? Recall that the first five pitches of the major scale follow the pattern . Examine the G-major scale in the margin, then write the letter names of the first five pitches (five-finger pattern) below.

____   ____   ____   ____   ____

• Play each note in the G-major five-finger pattern:

• Using these five pitches, try a melody that is heard in the final movement of Beethoven's *Ninth Symphony:*

CHORAL THEME (from *Ninth Symphony*)

Beethoven

The G-major chord and D₇ chord are the two chords most commonly used to accompany a song in G major. Note that the D₇ chord has *four* different tones.

• You can accompany this melody using two chords: the G-major chord and D₇ chord. The G-major chord (G–B–D) is built on the first step of the G-major scale. The D₇ chord (D-F♯-A-C) is built on the fifth step of the G-major scale. Play these two chords with the left hand, using the fingerings indicated.

G   D7   G

• These two chords—G and D₇—are in *root* position. Each chord is arranged with its *root* on the bottom.

Once a chord is built, its pitches can be rearranged. Such rearrangements are called *chord inversions.*

Often in piano playing, the tones of a *seventh chord* are rearranged for easier playing. Look at this new arrangement of the D₇ chord. Notice that the A is left out—the fifth of a seventh chord may be omitted without altering the chord's color or effectiveness.

G (I)   D7 (V7)   G (I)

• Try playing the two chords now in this position. You'll notice how easily you can move between the G (I) and the D₇ (V₇) chords in this "piano position." When you're comfortable with this progression, try adding this accompaniment to Beethoven's melody.

CHORAL THEME (from *Ninth Symphony*)

Beethoven

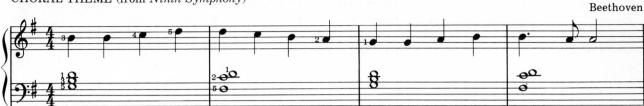

● Other songs using the first five pitches of the G-major scale: *Suo Gan,* SBM 2, *A La Claire Fontaine,* MMYO 3, *Cascabel,* MMYO 3.

14
C - major 5 - finger pattern
C, G₇ chords
broken chord accompaniment

● With two chords, you can play a left-hand accompaniment for many songs. The chord arrangement, fingering, and hand position used in G major may be used for other scales and keys. In C major, the chord built on the first tone of the scale is the C-major chord (C-E-G), and the chord built on the fifth tone is G seventh (G-B-D-F).

```
G                F
E                D
                 B
Ⓒ  D  E  F   Ⓖ⑦  A  B  C
I                V7
```

● Try playing these two chords with the G₇ chord inverted.

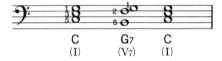

C   G₇   C
(I)   (V₇)   (I)

● Now accompany *Go Tell Aunt Rhody* with the C and G₇ chords used in the same places where you previously used the chord roots. The song is on p. 255.

● You can accompany *Love Somebody,* too, with the C and G₇ chords. Try the following left-hand accompaniment. It uses the chords, but in a different pattern: the *broken-chord* pattern. Play this pattern for each chord designated in the song *Love Somebody,* p. 256. Try this practice progression to get acquainted with the new pattern.

C (I)   G₇(V₇)   C (I)

15

E - minor
expanded
hand position

E - minor and
E - major
chords

● *This* time, alternate between two chords, but one chord will be major and one minor. The chord root will be E. Put your little finger of your left hand on the E below middle C. Put your thumb on the B directly below middle C. The E and B will be used in both the E-major chord and the E-minor chord. The middle finger will play G for the E-minor chord and G♯ for the E-major chord. Try changing between these two chords.

E min.   E maj.   E min.

● These two chords will serve as an appropriate accompaniment for the folk song *John the Rabbit.* Listen to a recording of the song in MMYO Kg. Follow the music as you listen, and observe where those chord changes occur.

● To play the melody of *John the Rabbit,* you will first use the five-finger pattern in E-minor (refer to unit 12). Later, at the same place that you play the E-major chord in the song, you will need to extend the five-finger pattern in order to play the C♯. Note the suggested fingerings. Try it!

JOHN THE RABBIT

American Folk Song
Collected by John W. Work

16
F - major expanded hand position
F, B♭, C₇ chords

● Most songs will require you to expand the five-finger hand position. *Lovely Evening* is an example. Notice below those places circled indicating the expanded hand position in F major. Try the right-hand part using the fingerings indicated.

$\frac{3}{4}$ or $\mathbf{3}$ = ♩ ♩ ♩   Steady beats can be grouped in threes (triple meter).

LOVELY EVENING

Traditional Round

● Play the chords indicated as an accompaniment for the song. F and B♭ are the chords built on the first step of the F-major scale and on the fourth step.

```
C        F
A        D
Ⓕ  G  A  Ⓑ♭  C  D  E  F
I        IV
```

● You'll find it easier to play the IV (B♭) chord, if you rearrange the tones like this:

● Add this chordal left-hand accompaniment to *Lovely Evening.*

● For variety, try the *broken-chord pattern* to accompany this song.

● Play *Row, Row, Row Your Boat*, p. 253, *Three Blind Mice*, p. 254, and *Are You Sleeping?* p. 259, using the expanded hand position.

F-major scale

F	
E	
D	
C	5 (V)
B♭	4 (IV)
A	
G	
F	1 (I)

• Some songs require three chords in order to provide an appropriate accompaniment. The three chords (usually known as the *primary chords*) most often used are the I, IV, and V₇ in any key. In F major, the three chords are the F (I), B♭ (IV), and C₇ (V₇). An easy "piano position" for these three chords is:

I   IV   V₇   I

• Add these three chords in the designated places as an accompaniment to *We Are Going Down the Numbers.* Listen to the song in MMYO 1. Notice that the melody extends beyond the five-finger pattern in only one place.

WE ARE GOING DOWN THE NUMBERS

Song from Nigeria
As Sung by Ernest Ikpe

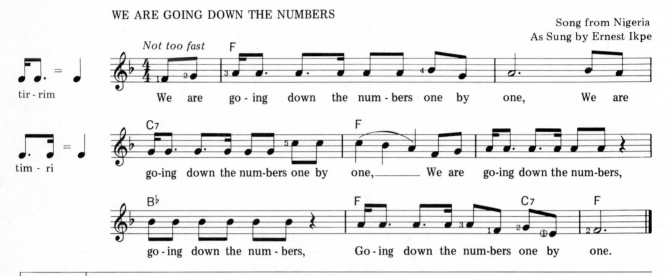

17
C - major expanded hand position
C, F, G₇ chords

• The I, IV, and V₇ chords in the key of C major may be used to accompany the song *When the Saints Go Marching In* (unit 6). Practice changing between chords in the "piano position," then go back and accompany the song.

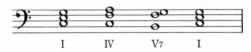

I   IV   V₇   I

● Try these chords with *Kum Ba Ya*. Notice that the melody extends beyond the five finger position.

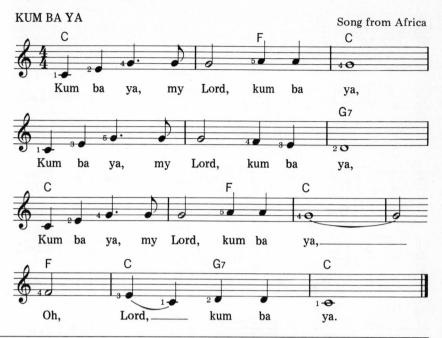

KUM BA YA

Song from Africa

Kum ba ya, my Lord, kum ba ya,

Kum ba ya, my Lord, kum ba ya,

Kum ba ya, my Lord, kum ba ya,_____

Oh, Lord,_____ kum ba ya.

18
C - major crossover, crossunder

● In addition to expanding the hand position in order to extend the range of notes, one can also shift the hand position by using the thumb on higher scale steps. For example, the third melody heard in *Pianists* from *The Carnival of Animals,* may be easily fingered by passing the thumb under the third finger without turning the hand:

Thumb under!

● Try the beginning part of *The First Noel.* Remember, just pass the thumb under.

THE FIRST NOEL

Carol

The first no - el the An - gel did say,
Was to cer - tain poor shep - herds in fields as they lay,
In fields where they lay keep - ing their sheep
On a cold win - ter's night that was so deep.
No - el, no - el, no - el, no - el,
Born is the King of Is - ra - el.

● Try all of *America, the Beautiful,* observing the fingerings, especially the crossunder (marked *).

AMERICA, THE BEAUTIFUL

Music by Samuel Ward
Words by Katharine Lee Bates

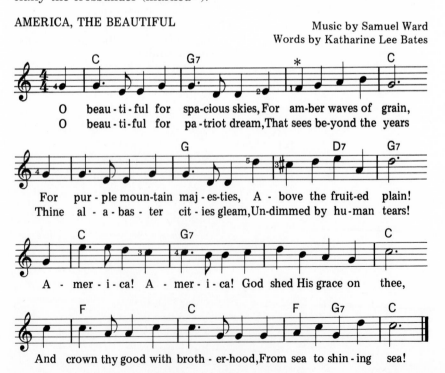

O beau - ti - ful for spa-cious skies, For am-ber waves of grain,
O beau - ti - ful for pa-triot dream,That sees be-yond the years

For pur - ple moun-tain maj - es-ties, A - bove the fruit-ed plain!
Thine al - a - bas - ter cit - ies gleam,Un-dimmed by hu-man tears!

A - mer - i - ca! A - mer - i - ca! God shed His grace on thee,

And crown thy good with broth - er-hood,From sea to shin - ing sea!

● When you play the beginning of *Joy to the World,* you will need to pass the third finger *over* the thumb without turning the hand.

JOY TO THE WORLD

Music by George F. Handel
Words by Isaac Watts

● Try all of *St. Paul's Steeple,* p. 133, observing the fingerings, especially the crossover spot.

● This basic introduction to playing the piano should provide you with enough information to read and play simple songs from the elementary basal music series. Try the lower-grade books first!

● You might want to use one of the following books to increase your piano skills as well as your repertoire of songs:

Starr, William, and Constance Starr. *Basic Piano Technique for the Classroom Teacher.* Dubuque, Iowa: Wm. C. Brown, Co., 1971. Many songs to play and many different accompaniments to try.

Winslow, Robert W., and Leon Dallin. *Music Skills for the Classroom Teacher.* Dubuque, Iowa: Wm. C. Brown, Co., 1970, pp. 96–125. Easy songs to play and numerous accompaniments to try.

Bastien, James W., and Jane Smisor Bastien. *Beginning Piano for Adults.* Park Ridge, Ill.: General Words & Music Co., 1968.

Mach, Elyse. *Contemporary Class Piano.* New York: Harcourt Brace Jovanovich, Inc., 1976.

Pace, Robert. *Piano for Classroom Music.* Englewood Cliffs, N.J.: Prentice-Hall, Inc., 1956.

Robinson, Helene. *Basic Piano for Adults.* Belmont, Calif.: Wadsworth Publishing Co., 1964.

The grand staff (key of C)

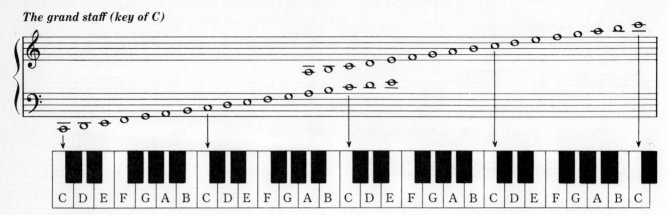

The piano keyboard

The Recorder Instructor

The recorder program offers beginning experiences playing the recorder. These experiences focus on learning to read and play simple melodies. The beginning melodies are based on pitches within the D-A range, widely used in initial song experiences for young children. Recorder players should also learn to sing these songs. Proceed through each unit at your own pace. Note the factual labeling of musical understandings and materials in the margins.

Songs (in order of study)

- RAIN, RAIN
- STARLIGHT, STARBRIGHT
- BYE BABY BUNTING
- A TISKET, A TASKET
- TAILS
- AU CLAIR DE LA LUNE
- POOR BIRD
- FAIS DO DO
- SKIN AND BONES
- BINGO (EXCERPT)
- MERRILY WE ROLL ALONG
- JAMAICA FAREWELL (COUNTER-MELODY)
- TRAMPIN'
- GOOD NEWS
- OLD PAINT
- GO TELL AUNT RHODY (KEY OF G)
- WE THREE KINGS
- THIS OLD MAN
- SCOTLAND'S BURNING

- O COME, EMMANUEL
- HARI KRISHNA
- SERAFINA
- GO TELL AUNT RHODY (KEY OF C)
- KHUKHABARA (KOOKABURRA)
- CHESTER
- SWEET POTATOES
- ZUM GALI GALI
- MINKA
- HANUKAH SONG
- THE FROG AND THE MOUSE
- HUSH, LITTLE BABY
- BILE THEM CABBAGE DOWN
- BATTLE HYMN OF THE REPUBLIC
- SHOO FLY
- YANKEE DOODLE
- SKIP TO MY LOU
- FRENCH CATHEDRALS
- DONA NOBIS PACEM

Skills and Techniques

- Fingering (C through high E, including F♯, B♭, C♯)
- Tonguing
- Slur
- Breath control
- Split-hole

Music Theory

- Pitch notation in treble clef
- Note durations and rest durations
- Duple, triple, quadruple and compound meters
- Fermata, repeat sign, D.C. al Fine, slur, phrase mark
- Pickup note
- Phrase structure (a a b a)
- Syncopation
- Sectional Form (AB and ABA)

The Recorder

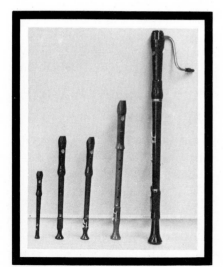

The recorder family (left to right): soprano recorder, alto recorder without key, alto recorder with key, tenor recorder with key, bass recorder.

The recorder can provide you with many hours of personal pleasure, as well as serving you as a valuable learning/teaching tool.

It has been in use for centuries and has been known by a number of names—*flûte-à-bec* (French), *blockflöte* (German), *flauto dolce* (Italian), and fipple flute. Today, the recorder family consists of the sopranino, the soprano (or descant), the alto, the tenor, and the bass. The entire family is often heard in ensemble playing.

With limited skill on the recorder you will be able to teach yourself many melodies and songs. Even if you are an insecure singer, you can teach your students a new song by playing it on your recorder. The instrument's portability makes it an ideal music maker for virtually any setting—the classroom, outdoors, ensemble-playing with friends, and many other situations. You are urged to add your recorder accomplishments to the musical activities of your college class as often as possible.

What follows is a brief introduction to playing the recorder (soprano or tenor). This material is not presented as a "method," but a one-quarter or one-semester beginning in playing the recorder. (Numerous recorder methods are currently available, and several are listed at the end of this section.)

Inexpensive wood and plastic recorders are available in most places. Fine wooden recorders are quite expensive but should be considered after you have enjoyed some success with your less expensive "beginning model."

CARE OF YOUR RECORDER

Wooden recorders should be oiled before they are used. Follow directions provided with your recorder, or (1) take the instrument apart, using a twisting motion to ease the joints apart; (2) with a small swab, apply a small quantity of woodwind oil to the insides of the joints *(do not oil aperture);* (3) allow oil to dry 10–12 hours, wipe off excess oil, and assemble recorder for playing.

Warm your recorder, especially the mouthpiece, in your hands before playing. Avoid blowing too hard, as this will eventually damage the instrument.

After playing, take the recorder apart and carefully dry the inside of each section with a soft, dry swab (often provided with the instrument). Again, avoid touching the aperture or the fipple. Allow recorder to dry completely before returning it to its case.

FINGERS

The left-hand thumb covers the hole at the back of the recorder. The top three holes are covered by the index (1), middle (2), and ring (3) fingers.

Support the recorder by placing the right-hand thumb underneath and behind the fourth and fifth holes from the top. The four fingers of the right hand are used to cover the lower four holes.

The length of the column of vibrating air in the recorder largely determines the pitch that will sound. When all holes are covered the column of vibrating air is longest and the pitch lowest. Higher pitches result from shortening the vibrating column of air (uncovering holes) and from overblowing (increasing the air pressure in the instrument).

Begin to get the correct feel of the fingers on the instrument by carefully covering the holes with the pads, rather than the tips, of your fingers. The fingers should (1) strike the holes, (2) hold firmly for the duration of the note, and (3) be lifted quickly when not needed.

ARMS

Allow your upper arms to remain relaxed and at a comfortable angle to the body. Keeping your elbows beside your rib cage will help keep your recorder at a proper angle as you play.

MOUTH (EMBOUCHURE)

Place the tip of the mouthpiece between your lips and *in front of your teeth.* Try for a relaxed, comfortable mouth position. *Never place the mouthpiece between your teeth.* Close your lips gently around the mouthpiece, opening them slightly to take a breath.

LET'S PLAY!

Warm your recorder mouthpiece in your hands. Warm the whole instrument by blowing gently through it for a few seconds.

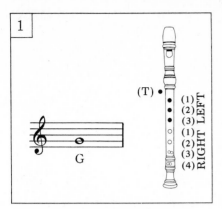

● Place your fingers as indicated for G. Carefully cover the proper holes with the *pads* of your fingers.

● Use your tongue to start the tone, saying "doo" for each *attack*.

● Maintain each tone with a gentle, even stream of air.

● Play the G four times, saying "doo" to begin each tone. *Don't allow your tongue to come up against your upper teeth except as you end the fourth G. The last G will resemble "doot."

doo - doo - doo - doot

*(Think "one-two" as you play these **half notes**.)*

● Notice that the vibrating column of air producing G is approximately half the length of your recorder. You will slightly shorten the column when you finger A and will hear that A is a slightly higher pitch than G.

(Baroque fingerings will be used throughout. Some beginning recorder players may find it easier to view printed fingerings as though they were looking *down* the instrument as it is held in playing position. Turn your book upside down and decide which is best for you. Also, see fingering chart, p. 295.)

● Sound A several times, as you did the G.

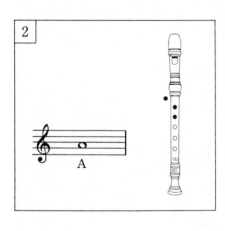

doo - doo - doo - doot

● Now, alternate A-G, A-G a few times. Remember to use the fingers like small hammers and be sure to cover the holes with the pads, not the tips, of the fingers. Attack ("doo") each tone.

doo - doo - doo - doo   *etc.*

● Playing first-line E will involve both hands. (You must create a longer column of vibrating air to sound this lower pitch.)

● Attack and blow gently, as lower notes are easily overblown. You'll recognize the shriek if you overblow!

● Play E a few times, striving for even pitch and volume.

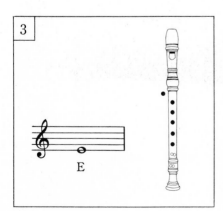

doo - doo - doo - doot

● Use first-line E to play the "Oh yes" responses of *John the Rabbit*. p 266 Play along with the song recording or with a partner who can play or sing the rest of the song.

Song notation, p. 266.

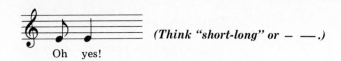
Oh   yes!

(Think "short-long" or – —.)

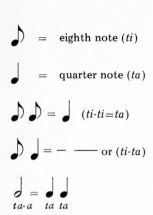

♪ = eighth note (*ti*)

♩ = quarter note (*ta*)

♪ ♪ = ♩ (*ti-ti=ta*)

♪ ♩ = – —— or (*ti-ta*)

♩ = ♩ ♩
ta-a   ta ta

● Experiment by playing E, G, and A in as many combinations as you can think of—E-G-A, A-G-E, G-A-E, GG-AA-G-E, etc. Here are some combinations in notation:

● You now have three pitches that can be combined into some familiar melodic fragments. Remember the "teasing chant" from childhood?

G   G   E   A   G   E
"Pat - ty's   got   a   boy - friend!"

● Now, play that chant from musical notation:

Here are some familiar childhood chants that use only G, A, and E. Remember to think of the note durations as you play.

RAIN, RAIN

Rain, Rain,   go a - way;   Come a-gain some oth - er day.

STARLIGHT, STARBRIGHT

Star - light   go bright,   First star I   see to - night,

Wish I may,   Wish I might,   Have the wish I   wish to night.

BYE BABY BUNTING

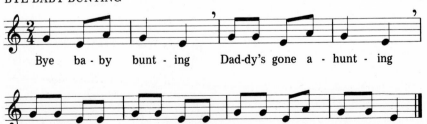

Bye   ba - by   bunt - ing   Dad-dy's gone a - hunt - ing

Catch a lit - tle   rab - bit skin to   wrap the ba - by   bunt-ing in.

′ = breathe here

Each measure contains two quarter notes or an equivalent of two quarter notes:

A TISKET, A TASKET

A tisk-et a task-et, a green and yel-low bask-et,

I sent a let-ter to my love and on the way I lost it,

I lost it, I lost it, yes, on the way I lost it.

= ti - ti-ri

= ti-ri-ti-ri

TAILS

Rac-coon's got a ring-ed tail; pos-sum's tail is bare;

rab-bit's got no tail at all, just a lit-tle bit-ty bunch of hair.___

*Slurs are indicated by curved lines connecting different pitches. Tongue only at beginning of slur, and maintain air flow as you finger successive pitches.

Congo Lullaby (NDM 2) will provide you with a longer melody using *G, A,* and *E.* Note that it is in quadruple meter (⁴⁄₄) and contains several equivalents of four quarter notes (♩♩ ♩, ♩ ♩, and 𝅝).

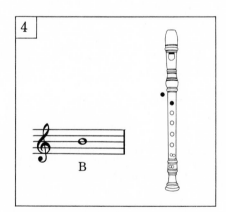

● Review the fingerings for G and A. B involves merely uncovering one more hole.

● Improvise for a few minutes, using G, A, and your new pitch, B. (B-G-A, A-B-G, B-A-G, etc.)

● Play the "a" phrases of *Au Clair de la Lune.* Notice that these phrases are identical. The third phrase ("b") is different, creating a phrase structure of a a b a. (You will be asked to play the "b" phrase later.)

AU CLAIR DE LA LUNE

French Folk Song

Au clair de la lu - ne, Mon a - mi Pier - rot. repeat sign

Prê - te moi ta plu - me, Pour é - crire un môt.

Au clair de la lu - ne, Mon a - mi Pier - rot.

● Here are some folk melodies using pitches you have already learned.

POOR BIRD

(ti ti - ri) (ta)

🎵 = **fermata**
(hold this tone slightly longer)

Ka - go - me, ka - go - me, Bird, oh bird in - side the cage.

(ti ti - ri ta)

When will you fly out and a - way? Ka - go - me, ka - go - me,

(solo)

Cir - cle round and stop in place. Who's be - hind you? Can you tell?

● Play the "a" phrases (bracketed) of *Fais do do*. The ⁶⁄₈ meter helps give this lullaby a gently rocking quality. See margin for help with note groupings and durations. Also note the "blank" notation (dashes) above the melody.

FAIS DO DO

French Folk Song

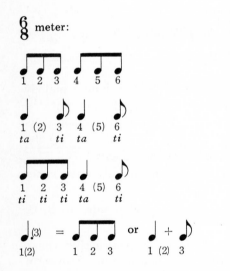

⁶⁄₈ meter:

1 2 3 4 5 6

1 (2) 3 4 (5) 6
ta ti ta ti

1 2 3 4 (5) 6
ti ti ti ta ti

♩.(3) = 🎵🎵🎵 or ♩ + ♪
1(2)   1 2 3   1 (2) 3

"Pick up" note or upbeat; see *anacrusis* in Glossary.

● *Skin and Bones* is also ⁶⁄₈ meter and has a "pickup" note at the beginning. This accounts for the presence of only five beats in the final measure. The last four notes of the melody should be *slurred* (tongue only the B). See *Chester,* p. 286, for further use of *slur.*

SKIN AND BONES

Collected by Jean Ritchie

𝄽 = quarter rest

𝄽 = ♩

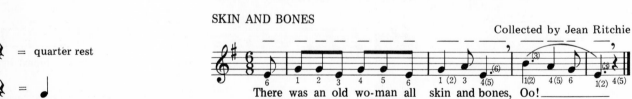

There was an old wo-man all skin and bones, Oo!_____

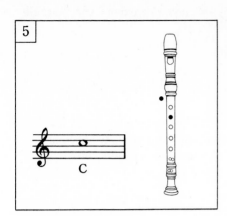

Song notation, p. 147.

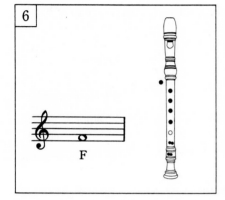

(♩.) A dot increases a note's duration by half its original duration. In this case:

♩ = 1 beat

♩. = 1 1/2 beats

Key of F major (one flat), but the B♭ is not used in this melody or in *Old Paint,* below.

- Review the fingering for B. Compare it to third-space C.
- Alternate between B and C several times. Try starting with C, then with B.
- Play these six measures of *Bingo.*

B - I - N-G-O, B - I - N-G-O, B - I - N-G-O,

- F is fingered simply, leaving just one hole uncovered. Try it:

doo - doo - doo - doot.

- As you alternate G and F, remember to "strike" the right-hand holes with the fingers. Remember to lift them quickly, too.

doo - doo - doo - doot,   etc.

- Be careful of the *dotted quarter note* (see margin) in *Merrily We Roll Along.* The duration of this note is a beat (ta) and a half (ti). To vocalize this rhythm say, "ta-i ti | ta ta." Play entire melody.

ta - i ti   ta   ta

MERRILY WE ROLL ALONG

Traditional

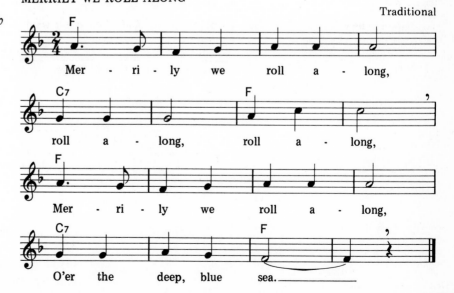

Mer - ri - ly   we   roll   a - long,
roll   a - long,   roll   a - long,
Mer - ri - ly   we   roll   a - long,
O'er   the   deep,   blue   sea._____

● The melody below has a skip in every measure except the last. Be careful!

repeat sign

Song notation, p. 241.

● Find an Autoharp player (or guitarist) who can play C, F, and G₇ chords, and practice the above together. This melody becomes a *countermelody* to *Jamaica Farewell*. As soon as you and your partner are ready, play your two parts over and over as the class sings the *Jamaica Farewell* melody.

Song notation, p. 259.
See Glossary for *ostinato*.

● Play the first two measures of *Are You Sleeping*? As soon as you feel ready, play these two measures as an *ostinato* while the class sings the song.

● Here are two spirituals you can play with just three pitches: F, G, and A.

TRAMPIN'

American Spiritual

I'm tramp - in', tramp - in', tryin' to make heav - en my home,

I'm tramp - in', tramp - in', tryin' to make heav - en my home.

GOOD NEWS

American Spiritual

Good news! Char - i - ot's com - in', Good news! Char - i - ot's com - in',

Good news! Char - i - ot's com - in' and I don't want you leav - in' me be - hind.

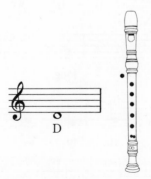

D

● Finger fourth-line D two ways. First, finger *low D* and roll the thumb *slightly* to *partially* uncover the thumbhole. Be sure the thumb remains in contact with your recorder. (This split-hole technique will be needed for other high pitches later.)

● Now, try playing the octave D-D, low to high *and* high to low. Remember to tongue each tone, and watch your breath control.

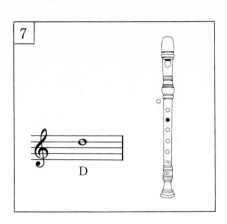

7

D

3/4   triple meter

Note: Each phrase begins with a "pickup" note. See (a) and (b) in the notation.

● Try the fingering shown here for fourth-line D. In some music one fingering will be more comfortable than the other. You be the judge.

● *Old Paint* has the same phrase structure (a a b a) as *Au Clair de la Lune* and *Fais do do.* With high D learned, you can now play the three "a" phrases of *Old Paint.*

OLD PAINT

Cowboy Song

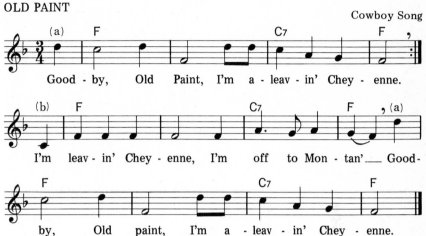

Good - by,   Old   Paint,   I'm   a - leav - in' Chey - enne.

I'm   leav - in' Chey - enne,   I'm   off   to Mon - tan'___ Good-

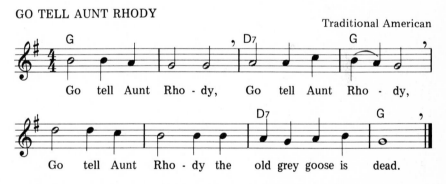

by,   Old   paint,   I'm   a - leav - in' Chey - enne.

● Go back to *Fais do do* (p. 278); practice the "b" phrase, and then play the entire melody.

● *Go Tell Aunt Rhody* should give you no trouble. Try it!

GO TELL AUNT RHODY

Traditional American

Go   tell Aunt Rho - dy,   Go   tell Aunt Rho - dy,

Go   tell Aunt Rho - dy the   old grey goose is   dead.

● Turn to p. 264 and try *Choral Theme.* Try *Amazing Grace,* p. 236.

8

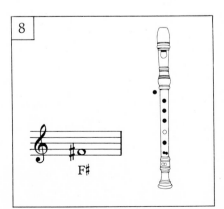

F♯

● F♯ will be found in many songs in the keys of G major, D major, and E minor. Finger F♯ and compare it to F♮ (F-natural) (see marginal box for unit 6).

● After sounding several F♯s, play this pattern several times:

F♯

● *We Three Kings* is a two-section (A B) song. Try the A section, which is in E minor. After learning low D, come back and play the B section (in G major.)

WE THREE KINGS

John H. Hopkins

Sharp sign (♯) appears on top line in key signature but affects *all F's* (in this case, first-space F).

$\frac{3}{8}$ triple meter

♪ = 1 beat

ta   *ti*

1   (2)   3

𝄾 = eighth rest

𝄾 = ♪

We three Kings of Or - i - ent are,

Bear - ing gifts we trav - erse a - far,

Field and foun - tain, moor and moun - tain,

Fol - low - ing yon - der star.

O___ Star of won - der, Star of night,

Star with roy - al beau - ty bright,

West - ward lead - ing, still pro - ceed - ing,

Guide us to thy per - fect light.

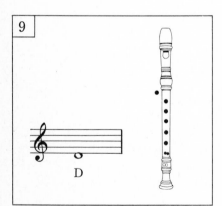

D

- Review first-line E. Now try the adjacent D. Practice alternating E and D. Remember the attack and the gentle, steady stream of air that will keep the pitch true.

- Both sections of the song *Hold On* end with this F-D-F-D-F-D pattern.

Hold on, hold on, hold on,

- Try playing the entire A section of *Hold On*, p. 262.

This Old Man will give you practice with both F♯ and low D.

THIS OLD MAN

● Play the "responses" in *Jane, Jane,* p. 227, and in *All Around the Kitchen,* p. 68. (Notice that the "cock-a-doodle, doodle, doo" is played two ways.)

Song notation, p. 261

● The syncopated responses in *Sing Hallelu* will give you a good chance to review A, G, F, and low D.

Syncopation. See Glossary.

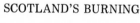

sing hal - le - lu
(syn - co - pa ta - a)

● Practice the "b" phrase of *Au Clair de la Lune* and then play the entire melody (p. 277).

● Low D will enable you to play the B section of *We Three Kings.* Go back to p. 282 and work on the B section, then try the entire song.

● Because of the D-D octave leap in *Scotland's Burning,* you will probably have better luck with the high D if you use the split-thumbhole technique described earlier (p. 280.) Try the last four measures first. Then play the entire melody.

Note: If you are having trouble with the lower pitches on your recorder, concentrate on breath support—a steady, gentle stream of air through the instrument. Use much less air than you think you need. Think of that stream of air as being *very* small, about the size of a pencil point. Also, practice often and for short periods of time. Don't risk the fatigue and frustration of overlong practice periods.

SCOTLAND'S BURNING

● Play this melody as smoothly (legato) as possible. Notice the slurs.

O COME, EMMANUEL

Traditional chant

O come, O come Em - man - u - el,

And ran - som cap - tive Is - ra - el;

That mourns in lone - ly ex - ile here,

Un - til the son of God _____ ap - pear.

Re - joice, re - joice, Em - man - u - el,

Shall come to thee, O Is - ra - el.

*Incomplete measure is completed at beginning of second staff.

● Play *Hari Krishna* and *Serafina*.

HARI KRISHNA

Ancient Indian Chant

Ha - ri Krish - na, Ha - ri Krish - na, Krish - na, Krish - na, Ha - ri, Ha - ri.

Ha - ri Ra - ma, Ha - ri Ra - ma, Ra - ma, Ra - ma, Ha - ri, Ha - ri.

SERAFINA

Sea Chantey

In Cal - ly - o there lives a girl whose name is Se - ra - fi - na!

Se - ra - fi - na! She works all day and sleeps all night, Oh,

yes, my Se - ra - fi - na. Se - ra - fi - na, oh, Se - ra - fi - na!

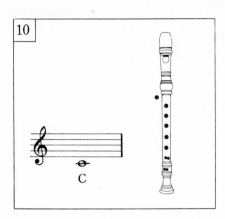

C

- Try sounding several low C's—gently.
- *Go Tell Aunt Rhody* (this time in the key of *C*) will give you several chances to practice low C. *Don't overblow!* A mere *thread* of air is enough for the lowest pitches.

GO TELL AUNT RHODY

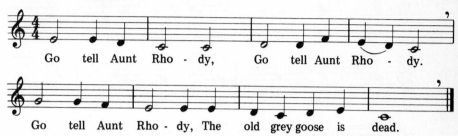

Go tell Aunt Rho - dy, Go tell Aunt Rho - dy.

Go tell Aunt Rho - dy, The old grey goose is dead.

- Return to *Old Paint* (p. 281) and try the "b" phrase. Then play the entire melody.
- Play *Khukhabara*, now that you can play low C. Some rather fast tonguing of *G, A*, and *E* will produce the first two measures of this African version of *Kookaburra*. If the rhythm looks difficult, sound it out with rhythm syllables and *think* the rhythm of the words.

Khukhabara uses the Swahili dialect of the Luhya people (Luo tribe).

♩ = ♫♫
ta   ti - ri - ti - ri

♩ = ♫♩
ta   ti   ti - ri

♩ = ♩♩
ta   ti   ti

♩ = ♩♫
ta   ti - ri ti

♩ = ♩.♫
ta   ti - i   ri

Notes are grouped in one-beat units (see above) in this *duple meter* song.

♪* *Grace note* (omit). See Glossary.

KHUKHABARA   (KOOKABURRA)

As sung in Kenya

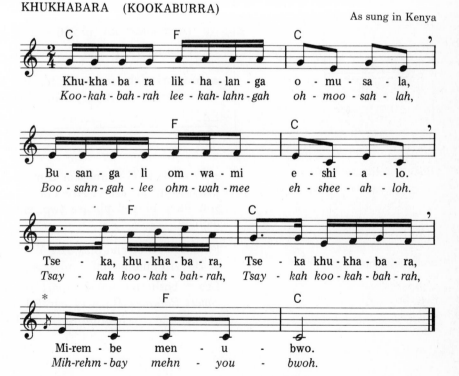

Khu-kha-ba - ra   lik - ha - lan - ga   o - mu - sa - la,
Koo-kah-bah-rah   lee - kah- lahn-gah   oh - moo - sah - lah,

Bu - san - ga - li   om - wa - mi   e - shi - a - lo.
Boo-sahn-gah - lee   ohm-wah-mee   eh - shee - ah - loh.

Tse - ka, khu-kha-ba - ra,   Tse - ka khu-kha-ba - ra,
Tsay - kah koo-kah-bah-rah,   Tsay - kah koo-kah-bah-rah,

Mi-rem - be   men - u - bwo.
Mih-rehm - bay   mehn - you - bwoh.

- *St. Paul's Steeple* contains descending and ascending C-major scales. Easy enough! (p. 133.)
- *Chester* uses all the pitches in the key of C major. *Slurs* are indicated by the curved lines and are marked with asterisks (*). Tongue only at the beginning of a slur. Do not tongue again until the first note following the slur.

CHESTER   o = 4 beats   William Billings

Let ty - rants shake their i - ron rod,

And slav - 'ry clank her gall - ing chains;

We fear them not, We trust in God;

New Eng - land's God for - ev - er reigns.

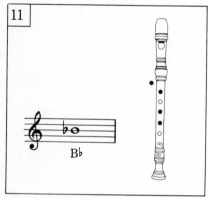

11

Bb

Song notation, p. 259

Song notation, p. 233

See Glossary.

● Additional melodies elsewhere in the text will give you good practice, especially for low C:

JINGLE BELLS, p. 255

WHEN THE SAINTS GO MARCHING IN, p. 256

LOVE SOMEBODY, p. 256

KUM BA YA, p. 269

● Memorize the fingering for B♭. You will find yourself needing to move from B♭ to A very often. Practice this alternation:

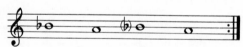

● A to B♭ to C is another combination of pitches you will often use. The second phrase of *Are You Sleeping?* is an example of this. After you have played phrase two, challenge yourself to play the entire melody.

Find a partner and play *Are You Sleeping?* as a round.

● B♭ will enable you to play *A Ram Sam Sam,* too.

Learn both the melody (part I) and the countermelody (part II) of *Sweet Potatoes.* Be very careful to observe the *quarter rests,* which help create *syncopation* in the melody.

SWEET POTATOES

Creole Folk Song

● Practice both melodies of *Zum Gali Gali.* Choose a partner and play the two melodies simultaneously.

ZUM GALI GALI

Palestinian Folk Song

2. Avodah le 'man hechalutz;
   Hechalutz le 'man avodah.

3. Hechalutz le 'man hab'tulah;
   Hab'tulah le 'man hechalutz.

4. Hashalom le 'man ha'amim;
   Ha'amim le 'man hashalom.

Approximately translated, the verses of *Zum Gali Gali* mean:
1. The pioneer's purpose is labor.
2. The pioneer's purpose is labor.
3. The pioneer is for his girl.
4. Peace for all the nations.

● Additional melodies elsewhere in the text will give you good practice, especially for *B♭*:

LADY COME, p. 259

LOVELY EVENING, p. 267

Key of G minor, harmonic form of the scale

● *Minka* is a song that uses both B♭ and F♯. Work it out phrase by phrase and be patient!

MINKA

Russian Folk Song
English words by Margaret Marks

Note: The curved lines above the notes are phrase marks. *Try to make each phrase flow from beginning to end.*

● Measures 11–12 of *Hanukah Song* will be good practice for B♭. After measures 11–12, try measures 11–16. (Play the entire melody as soon as you can.)

HANUKAH SONG

As sung by Allie Lindeman

- Try playing the "Whipsee diddle dee dandy O" fragment in *The Frog and the Mouse*. Review the $\frac{6}{8}$ note groupings accompanying *Fais do do*, p. 278.
- Challenge yourself to play the entire song.

THE FROG AND THE MOUSE

English Folk Song

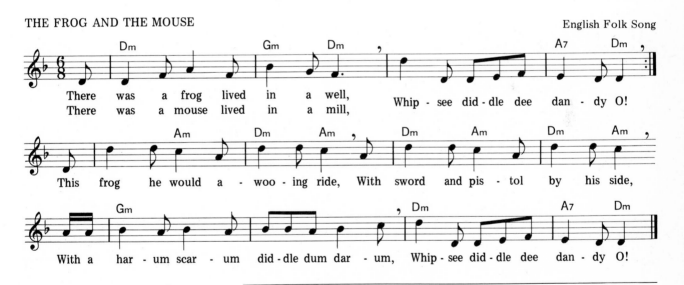

There was a frog lived in a well,
There was a mouse lived in a mill, Whip-see did-dle dee dan-dy O!

This frog he would a - woo-ing ride, With sword and pis - tol by his side,

With a har - um scar - um did-dle dum dar-um, Whip-see did-dle dee dan-dy O!

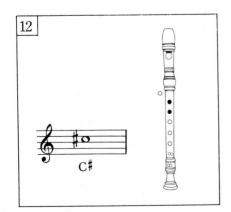

- Practice playing third-space C♯.

C♯ appears just once in *Hold On* (p. 262.) Practice moving from A to C♯ a few times before you try playing the entire B section of *Hold On*.

Play *Hush, Little Baby* in the key of A major.

HUSH, LITTLE BABY

American Folk Song

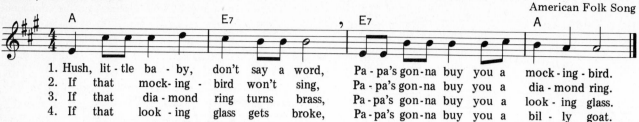

1. Hush, lit-tle ba - by, don't say a word, Pa - pa's gon-na buy you a mock-ing-bird.
2. If that mock-ing - bird won't sing, Pa - pa's gon-na buy you a dia-mond ring.
3. If that dia-mond ring turns brass, Pa - pa's gon-na buy you a look-ing glass.
4. If that look-ing glass gets broke, Pa - pa's gon-na buy you a bil - ly goat.

5. If that billy goat don't pull,
   Papa's gonna buy you a cart and bull.
6. If that cart and bull turns over,
   Papa's gonna buy you a dog named Rover.
7. If that dog named Rover don't bark,
   Papa's gonna buy a pony cart.
8. If that pony cart falls down,
   You'll be the saddest child in town.

● Have a guitarist play the A and E₇ chords as you play the melody. (Guitarist might use an *arpeggio strum*)

● Additional melodies elsewhere in the text will give you good practice, especially for third-space C♯.

JOHN THE RABBIT, p. 266

AMERICA, THE BEAUTIFUL, p. 270

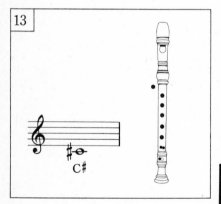

13

C♯

"Bile" means boil.

● To play low C♯, partially uncover the double hole under the fourth finger. Songs in D major or D minor will sometimes use this pitch.

● Practice Part II of *Bile Them Cabbage Down*. Find a partner to play part I, and you will have a harmonized version. Invite an Autoharp player or guitarist to play the chords with you.

BILE THEM CABBAGE DOWN

American Folk Song

If you're in a singing mood, here are some lyrics that are sometimes sung to *Bile Them Cabbage Down:*

Bile them cabbage down, boys,
Stir them hoecake 'round,
Craziest song I ever sung is
'Bile them cabbage down.'

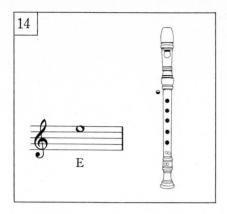

14

E

Review information at the bottom of p. 280.

For notes in the upper octave one generally fingers the lower-octave pitch, *partially* uncovers the thumbhole, and overblows *very slightly.*

Try the high E (fourth space) in this way. Alternate low and high E, and try for evenness of pitch and volume.

Turn to model experience *Ancient Chinese Temple Music* and examine the "Reading Objective." Try playing both the D and the E by fingering the lower D and E with the thumbhole slightly uncovered. Blow very gently.

(The bridge in *Ancient Chinese Temple Music* very clearly uses the melodic fragments shown in the "Reading Objective.")

Try playing *Battle Hymn of the Republic.* The melodies of verse and refrain are the same, but the refrain is a bit easier to read rhythmically. Try the refrain first.

You'll notice that many single beats (♩) are divided

ti - i ri

(dotted eighth note followed by a sixteenth note).

Remember that the dotted eighth is *three times as long* as the sixteenth.

BATTLE HYMN OF THE REPUBLIC

Civil War Song
Julia Ward Howe
Words attributed to William Steffe

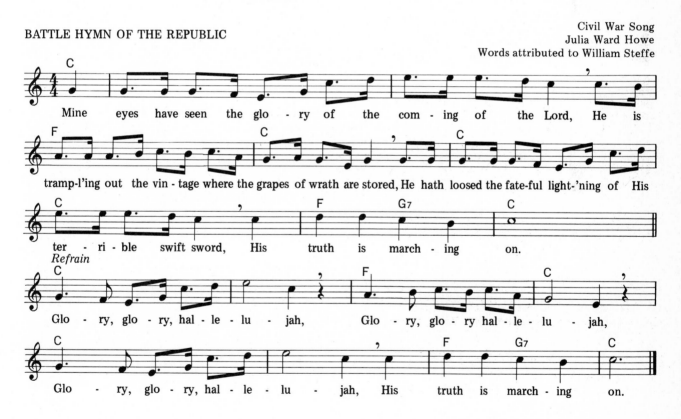

Mine eyes have seen the glo - ry of the com - ing of the Lord, He is tramp-l'ing out the vin - tage where the grapes of wrath are stored, He hath loosed the fate-ful light-'ning of His ter - ri - ble swift sword, His truth is march - ing on.

Refrain

Glo - ry, glo - ry, hal - le - lu - jah, Glo - ry, glo - ry hal - le - lu - jah,

Glo - ry, glo - ry, hal - le - lu - jah, His truth is march - ing on.

ENSEMBLE PLAYING

Here is a two-part arrangement of *Shoo, Fly.* Play part 2 alone, then find someone to play or sing the melody with you. Or play the melody as others sing or play the harmony part.

SHOO FLY

American Game Song

Repetition of the refrain ("A" section) makes the form of this song A B A, also called *ternary* form.

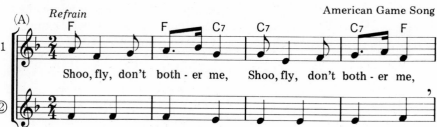

Shoo, fly, don't both - er me, Shoo, fly, don't both - er me,

Shoo, fly, don't both - er me, For I be-long to some-bod - y.

Fine

I feel, I feel, I feel, I feel like a morn-ing star,

⌢ = fermata

D.C. = "from the beginning." Repeat from beginning to the point marked *Fine* ("end").

I feel, I feel, I feel, I feel, I feel like a morn-ing star. So

D.C. al Fine

Here is a harmonized version of *Yankee Doodle*. Try the harmony part, part 2, alone. Then play it as others sing or play the melody.

YANKEE DOODLE

Traditional

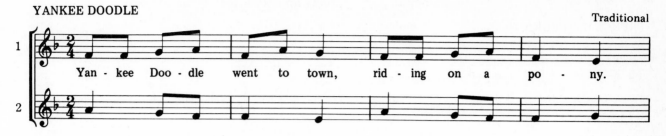

Play the melody *Skip to My Lou,* p. 238. Learn the following countermelody to *Skip to My Lou* and, with a partner, play the two parts. Add an Autoharp player (or a guitarist) to play the C and G₇ chords.

SKIP TO MY LOU (countermelody)

I Belong to This Band (SBM 5) has an interesting countermelody you might play as the melody is sung or played by others.

Also in SBM 5 you will find a very easy two-part arrangement of *Nani Wale Na Hala,* a folk song from Hawaii. The same song can be found in MMYO 5.

Quodlibets provide very interesting materials for ensemble playing. See model experience *Bow, Belinda* for one example.

Song notation, p. 176.

Tzena, Tzena (MMYO 5 and 6) can be played as a *quodlibet.* Play the A section (four measures repeated) as someone else plays the eight-measure B section. Listen to the recording if you have difficulty with this song.

French Cathedrals, though a simple melody, becomes very interesting played in three parts. Try it with three recorders or a combination of recorders and other melody instruments.

FRENCH CATHEDRALS

French Round

Or - lé - ans,   Beau - gen - cy,   No - tre Dam- e   de Cler - y,   Ven - dôm - e,   Ven - dôm - e.

Learn to play one of the three sections of *Dona Nobis Pacem* while two partners learn the other two. Play them as follows to quickly achieve the sound of the three-part round:

1. Player 1 plays his eight measures,

2. Player 1 plays his eight measures as player 2 adds his part, and

3. Players 1 and 2 repeat their parts as player 3 adds his part.

Learn all three sections so your ensemble can play *Dona Nobis Pacem* as a round in the usual way.

DONA NOBIS PACEM

Traditional Round

Do - na   no - bis   pa - cem, pa-cem, Do - na   no - bis   pa - - cem.

Do - na   no - bis   pa-cem,   Do - na   no - bis   pa - - cem.

Do - na   no - bis   pa-cem,   Do - na   no - bis   pa - - cem.

○ open   ● closed   ◕ slightly open

Fingering for soprano recorder (1, 2, and 3 indicate alternate fingerings)

Some beginning recorder players may find it more logical to view printed fingering as though they were looking *down* the instrument as it is held in playing position. Turn your book upside down and decide which is best for you.

RECORDER METHODS

Duschenes, Mario. *Method for the Recorder.* New York: Associated Music Publishers, Inc., 1957.

John, R. W., and C. H. Douglas. *Playing Social and Recreational Instruments.* Englewood Cliffs, N.J.: Prentice-Hall, Inc., 1972.

Trapp Family Singers, The. *Enjoy Your Recorder.* Sharon, Conn.: Magnamusic Distributors, Inc., 1954.

White, F., and A. Bergman. *Playing the Recorder.* New York: E. B. Marks Music Corp., 1955.

SECTION THREE
Backgrounds for Teaching Music

Musical Elements Provide a Framework for Music Learning

Music communicates through its melodies, rhythms, harmonies, forms, and expressive qualities. These musical elements provide the teacher with a "cognitive map" appropriate for use at every level of the learner's development. (15) Throughout this text, the following definitions of the elements are used:

● *Expressive qualities* are those qualities (dynamics, tempo, timbre) which, combined with other musical elements (melody, rhythm, form, and harmony) give a composition its unique musical identity.

> *dynamics* — the degree and range of loudness of musical sounds

> *tempo* — the rate of speed of the music

> *timbre* — the characteristic quality of sound that distinguishes one sound source from another

● *Melody* is a linear succession of pitches; the horizontal structure in music.

● *Rhythm* includes all of the durations that occur in music.

● *Form* is the shape, order, or design of a musical composition.

● *Harmony* is the simultaneous sounding of two or more pitches; the vertical structure in music.

The experience of the beginning student is a composite of undifferentiated perceptions. (3) Therefore, each model experience in *The Musical Classroom* has been designed to focus student perception on a single musical element and to lead to a fundamental understanding about that element. Because music is a temporal art, each experience will facilitate — simultaneously — perception and conceptualization. (12) Great care has been taken to suggest how this may be accomplished without diminishing the aesthetic impact of the art.

In the section which follows, each musical element is discussed as it is used within the model experiences of this text. Information is also given which suggests how and when each element may be introduced to children. The description of each element concludes with a list of related model experiences.

EXPRESSIVE QUALITIES

Tempo, dynamics, and timbre are the musical elements which often communicate most directly and forcefully. These elements are readily perceived, even by young children. (8) And to be understood, they require only a modicum of musical information.

Tempo is the speed of the musical sound. Young children understand tempo, at first, in two degrees: slow and fast. They can translate their understandings to a percussion instrument, and play fast and slow tempi. (13) Children must be somewhat older before they can remember and compare a graduated series of tempi from slow to fast.

The degree of loudness of musical sounds is known as *dynamics*. This quality is easily identified and requires only limited training. (6) (16) For the most part, this involves the proper application of the terms "loud" and "soft." Children sometimes mistakenly associate

Timbre = TAM-br

"down" or "lower" with soft dynamics. (14) This may be due in part to the fact that radio and television dials are turned "higher" or "lower." As pupils are ready to conceptualize about music, teachers of music help them acquire an accurate vocabulary to label their understandings (1) and associate the terms "loud" and "soft" with dynamics.

The *timbre* of musical sounds (vocal or instrumental tone quality) may dominate a listener's perceptual field. A preschool child who hears *Are You Sleeping?* played on a violin and later on a tuba may believe the melody itself has been changed. (11) With the teacher's help, even this young child can learn to focus on the tune as well as on the tuba. Students should have many opportunities to hear live or recorded performances on Western orchestral instruments such as violin and tuba. Non-Western vocal and instrumental timbres also fascinate many youngsters. (7) Music of 20th-century composers explores timbre, often using electronically expressed environmental sounds or electrical impulses. Lessons which focus on timbre may enable students to become familiar with a wide variety of musical styles.(4)

An expressive palette of tempo, dynamics, and timbre is introduced through the following model experiences:

Tempo

1. Music can move in a fast tempo or in a slow tempo. (THE ELE-PHANT)
2. Tempo, combined with other musical elements, gives a composition its unique musical identity. (SERAFINA; FOG)

Dynamics

3. Musical sounds can be soft or loud or can gradually become softer or louder. (PARADE)

Timbre*

4. Instrumental families (woodwind, string, brass, percussion) can be identified by their timbres. (TOCCATA FOR PERCUSSION, etc.)

Several qualities

5. Timbre, duration, and volume can be altered electronically. (OVEN GRILL CONCERTO; POÈME ÉLECTRONIQUE)

Timbre

6. Each instrument has a characteristic timbre which, combined with others, contributes to a composition's unique identity. (HAIKU SOUND PIECE)
7. Instruments can be grouped according to their vibrating material (membranophones, idiophones, chordophones, aerophones). (WOMAN'S WEDDING SONG, etc.)

---

*Timbre is a distinctive quality mentioned in several other model experiences, though it may not be the specific focus for music learning.

MELODY

Melody involves a linear succession of tones (pitches) moving through time. Each melody is a unique combination of pitches, which together create a discernible contour or sense of unity. Exactly how a melody achieves musical and emotional impact is difficult to analyze. But it is possible to discover how pitches relate to one another and to study their movement within the temporal flow of music.

Musical pitches are produced by a vibrating medium. It is the rapidity of vibration that creates the quality referred to as "high" or "low" *pitch*. A high pitch vibrates more rapidly than a low pitch. Young children need help in using the terms "high" and "low" accurately. (6) Children may be confused, at first, because terms which otherwise designate a spatial concept are to be associated with an aural perception. (18) Teachers can provide concrete experiences to clarify these concepts. For example, a small xylophone may be placed in a vertical position, with the highest-pitched bar (the smallest) at the top, and the lowest-pitched bar at the bottom. Preschoolers may even arrive at this solution independently. (14) As they do, the teacher must be ready to help the pupil by supplying the appropriate label. (18)

Intervals, contour, and high and low pitches are all governed by a kind of musical grammar called *scales*. To speak a language it is not necessary to have a conscious understanding of its rules. So it is in regard to musical scales. The knowledge that HEY, HO! NOBODY HOME uses a minor scale is probably of greater use to the teacher than it is to the child. Students might, of course, be taught how to construct a minor scale. But until the child is ready to use facts in a creatively expressive manner, this kind of knowledge is premature. (16) It requires a sensitive and experienced teacher to judge this readiness and to recognize when children have acquired the experience with musical sounds that makes knowledge of scales meaningful. Seldom would scales be studied prior to the upper grades.

The Musical Classroom is designed to provide introductory experiences in music. Those model experiences which focus on scale structure and other specific areas of music theory are labeled "work-through experiences," and are intended for use in the college classroom. They might also be used with children, but only with those having an appropriate musical background.

The following understandings about melody are presented through the model experiences of this text:

1. The pitches of melodies can be mostly connected or mostly disconnected. (BARCAROLLE; POLKA)

2. Pitches in a tonal pattern can repeat. (JOHN THE RABBIT)

3. Melodies can include skips of an octave. (THE FROG AND THE MOUSE)

4. A melody can include repeated tonal patterns. (SCOTLAND'S BURNING)

5. Pitches in a tonal pattern can repeat or can move by skipping up. (GRIZZLY BEAR)

6. Pitches in a tonal pattern can move by step. (JANE, JANE; ANCIENT CHINESE TEMPLE MUSIC)

7. Pitches in a tonal pattern can move by stepping up. (FIVE ANGELS)

8. Pitches in a melody can move by stepping up or down. (PIANISTS)

9. A song usually ends on the tonal center. (THIS OLD MAN)

10. Octave displacement and change of duration can be produced electronically. (SOUND PIECE 7)

11. Pitches in a melody can move stepwise through a scale. (ST. PAUL'S STEEPLE)

12. Pitches in a melody can move through chord tones. (HOLD ON)

13. A tonal pattern can be restated, beginning on different pitches (sequence). (MINKA)

14. Composers can alter melodies by displacing the pitches one or more octaves. (GREETING PRELUDE)

15. A melody can exhibit a distinctive contour as it moves up or down or repeats. (CORN GRINDING SONG)

16. A single melody can serve as the basis for an entire composition. (GAMBANGAN)

17. Melodies can be altered by replaying them in scales that reflect differing pitch relationships (major to whole-tone scale). (VOILES)

18. The twelve tones of a chromatic scale can be rearranged in a composition (tone-row music). (MINUET)

19. A melody can be varied by changing it from minor to major mode. (TUTÚ MARAMBA)

20. Musical texture results from the combining of melodic and harmonic elements (monophonic, polyphonic, and homophonic styles). (LECHU NIRANENO ARLAYIM SHOVA, etc.)

RHYTHM

Music is an art of motion—of continuous flow. Rhythm refers to the durations of the sounds (and silences) in the musical flow. All of the rhythms that occur in music may be translated into physical responses. Because of this, elementary music teaching has long utilized rhythmic movement to expand rhythmic perception and understanding.

A recurrent rhythmic pulsation is called a *beat*. A beat is perhaps the most fundamental aspect of rhythm, for it governs all the other sounds and silences in a composition. The kindergarten child can learn to play this steady beat (13), but a child may have difficulty coordinating this playing with that of another child, or adjusting his beat to the beat of music. With training, this skill may be developed by the age of seven or eight (10).

In addition to the beat, there are always musical tones that are longer or shorter than the beat. These long and short *durations* are only vaguely understood by kindergarten children. (9) Movement experiences focusing on long and short durations may be important at first. One helpful experience is for youngsters to move until they hear a single long sound in a composition, and to "freeze" when it occurs. Very young children may describe this long sound as "slower" and shorter sounds as "faster." In fact, they are describing the physical movements elicited by those sounds. With greater maturity and experience, they will make a distinction and also begin to use informal notation to represent duration.

For example, a *rhythm pattern* (as, — — – – —) can be expressed through movement, singing, or playing instruments. These patterns are combinations of long and short sounds. Ultimately they are combined into longer melodic rhythms. Tapping the words of *Row, Row, Row Your Boat* sounds a *melodic rhythm*. The musical meaning of these sounds is communicated, in part, through their rhythmic grouping.

Meter is another kind of rhythmic grouping. It is the grouping of the beats into sets of two or three. In some music the beat groupings are obvious to the ear; in other music, they are not. The "oom-pah-pah" of *The Blue Danube Waltz* is easy to identify as triple meter. (8) By the age of nine or ten, the child may clap, tap, or sing to arrive at a correct identification of meter. All modes of learning will be useful at first: motor, aural, visual, tactile, and verbal. With experience and maturity, the child's perception and understanding may be expanded. (5) Eventually the student will identify meter by internalized conceptual means, rather than by overt actions.

The following understandings about rhythm are presented through the model experiences of this text:

1. Chants can suggest the presence of steady beats. (ENGINE, ENGINE)

2. Music can suggest the presence of steady beats. (THE WIND BLEW EAST)

3. A melodic rhythm usually includes long and short sounds (KANGAROO)

4. The prevailing rhythm of a musical composition can include consecutive long sounds, consecutive short sounds, or combinations. (MARCH, LITTLE SOLDIER)

5. Rhythm patterns can include sounds of long and short duration. (BINGO)

6. A melodic rhythm usually includes long and short sounds. (A RAM SAM SAM I)

7. Steady beats can be grouped in twos (duple meter). (WE ARE GOING DOWN THE NUMBERS)

8. Steady beats can be grouped in threes (triple meter). (ELEPHANT)

9. A melodic rhythm usually includes long and short sounds. (POLKA)

10. Short and long sounds in a tonal pattern can be grouped to create syncopation. (SING HALLELU)

11. Different rhythm patterns can sound simultaneously within a composition (polyrhythms). (JIN-GO-LO-BA)

12. Music can suggest the presence or absence of steady beats and can include rhythm patterns. (WAR DANCE SONG, etc.)

13. The rhythm of a melody can be varied when the melody is repeated. (SYMPHONY NO. 94)

14. Duple and triple groupings of beats can alternate (asymmetric meter). (SAMIOTISSA)

FORM

Musical form is often compared to architecture because it refers to shape, order, or design. In both arts, unity and variety are achieved through details and through overall shape.

The *phrase* is an important building block in musical form. A phrase may be compared to a sentence in speech, for it is a segment with a clear musical beginning and ending. *London Bridge,* for example, is a brief song consisting of only two phrases, each eight beats long. Young children readily understand such paired phrases. (13)

The phrases in a song may be grouped into distinct *sections. Jingle Bells* is an example of a song with two sections: a verse and a refrain. The sections of this song contrast with each other. This musical design is referred to as A B (also called *binary* form). *Shoo, Fly* is an example of a song with three sections: the first and third sections are the same with the second contrasting. This musical design is referred to as A B A (*ternary* form). Songs are an ideal starting point for understanding longer compositions containing several sections.

Longer compositions can be more difficult for children to listen to and understand. Teachers must focus student perception on the musical qualities that will be meaningful to them. This will help them learn to hear what is the *same,* and what is *different.* Some students will listen particularly for instrumental timbre. Others will hear and remember melodies or rhythms. Such understandings usually develop as the music is heard.

Because it is a temporal art, music simply will not "sit still" for examination. Teachers will be better able to observe the degree of student understanding if they design experiences requiring overt behavior to express perception and comprehension. Techniques frequently used include moving the body or playing instruments along with the music. Another technique is to provide shapes which may be manipulated while listening to a composition. (9) A square might represent the initial section of the music, and a circle, the contrasting section. Experiences of this kind will focus perceptions that are otherwise vague and undifferentiated. For ultimately, teachers do not "teach." Rather, they help students identify and understand what they perceive.

The following understandings about form are presented through the model experiences noted in parentheses:

1. In "call-and-response" form, responses can be identical to the call, or contrasting (STOMP DANCE, etc.)

2. Repetition creates unity in games, poems, and songs. (ALL AROUND THE KITCHEN; THE CLAM)

3. Phrases in a melody can repeat. (LA VÍBORA)

4. Paired phrases can contrast with each other. (CHINESE DANCE) (CONTRASTING MELODIC PHRASES [Improvised])

5. Each phrase in "12-bar" blues consists of four measures (16 beats). (GOOD MORNING, BLUES)

6. Sections of a song can contrast with each other (A B). (CLAP YOUR HANDS)

7. Sections of a composition can contrast with one another and sections can be repeated (A B A, A B). (A RAM SAM SAM II) (CARILLON) (SCRATCH, SCRATCH, etc.)

8. Phrase length reflects stylistic and cultural traditions in folk songs. (ALA DAL'ONA)

9. The initial section of a composition may alternate with contrasting sections (rondo). (VIENNESE MUSICAL CLOCK)

HARMONY

Harmony results when two or more pitches are sounded simultaneously. Harmony gives an added dimension to melody, and it is broadly comparable to perspective in painting. Children are accustomed to hearing melodies against a background of harmonies. Yet melody nearly always dominates the perceptual field of the young child. (12) Therefore, the teacher must help students broaden their perception and help them to identify these multiple sounds of harmony.

In the elementary classroom, harmony may be introduced by adding sounds to a familiar melody. For example, a tonal pattern such as "ding, ding, dong" may be repeated over and over while the melody of *Are You Sleeping?* is sung. One or more of these *ostinati* can be sung or played along with a melody. Multiple sounds are also created when *Are You Sleeping?* is sung as a two- or three-voice round. Because the logic of this kind of harmony seems a mystery to children under eight years of age (12), rounds performed in several parts ought to be delayed until at least third grade. Combinations of separate, distinct melodies are a special kind of harmony labeled *polyphony*.

When a single melody is supported by a series of chords, *homophonic* style results. This "melody with accompaniment" occurs when classroom singing is accompanied with Autoharp, piano, or guitar. Children themselves can begin to play chordal accompaniments on the Autoharp when they are about eight. (18) Accompaniments which use only two or three different chords are easiest to play. Although beginners are better able to identify individual chords when only a few are heard (10), they may enjoy more varied harmonies.

Chords relate to melody, and the adult listener nearly always knows when the chords "fit" (are *consonant*) with the melody. Preschool children, however, demonstrate little discrimination one way or the other. (18) Yet by the age of nine they seem to develop a preference for consonant harmonies. (17) It is difficult to determine how much of this "conditioning" is accomplished in school, and how much through the media.

Ideas concerning consonance are relative, and have changed considerably over the course of music history. Non-Western music and 20th-century compositions do not always conform to traditional concepts of consonance. Music educators are beginning to identify a responsibility for providing an expanded musical environment—one conducive to understanding *all* of the sounds and styles of music.

Harmony is introduced through the following model experiences:

1. Chords can accompany melodies. (SKIP TO MY LOU)

2. Polyphonic texture can be created by vertically combining phrases of a round. (ARE YOU SLEEPING? I)

3. A phrase of a round can serve as an ostinato to accompany the entire melody. (THE GHOST OF TOM)

4. An ostinato can be created electronically. (STRING QUARTET NO. 4)

5. Chord roots can serve as a song accompaniment. (JOE TURNER BLUES)

6. Melodies based on differing scales can be combined (polytonality). (ARE YOU SLEEPING? II)

7. Aleatoric composition can be created electronically. (IMPROVISATION FOR SOLO PERFORMER AND FIVE TAPE RECORDERS)

8. Two melodies that use the same chords at the same time can be performed simultaneously. (BOW, BELINDA; SKIP TO MY LOU)

9. Chord tones can be played one after another as a song accompaniment. (JAMAICA FAREWELL)

10. Musical texture results from the combining of melodic and harmonic elements (monophonic, polyphonic, and homophonic styles). (LECHU NIRANENO ARLAYIM SHOVA, etc.)

SUMMARY

The musical elements which provide a framework for conceptual learning are melody, rhythm, harmony, form, and the expressive qualities of timbre, tempo, and dynamics.

While each element has been described separately, it must be emphasized that they never occur singly in music. Each is woven into the temporal tapestry of music and cannot be examined except as it is heard.

Teachers play an important role because they help students focus perception and increase their musical understanding. Each learning experience succeeds when it develops understandings which intensify the emotional and aesthetic impact of the music.

SECTION REFERENCES

1. Andrews, Frances M., and Ned C. Deihl. "Development of a Technique for Identifying Elementary School Children's Musical Concepts," *Journal of Research in Music Education,* 183 (Fall, 1970), p. 214.

2. Duell, Orpha K., and Richard C. Anderson. "Pitch Discrimination Among Primary School Children," *Journal of Educational Psychology,* 58, 6 (1967), p. 315.

3. Farnham-Diggory, Sylvia. *Cognitive Processes in Education.* New York: Harper & Row, Publishers, Inc., 1972.

4. Fowler, Charles B. "The Misrepresentation of Music," in *Perspectives in Music Education: Source Book III,* ed. Bonnie Kowall. Washington, D.C.: Music Educators National Conference, 1966.

5. Gordon, Edwin. *The Psychology of Music Teaching.* Englewood Cliffs, N.J.: Prentice-Hall, Inc., 1971.

6. Laverty, Grace E. "The Development of Children's Concepts of Pitch, Duration and Loudness as a Function of Grade Level," reviewed by David Swanzy in *Council for Research in Music Education,* 12, 23 (Winter, 1971), p. 33.

7. Malm, William P. "Preparing the Music Teacher for Handling the Music of Non-Western Traditions," in *International Seminar in Teacher Education in Music,* ed. Marguerite Hood. United States Office of Education, 1966, p. 194.

8. Moorhead, Gladys, and Donald Pond. *Music of Young Children.* Santa Barbara, Calif.: Pillsbury Foundation for the Advancement of Music Education, 1941–44.

9. Neidlinger, Robert J. "A Study in Teaching Musical Style and Form to Elementary School Children," as reviewed by Marilyn P. Zimmerman in *Council for Research in Music Education,* No. 18 (Fall, 1969), p. 39.

10. Petzold, Robert G. *The Development of Auditory Perception of Musical Sounds by Children in the First Six Grades.* Madison: University of Wisconsin Press, 1966. Report of United States Office of Education Cooperative Research Project No. 1051.

11. Pflederer, Marilyn, and Lee Sechrest, "Conservation-type Responses of Children to Musical Stimuli," *Council for Research in Music Education,* No. 13 (Spring, 1968) p. 19.

12. Pflederer, Marilyn, and Lee Sechrest, "Conservation in Musical Thought," *Psychology in the Schools,* 5, 2 (April, 1968), p. 99.

13. Piper, Richard M., and David M. Shoemaker, "Formative Evaluation of a Kindergarten Music Program Based on Behavioral Objectives," *Journal of Research in Music Education,* 21, 2 (Summer, 1973), p. 145.

14. Stecher, Miriam B., and Hugh McElheny. "The Structure of Music Can Box a Child In," *Music Educators Journal,* 56, 8 (April, 1970), p. 54.

15. Taba, Hilda, Samuel Levine, and Francis F. Elzey, *Thinking in Elementary School Children.* San Francisco, Calif.: U.S.O.E. Cooperative Research Project 1574, 1964.

16. Taebel, Donald K., "The Effect of Various Instructional Modes on Children's Performance of Music Concept Tasks," *Journal of Research in Music Education,* 11, 3 (Fall, 1974), p. 170.

17. Valentine, C. W. *The Experimental Psychology of Beauty.* London: Methuen and Co., Ltd., 1962.

18. Zimmerman, Marilyn P. *Musical Characteristics of Children.* Washington, D.C.: Music Educators National Conference, 1971.

OTHER REFERENCES

Elkind, David. "Cognitive Development and Reading," *Today's Education,* 64, 4 (November–December 1975), p. 34.

——. "Misunderstandings About How Children Learn," *Today's Education,* 64, 2 (March–April, 1975), p. 45.

Evenson, Flavis. "... And How They Are Applied," *Music Educators Journal,* 56, 6 (February, 1970), p. 55.

——. "The Study of Music in the Elementary Schools—A Conceptual Approach," *1968 Music Journal Annual Anthology,* p. 41.

Gary, Charles L., ed. *The Study of Music in the Elementary School.* Washington, D.C.: Music Educators National Conference, 1967.

Landeck, Beatrice. "Basic Ideas in Music Education," *Music Educators Journal,* 50, 4 (February–March, 1964), p. 67.

Leonhard, Charles, "Newer Concepts in Learning Theory as They Apply to Music Education," *Council for Research in Music Education,* No. 1 (June, 1963), p. 24.

Olsen, Rees G. "On Not Forgetting What We've Learned About Learning," *Music Educators Journal,* 55, 2 (October, 1968), p. 57.

Pflederer, Marilyn. "How Children Conceptually Organize Musical Sounds," *Council for Research in Music Education,* No. 7 (Spring, 1966), p. 1.

Pflederer, Marilyn. "A Study of the Conservation of Tonal and Rhythmic Patterns in Elementary School Children," *California Journal of Educational Research,* 17, 2 (1966), p. 52.

Behavioral Objectives Specify How Students Will Demonstrate Music Learning

There is an oft-quoted Chinese proverb which says:

> He who hears, forgets;
>
> He who sees, remembers;
>
> But he who *does,* **knows.**

Could the ancient poet-philosopher have known he was describing cognitive behaviorism? Active involvement (doing), as an observable behavior in demonstrating music learning (knowing), must be the focus in preparing behavioral objectives.

Behavioral objectives are statements that specify the observable behavior students will demonstrate at the end of learning experiences. Objectives of the behavioral type establish the criteria for an acceptable performance, and generally include as well the conditions under which the students will demonstrate their learnings. Those who teach music must first assess their students in terms of background, needs, and motivation, then define and formulate objectives to serve as the bases for planning and evaluating musical learnings.

Objectives need to be prepared not only for immediate learning experiences, but for intermediate and long-range learnings as well. The relationship of the immediate objectives (instructional-behavioral) to the intermediate objectives (program), and finally to the long-range ones (broad goals), is important for articulating the focus and direction of all learnings. If objectives are not prepared on all levels, learning will be fragmented and the objectives may be invalid.

Objectives, especially those concerned with the behavior expected of students, have long been an important aspect of outstanding music teaching. Perhaps this is because music learning often leads naturally to an overt response such as singing or playing an instrument. However, instructional objectives of the behavioral type have recently become an integral part of curriculum development and instruction in all subject areas. Teachers are often required to be accountable for the achievement of their students. By stating objectives in behavioral terms, teachers can specify in advance what behavioral changes they wish to see in their students. Instruction can then be planned and evaluation accomplished with greater clarity.

BIBLIOGRAPHY

Cram, David D. "Let's be Objective about Music," *Music Educators Journal,* 57, 5 (January, 1971), p. 51.

Dunham, Benjamin. "MENC Rings a Behavioral Change," *Music Educators Journal,* 55, 9 (May, 1969), p. 65.

Kibler, Robert J., et al. *Behavioral Objectives and Instruction.* Boston: Allyn and Bacon, Inc., 1970.

Schmidt, Lloyd. "The Process of Music Education," *Music Educators Journal,* 61, 6 (February, 1975), p. 50.

Sidnell, Robert. *Building Instructional Programs in Music Education.* Englewood Cliffs, New Jersey: Prentice-Hall, Inc., 1973.

CLASSIFICATION OF OBJECTIVES

Educational objectives have been classified in hierarchical order from the simplest behavioral outcomes to the most complex. These classifications are based on the assumption that learning outcomes can best be described in terms of changes in student behavior. The classification systems, referred to as taxonomies, deal with the three domains of learning—the cognitive, the affective, and the psychomotor domains.

The *cognitive domain* (Bloom, 1956) encompasses the intellectual outcomes: knowing, understanding, and thinking. The *affective domain* (Krathwohl, 1964) comprises changes in interest, attitudes, values, and appreciation. The *psychomotor domain* (Simpson, 1966, and Harrow, 1972) includes objectives that emphasize manipulative skills: singing, playing, moving, or performing music. Of these three, the cognitive domain is the principal focus of this text.

In music teaching, as in other teaching, the three domains do not exist in isolation, but are related one to another. For example, when students are asked to identify the steady beat of music, a cognitive objective is implied. However, if the students are to enjoy and to value the music, an affective objective is involved. When students are asked to create body movement in association with that steady beat, a psychomotor objective has been specified. All three domains are involved if a student verbally labels the steady beat, and then moves to the music with sensitivity.

Objectives in the cognitive domain, arranged in hierarchical order from the simplest to the most complex, are listed below. The six major categories, as described by Bloom, are presented because they are the bases of the objectives in this text:

1. *Knowledge:* remembering, by recall or recognition, ideas or material previously learned.

2. *Comprehension:* interpreting, translating, or summarizing the meaning of material.

3. *Application:* using learned material in new and concrete situations.

4. *Analysis:* breaking down material into component parts so that its organizational structure may be understood.

5. *Synthesis:* putting together parts to form a new whole.

6. *Evaluation:* judging the value of material for a given purpose.

Special attention is needed to identify objectives and develop musical experiences on the higher levels of the taxonomy. Students' cognitive abilities must be expanded at every level.

BIBLIOGRAPHY

Armstrong, Robert J., et al. *The Development and Evaluation of Behavioral Objectives.* Worthington, Ohio: Charles A. Jones Publishing Co., 1970.

Bloom, Benjamin S., et al. *Taxonomy of Educational Objectives. Handbook I: Cognitive Domain.* New York: David McKay Co., 1956.

Edwards, Larry. "Elementary School Students Should Make Value Judgments," *Music Educators Journal,* 61, 1 (September, 1974), p. 41.

Harrow, Anita J. *A Taxonomy of the Psychomotor Domain.* New York: David McKay Co., 1972.

Krathwohl, David R., et al. *Taxonomy of Educational Objectives. Handbook II: Affective Domain.* New York: David McKay Co., 1964.

Larson, Richard C. "Behaviors and Values: Creating a Synthesis," *Music Educators Journal,* 60, 2 (October 1973), p. 40.

Leonhard, Charles, and Robert W. House. *Foundations and Principles of Music Education* (2nd edition). New York: McGraw-Hill Book Co., 1972.

Simpson, Elizabeth J. *The Classification of Educational Objectives, Psychomotor Domain.* Urbana, Ill.: University of Illinois, Abstract, Contract No. OE 5-85-104, July 1, 1965–May 31, 1966. U.S. Office of Education.

WRITING BEHAVIORAL OBJECTIVES

Numerous books, articles, learning kits, and other materials are available to assist in the writing of behavioral objectives. The approaches and terminology vary, but the common denominator in all sources is that a behavioral objective must include a specification of how the learner will demonstrate learning *(observable behavior)*. In addition, many sources suggest that the important *conditions* under which the behavior is performed and the *criteria* for acceptable performance should be included.

The verb chosen to specify desired behavior must connote observable activity. Such *action verbs* as "sing," "move," "clap," and "play" are appropriate for formulating behavioral objectives in music. A teacher can readily listen to, or watch, a student clap, sing, play, or move. These action verbs clearly indicate how students will demonstrate their music learning. However, verbs such as "recognize," "understand," or "know" do not connote observable activity, and should be avoided.

BIBLIOGRAPHY

Gronlund, Norman E. *Stating Behavioral Objectives for Classroom Instruction.* London: The Macmillan Co., 1970.

Kapfer, Miriam B. "Behavioral Objectives in Music Education," in *Instructional Objectives in Music,* ed. J. David Boyle. Vienna, Va.: Music Educators National Conference, 1974, p. 20.

Leles, Sam, and Raymond Bernabei. *Writing and Using Behavioral Objectives.* Tuscaloosa, Ala.: Drake and Son Printers, Inc., 1969.

Mager, Robert F. *Preparing Instructional Objectives.* Belmont, Calif.: Fearon Publishers, 1962.

Radocy, Rudolf E. "Behavioral Objectives in Music: Shall We Continue?" *Music Educators Journal,* 60, 7 (March, 1974), p. 38.

CRITERION-REFERENCED EVALUATION OF BEHAVIORAL OBJECTIVES

Once objectives have been prepared and stated for music learning experiences, it is important to determine *if* and *how well* the behavioral objectives have been met. One approach which is emerging as an effective and useful way to evaluate learning is the *criterion-referenced* measure.

Criterion-referenced evaluation compares a student's behavior with stated standards of expected, observable behavior. This kind of evaluative measure contrasts with the more familiar norm-referenced measure which compares a student's behavior with the behavior of other students. Criterion-referenced evaluation has been applied and adapted successfully with a number of approaches focused on evaluating musical learnings. This kind of evaluation can readily serve as a measurement tool for making decisions about the effectiveness of instruction. The information yielded from the criterion-referenced approach may serve as the basis for planning future instruction.

BIBLIOGRAPHY

Boyle, J. David, and Rudolf E. Radocy. "Evaluation of Instructional Objectives in Comprehensive Musicianship," *Council for Research in Music Education,* 32 (Spring, 1973), p. 2.

"Contemporary Music Project," Special issue of *Music Educators Journal,* 59, 9 (May, 1973), p. 33.

Labuta, Joseph A. "Accent on the Output," *Music Educators Journal,* 59, 1 (September, 1972), p. 43.

——. *Guide to Accountability in Music Instruction.* West Nyack, N. Y.: Parker Publishing Corp., Inc., 1974.

Popham, W. James, ed. *Criterion-Referenced Measurement.* Englewood Cliffs, N. J.: Educational Technology Publications, Inc., 1971.

Radocy, Rudolf E. "Criterion-Referenced Testing of Behavioral Objectives," in *Instructional Objectives in Music.* ed. J. David Boyle. Vienna, Va.: Music Educators National Conference, 1974, p. 140.

Radocy, Rudolf E. "Computerized Criterion-Referenced Testing of Certain Nonperformance Musical Behaviors," *Council for Research in Music Education,* No. 28 (Spring, 1972), p. 1.

SUMMARY

By stating objectives in behavioral terms, teachers can specify in advance what behavioral changes they wish to see in their students as a result of instruction. Focus must be on the observable behavior that the learner will perform. Instruction can then be planned, and the educational processes and products evaluated. The criterion-referenced evaluation may be a useful and valid approach to evaluating musical learning.

BIBLIOGRAPHY

Boyle, J. David. "Behavioral Objectives: Is What People Are Saying About Them Really True?" *Music Educators Journal,* 63, 6 (February, 1977), p. 60.

Deihl, Ned C., and Ray H. Zeigler. "Evaluation of a C.A.I. Program in Articulation, Phrasing, and Rhythm for Intermediate Instrumentalists," *Council for Research in Music Education,* 31 (Winter 1973), p. 1.

Gerhard, Muriel. *Effective Teaching Strategies with the Behavioral Outcomes Approach.* West Nyack, N. Y.: Parker Publishing Corp., 1970.

Hansen, Kenneth H. "Accountability Is a Premise, Not a Promise," *Music Educators Journal,* 61, 4 (December, 1974), p. 40.

Modes for Translating Music Learning into Behavior Include Singing, Playing Instruments, Movement, Reading Music, and Creating Music

Concrete musical experiences are important, for they allow students to express their music learning through behavior. Modern educational theory suggests that learning is most effective when a concept is experienced through several modes: aural, motor, visual, tactile, and verbal. Teachers may design experiences so that music learning may be demonstrated through several modes of behavior: singing, playing instruments, movement, reading music, and creating music. These activities will then serve the cause of conceptualization and will not become ends in themselves.

The information which follows sketches the broad outlines of how these behaviors may be employed in classroom music. It suggests experiences which many music educators agree are important for children, and lists some materials which may be used in these experiences. Other references to music education literature note sources which describe specific techniques for teaching singing, instruments, movement, reading, and creative activities.

SINGING

Since colonial times, singing has been a popular means of expression in America. Fine choral singing for the church was a goal of the singing-schools of the late 18th century. And in 1838 Lowell Mason was able to persuade the Boston school board to add vocal music to the school curriculum. From these beginnings, singing has occupied an important place in American school music.

In the past, a fine vocal performance sometimes became an end in itself. In today's education, singing is valuable because it adds yet another dimension in the total growth of the child. The human voice can be a remarkably expressive musical instrument, and children must have opportunities in learning to use it enthusiastically and expressively.

Many children have not discovered their singing voices when they enter school. (5) At first, they must learn to listen to their own voices, and discover how singing differs from speaking, shouting, whispering, and other modes of vocal expression. (6) Dramatizing poems and stories may help draw attention to tone quality and to pitch differences. Children should be encouraged to experiment with higher and lower vocal registers in their characterizations. But in singing, youngsters must learn to use a light voice. Never elicit such vigorous singing that the tone sounds heavy or forced.

The singing range of most young children extends approximately from C or D up to A above middle C. (7) Songs which stay mostly within this five-note range are appropriate to use in first experiences. Chants containing only two or three pitches are also ideal and may be used for singing questions and answers between teacher and students. Teachers will want to provide opportunities for individual expression, as well as for group singing. Most of all, the teacher must always maintain an encouraging, positive attitude toward the efforts of each child. No student must ever be made to feel he has a limited potential because he is an unskilled singer.

Those adults who feel their own singing is less than adequate will have empathy for the child who has difficulty. Traditionally, elementary teachers have been expected to sing, and also to play the piano. These are very useful skills, and once begun, should be expanded through additional training and practice. However, the singing voice of the teacher is not as indispensable as once thought. This is due in part to the availability of sound recordings (which also make piano accompaniments less vital). Another reason is that children develop musical concepts more readily when they are experienced through several modes: aural, motor, tactile, visual, and verbal. Teachers must be able to utilize *all* of these modes in experiences which lead to fundamental understandings about music. Singing is but one avenue.

When songs are learned by rote (aurally), it may be through either direct or indirect teaching techniques. In the former, each phrase of a song is systematically presented and learned. Indirect techniques are especially appropriate when a conceptual understanding is the focus of music learning. For example, when students are meaningfully involved in tapping or clapping the beats of a song, they readily learn to sing the song. Only the difficult portions need to be isolated for special study. (See model experience *The Wind Blew East,* in which the song is learned indirectly.)

Children are quick to imitate what they hear. For this reason, songs must be presented to them in a style appropriate to the music, without exaggerated mannerisms. And when they are learning a song by rote, they must have a clear idea what pitches they are to imitate. (6) They will rely on the teacher's voice, or on a song recording. As soon as most of the children in a classroom sing the song accurately, they will become free of any dependency. This is an important goal.

Singing is important because it is a direct and satisfying human mode of expression. Every day, children should have opportunities to participate in singing. Vocal music deserves its role in today's classroom because it can serve the perceptual, cognitive, emotional, and musical development of every child.

REFERENCES

Of the songs in this text, these fall within the C to A range (see Music Index for page numbers):

ALA DAL'ONA

BILE THEM CABBAGE DOWN

BYE BABY BUNTING

GOOD NEWS (refrain)

GO TELL AUNT RHODY

HARI KRISHNA

JINGLE BELLS

JIN-GO-LO-BA

LOVE SOMEBODY

RAIN, RAIN

STAR LIGHT, STAR BRIGHT

A TISKET, A TASKET

TAILS

TRAMPIN' (refrain)

WHEN THE SAINTS GO MARCHING IN

These songs may be transposed to fall within the C to A range:

FRENCH CATHEDRALS

MERRILY WE ROLL ALONG

POOR BIRD

SKIN AND BONES

REFERENCES FOR TEACHERS

Valuable discussions of the singing program are to be found in many texts. It is extremely difficult to single out any one of the resources mentioned below and in the sections which follow.

Garretson, Robert L. *Music in Childhood Education* (2nd ed.), Englewood Cliffs, N.J.: Prentice-Hall, Inc., 1976, Chapter 3, "The Child Voice and Singing."

Nordholm, Harriet. *Singing in the Elementary School.* Englewood Cliffs, N.J.: Prentice-Hall, Inc., 1966.

Smith, Robert B. *Music in the Child's Education.* New York: The Ronald Press Company, 1970, Chapter 2, "The Early Childhood Vocal Program," and Chapter 3, "Vocal Activities for Older Children."

Swanson, Bessie R. *Music in the Education of Children* (3rd ed.). Belmont, Calif.: Wadsworth Publishing Company, Inc., 1969, Chapter 6, "Songs and Singing Voices," and Chapter 7, "Management of the Singing Situation."

SELECTED SONG COLLECTIONS.

Glazer, Tom. *A New Treasury of Folk Songs.* New York: Bantam Books, Inc., 1961.

Haywood, Charles. *Folk Songs of the World.* New York: John Day Company, 1966.

Landeck, Beatrice. *Songs To Grow On* (1950) and *More Songs To Grow On* (1953). New York: Edward B. Marks and William Sloan, Associates.

Landeck, Beatrice, and Elizabeth Crook. *Wake Up and Sing!* New York: Edward B. Marks Music Corp. and William Morrow and Company, Inc., 1969.

Lomax, Alan. *Folk Songs of North America.* Garden City, N.Y.: Doubleday and Company, Inc., 1975. In the Appendix of this book, see the annotated list of outstanding folk song recordings.

Nye, Robert, et al. *Singing with Children* (2nd ed.). Belmont, Calif.: Wadsworth Publishing Company, 1970.

Seeger, Ruth Crawford. *American Folk Songs for Children* (1948), *Animal Folk Songs for Children* (1950), and *American Folk Songs for Christmas* (1953). Garden City, N.Y.: Doubleday and Company, Inc.

Wood, Lucille F., and Louise B. Scott, *Singing Fun* (1954) and *More Singing Fun* (1961). St. Louis, Mo.: Webster Publishing Company. Recordings of these songs are available from Bowmar Records, 622 Rodier Drive, Glendale, California 91201.

SONGS TO SING IN HARMONY

Anderson, Ruth. *Rounds from Many Countries.* New York: G. Schirmer, Inc., 1961.

Beckman, Frederick. *Partner Songs* (1958) and *More Partner Songs* (1962). Boston: Ginn and Company.

Daniel, Oliver. *Round and Round and Round They Go.* Evanston, Ill.: Summy-Birchard Publishing Co., 1952.

Krone, Beatrice, and Max Krone. *Very Easy Descants.* Park Ridge, Ill.: Neil A. Kjos Music Company, 1951. The Krones have published many additional collections of descants.

Terri, Salli. *Rounds for Everyone from Everywhere.* New York: Lawson-Gould Music Publishers, Inc., 1961.

Wilson, Harry R. *Old and New Rounds and Canons.* Delaware Water Gap, Pa.: Shawnee Press, Inc.

PLAYING INSTRUMENTS

Young children may develop concepts about music as they play instruments. Through this playing they acquire concrete experiences upon which to base their musical understandings.

A variety of high-quality instruments, with a good musical tone, should be used in these experiences. The nonpitched percussion instruments must be available in every classroom. (See photos of these on p. 317. Young children, especially, learn about their world through texture and shape. (4) So musical instruments should be available to handle: to bang, stroke, and tap. Instruments used in specific grade levels will reflect the musical goals of the program and the maturity of the students. Nonpitched percussion instruments produce a variety of tonal effects, from sustained and ringing sounds to those which seem short and "dry." They may be used to supply rhythm patterns (and sound effects) for songs, stories, and body movement. Exploration of their timbre singly or in combination can result in many creative experiences for students.

Xylophone-type instruments are becoming more widely available for classroom use. Because they are pitched, these instruments are especially useful in developing understandings about melody and harmony. The bars on a xylophone may be attached or they may be removable. If unneeded bars are removed, beginning players can strike correct pitches with greater accuracy. On this type of instrument, students readily learn to play tonal patterns, extracted from songs or created themselves. Through continuing experience with xylophone-type instruments, students become able to play melodies and counter-melodies. Chords may also be played. Xylophone-type instruments are used in the Orff Schulwerk program, where they form the basic musical ensemble (see p. 332).

Of all the instruments which produce harmony, the Autoharp is the easiest to play. When a single button is pressed, several chord tones can be sounded. This makes it an ideal instrument for classroom use. Other chordal instruments require greater skill, and to teach them in the classroom, special instructional materials are desirable. (See the end of this discussion for a list of instruction books.) The ukulele and guitar are popular instruments and are often studied, beginning in about fourth grade.

The flute-like instruments most widely taught in school music programs have been the song flute and the tonette. Now it is possible to purchase a soprano recorder (made of either wood or plastic) that has an excellent tone quality and plays a wider range of pitches than the other two instruments. Beginning in third grade, students can be introduced to one of these wind instruments, which they may enjoy for years. The teacher must learn how to play these small wind instruments, and should utilize instructional materials which teach the fingerings and pitches that young children can manage. (See lists below.)

Instruments are sometimes designed and constructed in the classroom art program. If they are to be used for music, however, they must produce a good tone quality, and they should be durable. (Few meet these criteria!) Nonpitched percussion instruments—especially those patterned after non-Western models—often provide the most musical satisfaction. For example, a pair of stone castanets from Hawaii *(ili ili)* can be readily duplicated. Notched sticks and "shredded" bamboo poles are among several other possibilities. (See the "Bibliography" at the conclusion of Haiku Sound Piece, p. 99, for sources of information about homemade instruments.)

Experiences in playing instruments may lead to expanded sensorimotor skills and to cooperative ensemble performance. But above all, they provide the experiential basis for the cognitive understanding of melody, rhythm, harmony, form, and the expressive qualities of music.

SEQUENTIAL INDEX

Playing pitched and nonpitched instruments is an integral part of the model experiences listed below. "Another Time" and "Elaboration" portions of model experiences suggest many additional uses. (See Music Index for page numbers.)

Pitched

- THE FROG AND THE MOUSE
- JANE, JANE
- ANCIENT CHINESE TEMPLE MUSIC
- CONTRASTING MELODIC PHRASES (improvised)
- FIVE ANGELS
- PIANISTS
- THIS OLD MAN
- SOUND PIECE 7
- CARILLON
- ARE YOU SLEEPING? (I)
- GHOST OF TOM
- ST. PAUL'S STEEPLE
- HOLD ON
- ARE YOU SLEEPING? (II)
- MINKA
- GREETING PRELUDE
- GAMBANGAN
- VOILES
- MINUET
- TUTU MARAMBA

Nonpitched

- OVEN GRILL CONCERTO
- GOOD MORNING, BLUES
- HAIKU SOUND PIECE
- A RAM SAM SAM (II)
- SCRATCH, SCRATCH
- STRING QUARTET NO. 4
- JIN-GO-LO-BA
- IMPROVISATION FOR SOLO PERFORMER AND FIVE TAPE RECORDERS

Chordal

- SKIP TO MY LOU
- JOE TURNER BLUES
- BOW, BELINDA
- JAMAICA FAREWELL

REFERENCES FOR TEACHERS

Cheyette, Irvin, and Herbert Cheyette. *Teaching Music Creatively in the Elementary School.* New York: McGraw-Hill Book Company, 1969, Chapter 8, "Developing a Classroom Orchestra."

Gelineau, R. Phyllis, *Experiences in Music* (2nd ed.). New York: McGraw-Hill Book Company, 1976, Chapter 6, "Instrumental Experiences."

Nye, Robert Evans, and Vernice Trousdale Nye, *Essentials of Teaching Elementary School Music.* Englewood Cliffs, N.J.: Prentice-Hall, Inc., 1974. Chapter 4, "Learning Music with Songs and Instruments."

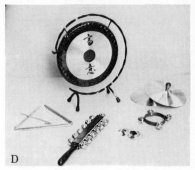

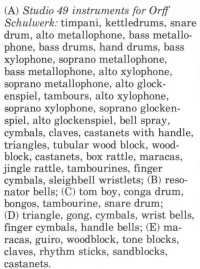

(A) *Studio 49 instruments for Orff Schulwerk:* timpani, kettledrums, snare drum, alto metallophone, bass metallophone, bass drums, hand drums, bass xylophone, soprano metallophone, bass metallophone, alto xylophone, soprano metallophone, alto glockenspiel, tambours, alto xylophone, soprano xylophone, soprano glockenspiel, alto glockenspiel, bell spray, cymbals, claves, castanets with handle, triangles, tubular wood block, woodblock, castanets, box rattle, maracas, jingle rattle, tambourines, finger cymbals, sleighbell wristlets; (B) resonator bells; (C) tom boy, conga drum, bongos, tambourine, snare drum; (D) triangle, gong, cymbals, wrist bells, finger cymbals, handle bells; (E) maracas, guiro, woodblock, tone blocks, claves, rhythm sticks, sandblocks, castanets.

INSTRUCTIONAL MATERIALS FOR THE ELEMENTARY CLASSROOM

Guitar, ukulele

Crook, Elizabeth, et al. *Silver Burdett Music.* Morristown, N.J.: Silver Burdett Company, 1974, "Playing the Guitar" satellites in levels 5 and 6, and "Guitar" in levels 7 and 8.

D'Auberge, Alfred, and Morton Manus. *The New Guitar Course.* New York: Alfred Music Co., Inc., 1966.

Marsh, Mary Val, et al. *Spectrum of Music.* New York: Macmillan Publishing Co., Inc., 1974, "Playing the Guitar and String Bass" module for level 7 and 8 (or slightly lower or higher grades).

Snyder, Jerry. *Basic Instructor Guitar,* I, II. New York: Charles Hansen Distributor, 1976.

See the introduction to the ukulele in Burton, Leon, et al., *Comprehensive Musicianship Through Classroom Music,* Zone 2, level B.

See the bibliography at the conclusion of the Guitar Instructor in Section Two of this text.

Soprano recorder

Burakoff, Gerald. *The Elementary Method for the Soprano Recorder.* New York: Hargail Music Press, 1967.

Crook, Elizabeth, *et al. Silver Burdett Music.* Morristown, N. J.: Silver Burdett Company, 1974, "Playing the Recorder" satellite in levels 5 and 6.

Marsh, Mary Val, *et al. Spectrum of Music.* New York: Macmillan Publishing Co., Inc., 1974, "Playing the Recorder" module in level 7 and 8 (or slightly lower or higher grades).

Nash, Grace C. *Music with Children,* Series I, II, III *Recorder Book.* Scottsdale, Ariz.: G. C. Nash, 1965.

See the introduction to the recorder in Burton, Leon, *et al., Comprehensive Musicianship Through Classroom Music,* Zone 3, level A.

See the bibliography at the conclusion of the Recorder Instructor in Section Two of this text.

Autoharp

Each basal music series contains suggestions for using the Autoharp.

See the bibliography at the conclusion of the Autoharp Instructor in Section Two of this text.

SELECTED LIST OF COMPANIES SUPPLYING CLASSROOM INSTRUMENTS

Children's Music Center, 5373 West Pico Blvd, Los Angeles, Ca. 90019.

Educational Music Bureau, 1834 Ridge Ave., Evanston, Ill. 60204.

Gamble Hinged Music Company, 312 So. Wabash Ave., Chicago, Ill. 60604.

H. Hohner, Inc., Andrews Road, Hicksville, Long Island, N.Y. 11802.

Kitching Educational Division of Ludwig Industries, 1728 North Damen Drive, Chicago, Ill. 60647.

Magnamusic-Baton, Inc., 6394 Delmar Blvd., St. Louis, Mo. 63130.

Oscar Schmidt-International, Inc., Garden State Rd., Union, N.J. 07083.

Peripole, Inc., 51-17 Rockaway Beach Blvd., Far Rockaway, Long Island, N.Y. 11691.

Rhythm Band, Inc., P.O. Box 126, Fort Worth, Texas 76101.

MOVEMENT

Because music is a temporal art, it often elicits bodily movement. Its rhythms, melodies, expressive qualities, and its harmony and form, too, may all be expressed through movement. Movement becomes an additional means for refining perceptions and understandings about music. Because movement requires total involvement, teachers are able to ascertain the level of student responses. And for many children, movement is the most satisfying of their musical experiences.

First, movements are child-created, free responses which use the large muscles. (11) Since very young children lack the coordination to follow a given tempo, the teacher should provide accompaniment to these movements, adjusting the tempo to that of the child. (11) Percussion instruments, piano, Autoharp, or even guitar may be used along with fundamental locomotor movements such as walking or running.

Kindergarten children can begin to refine small-muscle movements and participate in finger plays and body rhythms. Steady beats can be expressed through clapping and other nonlocomotor movements. Preschool children continue to enjoy free interpretive movement, pantomime, and dramatizations. All these physical activities help to provide a foundation for the cognitive understanding of music. (4)

In first or second grade, children begin to learn to adjust their movements to the tempi they hear in songs and recorded music. Soon they will be learning traditional singing games and, in upper grades, patterned folk dances. Students who have a rich background of movement experiences in lower grades will not be reluctant to participate in these activities when they are older. They continue many of the same movement experiences, but with greater maturity, they are able to interpret more subtle music, or music which is unfamiliar to them. Compositions by Debussy, Stravinsky, Cage, and others might elicit expressive, creative responses.

Movement experiences in music are related to programs in physical education and creative dramatics. And they serve many of the same objectives in providing for personality development, individual accomplishment, and physical control. All these goals may be met while at the same time refining the child's perception and understanding of *music*.

SEQUENTIAL INDEX

Many model experiences involve bodily movement. Often, movement is suggested in "Another Time" and "Elaboration" sections which follow every model experience.
(See Music Index for page numbers)

REFERENCES FOR TEACHERS

Brown, Margaret, and Betty K. Sommer. *Movement Education: Its Evolution and a Modern Approach.* Reading, Mass. Addison-Wesley Publishing Co., Inc., 1969.

Doll, Edna, and Mary Jarman Nelson. *Rhythms Today!* Morristown, N. J.: Silver Burdett Company, 1964.

Gray, Vera, and Rachel Percival. *Music, Movement and Mime for Children.* London: Oxford University Press, 1962.

Humphreys, Louise, and Jerrold Ross, *Interpreting Music Through Movement.* Englewood Cliffs, N. J.: Prentice-Hall, Inc., 1964.

Landis, Beth, "Realization in Movement as a Way of Comprehending Music," in Beth Landis and Polly Carder, *The Eclectic Curriculum in American Music Education: Contributions of Dalcroze, Kodály, and Orff.* Washington, D.C.: Music Educators National Conference, 1972.

Monsour, Sally, Marilyn Chambers Cohen, and Patricia Eckert Lindell. *Rhythm in Music and Dance for Children.* Belmont, Calif.: Wadsworth Publishing Company, Inc., 1966.

Sheehy, Emma D., *Children Discover Music and Dance.* New York: Holt, Rinehart and Winston, 1959.

READING MUSIC

Pitch and duration may be visually represented by music notation. This notation represents musical tones, and will have little meaning for children unless the abstract symbols are associated with sound. (9) Written language is used to express previously acquired speech or experience. This principle must be observed when teaching music notation.

Preschool children are not ready to use symbols for music notation because they perceive figures as wholes, devoid of their details. (4) It would therefore be premature to use formal music notation with these youngsters, because many symbols in music look more alike than different. Young children should be acquiring a background of musical experiences which may later provide the basis for meaningful use of music notation. (11)

There are several theories about how and when notation may be introduced to children. (5) Many music educators recommend initial use of "informal" notation using geometric shapes and lines. (9) (11) This can begin in first or second grade, and may enable students to understand that sound can be visually represented. This technique is exciting because students can use informal notation to express their own creative musical ideas. It is especially useful because it may be readily used with beginning students at nearly every grade level.

Instruction based on the principles of the Kodály method introduces a kind of "simplified" notation almost from the start. (2) First-grade children study notation using only note stems (⊓ and Ι). Notation for pitch begins not with a five-line staff, but with a two-line staff on which note heads are placed. (—o— o—) Rhythm syllables ("ta," "ti," etc.) are learned in association with rhythm notation, and sol-fa syllables for pitch notation. (See Appendix.) Symbols of increasing complexity are learned as children gain experience and maturity.

Music notation, informal or standard, is essentially a "retrieval system" for the student. (1) Notation must represent musical sounds already experienced. The ability to read notation is a desirable skill which should be neither neglected nor overemphasized. Music reading must be introduced when sensorimotor and perceptual skills permit optimum learning. The teacher who understands these principles will not ask preschool children to make paper hats adorned with quarter-note symbols.

SEQUENTIAL INDEX

Music-reading objectives accompany many model experiences in this text, though many times they are optional. Their use will depend on the readiness of the learners participating in the model experience.
(See Music Index for page numbers.)

Informal notation

- GRIZZLY BEAR
- BINGO
- HAIKU SOUND PIECE

Musical notation

- ANCIENT CHINESE TEMPLE MUSIC
- A RAM SAM SAM (I)
- CONTRASTING MELODIC PHRASES (improvised)
- FIVE ANGELS
- PIANISTS
- POLKA
- CARILLON
- ARE YOU SLEEPING? (I)
- GHOST OF TOM
- ST. PAUL'S STEEPLE
- HOLD ON
- ALA DAL'ONA
- SING HALLELU
- ARE YOU SLEEPING? (II)
- SYMPHONY NO. 94
- TUTÚ MARAMBA

CREATING MUSIC

Experiences in creating music are important because they can place students in the role of composer. Melody, rhythm, harmony, form, and the expressive qualities (timbre, tempo, and dynamics) become the raw materials for this creative work. The students combine and arrange these elements into an original creative product. Experiences in creating music are ideal for individuals and small groups and allow many opportunities for personal growth and expression.

To heighten aural perception and sensitivity, children need to explore the world of sound. Musical instruments are a part of this world, but should be supplemented by nontraditional sound sources. These include the sounds of countless objects from nature, and from manufactured metals and plastics. The human voice, too, may be used in other than traditional ways. These sounds may be combined, and by their juxtaposition acquire a new expressiveness. Upper-grade students may further transform these sounds when they manipulate a microphone while tape-recording. Playback—at the same and different speeds—will create new possibilities. And each tape may be cut into sections, then recombined, to create a collage of sound relationships.

Children also need many opportunities to experiment with their own variations on familiar songs. (11) Changes most easily manipulated and understood include those which alter tempo, instrumental timbre, or harmony. (12) For example, each "ding, ding, dong," at the conclusion of *Are You Sleeping?* might be played on a different instrument: drum, triangle, and wood block. Changes in pitch or rhythm are more complex and require greater skills. To play "Broth-er John, Broth-er John" on pitches *higher* and *slower* than normal will greatly alter the musical configuration of the song. (This may be readily accomplished on the tape recorder.) Creative experiences of this kind need to be more widely used in music teaching, because they help children understand how the musical elements interact and interrelate. (1)

A comprehension of musical form may be acquired when children are encouraged to create their own compositions in two sections (A B), three sections (A B A), or rondo form (A B A C A). Several media may be used: pitched or nonpitched percussion instruments, voices, nontraditional sound sources, or a combination of these. Students can better understand a rondo by Beethoven when they have created one of their own.

Improvisation within a familiar structure is a widespread folk and jazz device. Using the melody of a favorite song, very young children can invent their own text. Or, they might transform it into a percussion composition, with each instrument playing a different phrase. The process becomes more complex when upper-grade children devise a chord progression on Autoharp for their own "12-bar" blues. As they create their own text and melody, they will have composed an original blues song. Harmonic progressions on chordal instruments may provide the framework for individual students to create songs — in any style.

As children create their own compositions and perform them (or help others to do so), they experience several musicianly roles. They also become aware of the need to notate their musical sounds, so that they can be remembered, and played by others. Students become sensitive to a wide spectrum of sounds, and perhaps more accepting of unfamiliar music they may encounter. Most of all, they can begin to understand the principles of interaction of all the elements of music: melody, rhythm, harmony, form, and expressive qualities.

SEQUENTIAL INDEX

While several model experiences describe creative music making efforts, most often they are suggested as creative extension of the experiences in "Another Time" and "Elaboration."

(See Music Index for page numbers.)

- OVEN GRILL CONCERTO and POÈME ÉLECTRONIQUE (Sound Experiment with Tape Recorder: Timbre, Volume, and Duration)
- CONTRASTING MELODIC PHRASES (improvised)
- HAIKU SOUND PIECE

- ● SOUND PIECE 7 (Sound Experiment with Tape Recorder: Pitch and Duration)
- ● A RAM SAM SAM (II)
- ● STRING QUARTET NO. 4 (Sound Experiment with Tape Recorder: Tape Loop)
- ● JIN-GO-LO-BA
- ● IMPROVISATION FOR SOLO PERFORMER AND FIVE TAPE RECORDERS (Sound Experiment with Tape Recorder: Tape Delay)

REFERENCES FOR TEACHERS

Benson, Warren. "The Creative Child Could Be Any Child: Drawing Out Inherent Creativity in Compositional Experiences," *Music Educators Journal,* 59, 8 (April, 1973), p. 38.

Boardman, Eunice. "New Sounds in the Classroom," *Music Educators Journal,* 55, 3 (November, 1968), p. 62.

Carle, Irmgard Lehrer, and Isaiah Martin. "Enlarge Your Sound Repertory," *Music Educators Journal,* 62, 4 (December, 1975), p. 40.

"Electronic Music." Special issue of the *Music Educators Journal,* 55, 3 (November, 1968).

Elliott, Dorothy Gail, "Junk Music," *Music Educators Journal,* 58, 5 (January, 1972), p. 58.

Hoenack, Peg, "Unleash Creativity—Let Them Improvise," *Music Educators Journal,* 57, 9 (May, 1971), p. 33.

Holderrild, Elizabeth Swist. "Creativity in My Classroom," *Music Educators Journal,* 55, 7 (March, 1969), p. 37.

Jensen, Eric. "Creativity and Its Sources," *Music Educators Journal,* 55, 7 (March, 1969), p. 34.

Thackray, R. M. *Creative Music in Education.* London: Novello, 1965.

See the bibliography following model experience *Oven Grill Concerto* (Sound Experiment with Tape Recorder: Timbre, Volume and Duration), p. 55.

See the bibliographies in Section III of this text which follow the descriptions of the Contemporary Music Project and the Manhattanville Music Curriculum Project (p. 336.

SUMMARY

In working with children, the importance of singing, playing instruments, moving, reading music, and creating music soon becomes clear. But it is important to remember that these activities are not ends in themselves. Always ask, "Are these experiences leading to music learning?" For students must be able to understand the world of music when teachers are no longer present to help.

SECTION REFERENCES

1. Choate, Robert A., et al. *New Dimensions in Music,* teacher's edition, "Introduction," New York: American Book Company, 1970.
2. Choksy, Lois. *The Kodály Method.* Englewood Cliffs, N. J.: Prentice-Hall, Inc., 1974.
3. Dexler, Ethel N., "A Study of the Ability to Carry a Melody at the Pre-School Level," *Child Development,* 9 (September, 1938), p. 319.
4. Farnham-Diggory, Sylvia. *Cognitive Processes in Education.* New York: Harper and Row, Publishers, Inc., 1972.

5. Gordon, Edwin, *The Psychology of Music Teaching.* Englewood Cliffs, N. J.: Prentice-Hall, Inc., 1971.

6. Gould, Oren A., *Developing Specialized Programs for Singing in the Elementary School.* Interim report No. 2. United States Office of Education. Cooperative Research Project No. 5-0214, Western Illinois University, 1968.

7. Jersild, Arthur, and Sylvia Bienstock. "A Study of the Development of Children's Ability to Sing," *Journal of Educational Psychology,* Vol. 25 (1923), p. 481.

8. Moorhead, Gladys, and Donald Pond. *Music of Young Children:* Part I "Chant" (1941); Part II, "General Observations" (1942); Part III, "Free Use of Instruments for Musical Growth" (with Florence Sandvik and Don Wight, 1943); Part IV, "Musical Notation" (1944). Santa Barbara, Calif.: Pillsbury Foundation for the Advancement of Music Education.

9. O'Brien, James P. "Teach the Principles of Notation, Not Just the Symbols," *Music Educators Journal,* 60, 9 (May, 1974), p. 38.

10. Petzold, Robert. *Auditory Perception of Musical Sounds by Children in the First Six Grades.* Madison, Wisc.: University of Wisconsin Press, 1966. Report of U.S.O.E. Cooperative Research Project No. 1051.

11. Zimmerman, Marilyn P. *Musical Characteristics of Children.* Washington, D.C.: Music Educators National Conference, 1971.

12. Zimmerman, Marilyn P., and Lee Sechrest. "Brief Focused Instruction and Musical Concepts," *Journal of Research in Music Education,* 18, 1 (Spring, 1970), p. 25.

Basal Music Series Provide Materials for Classroom Music

Elementary teachers should prepare to teach music in their classrooms. Music teachers are sometimes employed, but in an era of restricted resources, these specialists are among the first to be eliminated when budgets are reduced. As a teacher of music, the classroom teacher has a very real advantage in knowing the capabilities of each student, and can relate the music program to the child's life and to the total school curriculum.

In most American classrooms, teachers have a fair degree of latitude in selecting music to use with students. Basal music series adopted by city, district, or state boards of education are the most readily available and comprehensive source of materials for curriculum development. Teachers will need to become thoroughly familiar with these materials. Curriculum consultants are often available to provide information and assistance.

CONTENT OF THE BASAL MUSIC SERIES

Songs and recorded instrumental music form the basis for music learning experiences in every basal music series. Current publications make a very real effort to put students in touch with music which reflects the diversity of our artistic and cultural heritage.

Every series contains a wide variety of songs, and each of these songs is recorded. The recordings feature performances by children, by trained adult voices, and recently, by contemporary folk and youth musicians. Classroom teachers will find these recordings of great help in teaching music. As an added plus, they are an easy and enjoyable means to help the teacher become familiar with the musical selections in each textbook.

The instrumental compositions on these recordings are described in annotated teachers' editions, as are the songs. The majority of these instrumental selections are from the repertoire of Western orchestral compositions (from 1700 to about 1875), but other musical periods are increasingly represented. Several basal series contain performances of non-Western music from Africa, Asia, and the Middle East.

Creative music-making activities are suggested in every series. Composition and improvisation by pupils are often integral to this work, which emphasizes exploration and discovery.

Basal music texts differ in their approach to the teaching of music reading. Some introduce notation in a sequential manner, often utilizing small wind instruments, xylophones, or ukuleles. Others focus on conceptual learning, and introduce reading skills only as they become relevant. Teachers who wish to emphasize music-reading skills frequently select additional materials to supplement the basal texts.

Several series make provision for measuring pupil achievement and provide worksheets or tests. Often these are obtainable on spirit masters so that they may be duplicated. These workbook activities sometimes accompany programmed cassettes for individualized music learning. Thus paper-and-pencil work can be associated with sound—the *sine qua non* of music.

The currently available basal music series are described below. Each has its own special distinctions and strengths.

CURRENT BASAL MUSIC SERIES

Burton, Leon, dir. *Comprehensive Musicianship Program.* Menlo Park, Calif.: Addison-Wesley Publishing Co. (2725 Sand Hill Road), 1973/4.

The Comprehensive Musicianship Program was developed under the sponsorship of the College of Education Curriculum Research and Development Group at the University of Hawaii. Project director Dr. Leon Burton was assisted by a staff of nine music and education specialists with many years of classroom experience.

That part of the program designed for elementary grades is titled *Comprehensive Musicianship Through Classroom Music.* The book organization is by zones rather than grades. The zone and approximate grade designation for each book appears on the title page of each Teacher's Edition:

Zone 1	Zone 2	Zone 3
Book A — Kindergarten	Book A — Grade 2	*Book A — Grade 4*
Book B — Grade 1	Book B — Grade 3	*Book B — Grade 5*
		Book C — Grade 6

Zone 4	Zone 5
Junior High School	High School

Recordings are available for parts of the program and may be obtained from Westmont Recording Studio, San Jose, Calif. Worksheets and Answer Sheets for the evaluation components are available on duplicator masters.

The *Comprehensive Musicianship Program* is designed to help students develop an understanding of musical concepts by involving them in a variety of musical activities. The curriculum study focuses on seven basic musical concepts—rhythm, melody, harmony, tone, texture, tonality, and form—which are introduced, reinforced, and extended throughout the K–12 program. Each of the seven concepts is divided into a number of subconcepts which are arranged from simple to complex, or from the more concrete to the more abstract. This arrangement of the subconcepts reflects the CMP approach toward gradually expanding or broadening conceptual understandings during the years K–12. Students develop an understanding of the seven concepts and their subconcepts by participating in activities such as moving, singing, playing instruments, improvising, composing, analyzing, listening, and evaluating.

The goal of the program is to help each student become involved with music to the extent that his abilities, inclinations, and environment allow. The program aims to develop a person committed to and moved by music. Thus the aesthetic response of the learner is stressed at each instructional level. It aims to develop an individual aware of the world's music by presenting music from various cultures, historical periods, and styles in a one-world perspective. It aims to develop one who can evaluate the world's music, and analyze it to see what makes each work unique. Further, the *Comprehensive Musicianship Program* strives to develop a person who can communicate using the language and symbolic systems of music. In essence, the *Comprehensive Musicianship Program* strives to develop a *comprehensive musician.*

● Leonhard, Charles, Beatrice Perham Krone, Irving Wolfe, and Margaret Fullerton. *Discovering Music Together.* Chicago, Ill.: Follett Publishing Co. (1010 W. Washington Blvd.), 1970.

This elementary music book series is organized as a sequential program based upon specific objectives. The objectives of the *Discovering Music Together* music program include three types of learning products: musical concepts, musical competencies, and appreciation. The objectives in the areas of appreciation and musical competencies are stated in terms of desired behaviors, while musical concepts are presented as generalizations about music. These objectives, presented at the beginning of each Teacher's Edition, represent the goals toward which the music teaching should be directed. The program of musical learnings in *Discovering Music Together* is structured to enable students to achieve these goals.

The Teacher's Editions of each grade-level book include all the pages of the student's book. In addition, a teacher's page for each song presents: general information, specific suggestions for guiding the students' learning, and piano accompaniments. Classroom charts are available for some texts, while recordings, which include all songs and listening lessons, are available for all texts.

Each grade-level book focuses on: presenting songs; teaching music reading (sol-fa syllables with hand signs and rhythm syllables are stressed); teaching listening; teaching rhythmic responsiveness; and encouraging creativity. Parts for bells, piano, and small winds, and chord symbols for chordal instruments are provided for a number of songs in each book.

Evaluating the results of the music program is an important ingredient in the *Discovering Music Together* program. Informal but systematic and continuous observation of students' behavior during musical experiences is recommended. Suggestions for specific evaluative procedures are presented in some of the textbooks. The *Music Achievement Tests,* available from Follett Educational Corporation, are suggested for beginning and end-of-year achievement measurements.

● Boardman, Eunice, Beth Landis, and Barbara Andress, *Exploring Music.* New York: Holt, Rinehart, and Winston, Inc. (CBS Inc., 383 Madison Ave.), 1975.

Exploring Music 1975 is a music textbook series for kindergarten through eighth grades. In addition to pupil books and Teacher's Editions, recordings of all songs and listening selections are available for each book.

The goal, specified by *Exploring Music 1975* authors, is to help students develop an awareness of the kinds of music they will enjoy and perform throughout their lives. As students progress through each level of the series, they hopefully will grow in the ability to understand, organize, and interpret musical ideas.

The *Exploring Music* kindergarten and first-grade books present activities and songs to offer the young child an exploration of all the elements of music. The second- and third-grade books offer material arranged sequentially around each of the major concepts, presenting an exposure to all of the elements of music. The fourth-, fifth- and sixth-grade books continue to develop the student's understanding of the major concepts while applying these skills to studies of specific styles. Book 4 stresses how all the world's peoples use music in similar ways. Book 5 stresses the development of American music through history. Book 6 stresses the unique characteristics of music from different cultures and contemporary forms, including 12-tone techniques and electronic music.

The Teacher's Editions for all the books are designed to provide the necessary help for teaching the program. Each Teacher's Edition specifies a sequential development of songs, teaching suggestions, and listening lessons for each quarter of the school year. Behavioral and concept charts are included, as well as accountability charts for students and teachers to use in evaluating musical learnings.

As a part of the total *Exploring Music* program, a cassette kit with student activity sheets, *Holt Individualized Music Program,* is available to be used at the teacher's discretion as a supplement to and extension of large-group activities. The *Individualized Music Program* can be used with the *Exploring Music* series or with any other elementary music program.

● Landeck, Beatrice, Elizabeth Crook, Harold C. Youngberg, and Otto Leuning. *Making Music Your Own.* Morristown, N. J.: Silver Burdett Company, 1971.

In *Making Music Your Own,* programs throughout the grades explore music as an expression of people who create it. Diversified classroom experiences call for children's responses to listening, involving singing, rhythmic activities, learning to read the score, playing instruments, creating music individually and collectively, and perceiving music as it relates to its particular social setting. Children are encouraged to learn by sharing their thoughts with others in class discussions.

The outstanding strength of the program is in the quality of the material presented. (None of it is *contrived* for teaching purposes.) The song material falls into four main categories.

1. Genuine American folksongs—without dilution lyrically or musically. (The proportion of material of Afro-American and Latin-American origin exceeds the proportion of these ethnic groups in the population.)

2. Folk songs from other countries with lyric adaptations that reflect the meaning and spirit of the original in colloquial English. (Original lyrics in French and Spanish are often included.)

3. Composed songs of intrinsic value by noted contemporary composers.

4. Art songs of other periods that are singable and related to children's interest.

In addition to song material, the series includes meaningful poetry, Afro-American fables, stories, and historical narratives to stimulate creative thinking and active responses.

The listening program is a unique feature of the series in three ways:

1. Recorded interviews with outstanding contemporary composers are followed by a selection of their works.

2. Listening materials are closely integrated with social studies.

3. In each grade, there are at least two recordings called "Sounds of Music" which are theory lessons by the distinguished composer and educator Otto Luening, carefully graded to the comprehension level of the age group.

The reading program, built on eye and ear perception, is developed on sequential learning of musical concepts derived from a familiarity with contents of a particular book and its recordings and from the immediate environment. *(Description provided by Beatrice Landeck.)*

● Choate, Robert A., Richard C. Berg, Lee Kjelson, Eugene W. Troth, Barbara Kaplan, and James Standifer. *New Dimensions in Music.* New York: American Book Company (450 West 33rd Street), 1970. Basal music series for preschool through level eight.

The general objective of this series is the aesthetic education of children in and through music. To develop the innate musical capacities and potentials of children, many kinds of interrelated experiences are provided. *New*

Dimensions in Music emphasizes the aesthetic component in the aural art of music as children hear, sing, play, read, and write the music of many periods, styles, and cultures. It is designed to help children experience music as an expression of human feelings and values; to recognize music as a cultural force; and to explore music as a creation of science and technology.

Each book is organized into units which reflect the elements of music: rhythm, line and melody, harmony, musical architecture, and musical colors. Subsections include the music of Africa, the Orient, the Middle East, and India. Each book concludes with a section to further enhance its usefulness: music for special times, poems and stories, songs for chorus, etc.

Every song in the series can be heard on a recording (or cassette), sung either by children or adults. The songs are selected from a wide variety of cultures, and many provide foreign-language texts. Instrumental recordings include selections from the standard orchestral repertory. Authentic recordings of the music of other cultures are provided, as are recordings of electronic and experimental music. Programmed learning tapes are also available.

The teacher is given many suggestions for helping students discover and solve musical problems. In the annotated Teacher's Edition, each song is accompanied by many specific suggestions about (1) the musical understandings which may be explored through the song, (2) ideas for participation through which students can demonstrate their understandings, and (3) related activities. Throughout, many opportunities are provided for student growth in music reading and in performance skills.

● Crook, Elizabeth, Mary E. Hoffman, Albert McNeil, Bennett Reimer, and David S. Walker. *Silver Burdett Music*. Morristown, N. J.: Silver Burdett Company, 1974. Basal music series for early childhood through level eight.

Silver Burdett Music, a program starting with early childhood education, is designed for parents, teachers, and children, to be used in a variety of teaching-learning situations. It provides for individual, small-group, and large-group instruction in school and can be a resource for individual and group participation in the home.

The program, based on a philosophy of aesthetic education, is organized into learning modules, each one focusing on a particular quality of music (tone color, tempo, register, duration, dynamics, rhythm pattern, etc.). Through a series of child-centered activities, including singing, listening, playing instruments, and moving, both children and teachers are led to an ever-deepening perception of the components of music—how music "works." The involvement through performing, analyzing, conceptualizing, and evaluating becomes a workable means to this end. Every effort has been made throughout the series of books to keep a balance between the challenge to understanding and perception needed to learn and the successes necessary to enjoyment. In the introduction printed in each book, Bennett Reimer writes: "As perception deepens, enjoyment deepens. As children are moved by the power of music, their ability and desire to perceive increases. Thinking and feeling become inseparable as both are exercised in the experience of music."

The literature in *Silver Burdett Music* offers a wide variety of styles and mediums, and all selections are available on cassettes and recordings for easy use at home or at school. From the beginning, the contemporary child is exposed to music literature of great diversity, including avant-garde music. In this way he can sample what really exists outside of the classroom.

A popular feature of the program is the inclusion of arts lessons. In addition to making teachers and children aware that music is a part of a larger family of arts, the purpose of the lessons is to show how a particular quality exists in several arts. One is led to explore painting as painting, music as music, poetry as poetry, and dance as dance.

The many contributors to *Silver Burdett Music* hope that the material continues to be a rich resource for all who are dedicated to teaching and learning. *(Description provided by Elizabeth Crook.)*

● Marsh, Mary Val, Carroll Rinehart, and Edith Savage. *The Spectrum of Music*. New York: Macmillan Publishing Co., Inc. (200F Brown St., Riverside, N. J.), 1974.

The Spectrum of Music is an integrated music and art textbook series for kindergarten through junior high school. It is designed for successful use by both general classroom teachers and music specialists. Outstanding features of the series are as follows:

1. The books are written **to** and **for** students. They invite pupils to become involved in a wide variety of music and art activities. Emphasis is given to creative approaches which will bring about growth in both music and the visual arts.

2. The focus of the series is upon *what music is—organized sound.* Through purposeful, sequential experiences in singing, playing instruments, conducting, body movement, improvising and composing, listening and analyzing, and using notation, students become increasingly aware of the nature of sound and of the ways in which sounds are combined and organized into music.

3. Consistent organization of content throughout the series facilitates a developmental program from one level to the next. Each book is organized into four areas—*Media* (the voices and instruments that make music); *Components* (the building blocks of music—rhythm, melody, harmony, and expression); *Structure* (the internal and external forms of music); and *Perspectives* (the significance of music in people's lives.)

4. The Teacher's Annotated Edition of each book provides a specific six-point plan for each teaching experience. Each plan suggests *purposes, materials needed, motivation, exploration, extension,* and *desired responses.* These plans offer specific guidance for the less secure teacher of music, as well as a multitude of ideas for the musically confident teacher. Each Teacher's Edition contains full-color reproductions of corresponding pages in the pupil's book. Also included are curriculum correlation notes pertaining to social studies, reading, and language arts; a "minimum program" chart for each level; notes that relate *Spectrum of Music* materials to both Kodaly and Orff approaches, and much other resource material.

5. All songs and listening materials presented in the series are available on both stereo records and cassettes.

6. Macmillan MusicCenter Materials, designed for individualized or small-group instruction, are available for levels 2 through 6. MusicCenter Materials for each of these levels consist of a sturdy box of 60 laminated cards which may be written on with crayon or grease pencil and erased for repeated use, and an accompanying teacher's guide. MusicCenter Materials may be used with or without the textbooks. *(Description provided by Mary Val Marsh.)*

● Tipton, Gladys, and Eleanor Tipton. *Adventures in Music.* RCA Victor. Basic collection of orchestral music for elementary schools. A twelve-volume collection of standard orchestral music, two volumes for each grade. Teacher's guides provide pertinent musical information about each composition, ideas for classroom presentations, and suggestions and resources for relating music to other arts.

● Wood, Lucille, ed. *Bowmar Orchestral Library.* Educational Records, Glendale, Calif., 1967. Collection of orchestral and chamber music, thirty-five volumes. Organized topically under such headings as: "Nature and Make-Believe" and "Twentieth Century America." Record sleeves contain teaching suggestions, musical analyses, and principal themes and rhythms. Wall charts of the themes are available.

POSTSCRIPT

Adolescents often express a desire for music that is different from the school music of earlier grades. This usually means the currently popular "top 40." Many students enjoy this music because it speaks the language of their peer group and their emotions. This youth music cannot be found in basal music texts, though students can of course provide the recordings to teachers who wish to play them. For teachers, instructional materials are available which describe and analyze this music in terms of musical elements: melody, rhythm, harmony, form, etc. Many times, these understandings about youth music can be transferred to other styles of music.

Yet not every student prefers this youth music. Many will be fascinated by the performances of non-Western music now beginning to be included in basal music texts. As they listen to African or Native American singers, many can even learn to sing along with the performers. Children are quick to imitate the vocal mannerisms which contribute so much to the distinctive sound of non-Western music. Familiarity with other styles may help to develop listeners who truly enjoy the *sound* of other music.

Teachers must help students discover *the world of music*. As sensitive music lovers, teachers will want to understand and teach the most powerful and enduring music within each style. Students will become music listeners; few will be performers. At best, one can hope that they will enjoy and understand what has been introduced to them, and that they will keep open ears in regard to the unfamiliar. Teachers have the joyful responsibility of introducing students to this kaleidoscopic world of sounds with its incredible variety of musical riches.

BIBLIOGRAPHY

Bennett, Michael D. "Make the Top 40 Work for You," *Music Educators Journal,* 61, 5 (January, 1975), p. 32. Specific suggestions for classroom lessons.

Carlsen, James C., "Concept Learning—It Starts with a Concept of Music," *Music Educators Journal,* 60, 3 (November, 1973), p. 34. An eloquent plea to use the world repertory as the basis for music teaching.

Fowler, Charles B., "The Case Against Rock: A Reply," *Music Educators Journal,* 57, 1 (September, 1970), p. 38.

Fox, Sidney. "From Rock to Bach (youth music on our terms)," *Music Educators Journal,* 56, 9 (May, 1970), p. 56.

"Facing the Music in Urban Education," special issue of the *Music Educators Journal,* 56, 5 (January, 1970).

"I is In: Individualization in Music Education," special issue of the *Music Educators Journal,* 59, 3 (November, 1972).

McAllester, David P. "The Substance of Things Hoped For," *Music Educators Journal,* 54, 6 (February, 1968), p. 48. A vivid discussion, by a noted anthropologist-musician, of the role of the music educator in today's world.

Maslow, Abraham H. "Music Education and Peak Experience," *Music Educators Journal,* 54, 6 (February, 1968), p. 72. Because the arts are close to our psychological and biological core, they are the kind of education that "can be a glimpse into the infinite, into ultimate values."

Malm, William P. "Preparing the Music Teacher for Handling the Music of Non-Western Traditions," in *International Seminar in Teacher Education in Music,* ed. Marguerite Hood. United States Office of Education, 1966, p. 250–56.

May, Elizabeth, "Teaching a Music Teacher to Use the Music of Other Cultures," in *International Seminar in Teacher Education in Music,* ed. Marguerite Hood. U.S.O.E., 1966, p. 257–69.

"Music in World Cultures," Special issue of the *Music Educators Journal,* 59, 2 (October, 1972).

Newman, Grant. "Doublethink and Music Education," *Music Educators Journal,* 56, 8 (April, 1970), p. 59.

Reeder, Barbara. "Afro Music: As Tough As a Mozart Quartet," *Music Educators Journal,* 56, 5 (January, 1970), p. 88.

Trimillos, Ricardo D. "Expanding Music Experience to Fit Today's World," *Music Educators Journal,* 59, 2 (October, 1972), p. 90.

"Youth Music—A Special Report." Special issue of the *Music Educators Journal,* 56, 3 (November, 1969), p. 43.

INSTRUCTIONAL MATERIALS

Bennett, Michael D. *Pop Hit Listening Guides.* Memphis, Tenn.: Pop Hits Publications. Monthly student worksheets, teacher's supplement, and a "top 40" recording in each of the nine issues.

Crook, Elizabeth, et al. *Silver Burdett Music.* Morristown, N. J.: Silver Burdett Company, 1974. Satellites for levels 7 and 8 include "Music of North American Indians," "Afro-American Music and Its Roots," "Spanish-American Music and Its Roots," and "Country Music and Its Roots." Booklets and recording.

Fox, Sidney, et al. *The World of Popular Music.* Chicago, Ill.: Follett Publishing Company, 1974. Books for junior-high-school level include "Afro-American Music," "Folk and Country," "Jazz," and "Rock." Books and recordings.

Marsh, Mary Val, Carroll A. Rinehart, and Edith J. Savage, *The Spectrum of Music.* New York: Macmillan Publishing Co., Inc., 1975. Booklets for students, with recordings and teacher's annotated editions; levels 7 and 8, but also appropriate for students somewhat older or younger. Includes "Afro-American Music," "Music of Latin Americans," "Music of the Orient," and "The Rock Story."

The Eclectic Curricula in American Music Education Reflect the Needs of a Diverse Population

The philosophy and practice of teaching have evolved in music as in other curricular areas. Aesthetic involvement in performance has often been a goal. Periodically, skills in music reading have been emphasized. Not too long ago, the activity approach, referred to as the "ings" (singing, playing, and so forth), was the core of elementary classroom music. Recently, educational objectives have stressed learning fundamental concepts about music. The philosophies, techniques, and materials of various European approaches to music education have also been imported and adapted. Those European approaches frequently incorporated in the American classroom music program are the Kodaly Method, Orff Schulwerk, and Dalcroze Eurhythmics. In addition, the influences of the Manhattanville Music Curriculum Project (MMCP) and the Contemporary Music Project (CMP) are apparent in the music education program. In fact, nearly *all* approaches, often in varying combinations, are used today in classroom music.

THE KODÁLY METHOD

Zoltan Kodály (Hungarian, 1882–1967), composer and educator, developed a sequential music education program for the schools of Hungary. The music education of Hungarian children is begun as early as age three, with singing and rhythm games. Sight-singing is taught using sol-fa syllables along with the Curwen hand signs corresponding to those syllables (see Appendix). Melody study begins with songs that use sol-mi, the two tones of a child's natural chant. It progresses to songs with three tones (sol-mi-la), then to songs with five tones (pentatonic scale), and finally to songs that use all tones of the major and minor scales. Rhythmic study involves the use of rhythm syllables: "ta" for quarter notes (♩), "ti" for eighth notes (♪), and so on. (See Appendix). Musical sounds are gradually and systematically associated with written musical notation. Hungarian folk songs are used to develop a national cultural identity, and Kodály himself wrote many compositions especially for the curriculum. Many adaptations are used in this country, but all are faced with the problem of substituting relevant American folk music for the material used in Hungary.

BIBLIOGRAPHY

● *Material to be used in the classroom*

Bachmann, Tibor. *Reading and Writing Music.* 2 vols. Elizabethtown, N.J.: Continental Press, 1968.

Dániel, Katinka Scipiades. *The Kodály Approach.* Belmont, Calif.: Fearon Publishers, 1973. Workbook, Nos. 1 and 2.

Darazs, Arpad, and Stephen Jay. *Sight and Sound.* New York: Boosey & Hawkes, 1965.

Lewis, Aden G. *Listen, Look and Sing.* Morristown, N. J.: General Learning Corporation, 1971/2.

Richards, Mary Helen. *Threshold to Music.* Belmont, Calif.: Fearon Publishers, 1964. See also second edition by Eleanor Kidd, 1974.

——. *The Music Language,* 2 vols. Portola Valley, Calif: Richards Institute of Music Education and Research, 1974.

Young, Percy, comp. *Choral Method.* London: Boosey & Hawkes.

● *General Information on the Kodály Method*

Choksy, Lois, "Kodály: In and Out of Context," *Music Educators Journal,* 55, 8 (April, 1969), p. 57. Excellent; somewhat technical.

——. *The Kodály Method: Comprehensive Music Education from Infant to Adult.* Englewood Cliffs, N.J.: Prentice-Hall, Inc., 1974. Parts are technical.

Edwards, Loraine. "The Great Animating Stream of Music," *Music Educators Journal,* 57, 6 (February, 1971), p. 38.

Kodály Musical Training Institute, *Teaching Music at Beginning Levels Through the Kodály Concept.* Wellesley, Mass.: Kodály Musical Training Institute (524 Worcester St.), 1973.

Landis, Beth, and Polly Carder. *The Eclectic Curriculum in American Music Education: Contributions of Dalcroze, Kodály, and Orff.* Washington, D.C.: Music Educators National Conference, 1972. Parts are technical.

Szabo, Helga. *The Kodály Concept of Music Education.* London: Boosey & Hawkes, 1969. Three LP recordings with 36 pages of notes.

Szöny, Erzébat. *Kodály's Principles in Practice.* London: Boosey & Hawkes, 1973.

ORFF SCHULWERK

Carl Orff (b. 1895), a German composer and man of wide-ranging interests, has developed a child-centered approach to music education. Not really a "method," the philosophy suggests a parallel in the historical development of music and the musical growth of an individual. Orff Schulwerk treats music, movement, and speech as inseparable elements, stemming from the natural play of childhood. Words, rhymes, chants, and European folk songs are used to create what Orff calls an elemental music. Reading music notation is a peripheral goal. Emphasis is placed on rhythmic games and on using body rhythms: finger snapping, clapping, *patschen,* and foot tapping. Students are soon transferring their manipulative and musical skills to instruments designed by Orff. They create original compositions and accompaniments to songs, using repetitive *ostinati* at first, but progress later to accompaniments of considerable complexity. The objective is to achieve a total ensemble sound. The instruments (which are vital to the program) include tuned drums, Baroque recorders, and xylophone-type instruments which resemble Indonesian gamelan instruments. American adaptations of the Orff Schulwerk must include a wide assortment of music to replace much of the European material.

BIBLIOGRAPHY

● *Materials to be used in the classroom*

Nash, Grace C. *Chamber Music for Tonebar Instruments and Recorder.* La Grange, Ill.: Kitching Educational, 1971.

——. *Creative Approaches to Child Development with Music, Language and Movement,* ed. J. Robert Welsh. New York: Alfred Publishing Co., Inc., 1974.

——. *Music With Children.* La Grange, Ill.: Kitching Educational, 1965. Series I, II, III; also Teacher's Manual, 1966.

——. *Music with Children: Rhythmic Speech Ensembles.* La Grange, Ill.: Kitching Educational, 1966.

——. *Today with Music.* New York: Alfred Publishing Co., Inc., 1973.

Nichols, Elizabeth. *Orff Instrument Source Book,* 2 vols. Morristown, N. J.: General Learning Corporation, 1971.

Orff, Carl, and Gunild Keetman. *Music for Children,* 5 vols., English adaptation by Doreen Hall and Arnold Walter. Mainz: B. Schott's Sohne, 1960.

● *General Information on Orff Schulwerk*

Bevans, Judith. "The Exceptional Child and Orff," *Music Educators Journal,* 55, 7 (March, 1969), p. 41. Also in *Education of the Visually Handicapped,* 1, no. 4 (December, 1969), p. 116.

Flagg, Marion. "Orff Defended," *Music Educators Journal,* 50, 5 (April–May, 1964), p. 90.

——. "The Orff System in Today's World," *Music Educators Journal,* 53, 4 (December, 1966), p. 30.

Landis, Beth, and Polly Carder. *The Eclectic Curriculum in American Music Education: Contributions of Dalcroze, Kodaly, and Orff.* Washington, D.C.: Music Educators National Conference, 1972.

——. "Orff-Schulwerk . . . Innovation at Bellflower (Calif.)," *Instructor,* 9, 76 (May, 1967), p. 76.

Liess, Andreas. *Carl Orff,* trans. Adeheide Herbert Parkin. New York: St. Martin's Press, 1966.

Mittleman, Lois. "Orff and the Urban Child," *Music Educators Journal,* 55, 7 (March, 1969), p. 41.

Nash, Grace. "Orff," *The Instrumentalist,* 20, 3 (October 1965), p. 47.

——. "Orff can Work in Every Classroom," *Music Educators Journal,* 57, 1 (September, 1970), p. 43.

Orff, Carl. "Orff-Schulwerk: Past and Future," in *Perspectives in Music Education: Source Book III,* ed. Bonnie Kowall. Washington, D.C.: Music Educators National Conference, 1966, p. 386.

Ponath, Louise, and Carol H. Bitcon. "A Behavioral Analysis of Orff-Schulwerk," *Journal of Music Therapy,* 9 (Summer, 1972), p. 56.

Thresher, Janice M. "The Contributions of Carl Orff to Elementary Education," *Music Educators Journal,* 50, 3 (January, 1964), p. 43.

Thomas, Werner, *et al. Carl Orff: A Report in Words and Pictures.* Mainz, Germany: B. Schott's Söhne, 1955.

Wheeler, Lawrence, and Lois Raebeck. *Orff and Kodály Adapted for the Elementary School.* Dubuque, Iowa: Wm. C. Brown Co., 1972.

DALCROZE EURHYTHMICS

Émile Jacques-Dalcroze (Swiss, 1865–1950) formulated a comprehensive philosophy of music teaching. His approach begins with experiencing rhythm through body movements *(eurhythmics).* Instruction in Dalcroze eurhythmics can begin at any age, but the age of four or five is considered ideal. The Dalcroze approach encourages free bodily movements in response to improvised piano music. Focused listening to piano music is essential for responding with appropriate body movements. For example, walking movements may be a correct response for music improvised in a moderate tempo, while running movements would be more appropriate for faster tempos. These rhythmic responses are simple beginning experiences, but will lead to more complex responses, such as walking to the music of the pianist's left-hand part and clapping the music of the pianist's right-hand part. In these eurhythmics experiences, students actually use their bodies as musical instruments. They show their musical understandings through movement.

BIBLIOGRAPHY

Aronoff, Frances Webber. "Games Teachers Play," *Music Educators Journal,* 57, 6 (February, 1971), p. 28.

Driver, Ann. *Music and Movement.* London: Oxford University Press, 1936.

Driver, Ethel. *A Pathway to Dalcroze Eurythmics.* 1951; repr. London: Thomas Nelson & Sons, 1963.

Findlay, Elsa. *Rhythm and Movement: Applications of Dalcroze Eurythmics.* Evanston, Ill.: Summy-Birchard Co., 1971.

Jacques-Dalcroze, Emile. *Eurhythmics, Art and Education.* London: Chatto and Windus, 1930.

——. *Rhythm, Music and Education,* trans. H. F. Rubenstein. London & Whitstable: The Riverside Press, Ltd., Abridged Reprint Edition, 1967.

Landis, Beth, and Polly Carder. *The Eclectic Curriculum in American Music Education: Contributions of Dalcroze, Kodály, and Orff.* Washington, D.C.: Music Educators National Conference, 1972.

Willour, Judith. "Beginning with Delight, Leading to Wisdom: Dalcroze." *Music Educators Journal,* 56, 1 (September, 1969), p. 72.

THE CONTEMPORARY MUSIC PROJECT

The beginnings of the Contemporary Music Project can be traced back to 1959 with the initiation of the Young Composers Project (YCP). This project, supported by the Ford Foundation, involved placing young composers in the public schools where they could gain experience composing for the musical groups in their particular schools and at the same time provide students the unusual opportunity of witnessing the creative processes "at work." The YCP became known in 1965 as the Composers in Public Schools (CPS) program. About that time, it developed more of a focus on contemporary music, including aleatoric and electronic compositional techniques. In 1968, the CPS program was extended to include Professionals-in-Residence in communities as well as in schools.

Through these three programs, it became apparent that music educators lacked understanding in dealing effectively with contemporary music. The Music Educators National Conference in 1962 received funding from the Ford Foundation to expand the YCP by offering contemporary music seminars and workshops in colleges and universities for teachers and by offering pilot projects which focused on developing creative talent among students. This project, from 1963 to 1969, became known as the Contemporary Music Project for Creativity in Music Education (CMP). Those preservice and in-service teachers who participated in the seminars and workshops were encouraged to introduce their students to contemporary music and to use at all levels a more creative, hands-on approach in their teaching.

BIBLIOGRAPHY

Experiments in Musical Creativity. Washington, D.C.: Music Educators National Conference, 1966.

"Contemporary Music Project," *Music Educators Journal,* 59, 9 (May, 1973), p. 33.

Benson, Warren. *Creative Projects in Musicianship.* Washington, D.C.: Music Educators National Conference, 1967.

Comprehensive Musicianship, The Foundation for College Education in Music. Washington, D.C.: Music Educators National Conference, 1965.

Comprehensive Musicianship: An Anthology of Evolving Thought. Washington, D.C.: Music Educators National Conference, 1971.

Willoughby, David. *Comprehensive Musicianship and Undergraduate Music Curricula.* Washington, D.C.: Music Educators National Conference, 1971.

FILM

What is Music? Reston, Va.: Contemporary Music Project, Music Educators National Conference, 1973. A 20-minute color film on the basic elements of music. Suitable for any age level.

THE MANHATTANVILLE MUSIC CURRICULUM PROJECT

The Manhattanville Music Curriculum Project (MMCP), a U.S. Office of Education Research Project, was developed between 1965 and 1970 as an alternative for music educators. Under the direction of Ronald B. Thomas, the project was designed for students to explore as total musicians the concepts of music. Contemporary music serves as the musical focus for MMCP with music of earlier times incorporated within a frame of reference that is meaningful today.

MMCP places great emphasis on discovery as a technique for learning musical concepts. The understanding of concepts is accomplished through the spiral curriculum, and organized by cycles, from the simplest to the most complex.

Seven major areas of activities are included in the Manhattanville Music Curriculum Project:

1. Strategies involving composing, performing, evaluating, conducting, and listening

2. Listening to recordings

3. Singing (for joy and pleasure)

4. Research and oral reports

5. Skill development

6. Student performances

7. Guest performances

BIBLIOGRAPHY

Manhattanville Music Curriculum Program Final Report. U.S. Office of Education, Bureau of Research, Project 6-1999 (Grant #OEG-1 001999-0477).

Thomas, Ronald B. *MMCP Synthesis: A Structure for Music Education.* Bardonia, N.Y.: Media Materials, Inc., 1971. This guide, prepared for use with students from third grade through high school, and the *Early Childhood Music Curriculum,* a learning program for children ages four to eight, are the curricular results of the MMCP project.

SUMMARY

Yes: the search for the ideal music program continues. Probably there is no single approach that is best for every student. An eclecticism may be inevitable in our heterogeneous country with its distinct regional traditions. We can hope this eclecticism will lead to research and study, providing insights into music teaching both as skill and as art.

SOURCES FOR OTHER APPROACHES

Caylor Florence. "On the Trendmill of Elementary Music Education," *Music Educators Journal,* 58, 7 (March, 1972), p. 33.

Crews, K. "Music Every Day: What's New in Music Teaching," *Instructor,* 80 (December, 1970), p. 44.

Curatilo, Joseph S., Richard C. Berg, and Marjorie Farmer. *The Sight and Sound of Music.* Delaware Water Gap, Pa.: Shawnee Press. A two- or three-year program to develop sight-reading skills, beginning in grades 2, 3, or 4. Includes pupil's and teacher's books, cassette tapes, overhead projector transparencies, and spirit masters.

Garson, Alfred. "Learning with Suzuki: Seven Questions Answered," *Music Educators Journal,* 56, 6 (February, 1970), p. 64.

Garson, Alfred. "Suzuki and Physical Movement," *Music Educators Journal,* 60, 4 (December, 1973), p. 34.

Holt, John. "What You See Isn't Necessarily What You Get," *Music Educators Journal,* 60, 9 (May, 1974), p. 35.

Lekberg, Charles. "Suzuki: Pied Piper of Fiddledom," *Music Journal,* 26, 5 (May, 1968), p. 21.

Ling, Stuart. "The Work of Anna Lechner, Viennese Music Educator," in *The Eclectic Curriculum in American Music Education,* ed. Beth Landis and Polly Carder. Washington, D.C.: Music Educators National Conference, 1972, p. 191.

SECTION **FOUR**

Appendix

Glossary

Music Index

Subject Index

Appendix

Music in Special Education Index and Bibliography

Music is an important force in the life of the child with special needs. The need for musical participation is very real. Specialists in the field should diagnose particular problems and formulate goals for these students.

The model experiences listed below can provide meaningful experiences for many children in special education.

SEQUENTIAL INDEX

(See Music Index for page numbers.)

- ENGINE, ENGINE
- THE WIND BLEW EAST
- SKIP TO MY LOU
- THE ELEPHANT
- SERAFINA; FOG
- BARCAROLLE; POLKA
- JOHN THE RABBIT
- GRIZZLY BEAR
- PARADE
- KANGAROO
- MARCH, LITTLE SOLDIER

- BINGO
- TOCCATA FOR PERCUSSION, etc.
- ALL AROUND THE KITCHEN; THE CLAM
- A RAM SAM SAM (I)
- CHINESE DANCE
- FIVE ANGELS
- PIANISTS
- WE ARE GOING DOWN THE NUMBERS
- CLAP YOUR HANDS
- SCRATCH, SCRATCH, etc.

BIBLIOGRAPHY

While the following references can aid work or study in the field, they are not intended to supplant professional training. They include literature specifically relating to music in special education.

General information

Gaston, E. Thayer, ed. *Music in Therapy.* New York: Macmillan Publishing Co., Inc., 1968. Forty articles discussing all problems.

Graham, Richard M., ed., *Music for the Exceptional Child,* Washington, D.C.: Music Educators National Conference, 1975. Includes articles by experts in the fields of speech handicapped, hearing impaired, blind, mentally retarded, emotionally disturbed, learning disabilities, and the gifted. See the comprehensive bibliographies, pp. 203–223, and the Addenda, which includes lesson planning.

Kondorossy, Elizabeth. "Let Their Music Speak for the Handicapped," *Music Educators Journal,* 52, 4 (February–March), 1966, p. 115.

Nordoff, P., and C. Robins. *Music Therapy in Special Education.* New York: John Day Co., 1970.

Rosenkranz, Peggy A. "Perceptual-Motor Development," *Music Educators Journal,* 61, 4 (December, 1974), p. 57.

Warren, Linda C., "Help the Exceptional Child!" *Music Journal,* 26, 9 (November, 1968), p. 27.

Information relating to specific needs

Allen, Mariam. *Dance of Language.* Portola Valley, Calif.: Richards Institute of Music Education and Research, 1974. (deaf)

Alvin, Juliette. *Music for the Handicapped Child.* London: Oxford University Press, 1965.

Boardman, Eunice, et al. "The Art and Music Program at the Institute of Logopedics, Wichita, Kansas," *Cerebral Palsy Review,* 22, 1 (January–February, 1961), p. 8.

Breinholt, Verna, and Irene Schoepfle. "Music Experiences for the Child with Speech Limitations," *Music Educators Journal,* 47, 1 (September–October, 1960), p. 45.

Campbell, Dorothy Drysdale. "One Out of Twenty: The LD," *Music Educators Journal,* 58, 8 (April, 1972), p. 38.

Carey, Margaretta. "Music for the Educable Mentally Retarded," *Music Educators Journal,* 46, 4 (February–March, 1960), p. 72.

Epley, Carol. "In a Soundless World of Musical Enjoyment," *Music Educators Journal,* 58, 8 (April, 1972), p. 55.

Fahey, Joan Dahms, and Lois Birkenshaw. "Bypassing the Ear: The Perception of Music by Feeling and Touch," *Music Educators Journal,* 58, 8 (April, 1972), p. 44.

Giacobbe, George A. "Rhythm Builds Order in Brain-Damaged Children," *Music Educators Journal,* 58, 8 (April, 1972), p. 40.

Graham, Richard M. "Seven Million Plus Need Special Attention. Who Are They?" *Music Educators Journal,* 58, 8 (April, 1972), p. 22. (retarded)

Hoem, Jean C. "Don't Dump the Students Who 'Can't Do'," *Music Educators Journal,* 58, 8 (April, 1972), p. 29. (retarded)

Hollander, Fred M., and Patricia D. Juhrs. "Orff Schulwerk: An Effective Treatment Tool with Autistic Children," *Journal of Music Therapy,* 11 (Spring, 1974), p. 1.

Kaplan, Max. "Music Therapy in the Speech Program," *Exceptional Children,* 22, 2 (December, 1955), p. 112.

Kirkland, Evelyn. "Music for Blind Children," *Music Journal,* 30, 9 (November, 1972), p. 19.

May, Elizabeth. "Music for Children with Cerebral Palsy," *American Journal of Physical Medicine,* 35, 5 (October, 1956), p. 320.

Morgan, Elaine. "Music—A Weapon Against Anxiety," *Music Educators Journal,* 62, 4 (January, 1975), p. 38.

Pirtle, Marilyn, and Kay P. Seaton. "Use of Music Training to Actuate Conceptual Growth in Neurologically Handicapped Children," *Journal of Research in Music Education,* 21, 4 (Winter, 1975), p. 292.

Welsbacher, Betty T. "More Than a Package of Bizarre Behaviors," *Music Educators Journal,* 58, 8 (April, 1972), p. 26. (neurologically handicapped)

Music in Early Childhood Index and Bibliography

Young children need to be actively involved in moving to music, singing, exploring and playing instruments, creating, improvising, and listening to music. As a result of these active experiences in music, children will develop basic understandings *about* music. In demonstrating their understandings, young children will *show* rather than verbalize these perceptions.

These model experiences may be adapted for use with young children:

SEQUENTIAL INDEX

(See Music Index for page numbers.)

- ENGINE, ENGINE
- THE WIND BLEW EAST
- THE ELEPHANT
- BARCAROLLE; POLKA
- JOHN THE RABBIT
- PARADE
- KANGAROO
- MARCH, LITTLE SOLDIER
- BINGO
- JANE, JANE
- LA VÍBORA
- CHINESE DANCE (use without cards)
- WE ARE GOING DOWN THE NUMBERS
- CLAP YOUR HANDS

BIBLIOGRAPHY

Andress, Barbara L. *Music in Early Childhood.* Washington, D.C.: Music Educators National Conference, 1973.

Aronoff, Frances Webber. *Music and Young Children.* New York: Holt, Rinehart and Winston, Inc., 1969.

——. "No Age is too Early to Begin," *Music Educators Journal,* 60, 7 (March, 1974), p. 18.

Austin, Virginia D. "Striking a Balance Between Participation and Perfection," *Music Educators Journal,* 60, 7 (March, 1974), p. 33.

Barnett, Elise Braun. *Montessori and Music: Rhythmic Activities for Young Children.* New York: Schocken Books, 1973.

Batscheller, John. *Music in Early Childhood.* New York: Classroom Music Enrichment Units, 1975.

Gelvin, Miriam P. "Arts Experiences in Early Childhood Education," *Music Educators Journal,* 60, 7 (March, 1974), p. 26.

Kemper, Marjorie. "How Young is Early Enough?" *Music Educators Journal,* 57, 6 (February, 1971), p. 36.

Mankin, Linda. "Are We Starting Too Late?" *Music Educators Journal,* 55, 8 (April, 1969), p. 36.

Moorehead, Gladys, and Donald Pond. *Music of Young Children.* 4 vols. Santa Barbara, Calif.: Pillsbury Foundation, 1941–51.

Reilly, Mary L. "Preschool Teachers Need Music," *Music Educators Journal,* 55, 8 (April, 1969), p. 40.

Rowen, Betty J. "Let Them Move," *Music Educators Journal,* 55, 8 (April, 1969), p. 43.

Schmitt, Sister Cecelia. "The Thought-Life of the Young Child," *Music Educators Journal,* 58, 3 (December, 1971), p. 22.

Stecher, Miriam B., and Hugh McElheny. "The Structure of Music can Box a Child In," *Music Educators Journal,* 56, 8 (April, 1970), p. 54.

——. *Joy and Learning Through Music and Movement Improvisation.* New York: Macmillan Publishing Co., Inc., 1972.

Reference Material for Music Notation and Music Theory

TEMPO TERMS

largo (very slow and broad)

lento (very slow)

adagio (leisurely)

andante (moderate and walking)

moderato (moderate)

allegretto (moderately fast)

allegro (quick, lively)

vivace (brisk, fast)

presto (very fast)

DYNAMIC TERMS

pp   pianissimo (very soft)

p   piano (soft)

mp mezzo piano (medium soft)

mf mezzo forte (medium loud)

f   forte (loud)

ff fortissimo (very loud)

NOTES AND RESTS

Kodály syllables   *rests*

𝅝
ta - a - a - a   1 whole note   𝅝   ▬

                                  equals

♩
ta - a   2 half notes   𝅗𝅥   𝅗𝅥   ▬

                                  or

♩
ta   4 quarter notes   ♩   ♩   ♩   ♩   𝄽

                                  or

♫
ti - ti   8 eighth notes   ♫   ♫   ♫   ♫   ♪

                                  or

♬
ti - ri - ti - ri   16 sixteenth   ♬   ♬   ♬   ♬   𝄿
                                      notes

Combinations:

♪ ♩ ♪
syn - co - pa

♩. ♫   1 dotted   ▬.
tim - ri   whole note   𝅝·

                                  equals

♫ ♩.   2 dotted   𝅗𝅥·   𝅗𝅥·   ▬·
tir - rim   half notes

                                  or

⌐3⌐   4 dotted   ♩·   ♩·   ♩·   ♩·   𝄽·
♫♪   quarter notes
tri - o - la

                                  or

                                  12 eighth   ♫   ♫   ♫   ♫   ♪·
                                      notes

                                  or

♩.⌣♪   24 sixteenth   ♬   ♬   ♬   ♬   𝄿·
(ta - i - ti)   notes

Curwen hand signs

do

ti

ta (or li)

la

si (or le)

so

fi (or se)

fa

mi

re

do

Meter signatures

2 = 2 beats in a measure
4 = quarter note is basic beat

Frequently used meter signatures

(or "common time")

 (slow tempo)

(fast tempo)

 *alla breve*
(or "cut time")

The staff

Clef signs

G

G or Treble Clef

F

F or Bass Clef

Accidentals

♭ (flat): lowers the pitch one half step
♯ (sharp): raises the pitch one half step
♮ (natural): cancels a flat or sharp

SCALES AND CHORDS   *The grand staff (key of C)*

Frequently used major scales and their primary chords

Frequently used minor scales and their primary chords

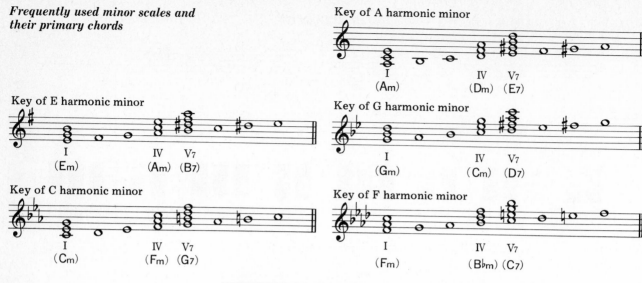

Key of A harmonic minor
I (Am)   IV (Dm)   V7 (E7)

Key of E harmonic minor
I (Em)   IV (Am)   V7 (B7)

Key of G harmonic minor
I (Gm)   IV (Cm)   V7 (D7)

Key of C harmonic minor
I (Cm)   IV (Fm)   V7 (G7)

Key of F harmonic minor
I (Fm)   IV (Bbm)   V7 (C7)

IDENTIFYING MAJOR AND MINOR TONAL CENTERS FROM KEY SIGNATURES

● In a key signature of sharps, the sharp farthest right is *7* or *ti*. The next line or space above is *8* or *do*, the tonal center for *major*. The next line or space below is *6* or *la*, the tonal center for *minor*.

● In a key signature of flats, the flat farthest right is *4* or *fa*. Count downward on the lines and spaces to *1* or *do* for the *major* tonal center; count upward to *6* or *la* for the *minor* tonal center.

KEY SIGNATURES AND TONAL CENTERS

name of major key: C   G   D   A   E   B   F#   C#

name of major key: C   F   Bb   Eb   Ab   Db   Gb   Cb

name of minor key: A min   E min   B min   F# min   C# min   G# min   D# min   A# min

name of minor key: A min   D min   G min   C min   F min   Bb min   Eb min   Ab min

Intervals

Prime, or Unison   Second   Third   Fourth   Fifth   Sixth   Seventh   Octave

Splicing Recording Tape

If a splicing block is not available, use scissors.

Overlap the two pieces of tape to be spliced. Cut both pieces simultaneously on the diagonal. Discard the scrap ends.

On a flat surface, butt the two diagonally cut ends together, *shiny sides up. Do not overlap the tape segments or leave a gap between them.*

Fasten the two segments firmly with *splicing tape,* on the *shiny side. Do not use any other kind of tape!*

Carefully trim any splicing tape extending over the edges of the tape.

Tapes have multiple tracks on which sound is recorded. When cutting and splicing tapes, care must be taken to keep all tape segments *correct edge up,* as the recorded sound appears only on certain tracks of the tape. If the tape is inserted into the tape recorder upside down, only the unrecorded tracks play back, resulting in silence. As *recorded* tape is cut from the reel, the pieces should be laid down (or hung from a line by miniature clothespins) in such a way that the person splicing knows top edge from bottom edge.

Cutting for splicing

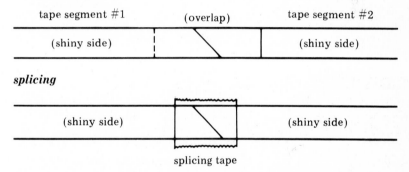

splicing

Attach splicing tape firmly. With scissors, cut a gentle curve into each edge of the recording tape to assure removal of all exposed adhesive. (Exposed adhesive will damage the tape recorder.)

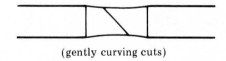

(gently curving cuts)

TAPE LOOPS

Make a *tape loop* following the above procedure. Overlap the two ends of the single piece of tape. Cut diagonally and splice butted ends together, as before. (See model experience *String Quartet No. 4.*)

Glossary

A B A musical design consisting of two sections, A and B, that contrast with each other (binary).

A B A A musical design consisting of three sections, A B A. Two are the same and the middle one is different (ternary).

accent A stress or emphasis given to certain tones. An accent sign is <.

accidental A sign introduced before a note of a composition that changes the pitch for one measure only: ♯ (sharp), ♭ (flat), ♮ (natural).

accompaniment Music that goes with or provides harmonic or rhythmic support for another musical part (usually a melody).

aleatory, aleatoric (al-ee-uh-TORE-ik) "Chance" music emphasizing improvisation within limitations set by the composer.

anacrusis (ana-CREW-sis) See **up-beat.**

arrangement The adaptation of a composition for performance in a medium other than the medium for which it was conceived.

asymmetric meter Meter in which the beat groupings are irregular, as 5/4 or 7/4. Often created by combining two meters: 2/4 and 3/4 = 5/4.

atonal Without a tonal center.

bar or **bar line** A vertical line through the staff to indicate a boundary for a measure of music.

bass clef The symbol 𝄢, which determines that the fourth line of the staff is F below middle C.

beam A line connecting stems of notes in rhythmic groups; flags are used for single notes.

beat The underlying pulse present in most music; the rhythmic unit to which one responds in marching or dancing.

bridge A passage that connects two sections which are more important than itself.

cadence (KAY-dns) A point of arrival which punctuates a musical phrase.

call-and-response form A responsorial form in which there is alternating (and sometimes overlapping) of solo and chorus.

calypso A kind of music developed in the West Indies; characterized by its rhythms and commentary on contemporary events and personalities.

canon A contrapuntal composition in which all parts have the same melody throughout, but start at different times. A round is a type of canon.

chord A combination of three or more tones sounded together.

chord progression A series of chords sounding in succession.

chord root The pitch on which a chord is constructed.

chromatic scale A 12-tone scale consisting entirely of half steps.

clef A symbol placed on a staff to designate a precise pitch which identifies the other pitches in the score.

coda A short passage added to the end of a composition; a musical way of saying "the end."

compound meter A grouping of beats in which a simple meter ($\frac{2}{4}$) is multiplied by three ($\frac{6}{4}$). $\frac{6}{8}$ is a frequently encountered compound meter.

conjunct Stepwise pitch movement, such as C to D to E.

conservation The realization that one aspect of something, e.g., quantity, remains the same while another aspect is changed (e.g., shape, position.).

consonance A relative term used to describe the pleasant, agreeable effect of certain tones sounded simultaneously. Intervals of thirds, sixths, and octaves are generally considered to be consonant.

348

contrapuntal (kontrah-PUN-tal) A musical texture created when two or more melodic lines are combined simultaneously (see **polyphonic**).

countermelody A melody sounding simultaneously with another melody.

counterpoint Music consisting of two or more melodies sounding simultaneously. (See **contrapuntal**.)

crescendo Gradually becoming louder.

decay Sound dying away.

decrescendo Gradually becoming softer.

descant A second melody less important than and usually sung above the principal melody.

diatonic (dye-ah-TAH-nik) A seven-tone scale, consisting of five whole steps and two half steps, utilizing every pitch name. Major and minor scales are diatonic scales.

disjunct Pitch movement by intervals larger than a second, such as C to F to A.

dissonance A relative term used to describe the disagreeable effect of certain tones sounded simultaneously. Intervals of seconds and sevenths are considered to be dissonant.

dominant The fifth degree of the scale; a chord constructed on the fifth degree of the scale.

downbeat The first beat of a measure (beat grouping), usually accented.

drone An accompaniment created by sounding one or more tones (usually two, five notes apart) simultaneously and continuously throughout a composition or section of a composition; a special type of harmony.

duple meter A grouping of beats into two ($\frac{2}{4}$, $\frac{2}{2}$).

electronic music Creating, altering, and imitating sounds electronically. The basic tools of this kind of music are the tape recorder and the electronic synthesizer.

enharmonic tones Tones sounding the same pitch but written differently, as E♭ and D♯.

ethnomusicology The study of all the music of people in a specified area, frequently in a cultural context.

falsetto A method of singing used by male singers, particularly tenors, to reach tones above the normal range of their voices.

fine (fee-NAY) Italian term meaning "the end."

flat A symbol that indicates that the written pitch is to be lowered a half step: ♭.

folk song A song having no known composer, usually transmitted orally, and reflecting the musical consensus of a cultural group.

form The shape, order, or design in which a piece of music is organized.

grace note A short note, printed in small type, which ornaments the note which follows it. A grace note is not counted in the rhythm of the measure.

half step The narrowest interval from one tone to another (in Western music); a semitone.

harmony A simultaneous sounding of two or more tones.

heterophonic (he-ter-oh-FAHN-ik) A musical texture in which slightly different versions of the same melody are sounded together.

homophonic (HOMO-fahn-ik) A musical texture in which all parts move in the same rhythm but use different pitches, as in hymns; also, a melody supported by chords.

imitation The restatement of a theme in different voices (parts).

impressionism A musical style of the late 19th and early 20th centuries, in which musical textures and timbres were used to convey impressions (hint) rather than make precise "statements."

improvisation Music performed extemporaneously, often within a framework determined by the musical style.

interlude A brief section of music inserted between stanzas of a song or sections of a larger work.

interval The distance between two tones, named by counting all pitch names involved:

introduction A brief section of music that precedes the main body of a composition.

inversions Rearranging the pitches of a chord (for example, C E G becomes G C E).

key The tonal raw materials of a composition, formed by the tonal center and the notes related to this tonal center. (Key may be said to be identical with scale.)

key signature The sharps or flats at the beginning of the staff, after the clef sign, indicating in which key or on what scale the composition is written.

legato (leh-GAH-toe) Tones moving in a connected, smooth manner (opposite of staccato).

leger lines (LEH-jer) Short lines above or below the five-line staff on which higher or lower pitches may be indicated.

major interval An interval a half step larger than the corresponding minor interval.

major scale A scale in which the pattern of whole and half steps is: whole – whole – half – whole – whole – whole – half.

melodic rhythm Durations of pitches used in a melody.

melodic sequence See **sequence**.

melody A succession of pitches moving one at a time through time.

melody bells Pitched metal bars fastened to a single frame; sometimes called **songbells**.

measure A unit of beats delineated by bar lines.

meter The grouping of beats in music.

meter signature Two numerals that show the number of beats grouped in a measure and the basic beat:

$\frac{4}{4}$ or $\frac{4}{♩}$ = four beats in a measure
= quarter note (♩) is basic beat.

middle C The *C* midway between the treble and bass clef; approximately midway on the piano keyboard.

minor interval An interval a half step smaller than the corresponding major interval.

minor scale A scale in which one characteristic feature is a half step between the second and third tones.

monophonic music A musical texture created when a single melody is heard without harmony.

musique concrète (kohn-KREHT) Music in which pre-existing sounds are altered by tape or electronic means.

natural A sign that cancels a sharp or flat: ♮. A note that is neither sharp nor flat, as C D E F G A B on the piano keyboard.

octave The interval in which two pitches share the same letter name (C-C), one pitch with twice the frequency of the other.

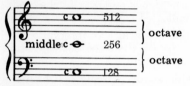

octave displacement A technique for altering a melody by replacing certain pitches with the same-named pitches from different octaves.

ostinato (ah-stih-NAH-toe) A continuous repetition of a melodic or rhythmic pattern.

patschen or **patsch** (PAW-chn) A thigh slap.

pedal point A long-held note, usually in the bass, sounding against changing harmonies in other parts.

pentatonic scale A five-tone scale often identified with the pattern of the black keys of the piano. Many other five-tone arrangements are possible.

perception A cortical activity in which sensory data are synthesized into an awareness of an object.

phrase A musical segment with a clear beginning and ending, comparable to a sentence in speech.

pitch The vibrations per second of a musical tone; the "highness" or "lowness" of a tone.

polyphonic A musical texture created when two or more melodies sound simultaneously.

polyrhythms Two or more contrasting rhythmic patterns that occur simultaneously.

polytonal Music that employs two or more tonalities (or keys) simultaneously.

quadruple meter A grouping of beats into four ($\frac{4}{4}$, $\frac{4}{8}$, $\frac{4}{2}$).

quodlibet (kwoad-LIH-bet) A combination of melodies, often with parallel harmonic and rhythmic design; sometimes called "partner" songs.

resonator bells Individual pitched bells consisting of metal bars fastened to hollow resonator blocks.

rest The notation for silence.

retrograde Backward motion; beginning with the last note of a melody and ending with the first.

rhythm All of the durations that occur in music.

rhythm pattern Any grouping, generally brief, of long and short sounds and silences.

rondo A musical form consisting of a recurring section with two or more contrasting sections, as: A B A C A.

root The tone on which a chord is built. A chord using C as its root is labeled a C chord.

round A melody performed by two or more groups entering at stated and different times.

scale A pattern of pitches arranged in ascending or descending order. Scales are identified by their specific arrangement of whole and half steps. See major scale, minor scale, chromatic scale, and whole-tone scale.

score A composite of all the written notational parts of a composition—an orchestral score.

sequence The repetition of a melodic pattern on a higher or lower degree of the scale.

sharp A symbol that raises the pitch a half step (♯).

shifting meter The changing of beat groupings in music, as from twos to threes.

skip A melodic interval exceeding a second or whole step.

staccato (stuh-CAH-toe) Detached, short sounds often indicated by a dot over or under a note (opposite of *legato*).

staff Five parallel lines used in traditional music notation.

step An interval of a second, as, A to B.

subdominant The fourth degree of the scale; a chord constructed on the fourth degree of the scale.

suite A group of musical pieces related to one idea.

syncopation (sin-co-PAY-shun) Placement of emphasis on normally weak beats or weak parts of beats.

tempo The rate of speed of music.

texture The distinguishing character of the music resulting from the ways in which the vertical (harmonic) and horizontal (melodic) elements are combined.

theme and variations A composition in which each section is a modified version of the original musical theme.

timbre (TAM-br) The quality or color of sound; the characteristic sound of an instrument. Synonyms: tone color, tone quality.

time Commonly used in place of more precise terms, namely, meter, rhythm, tempo, duration.

time signature See **meter signature.**

tonal center The central tone of the key and the first note of the scale. (Also called "tonic.")

tonality The relationship of tones in a scale to a tonal center.

tone A sound of definite pitch. Tones also have duration, intensity, and timbre.

tone row A series of 12 tones (the tones of the chromatic scale), arranged in a specific order by the composer.

transposition Changing a piece of music from one key to another.

treble clef The symbol 𝄞, which determines the second line of the staff as G above middle C.

triple meter A grouping of beats into threes ($\frac{3}{4}$, $\frac{3}{8}$, $\frac{3}{2}$).

unison Sung or played on the same pitch.

upbeat An unaccented beat, often the last beat of a beat grouping or measure. In conducting, the upbeat is indicated by an upward motion of the hand.

whole step An interval comprised of two consecutive half steps; as C to D.

whole-tone scale A scale of six different tones, each a whole step apart.

Music Index

351

OTHER SELECTIONS

Subject Index